SUFFERERS
& HEALERS

SOCIAL & ECONOMIC HISTORY SERIES

SUFFERERS
& HEALERS

The experience of illness in
Seventeenth-Century England

LUCINDA McCRAY BEIER

ROUTLEDGE & KEGAN PAUL
LONDON AND NEW YORK

First published in 1987 by
Routledge & Kegan Paul Ltd
11 New Fetter Lane, London EC4P 4EE

Published in the USA by
Routledge & Kegan Paul Inc.
in association with Methuen Inc.
29 West 35th Street, New York, NY 10001

Set in Bembo
by Columns of Reading
and printed in Great Britain
by Richard Clay Ltd.,
Bungay, Suffolk

Library of Congress Cataloging in Publication
Data
Beier, Lucinda McCray.
Sufferers and healers.
Bibliography: p.
Includes index.
1. Physician and patient – England – History –
17th century.   2. Medicine – England – History – 17th century.
I. Title.
R727.3.B43   1987   610′.941   87–20771
ISBN 0–7102–1053–1

British Library CIP Data also available
ISBN 0–7102–1053–1

To Lee, with gratitude and love.

CONTENTS

N.B. In quotations from original sources, spelling and punctuation have been modernised and abbreviations and suspensions have been extended. Dates are given in new style, the year beginning on 1 January.

ACKNOWLEDGMENTS

No book can be attributed to its author alone. This is especially true of first books, even truer of the books resulting from Ph.D. theses. If I were to thank all of those who influenced the conception, preparation and execution of this work, this brief note would be longer than the book itself. Thus, I must be economical.

First of all, thanks are due to my parents, Robert and Janet McCray, who encouraged my earliest interest in history and medicine. I also wish to thank my first history teachers, foremost among them Professor A. R. Hogue of Indiana University. Later inspiration, support and criticism came from the history faculty at the University of Illinois at Urbana, especially from Professor Walter Arnstein and Dr Caroline Hibbard. My thesis would never have been finished without the help of my supervisor at the University of Lancaster, Dr Roger Smith. My external examiners, Dr Paul Slack and Dr Roy Porter, have rendered assistance above and beyond the call of duty. I am grateful to Dr David Hamilton for his careful reading of Chapter 3. I would also like to thank the Cambridge University Press for allowing me to reprint material on the Josselins' experience contained in my essay 'In sickness and in health: a seventeenth-century family's experience' (in *Patients and Practitioners*, ed. Roy Porter, Cambridge University Press, 1985).

I am especially grateful to the Interlibrary Loan department at the University of Lancaster and the staffs of the Library of the Wellcome Institute for the History of Medicine and the British Library. I also wish to thank the Royal Society, without whose grant I would have been unable to complete my research. Andrew Wheatcroft, my editor at Routledge & Kegan Paul, has provided practical and moral support throughout the process of converting thesis to book, proving that the clichéd enmity between publishing staff and writers need have no basis in fact.

Finally, I must thank my family. My sons, Robert Joseph, Jesse, Jacob and Zachary, were all born during the years spent researching and writing this book. They have tolerated the haphazard housekeeping resulting from 'mummy's work' without complaint and with much good humour. To my husband, Lee, I owe a debt which can never be repaid. His practical aid, imaginative criticism and expert advice have helped turn a vague fantasy into a reality. The faults in this book are my own; much of the good in it is his.

INTRODUCTION

Along with death, taxes and the poor, illness, injury, childbirth and old age are always with us. These human universals are, and have always been, intrinsically interesting, permeating day-to-day conversation, providing comedy and tragedy in entertainment, and forming the subject matter of research in a multitude of disciplines.

Today we are obsessed by various aspects of health and illness. We exercise and diet according to infinitely mutable theories. Endlessly we debate the moral and ethical issues of abortion, contraception and euthanasia. We criticise, exploit and are addicted to our medical services, expecting far more than we can ever receive. We live in fear of diseases such as cancer, multiple sclerosis and AIDS, enraged because they are beyond our control.

Our vulnerability, fear and anger are not new. These also are common aspects of the human condition, products, like other pieces of mental baggage, of the Western tradition which has never become reconciled to the existence of evil and mortality. Some things do not change. Suffering and death come to us all.

However, the twentieth century has produced a major change in our expectations. We expect our children to be born alive and perfect. We expect health and a sense of well-being. We expect to live for at least the biblical three score and ten years. We expect our healers, like trained auto mechanics, to be able to fix damaged parts of us with a minimum of fuss and discomfort, putting us back on the road in peak running condition. We are losing the concept of natural death, that ancient loop-hole which comforted and exonerated survivors in ages past. These days death, regardless of age or circumstances, is usually somebody's fault.

Our inflated expectations have resulted, in part, from a combination of public health measures and developments in medical science. Perhaps understandably, in the past century medical historians have concentrated upon tracing the progress of medical science and eulogising the great doctors whose discoveries contributed to that progress. Scholars such as Charles Singer, Erwin Ackerknecht and Lester King produced general studies which concentrated on the development of rational, scientific medicine.[1] Biographers like Kenneth Dewhurst and Geoffrey Keynes described the lives and discoveries of those practitioners who contributed to that development.[2] These historians and others like them inter-nalised the values and prejudices of the twentieth-century medical community. For them, the learned and licensed medical practitioners of the past might have been mistaken, but were always altruistic; unlearned and unlicensed healers were quacks, deliberately taking advantage of a vulnerable lay population; 'modern medicine' represented a victory of reason over superstition, knowledge over ignorance, life over death. This Whig interpretation of the history of medicine protects the medical status quo by creating and articulating the myth of uninterrupted medical heroism and inevitable progress. Our doctors inherit the mantle of their sainted ancestors.

Until fairly recently traditional medical history satisfied the needs of both the medical profession and the general public. The medical profession as we know it is a recent phenomenon. The pedigree provided for it by medical historians contributed to a necessary *esprit de corps* and allowed for a gradual inflation of its demands for respect and rewards. The general public, relieved from the age-old tyranny of infection and encouraged by a rise in living standards, gave its gratitude to the doctors who were the most visible agents of the improvements it perceived. Miracle medicine and miracle surgery heralded the dawn of a new age. People wanted to believe in 'modern medicine' because this belief offered an irresistible combination of confidence in the future and relief from personal responsibility for the health and illnesses of themselves and their loved ones.

Predictably the second half of the twentieth century has witnessed a re-examination of medicine and the provision of medical care. Developments in medical science have outrun the cultural context within which they operate. People are not sure about how to use the opportunities now available to them. By the same token, despite its enormous capabilities, medicine still cannot provide a guarantee of health and happiness for all. Disappointed consumers, like naïve children, blame the medical profession for its all-too-human frailties. Furthermore, there is the feeling that lay-people, in their enthusiasm for the medical revolution, have given too much responsibility and power to doctors. Childbirth has become an arena where mothers struggle for good birth experiences, while medical professionals fight for safety and domination. Patient–doctor relationships are examined for evidence of control strategies on the part of the doctors, passivity and lack of satisfaction on the part of patients. In the Age of the Expert, lay-people grow increasingly uncomfortable about their own powerlessness.

Like the profession with which it is associated, the history of medicine is undergoing a process of reassessment and change. Traditional historians, concerned with mapping the advance of medical science, implicitly treated patients as irrelevant, except as the vehicles or beneficiaries of medical discoveries. Doctors were expected and seen to be totally in control of the experience of illness. However, it is impossible to relate illness and medicine to its social context without recognising the significance of the sufferer's feelings, attitudes and behaviour. Thus, medical historians increasingly study the experiences of both healers and sufferers, examining the social impact of epidemics, gathering information about the provision of medical care, and re-examining the development of medical occupations.[3]

The social history of medicine might more correctly be called the social history of suffering because it combines the study of medical theories, treatments and practitioners with the study of the disorders people underwent and the ways they experienced and dealt with those disorders. Because it is a young field, it has the advantage for the historian of being relatively uncharted territory. It has the complementary disadvantage of providing few standard authorities either to build upon or to disagree with. Like general social history, it borrows analytical techniques from anthropology and sociology, attempting to place medical events, along with the participants in those events, in their appropriate cultural and social contexts.

This book examines the experience of ill-health in seventeenth-century England. It is essentially a one-question study: what did people of that time do when they became ill, were injured, or had babies? Neither the approaches to this question nor the conclusions reached are simple. One must first examine the conditions surrounding the experience of suffering, then allow for the great diversity in individual responses to these conditions. This book will describe the ailments seventeenth-century English people had and the many ways they dealt with these ailments. It will also describe the enormous variety of healers available in the period. In addition, it will investigate popular attitudes regarding illness and medical practitioners. Although the diversity of medical ideas and behaviour will be emphasised, several case studies of individual healers and sufferers will be included. These will allow us to experience vicariously what seventeenth-century illness and therapy could be like in a way general discussion cannot. One study cannot hope to provide a definitive view of seventeenth-century illness experience. Limits must be imposed. This book will not give a demographic or epidemio-logical view of seventeenth-century diseases. It will not attempt to describe contemporary living conditions or suggest any cause-effect relationship between these conditions and the disorders people suffered from. It also will not attempt indepth analysis of the relationship between medical theories and therapies.

Because of the nature of the questions asked and the source materials consulted, arguments and conclusions will be impressionistic rather than quantitative. The question of how representative these conclusions can be is justifiable. However, this study will argue that few generalisations about human experience can successfully be made. Despite common living conditions and the options generally available for handling illness, injury and childbirth, the individual's experience is ultimately unique. It depends on numerous factors, such as individual character, religious orientation, geographical loca-tion, social class, economic status, pain threshold and personal 'medical history', in combinations which prove quite resistant to attempts at generalisation. One can describe what indivi-duals suffered and what they did about their problems. The more similar the accounts available, the more possible tentative generalisations become.

With the above reservations always in mind, some argu-ments will be made. In seventeenth-century England the most commonly used kinds of medical therapy were self-treatment and treatment rendered by lay-people – relations, friends and neighbours. Women acted as amateur healers, regardless of their social status. Medical information was widely dis-seminated in the population. Although certain types of medical knowledge, such as learned medicine, based on academic training, and popular medicine, based on oral tradition, can be identified, there is no clear demarcation between these types. Rather, there was a spectrum of medical knowledge shared by the population as a whole. Licensed physicians sometimes used popular therapies; lay-people were acquainted with learned medical theories and prescribed officially endorsed remedies for themselves and their friends.

Further, it will be argued that despite the efforts and aspirations of occupational organisations, there was no medical profession in seventeenth-century England. Providers of medical services, licensed and unlicensed, competed in an open market where the consumer remained largely in charge of his or her own care. Licensed medical practitioners had a monopoly over neither practice nor medical knowledge. Thus, although they and their unlicensed competitors might make claims of expertise, there was no consensus in the general population that licensed healers were the sole authorities in medical matters. The creation of a profession requires such a consensus.

Seventeenth-century sufferers' experience of illness and medicine was very different from that of their twentieth-century descendants. The modern inflation of expectations has been mentioned above. In the early modern period, whatever their hopes, people did not actually expect healers and medicines to cure them. Furthermore, as we shall see, they did not expect medicine-taking to make them feel better; most of the time, medicine made people feel very ill.

In addition, seventeenth-century illnesses, births and deaths were very social, in contrast to the privacy required by twentieth-century conventions. All of these events took place at home, witnessed by crowds of family members, friends and neighbours, as well as healers. All women were expected to prescribe for and nurse relatives, friends and neighbours. A married woman who had not been invited to the childbirth of someone closely connected to her might justifiably feel slighted. Visiting the sick was a religious and social duty performed by both sexes. Routine responsibility for and witnessing of birth, illness and death brought seventeenth-century people closer to the events of their own mortality than are those living in the twentieth century.

Source materials for this book are of six major types. The secondary literature dealing with both the general social history and the medical history of seventeenth-century England has been widely drawn upon. Indeed, the debts owed by this study for aid in articulating questions, finding resource materials and formulating conclusions are too great to be accurately enumerated. Keith Thomas's *Religion and the Decline of Magic* and Lawrence Stone's *The Family, Sex and Marriage in England 1500–1800* provided an enormous amount of background information and bibliographical help.[4] Although many of the arguments and conclusions of these seminal works may be challenged, their wide-ranging scholarship, imaginative approaches and superb readability were inspirational. Alan Macfarlane's *Witchcraft in Tudor and Stuart England: A Regional and Comparative Study*, along with Thomas's work, suggested ways in which anthropological perspectives could be brought to bear upon historical questions. It also added to the information gleaned from Thomas's book concerning unlearned and unlicensed healers.[5] A collection of essays edited by Charles Webster on *Health, Medicine and Mortality in the Sixteenth Century* suggested numerous ways of approaching that subject in the following century.[6] Michael MacDonald's pioneering study *Mystical Bedlam: Madness, Anxiety and Healing in Seventeenth-Century England* offered one method of using a healer's casebook as the primary source material for a discussion of seventeenth-century illness.[7] And Paul Slack's *The Impact of Plague in Tudor and Stuart England* illuminated ways in which disease can be viewed in its social context.[8] Unfortunately, I have been unable to cite Harold J. Cook's useful *The Decline of the Old Medical Regime in Stuart London*, which appeared after this book was completed.[9]

Such secondary reading served as the conceptual foundation upon which the information gleaned from primary sources was built. Casebooks kept by seventeenth-century medical practitioners give insight into the therapeutic routines and clienteles of healers. Diaries and correspondence of lay-people provide information about the disorders people suffered from, the treatments they used and the healers they consulted. These private papers also reveal general religious and theoretical orientations which are useful in explaining the medical behaviour of their writers. As historical sources they have obvious limitations. Writers of such documents are usually of upper or middling social origins. How representative can their records be of general experience? Firstly, it should be observed that the illness experience of even upper-class sufferers is rarely studied. As part of the wider picture, forming one end of the spectrum of observation and therapeutical attention, this experience offers a necessary perspective from which to view contemporary illness and medicine. Secondly, half a loaf is better than none at all; the historian must make the best possible use of whatever documents exist. Thirdly, although the writers of medical and surgical casebooks were of middling and upper status, many of their patients were not. Thus, casebooks allow inferences to be made about the general experience of medical and surgical care. Finally, sources originating with the social elite can be balanced by those having more direct links with a broader cross-section of the population.

The London Bills of Mortality and selected parish records have been consulted for evidence about causes of death. While the diseases people died from are not necessarily the same as those people lived with, they do act as a partial guide to the seventeenth-century medical 'scene'. For instance, the large number of plague deaths in the period helps to explain the general fear of plague felt even by people who lived far from the places usually threatened by epidemics.

Seventeenth-century popular literature and vernacular medical literature have been examined for information about attitudes concerning disease, healers and patients. This large body of writing tells a confused and sometimes contradictory tale. However, its complex character is useful in itself, underlining the general impression of complexity and diversity in matters relating to illness and medicine given by the other source materials.

This book is an exploratory study. It joins the small but growing body of work dealing with the sufferer's experience.[10] Rather than providing a complete picture of suffering and healing in seventeenth-century England, it hopes to suggest a number of directions for further research.

History is all about continuity and change. Historians have traditionally seen the seventeenth century as a watershed in the development of English medicine. Significant changes took place during the period. William Harvey discovered the circulation of the blood. Thomas Sydenham, the great clinician, advocated a return to empirical observation in the practice of medicine. The apothecaries stepped out of their medieval role as the servants of licensed physicians, increasingly becoming general practitioners in their own right. Man-midwives grew in number and power, giving promise of their eventual takeover of the practice of 'obstetrics' in the subsequent two centuries. Metallic 'Paracelsian' remedies increased in popularity, rivalling traditional herbal medicines. The spa became well established, offering a combination of fashionable social life and medicinal waters which would not decline in popularity until the late nineteenth century.

More examples could be given. However, for the individual sufferer, the early seventeenth century appears to have been much the same as the late seventeenth century. Remedies came in and out of fashion, but therapeutic evacuation was a constant. The medical marketplace was staffed by the same population of vendors at the beginning as at the end of the period. Although the plague disappeared after 1666, other seventeenth-century diseases remained to be suffered, feared and treated well after the new century began. Thus, this study concentrates on continuity rather than change, leaving the discussion of medical innovation to those not primarily concerned with the sufferer's point of view.

2

THE MEDICAL MARKETPLACE

In order to describe the seventeenth-century medical market-place, we must first divest ourselves of the assumption that the licensed medical practitioner belonged to a recognised profession. Professor Geoffrey Holmes defines professional status as follows:

> a profession is a calling or vocation, exclusive . . . of occupations 'purely commercial, mechanical, agricultural or the like'; and . . . what gives it its distinctive social stamp is the fact that, through education and a career-oriented training, a particular body of specialised knowledge is acquired and is then applied to the service . . . of others.[1]

Only seventeenth-century physicians could have claimed to fulfil the requirements of such a definition. And even the physicians' claims were suspect. Their numbers were very small.[2] Relatively few sufferers ever became their patients. Even the patients of physicians were not in uniform agreement about the physicians' service motivations.[3] And the physicians themselves were quite vocally insecure about their status, complaining about their many competitors and about the insufficient respect they received from lay-men.

Other medical occupations had no pretensions to such 'professional' status in the seventeenth century. Healers such as surgeons, apothecaries, midwives, empirics and cunning-folk sold their services quite openly. Their training, usually by some form of apprenticeship, was similar to that employed by other trades and crafts.

Margaret Pelling describes the approaches of traditional historians to the analysis of the medical occupations for the period before 1800 as follows:

> Some of these emphasised the literary qualifications of a minority; some, to point a contrast, stressed earlier credulity or eccentricity;

others entered into controversy over the craft origins of surgeons and apothecaries. Analysts have followed these leads without embarking on a freer discussion of the earlier period in terms outside those period–specific concepts used to describe the modern professions. This has had three main effects. First, by far the larger part of medical activity remains undescribed. Secondly, there is a disguising of the elements of continuity before and after 1800. Thirdly, there is a persistent underestimate of the connections between medicine and other economic and social activities.[4]

While the period after 1700 is outside the scope of this study and enterprises other than healing engaged in by medical practitioners will not be explored, an attempt will be made to describe as much of seventeenth-century medical activity as possible, and to place that activity in the context of the general social life of the period.

In order to do this, the links between seventeenth-century healers and the twentieth-century medical profession will be forgotten. The healers whose activities will be described will be seen, rather, as inhabiting a medical marketplace where services were advertised and sold to those sufferers who cared to shop. As this study can derive no benefit from attempting to make a qualitative distinction between medical and other occupations, no such distinction will be made. The society physician, in his red robe and full wig, may as easily be compared to the prosperous London merchant as to the bishop. Whether or not he was professional is unimportant; use of that label may well obscure more than it clarifies.

The following chapter will describe the many types of seventeenth-century healers. It will go on to examine healers' attitudes about themselves, other healers and the lay-population. Finally, it will turn to the question of healers' aspirations and public responses to them.

I LICENSED HEALERS

The truly licensed healers of seventeenth-century England were the physicians, surgeons and midwives. Physicians were licensed by bishops, universities and the Royal College of Physicians of London. They also sometimes became members of provincial medical guilds.[5] Surgeons were licensed by bishops and universities. They were also admitted to practise by the London Company of Barbersurgeons and provincial surgeons' companies or craft guilds. Midwives were licensed by bishops.[6]

Apothecaries, although they were technically neither healers nor licensed, will be included in the category of licensed healers. In London their position was legitimised by the Worshipful Society of Apothecaries (founded in 1617). They were alternately protected and persecuted by the physicians, depending upon whether they were perceived by their superior colleagues as loyal servants or renegade competitors. And, although their official function was merely to prepare medications, they often gave medical advice to those who patronised their shops.[7]

Theoretically the functions of these practitioners were very different. Physicians, although empowered by law to practise surgery and make up medications, were mainly expected to diagnose internal maladies and prescribe internal remedies. Partly because of their humanist training, partly because of their high social status, they were expected to be authorities, delegating most of the physical aspects of treatment to surgeons, apothecaries, nurses and servants. Surgeons were entrusted with injuries and the outward manifestations of disease. They set fractured bones, lanced infected swellings, dealt with obstructions such as bladder stones and treated skin rashes. They also treated venereal diseases and helped in difficult childbirths. They were expected to use only 'outward' remedies, leaving internal medicine to the physicians. Apothecaries, as indicated above, were expected to be experts in medical ingredients. Their function was to prepare remedies according to the directions given by physicians and surgeons.

Again theoretically, apothecaries and surgeons were expected to act under the direction of the learned physicians. The theory is well stated by Francis Herring, an early seventeenth-century Fellow of the Royal College of Physicians:

> So that the Physician, as a great Commander, hath as subordinate to him cooks for Diet, the surgeons for manual Operation, the Apothecaries for confecting and preparing medicines. You see then how goodly large and ample patrimony Physick hath, and that all her store and skill, consisteth not in compounding and mingling of a medicine. If that were all, then all our skillful chirurgeons and apothecaries . . . should be absolute and complete physicians. . . . And yet how far the cunningest of them are, from being able to give counsel in physic, both themselves will . . . freely acknowledge.[8]

Physicians had the highest social and economic status among all seventeenth-century medical practitioners. Their training was long and academic. They were expected to be able to read, write and speak in Latin and classical Greek. They were also expected to be familiar with a small library of classical and medieval medical works.[9] They obtained this education at university, attending Oxford or Cambridge and sometimes continuing their training at a continental university, such as Padua, Montpellier or Basel.

Several options were open to seventeenth-century medical students. For example, after 1570 Cambridge students became qualified physicians in one of two ways. Some obtained the MB by spending six years in residence, attending medical lectures, viewing dissections and participating in disputations in the schools, and acquired the MD five years later. Others took an MA, requiring seven years in residence, and then obtained a university medical licence which was both less expensive and easier to get than the MB.[10] English medical students who completed their educations at continental universities often returned to incorporate their degrees at one of the English universities, thus qualifying for membership of the Royal College of Physicians.

Not all of those who practised 'physic' in seventeenth-century England bothered to obtain English university degrees or licences. Some held bishops' licences which simply involved examination by the bishop of the diocese (or, in London, the Dean of St Paul's) and a panel of four physicians.[11] Many holders of foreign medical degrees practised both within and outside immigrant communities without bothering to obtain English accreditation.[12] All of the above practitioners, however, considered themselves learned and opposed the multitude of unlearned practitioners, be they surgeons, apothecaries, midwives, or part of the multitude of 'smiths, weavers and women' who prescribed internal remedies in spite of all legal and organisational attempts to stop them.[13]

Not all of those licensed to practise medicine were full-time physicians. Many, like the Buckinghamshire astrological physician, Richard Napier, were also clergymen.[14] The minister's duty to visit and comfort the sick made a combination of roles quite natural. The academic skills required for studying theology and medicine were similar. A suggestion has even been made that during times of religious turmoil, 'clerics prudently studied medicine as a safeguard'.[15] The Royal College of Physicians objected to the granting of licences to scholars who ultimately became clergymen.[16] However, this practice continued throughout the seventeenth century. The relationship between medicine and theology was a two-way street. While vicars sometimes were licensed physicians, physicians, such as the late sixteenth-century author, Timothy Bright, abandoned medicine for the church.[17]

At the top of the medical elite was the Royal College of Physicians of London (RCP), founded in 1518. From the beginning its members had a monopoly over the practice of medicine within the City of London and a seven-mile radius around the metropolis. After 1523 its monopoly was extended to include the whole country in an attempt to take the licensing of physicians out of the hands of the bishops and make it the responsibility of the RCP. Despite an unsuccessful attempt at regulating provincial practice by using 'Visitors', the RCP never developed the administrative machinery necessary to enforce its power outside London.[18] The RCP had the power to fine, imprison and bar from practice any person they found to be violating its monopoly. Numerous efforts were made to enforce this monopoly.[19] However, membership of the RCP was exclusive. At no time in the seventeenth century did it recognise more than forty Fellows. The membership of the RCP was so small and the numbers of those illegally prescribing internal medicines so large that attempts at enforcement were doomed to failure.

Furthermore, although the RCP's monopoly had been awarded in the first place to protect the populace from the depredations of the unlearned and unskilled, it frequently attacked practitioners such as Thomas Bonham, holder of a Cambridge MD, and John Banister, a learned surgeon, writer and translator.[20] Such actions make a nonsense of the RCP's claims of altruism and suggest questions about the reasons for its exclusivity, despite the obvious demand for medical services in London. The RCP appears to have been defeated by its own desire to protect its increasingly old-fashioned allegiance to lengthy classical education and its somewhat dubious claims regarding the gentility of physicians. By enlarging its membership and lowering the fees physicians charged, the RCP could most likely have made real the monopoly it claimed by law. However, to do so might have cheapened the physician in both his own estimation and in the eyes of the general public. For the RCP, such a result would have made the effort futile.

Surgeons were the most numerous of all licensed seventeenth-century healers.[21] Although the English universities licensed surgeons, most received their training by apprenticeship. They then could apply for bishops' licences, which were granted upon successful examination by the bishop and four expert

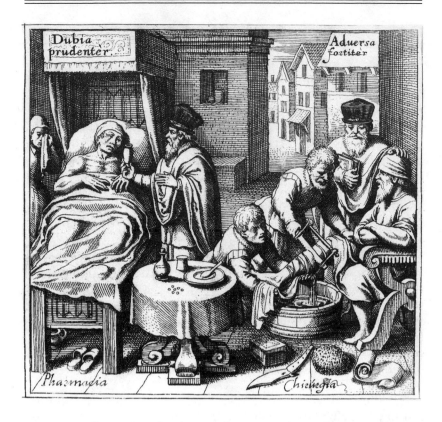

Engraving illustrating the duties of seventeenth-century apothecaries and surgeons. (Matthaeus Merian, *c.* 1646, Wellcome Library)

surgeons.[22] They could, alternatively, practise under the protection of one of the many craft organisations regulating surgeons which operated in towns and cities throughout the country.[23] In London the Barbersurgeons' Company, founded in 1540, was the largest of all the City Companies, numbering 293 members in 1641, of whom approximately half were surgeons.[24]

Surgeons were not expected to be multilingual or learned to the same degree as the physicians. However, they were expected to be literate in English and to have a sound basic understanding of such subjects as anatomy. Within the occupation there was an enormous diversity in training and social status, ranging from the learned surgeons, such as the sixteenth-century luminary William Clowes, to the local barbersurgeon who cut hair and drew teeth, in addition to performing surgical operations. The surgical elite pressed for higher standards. In 1564 the 'Master Surgeon' Thomas Gale lamented that 'every person good and bad, learned and unlearned, Chirurgeon or no Chirurgeon, do without penalty and correction of laws . . . take on them the practice of Chirurgerie'.[25] In order to remedy the situation, numerous handbooks for surgeons were published in English.[26] However, the craft organisations were most important in maintaining standards. The Barbersurgeons' Company of London punished its own members for malpractice and supervised the treatment of patients thought to be in danger of death.[27] It also prosecuted those who undertook surgical cases without the approval of the Company.[28] In addition, it housed surgical lectures and public dissections, thus contributing to the education of London surgeons.

Although surgeons shared neither the relatively high social status, nor the upward mobility aspirations of the physicians, the potential existed for them to make a good living and socialise with well-to-do people. Samuel Pepys numbered several surgeons among his friends. By performing a necessary function and providing relief from pain and handicap, the surgeons demonstrated their utility far more easily than could the physicians. It is therefore not remarkable that they were so numerous.[29]

For the apothecaries, the seventeenth was a very important century. Having formed their Worshipful Society in 1617 with the aid of the Royal College of Physicians, the apothecaries, both within and outside London, proceeded to spend the rest of the century challenging their erstwhile patrons for the right to practise internal medicine.[30] Their shops served both as outlets for merchandise and as consulting-rooms.

Like the surgeons, apothecaries were trained by apprenticeship. They were literate and, because of the demands made upon them by physicians, knew more than a little Latin. They were expected to be familiar with an enormous variety of medical ingredients, vegetable, animal and mineral, and were entrusted with the task of compounding the complicated recipes dear to the hearts of seventeenth-century physicians and patients. In addition to their familiarity with these ingredients, they were expected to understand the humoral qualities of the ingredients they used. Partly to standardise the remedies available and partly to help apothecaries in their work, the Royal College of Physicians published the first London *Pharmacopoeia* in Latin in 1618. This, in addition to the physicians' official duty to inspect apothecaries' shops, was expected to help the physicians control the apothecaries.

The apothecaries benefited from the general seventeenth-century greed for medicines. They also were able to capitalise on two important trends in the drug trade. English exploration and colonial expansion sent a steady stream of exotic foreign substances home throughout the century. Remedies such as tobacco, guaiacum and, late in the century, 'Jesuit's bark' increased apothecaries' incomes. Perhaps more important were the non-herbal Paracelsian remedies, such as mercury, antimony and vitriol, which were becoming popular by the beginning of the century. Shunned at first by the conservative 'Galenical' physicians, apothecaries and their Paracelsian colleagues, the chemists, prepared and sold these medicines alongside the surgeons.

Although the physicians tried to control the apothecaries, both by prosecuting individuals for practising medicine and by encouraging physicians to make their own remedies, the apothecaries were ultimately victorious.[31] For one thing, there were many more apothecaries than there were physicians. For another, what happened in apothecaries' shops was a private matter between the apothecary and the client. It was difficult for a physician to prove that an apothecary had been prescribing unless the apothecary wished to be found out.[32] By the end of the century, apothecaries were routinely acting as general practitioners, particularly in provincial areas.[33]

Last under the heading of officially recognised medical personnel, the midwives were uneasy companions of their more learned male colleagues. Although, like physicians and surgeons, they were licensed by the bishops, the licensing of midwives had more to do with their moral character than with their skill.

From the middle ages until the late sixteenth century at least, midwives were obliged to baptise infants who seemed likely to die before the sacrament could be administered by a priest.[34] Clergymen were expected to instruct midwives in the orthodox baptismal formula.

In addition, the midwife served a legal function, acting, along with the other women present, as a witness of the birth and an informal inquisitor of the labouring woman. A sixteenth-century midwife's licence makes her duties clear:

> ITEM you shall neither cause nor suffer any woman to name or put other father to the child, but only him that is the very father indeed thereof. ITEM you shall not suffer any woman to p'tend feign surmise herself to be delivered of a child which is not indeed neither to claim any other woman's child for her own. ITEM that

ye shall never consent agree give or keep counsel that any woman be delivered secretly of that she goeth with but that in the presence of two or three honest women and that there be two or three lights always ready.[35]

It was obviously in the interests of both church and state that midwives be honest, loyal and spiritually orthodox.

Midwives were, of course, employed to deliver babies. They were summoned early in labour and stayed with their clients until the baby was born. In addition, like sick-nurses, they often performed household tasks during labour and sometimes after delivery.[36] Midwifery training was generally informal, although, according to the seventeenth-century man-midwife, Percival Willughby, 'The young midwives at London be trained seven years first under the old midwives, before they be allowed to practise for themselves'.[37] For the most part, the midwife was trained through her own experience and her observation of many births. Since not only she, but also a number of other neighbour women were present during the birth process, all had the opportunity to add to the local stock of information on the subject.[38] The midwife also served as an authority on matters of women's diseases and sexual relations.

Until the eighteenth century midwives delivered almost all of the babies born in England. Only occasionally were surgeons summoned to difficult births. In these cases the infant was usually delivered in pieces, and the woman endangered as well. Beginning in the sixteenth century, however, male healers began to show an interest in midwifery techniques, which was reflected in a gradually increasing body of literature published on the subject.[39] A few seventeenth-century practitioners became man-midwives. One of these, Peter Chamberlen, is traditionally credited with the invention of the midwifery forceps. However, the instrument was jealously guarded as a family monopoly by generations of Chamberlen accoucheurs. Not until it was reinvented by Edmund Chapman in 1733 did it come into general use.[40]

Surgeons accused midwives of ignorance. Indeed, midwives themselves were aware of their own need for reliable training. In 1616 several London midwives, with the help of Peter Chamberlen, petitioned the King and Parliament for the incorporation of a midwives' company which would be responsible for the training and licensing of midwives.[41] However, the formation of such a company was blocked by the Royal College of Physicians on the following grounds:

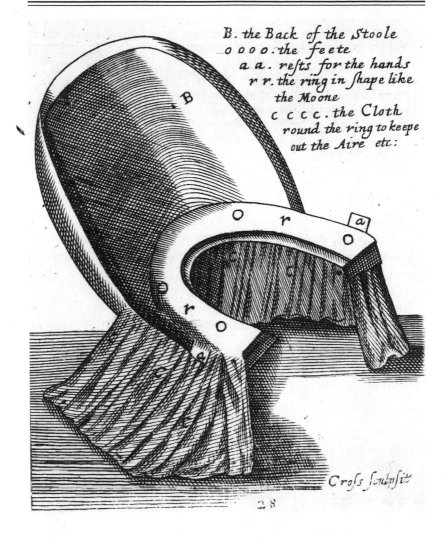

B. the Back of the stoole
o o o o. the feete
a a. rests for the hands
r r. the ring in shape like
the Moone
c c c c. the Cloth
round the ring to keepe
out the Aire etc:

Cross sculpsit

A birthing chair recommended by a seventeenth-century author of a book on midwifery. (J. Wolveridge, *Speculum Matricis*, London, 1671.)

> Nevertheless they [the RCP] think it neither necessary nor convenient that they [the midwives] should be made a Corporation to govern within themselves, a thing not exampled in any Commonwealth.[42]

Two more efforts were made to incorporate midwives. In 1634 another Peter Chamberlen (son of the first mentioned of that name) proposed a scheme for the training and licensing of midwives. Unfortunately he wanted to control the programme himself. His proposal was opposed by the midwives Mrs Hester Shaw and Mrs Whipp as follows:

> That through the molestation of a Dr. Chamberlen by appointing them [the midwives] to meet at his house once every month without authority, and with intention, as they suppose to bring about a project of his to have the sole licensing of them or approving of all such as shall hereafter be licensed out of an opinion of himself, and his own ability in the art of midwifery, implying a necessity of using him and no other both in those cases and in all other occasions that shall happen to women with child, presuming that he shall not repair unto such women as are distressed whose midwives have refused to conform themselves to him.[43]

They went on to accuse Chamberlen of extreme violence in his use of instruments. Chamberlen's attempt to monopolise midwifery in London failed.

In 1687 the midwife Elizabeth Cellier petitioned James II for 'the Foundation of a Royal Hospital and raising a Revenue of five or six thousand pounds a year by, and for the Maintenance of a Corporation of skilful midwives, and such Foundlings or exposed children, as shall be admitted therein'.[44] Her scheme was unsuccessful, partly because of her own notoriety (she was a convert to Catholicism, accused of involvement in the obscure Meal-Tub Plot), and partly, perhaps, because the monarch had other things on his mind. Not until 1902 were the midwives successful in obtaining their own corporation, including adequate training facilities and licensing rights.

Midwives may be viewed as being more similar to unlearned unlicensed healers than they were to physicians, surgeons and apothecaries. Like their unlicensed brethren, they were attacked by licensed healers for ignorance and immorality. Worse, their occupation was traditionally linked with witchcraft. Visitation articles of 1559 included the question,

> Whether you know of any that do use charms, sorcery, enchantments, invocations, circles, witchcrafts, soothsayings, or any like crafts or imaginations invented by the Devil and specially in time of women's travail.[45]

Although by the eighteenth century midwives were no longer being accused of witchcraft, they retained the negative reputation publicised by their detractors. The eighteenth-century midwife, Margaret Stephen, wrote,

> Those who have found it in their interest to bring midwives into
> disrepute, have charged them with intemperance, and even
> obscenity. How the being a midwife should make women possess
> such vices is to me a mystery. I know no way of life in which a
> woman can be engaged, that is more calculated to fix sentiments
> of piety and morality upon the mind, nor have I ever been
> acquainted with any midwife who did not possess them.[46]

Despite such defenders, and despite the support of those who
viewed as immoral the presence of man-midwives in the birth
chamber, the stereotype, of which Dickens's Sairey Gamp was
but one example, stuck to midwives.[47]

Rather than offering them training, the physicians and
surgeons attempted to drive midwives and other unlearned
healers from medical practice altogether. Their methods of
attack and the probable reasons for their success will be
discussed in greater detail below. Although licensed male
practitioners were unable entirely to rid England of female
midwives, they were able to take over the practice of
'obstetrics' among all but the poorest classes of patients, thus
essentially eliminating their competition.

II UNLICENSED HEALERS

> Forasmuch as the science and cunning of Physick and surgery (to
> the perfect knowledge whereof be requisite both great learning
> and ripe experience) is daily within the Realm exercised by a great
> multitude of ignorant persons, of whom the greater part have no
> manner of insight in the same, nor in any other kind of learning:
> Some also can no letters on the Book, so far forth that common
> Artificers, as smiths, weavers, and women boldly and
> accustomably take upon them great cures, and things of great
> difficulty: in the which they partly use sorcery and Witchcraft,
> partly apply such Medicines unto the disease as be very noxious,
> and nothing meet therefore; to the high displeasure of God, great
> infamy to the Faculty, and the grievous hurt, damage, and
> destruction of the King's liege people; most especially of them
> that cannot discern the uncunning from the cunning.
>
> An Act for the Appointing of Physicians and Surgeons (1512)[48]

The vast majority of people practising medicine in seventeenth-
century England did so without the blessing of church, state
or occupational organisation. It is difficult to obtain reliable
information about either the activities or the numbers of these
healers, because so much of what was written about them was
written by their enemies. Nevertheless, it is certain that both

urban and rural areas supported a host of unauthorised healers, some learned, most unlearned; some practising medicine as a full-time occupation, others dividing their attention between medicine and other trades; some engaging in general practice, others specialising in the treatment of a particular condition; some long-term members of a community, others itinerants who were subject to prosecution as vagrants in addition to their vulnerability to attack from licensed practitioners.[49]

Not all of these healers were the ignorant charlatans their competitors accused them of being. Some had received university training – a few holding foreign medical degrees.[50] A few were learned physicians or surgeons who, for one reason or another, had fallen foul of the medical organisations.[51] The group which provoked the most serious and sustained attacks from the supporters of learned licensed medicine, however, was the large number of empirics, who maintained that in medical practice experience was more important than theory and, thus, that the extensive book-learning of physicians was unnecessary. One popular sixteenth-century empirical writer, Leonardo Fioravanti, stated his position as follows:

> there is no science in the world wherewith a man may do good if therewith be no practice or experience, as a man may say. The which experience is master of all things, as it is plainly seen.[52]

That his common-sense approach to healing appealed to many simply made the attacks on empirics more vicious.

It is interesting to note that Fioravanti's scepticism regarding medical theory was echoed by the great clinician, Thomas Sydenham, a century later. In an unpublished treatise on dysentery, written in 1669, he wrote

> This way of cure will not be thought less expeditious and certain then [sic] courses usually prescribed are both tedious and dangerous, when the world valuing learning for that only therein which is necessary for the good of human life shall think as well of him that taught to cure diseases as those that taught to discourse learnedly about them.[53]

Although Sydenham himself came under attack for both his anti-intellectual views and his unorthodox methods, his general attitude was prophetic. Empiricism, or, at least, an empirical 'style', would characterise medical research and practice long after empirics themselves had been driven from the field.

None the less, for seventeenth-century orthodox physicians, their academic achievements were the basis for their claims of superiority and the right to a monopoly over medical care. The activities of those who openly professed a disregard for theory was both insulting to the *amour propre* of learned physicians and potentially injurious to their incomes.

The relatively large number of medical works produced by empirics and their sympathisers indicates that the medical establishment had cause for alarm.[54] Not only did these writers maintain that classical medical education was virtually useless, but also they wrote that the general public had the right to medical information which learned practitioners were deliberately keeping from them.

> How long would they [the physicians] have the people ignorant? Why grudge they physic to come forth in English? Would they have no man to know but only they? Or what made they themselves Merchants of our lives and deaths, that we should buy our health only of them, and at their prices?[55]

While some of the empirical writers demonstrate a tendency towards keeping as personal monopolies certain medical 'secrets', a practice their enemies often accused them of, most appear to have encouraged the popular penchant for self-medication.[56]

The term 'empiric' was a general one, intended by the enemies of unauthorised healers to have the same meaning as the word 'quack' has in modern parlance. Thus, the label stuck to a multitude of practitioners, some of whom were in general practice, and some of whom specialised in the treatment of particular disorders. Many specialists were quasi-respectable, so long as they did not poach on the territory of higher-status healers. The Barbersurgeons' Company of London awarded special licences to practitioners who specialised in bone-setting, scrofula, cutting for the stone and operating on ruptures, fistulae and cataracts.[57] Many such practitioners operated outside London as well – some living in towns and villages, some travelling from place to place.[58] Perhaps typical of these healers was the travelling shoemaker who showed up in Maidstone in the mid-sixteenth century, claiming to be able to heal sore eyes.[59]

It is difficult to generalise about the therapeutic methods of empirics, partly because they differed widely, one from another, partly because their methods are most often described by enemies, eager to discredit them. Empirics were accused of employing 'secret' remedies and of applying a single panacea

Woodcut of a sixteenth-century physician surrounded by a ring of urine flasks. Until the seventeenth century the distinctively-shaped urine flask was the major symbol of the service provided by physicians. Although diagnosis and treatment based upon the examination of a urine sample was increasingly frowned upon by learned physicians, many seventeenth-century healers and sufferers continued to use this technique.

to all disorders. However, licensed healers might with justice have been attacked for the same practices.

Certainly empirics borrowed techniques from higher-status colleagues. Two who specialised in the treatment of syphilis in mid-seventeenth-century London, 'one Bonorenige' and Kixton the Quack, used mercury preparations as did many licensed surgeons.[60] And a much-maligned group of healers, the so-called 'piss prophets', diagnosed and prescribed after examination of the patient's urine – a technique which had simply become out of date among most physicians by the mid-seventeenth century.

A revealing description of diagnosis from urine appeared in Thomas Brain's *The Piss-Prophet, or Certain Piss-Pot Lectures . . .*, published in 1637. Brain, a licensed physician, admitted that he had diagnosed pregnancy from examining urine samples, but wrote that he had known he was practising 'trickery' and had stopped using that method.[61] He claimed that his book had been written in order to give patients 'inside information' about how piss prophets operated, describing how a practitioner could tell a lot about the patient and the patient's condition by carefully observing the person who delivered the urine sample and questioning that person in so subtle a way that he or she would never realise that information had been divulged.

In spite of the scepticism of Brain and other physicians regarding the usefulness of the examination of urine samples, the practice continued for a long time, both among healers and among patients. The diarists Samuel Pepys and Ralph Josselin routinely examined their own urine during times of illness.[62]

A group of practitioners whose methods diverged more widely from those of licensed healers were the magical practitioners. A wide variety of such healers existed. At the top of the scale, in terms of both social status and expense, was the magical astrologer. His position, *vis-à-vis* learned physicians, the state and the church, was an uneasy one.

In the seventeenth century astrology was a respectable science, taught in the universities and frequently employed by physicians and apothecaries to help them gather herbs, prepare medicines and administer treatment at the most propitious times.[63] However, astrology's associations with 'art magic' were both recognised and practised. For Tudor and Stuart Englishmen, conscious of the presence and danger of witch-craft, high magic was simply a learned cousin of sorcery and demonianism. The physician John Cotta wrote

> As it is not obscure, that some men under the colour of astrology
> have practised magic and sorcery, so it is no less evident that
> many others under the pretense of advising and counselling in
> physick for curation or Prognostication of disease have likewise
> exercised the same devilish practice.[64]

Famous magical practitioners, such as Simon Forman and John Dee, testify both to the popularity of their services and the upper-class patronage such services could command.[65] Less notorious astrological physicians, such as Richard Napier, mentioned above, illustrate the respectability of such practices in some hands.[66] However, astrological physicians were in danger of being accused of sorcery. Simon Forman was accused of practising magic (which, indeed, he admitted doing), and was many times imprisoned for practising medicine without a licence.[67] Dr John Lambe, another magical practitioner patronised by the great, faced an even worse fate. After having been imprisoned and examined by the Royal College of Physicians for his unlicensed practice, Lambe was battered to death in the streets.[68]

Lower in status than the astrological physicians were the cunning-folk, wise-men and -women, white witches and wizards who, in addition to healing, found lost or stolen goods, identified thieves and witches, made love potions and foretold the future.[69] These practitioners treated a full spectrum of diseases in both animals and humans, ranging from readily diagnosable physical ailments to disorders caused by witchcraft. Their fees varied considerably, but compared favourably with the charges of other types of healers. Some charged only when the treatment was successful. Others would accept no money at all, but took their fees in foodstuffs.[70]

These healers mingled traditional medical knowledge, folk magic and prayer to produce their cures. They employed word charms which were either recited or written on pieces of paper and hung around the sufferer's neck.[71] They used other magical techniques, such as 'girdle-measuring' and transferring the illness from the sick person to themselves.[72] They also employed herbal preparations similar to those used by empirics and licensed medical practitioners.

Unlearned magical practitioners were open to attack on many fronts. They were prosecuted for unlicensed medical and surgical practice. They were also particularly vulnerable to the charge of witchcraft. For one thing, they were frequently employed to diagnose illnesses which had been caused by witchcraft, and could identify witches. For another, they claimed to be able to cure diseases caused by witchcraft. Such talents were dangerous, for, it was reasoned, magic was identified by magic. Although art magicians like Richard Napier argued in favour of angelic magic (Napier conjured up the Archangel Raphael), the consensus of opinion was that to traffic with the unseen world was either to invoke Satan or to act in obedience to him.[73] Thus, although the magical healer might use magical arts only for the benefit of mankind, he or she was as guilty of treating with the Devil as was the black witch.

Akin to such magical healers were those who healed by touch. Some, such as seventh sons – and particularly seventh sons of seventh sons – healed by virtue of their peculiar genealogical circumstances. Others, like modern faith healers, healed as a result of powers given them by God.[74] Most famous of the latter type of healer was Valentine Greatrakes, an Irish gentleman who began by healing his neighbours of the King's Evil (scrofula or struma – a tubercular inflammation of the glands of the neck) in 1662.[75] In 1665 Greatrakes found he could heal other diseases.[76] He gained a great reputation, first in Ireland, then in England, healing by stroking the patient.[77] Philosophers, scientists and physicians observed him at work, and testified to his cures.[78] Such intellectuals as Robert Boyle and Henry More believed in him.

Greatrakes took no payment for his work. Indeed, he cited this as the reason why he had not applied for an episcopal licence to practise medicine when he was examined at the Court of Lismore.

> Then the Judge asked me, where is your licence for practising, as all Physicians and Chirurgeons ought to have from the Ordinary of the Diocese? My answer was, that I knew no reason I had to take a licence, since I took no reward from any one, and that I knew no law of the Nation which prohibited any person from doing what good he could to his neighbours.[79]

Greatrakes claimed to have had

> no further design in the distribution of that talent which the all-healing God has entrusted him withal, than the honour of his maker, and the good of his poor fellow-creatures, whose Distempers (many of them) neither Art nor Physick probably could reach.[80]

His career as a healer ended abruptly in May 1666, when he failed to cure in a demonstration before Charles II and his court.[81]

This monarch must have been most interested in Greatrakes's claims, since he made similar ones himself. Beginning with Edward the Confessor, English monarchs had touched people suffering from the King's Evil.[82] This practice reached its height under the Stuarts. Charles II touched 90,798 people in the years 1660–4 and 1667–82.[83] Keith Thomas describes the ceremony as follows:

At a special religious service conducted by leading Anglican clergy the monarch laid his hands upon each member of the long queue of sufferers. The patients approached one by one and knelt before the monarch, who lightly touched them on the face, while a chaplain read aloud the verse from St. Mark: 'They shall lay hands on the sick and they shall recover'. They then retired and came forward again so that the king might hang round their necks a gold coin strung from a white silk ribbon.[84]

The monarch did not guarantee a cure, and did not charge for his or her services. Patients resorted to the royal touch very much as they did to other medical and surgical aid. Mrs Elizabeth Barker was treated for scrofula for four years by the London surgeon, Joseph Binns, before being touched by Charles II.[85] Queen Anne was the last English monarch to touch for the King's Evil.[86]

Scrofula was not the only ailment monarchs cured. Until the reign of Elizabeth I, monarchs also ministered to sufferers from epilepsy and associated disorders, such as convulsions, rheumatism and muscle spasms. Applicants were given 'cramp rings' which the monarch had rubbed between his or her fingers in a special ceremony.[87] The rings had originally been made of the money offered by the king on Good Friday. This money was believed to have magical properties.[88] Upon the accession of Elizabeth I, the blessing of cramp rings was abandoned.

Of all the unlicensed healers discussed above, only the monarch was immune from prosecution for practising without a licence. Unauthorised healers did claim some protection under the law, however. In 1543 the so-called 'Quack's Charter' was enacted which empowered

every person being the King's subject, having knowledge and experience of the nature of Herbs, Roots and Waters, or of the operation of the same, by speculation or practice within any part of the Realm of England, or within any other the King's Dominions, to practise, use and minister in and to any outward sore . . . , wound, apostemations, outward swelling or disease, any herb or herbs, ointments, baths, poultices and plasters, according to their cunning, experience and knowledge in any of the diseases, sores and maladies beforesaid, and all other like to the same, or drinks for the stone and strangury, or agues, without suit, berations, trouble, penalty or loss of their goods.[89]

The act was passed in order to enable poor people who could not pay surgeons' fees to obtain help.

There is no doubt that unlearned unlicensed healers were widely consulted in seventeenth-century England. Their licensed competitors and detractors, about whom more will be said below, were convinced that their numbers were growing. Although such allegations cannot be proven, recent scholarship has shown that unlicensed healers were widely distributed throughout the country and that sufferers did use their services. Alan Macfarlane writes, 'Nowhere in Essex was there a village more than ten miles from a known cunning man'.[90] And Margaret Pelling and Charles Webster estimate that some 250 unauthorised healers were practising in London between 1581 and 1600.[91] Their fees were, by and large, lower than those of licensed surgeons and apothecaries. And sometimes, as in the case of magical practitioners, they provided services not usually offered by their competitors.

Medical coverage in the seventeenth century is a difficult subject to tackle. Those who have undertaken it now agree that there were more medical practitioners available – both licensed and unlicensed – than has heretofore been thought. John Raach's pioneering study identified 814 known physicians practising in the period.[92] Of these, 635 matriculated at a university, 328 received a BA, 280 an MA and 246 an MD. Most of these physicians studied at English universities, but some 137 attended a continental university, 75 taking a foreign MD.[93] Concerning geographical distribution, Raach found the largest concentrations of physicians in the coastal counties, especially Kent, Sussex, Lincoln, Norfolk, Suffolk and Devon, as well as in the Home Counties.[94]

Needless to say, Raach's work only scratches the surface. He was interested only in 'reputable' physicians. Further, as R. S. Roberts points out, it remains to be demonstrated that the holders of medical degrees Raach included actually practised, some such people apparently appearing in the *Directory* simply on the strength of possessing a degree. 'This is particularly true of the seventy-odd physicians listed for the cities of Oxford and Cambridge, for such a figure is quite disproportionate to the population.'[95]

In addition, Raach was uninterested in the practices of surgeons and apothecaries, many of whom were in general practice. Some of these healers were formally licensed to practise, either by ecclesiastical authorities or by local occupational organisations. For instance, Margaret Pelling has identified 150 members of the Barbersurgeons' Company of Norwich (which included physicians) for the period 1550–1640.[96] Many locally recognised practitioners were never licensed, yet practised alongside their licensed colleagues without being challenged.

Still other practitioners changed their occupational 'tags' or combined the characteristics of several medical occupations in the course of their careers. For instance the inventory attached to the 1637 will of John Periam, 'physician' of Plymouth, indicated that he kept a shop with merchandise in it worth £20.[97] The use of the term 'Doctor', which became increasingly common toward the end of the seventeenth century, also confuses matters. Torrington Churchwardens referred to Dr Bradford and Dr Potter who were, respectively, a surgeon and an apothecary who was also called surgeon in other documents.[98]

Indeed, one can say only that the seventeenth-century medical marketplace was plentifully staffed. This is not to say that qualified practitioners were always available wherever and whenever they were needed. On 26 August 1601 Lady Margaret Hoby, who lived in a remote part of Yorkshire and practised medicine informally among her family and neighbours, reported

> this day in the afternoon I had had a child brought to see [me] that was born at Silpho, one Talliour son, who had no fundament [anus], and had no passage for excrements but at the mouth: I was earnestly entreated to cut the place to see if any passage could be made, but, although I cut deep and searched, there was none to be found.[99]

Lady Hoby had received no formal training in surgery. We must assume that the desperate parents of this unfortunate baby consulted her as a last resort. Either no trained surgeon was available to them, or the local surgeon had refused to perform an operation so likely to end in the patient's death. However, there were multitudes of healers offering a variety of medical and surgical wares throughout the country. The evidence indicates that prospective patients shopped around for the practitioners and therapies which best suited their needs, means and tastes.

Distinctions made among licensed practitioners and between licensed and unlicensed healers are by no means as clear as some would have us believe. Apothecaries and surgeons prescribed internal medicines. Physicians compounded and sold physic from their own shops, as did apothecaries.[100] Clients made no distinction between licensed and unlicensed healers. With the exception of the relatively few academically trained practitioners, training in all cases was composed of apprenticeship (formal or informal) and personal experience.

Furthermore, the practice of medicine and surgery was often combined with other trades. The connection between medicine and the ministry has been mentioned above. The relationship between the apothecaries and the grocers, although formally dissolved in London by the foundation of the Society of Apothecaries in 1617, still exists in the present day in the form of non-prescription drugs sold in food stores. The association between barbering and surgery was an ancient one. Indeed, barbers were still pulling teeth and letting blood well into the eighteenth century. Not until 1745 were London barbers and surgeons governed by separate companies.[101]

Barbersurgeons exercised many skills in addition to the obvious ones. With wax-chandlers they shared the task of embalming the dead. Other associated trades included music-making, the brewing and selling of drink, net-making and school-teaching.[102]

Midwives occasionally kept lodging houses where they cared for women before, during and immediately after delivery. They also sometimes served as cunning-women. Indeed, the association of midwifery with magic was a time-honoured one, as we have seen.[103] In addition, midwives had the unfortunate reputation of being bawds and abortionists. Thomas Heywood's *The Wise-woman of Hogsden*, a play published in 1638, has as its central character a woman who undertook many of these activities. She says of herself,

> Let me see how many Trades have I to live by: First, I am a Wise-woman and a Fortune-teller, and under that I deal in Physick and Fore-speaking, in Palmistry, and recovering of things lost. Next, I undertake to cure Mad folks. Then I keep Gentlewoman Lodgers, to furnish such Chambers as I let out by the night: Then I am provided for bringing young Wenches to bed: and for a need, you see I can play the Match-maker.[104]

In addition, there were a number of occupations traditionally associated with medicine and surgery. Housewives and gentlewomen were expected to be able to keep herb gardens, compound remedies and treat the illnesses and injuries of their families and neighbours. As the 1512 *Act for the Appointing of Physicians and Surgeons* indicates, smiths and weavers sometimes healed. The sixteenth-century surgeon, Lanfranc of Milan, wrote that

> Cutlers, Carters, Cobblers, Coopers, Coriars of Leather,
> Carpenters, and a great rabble of women . . . foresake their
> handicrafts, and for filthy lucre abuse physick and Chirurgerie.[105]

Lanfranc was certainly biased about the motivations of those who attempted to cure in addition to exercising their original trades. However, he was right about the diversity of tradesmen and women who practised medicine and surgery.

Thus, the task of classifying, counting or even identifying the healers practising in seventeenth-century England is a virtually impossible one. Instead of the relatively neat categories available to us today – consultant, general practitioner, chiropractor, homeopath – medical personnel of that time can be viewed as inhabiting a spectrum where all distinctions were blurred, ranging from the university-trained physician to the housewife, all of whom spent at least some of their time treating the sick.

A distinction has traditionally been made between 'folk' (or 'traditional' or 'popular') and 'learned' (or 'Western' or 'modern') medicine. This distinction is most useful in medical anthropology, where two discrete systems of medical theory and provisions are often seen in opposition. Thus, the anthropologist David Landy writes on 'Role Adaptation: Traditional Curers under the Impact of Western Medicine' and his colleague, Harold A. Gould, on 'Modern Medicine and Folk Cognition in Rural India'.[106]

The distinction between 'popular' and 'modern' medicine also is found in the works of medical historians, however. F. N. L. Poynter writes,

> Many of the most important problems which confront man today arise from the conflict between new ideas and traditional beliefs, whether these be religious, social or economic. . . . In two great societies of Asia, for example, China and India, there are two rival systems of medicine, the one traditional and popular, the other modern and scientific.[107]

The earlier popular medical historian, Howard M. Haggard, wrote, 'There are two philosophies of medicine: the primitive or superstitious, and the modern or rational. They are in complete opposition to one another.'[108]

In the hands of medical historians, the opposing categories of learned and popular medicine have been applied, respectively, to literary medicine, with its Greek, Roman, Arabic, scholastic and humanist associations, and to an oral tradition of superstition and herb-lore only sporadically mentioned in any sort of written record.[109] This categorisation is dangerous for several reasons. It is self-congratulatory, viewing the adherents and beneficiaries of 'modern' medicine as rational and civilised, while the users of 'traditional' medicines are at best old-fashioned, at worst uncivilised, furry little natives. It also supports the claims of the learned physicians of past ages to have been lonely protectors of enlightened knowledge in periods darkened by superstition and ignorance. And finally, it suggests a total polarity between those believing in learned medicine and those believing in popular medicine.

Although this polarity may have existed in some places at some times, even among so-called 'primitive' peoples in today's world the reality is far more complex. The anthropological evidence indicates that sufferers generally adapt the medical systems existing in their societies to their own needs.[110] This observation certainly applies to the medical choices made by seventeenth-century English sufferers. While it is possible to identify 'traditional' and 'classical' elements in seventeenth-century medicine, a polarisation between folk and learned medicine simply did not exist.[111] Licensed and unlicensed, educated and unlearned healers shared both theories and therapies among themselves.

Virtually all healers and sufferers subscribed to a humoral view of disease and therapy. Illness or injury caused an imbalance in the body's idiosyncratic humoral complexion which was rectified by evacuation. A traditional body of herbal and astrological lore was directed at maintaining or restoring the equilibrium of the sanguine, choleric, melancholic and phlegmatic humours.[112] The great arsenal of medical texts by such sages as Hippocrates, Galen and Avicenna was directed at the same goal. Even Paracelsus, who wished to cure by sympathy rather than antipathy, was basically humoral in his therapeutic orientation.[113]

Thus, from the sufferer's point of view, it mattered little whether the healer he or she consulted was a learned physician, an empiric or a wise-woman. Treatment was almost certain to include a purge or emetic. Blood-letting or sweating might be recommended. Both herbal and metallic remedies were classified, in part, by the evacuative result they were likely to achieve.

By the same token, both licensed and unlicensed healers used techniques which were related to magical lore. Both used the aetites or eagle stone to aid in difficult births.[114] Both sanctioned stroking an afflicted part with a dead hand and putting pigeons to the feet of a person thought to be in danger of death.[115]

As Keith Thomas points out, it is difficult to distinguish between the natural properties thought to be inherent in some substances and objects and magical practices sanctioned either by local tradition or by the Neoplatonist belief in occult influences and sympathies.[116] The example he cites is the notorious weapon salve, the use of which was advocated in a book by Sir Kenelm Digby which went into twenty-nine editions.[117] This salve was applied to the weapon rather than to the wound itself. Digby claimed that the resulting cure was obtained through natural rather than magical means. However, it is doubtful whether patients made this sort of sophisticated distinction in their understanding of sympathetic cures.

In place of the generally assumed polarity between folk and learned medical theories, then, there existed a collection of medical lore which was drawn upon by both healers and lay-people. This information existed partly in the oral tradition passed from generation to generation. It was also disseminated in a large and growing vernacular medical literature which was directed at both medical practitioners and the general reading public.[118]

This is not to say that specialised medical knowledge did not exist. Astrological healers used a literature and language inaccessible to other healers and lay-men. Wizards and witches had occult secrets, rituals and incantations which they used to heal. Paracelsians and iatrochemists utilised literature and techniques wellnigh incomprehensible to the uninitiated. Learned physicians had encyclopedic knowledge of texts in languages unknown to uneducated people. Such works often remained unpublished, circulating in manuscript.

In spite – or, perhaps, because – of these arcane specialisms, the general public remained interested and comparatively well-informed in medical topics. It cultivated a healthy scepticism regarding professors of medical authority. And it reserved the right to choose healers or resort to self-treatment regardless of the efforts made by licensed healers to control its behaviour.

III ATTEMPTS TO PROFESSIONALISE: THE CREATION OF THE MYTH

Although licensed medical practitioners had the support of both the state and the church, their achievements concerning the control of medical care and provision lagged far behind their aspirations. The public, like the horse in the old adage, could be led to the wholesome waters of authorised medicine and surgery, but it could not be forced to drink. Thus, motivated partly by a desire to raise medical standards and protect gullible patients, and partly by the wish to protect and increase their own practices, incomes and social status, licensed medical practitioners launched what might be described as an advertising campaign to sell their own point of view. It was a two-pronged campaign which sought, on the one hand, to create a favourable image for licensed healers and, on the other, to destroy the reputation and practices of unlicensed healers. As its main agencies it used the powers of its occupational organisations and the vernacular medical literature referred to above.

This study will not address itself to the numerous prosecutions launched against unlicensed practitioners by the Royal College of Physicians and the Barbersurgeons' Company of London. These prosecutions have been ably discussed by other scholars.[119] Rather, we will be concerned with the medical propaganda which appeared in print. This approach to the efforts of licensed healers to consolidate and improve their own position in the medical marketplace has not been taken before. The utility of the popular press for forming popular opinion was not neglected by sixteenth- and seventeenth-century medical writers. Because the medical writers of these two centuries said substantially the same things about themselves and their competitors, sixteenth-century works will be quoted as well as those belonging to the century principally under examination.

Foremost among medical propagandists were the physicians. This is easy to understand, for they had much to gain by victory. Their aspirations, including control over all of licensed medical practice, extinction of unlicensed practice, public recognition of their rights to a high income, and general acceptance of their claims to be gentlemen, were very high. Their status was already higher than that of the surgeons and apothecaries. However, their position was insecure. Despite their officially endorsed privileges, they found competitors on all sides. And their numbers were too small, their administrative machinery too weak, to enforce the powers they had been given by law. Since their competitors were unlikely simply to disappear at a wish or command, the physicians directed some of their efforts at the market for medical services – the patients themselves.

The physicians were joined in their efforts by a small

number of learned surgeons. These surgeons were concerned
about the activities of unlearned but licensed surgeons as well
as about the behaviour of unlicensed healers. Together the
physicians and learned surgeons attempted to create a pedigree
for their crafts and distrust of the medical and surgical outlaws
who surrounded them.

The pedigree constructed by licensed learned physicians and
surgeons drew upon two resources dear to the hearts of
educated Englishmen – classical tradition and religion. As
ancestors for themselves, the physicians recalled Aesculapius
and Hippocrates. And the sixteenth-century surgeon, Thomas
Vicary, wrote,

> For did not that worthy and famous captain of the Greeks,
> Agamemnon, love dearly and reward bountifully both Podalerius
> and Machaon, through whose cunning skill in surgery, thousands
> of worthy Greeks were saved alive and healed, who else had died
> and perished.[120]

Similar efforts were made by early man-midwives who
claimed direct descent from Adam – the first *accoucheur*.[121]

Furthermore, the ministrations of learned physicians and
surgeons were authorised by God. John Cotta argued,

> For as God hath created all things for the good of man, so hath he
> appointed the physician to fit and accommodate all things unto
> the necessity and need of man, and hath farther also deputed him
> to supply unto man even those things which nature herself
> ofttimes cannot.[122]

Having mustered to their side God and the ancients, the
learned healers lamented that their occupation had recently
fallen into disrepute. The surgeon Franciscus Arcaeus wrote in
1588,

> But oh good God, is it tolerable that the ancient glory and renown
> of chirurgerie should be so defaced? Or that such men as have
> spent all their time in it, should so injuriously be put from the
> benefit of the same.[123]

The physician Francis Herring complained that the noble
Romans had paid their physicians much more than seventeenth-
century patients were willing to. He felt the smaller fees
showed a decline in the physician's status, 'to the stain and
blush of our present age'.[124]

Learned healers believed that the divinely sanctioned

services they offered and their arduous training entitled them to a monopoly over medical care. The great sixteenth-century physician, Andrew Boorde, described the education of a physician as follows:

> every physician ought to know first learning, and then practice, that is to say, first to have Grammar to understand what he doth read in Latin. Then to have logic to discourse or define by argumentation the truth from the falsehood. . . . And then to have a rhetoric or an eloquent tongue. . . . And also to have geometry, to ponder and weigh the drugs or portions the which ought to be ministered. Arithmetic is necessary to be had concerning numeration: but above all things next to Grammar, a physician must have surely his Astronomy, to know how, when, and at what time every medicine ought to be ministered, and then finally to know natural philosophy, the which consisteth in the knowledge of natural things.[125]

Physicians were particularly eager to defend their use of classical languages. The great body of classical medical texts were available only in Latin and Greek. In the words of the physician E. D., the books published in English were 'very little and light'.[126] More to the point, the physician John Securis argued:

> If English books could make men cunning physicians, then pouchmakers, threshers, ploughmen and cobblers might be Physicians as well as the best if they could read.[127]

So pervasive was the respect for Latin and Greek that almost every vernacular work on a medical subject, whether it supported or attacked the position of learned practitioners, opened with an apology and justification for publishing in English. Many physicians apparently feared that English works on medical topics would open the field to the unlearned. About such fears, Peter Levins, Oxford MA and student in physic and surgery, wrote,

> Certainly, these kind of people cannot abide that good and laudable arts should be common to many, fearing that their name and practice should decay, or at the least should diminish.[128]

Those who published in English claimed that their aim was to benefit the unlearned who otherwise might come to harm for lack of medical knowledge. Furthermore, they argued, physicians of other nations, including such writers as

Hippocrates, Galen and Avicenna, had published in their native languages. Thomas Brugis, whose book was intended for lay household use, wrote,

> for a great number of people perish for want of means to procure the advice of a physician; when perhaps with a little instructions they might have cured themselves; but we are to consider the general good and commonwealth; for in Italy, France, and other countries, scarce any Physician but hath published some book in his mother tongue, and rather than in any other language.[129]

The very defensiveness of such writers demonstrates that general respect for the physicians' academic attainments was one of their strongest cards. Another important selling point was the great length of the physicians' training. One physician maintained that it took a lifetime to learn physic, and used this argument against Paracelsians and empirics:

> And therefore it is a great error in such men, that do dream that the art of physick may be easily attained unto: so that if they have gotten two or three chemical medicines, without any other grounds; they profess themselves to be great Doctors and cunning physicians.[130]

Diagnosis and treatment depended upon an in-depth examination of the individual sufferer's symptoms, his general physical state and humoral complexion, the time of year and the humoral cause of the disorder. Therapy included a specially ordered diet, properly composed medicines and well-monitored habits of exercise, sleep and dress. Unlearned practitioners were often accused of taking a simplistic approach to disease, offering a standard treatment rather than one dictated by the particular circumstances of a particular patient.

Because of their sophisticated education and skills, physicians demanded respect and obedience from their patients. Punishment for failure to heed the physicians' instructions was death. Furthermore, the relatives and friends surrounding the patient should also obey the physician. Criticisms abound of the loving women who countered doctor's orders. For example:

> And from hence it may be evinced the erroneous practice of many, of women especially, who think the sick hath never food enough; and for this purpose they never cease to urge them to eat, morning and evening, night and day, all is one, their too too officious love and kindness having neither rhyme nor reason, as

we say, produceth often this contrary effect, that, according to the vulgar saying, *They kill their friend with kindness.*[131]

In contrast to such unhelpful meddling, members of the sick person's household should behave as follows:

> if there be any Physician or surgeon, which is with any sick man, woman or child, let no man disquiet them that be in the house nor tell them what they should do, let every person be tendable about them. And let every man in the house please and serve the Physician and Surgeon honestly, and let them lack nothing, to the end that they may be the more diligent to do the thing they go about.[132]

Above all, patients must not treat themselves:

> let not patients turn medicine mongers, but containing themselves within their proper spheres of Prayer, Confidence and Regularity, refer each cure to the honest care of the Rational Artist.[133]

Although learned healers were concerned about patients' behaviour, they would not bite the hands they hoped would feed them by directing their anger and scorn at the general public. They chose to believe that disobedient and fickle patients were duped. They saved their big guns for unauthorised healers.

So general was the concern displayed by medical authors about the dangers posed to an unsuspecting public by unlearned, unlicensed and unscrupulous medical practitioners that even works which dealt with practical subjects – handbooks for apprentice surgeons, plague tracts and herbals, for example – found space in dedications or introductions to criticise such healers. These attacks served as both a central part of the argument in favour of legal limitation of the practice of medicine and as a method of encouraging licensed practitioners to help raise educational and service standards within their own occupations.

In addition to these virtually automatic endorsements of conventional sentiment, a number of works were published in the sixteenth and seventeenth centuries which were exclusively devoted to the attack on unlearned healers.[134] The authors of what might be called the anti-quack literature were all licensed physicians or surgeons. They claimed that their motivation for writing was a public-spirited desire to open the eyes of unwary patients to the dangers which threatened them and to raise the general standards of medical care. The works of the anti-quack writers represent the most extreme and extensive statements of the conventional viewpoint. They were directed at licensed practitioners and at the general reading public. They were intended to inform, to shock, to convince and to entertain. They resemble nothing more than very early examples of yellow journalism, complete with villains, heroes, victims and the plea for a public meting out of justice to all concerned.

Unauthorised healers were accused of many errors and crimes. Chief among these was ignorance. One early-seventeenth-century anti-quack author wrote:

> But our Empirics and Imposters, as they are too ignorant either to teach or to practice Physic . . . and too insolent, and too arrogant to learn of the Masters of that Faculty, or to be reduced into order: so are they most dangerous and pernicious unto the Weale public. . . . These Crocodiles, disguised with the vizard of feigned knowledge and masking under the specious titles of Physicians and Doctors, not attained in Schools, but imposed by the common people, do with their Absolonicall Salutations steal away the affections of the inconstant multitude, from the Learned Professors of that Faculty, and with their Ioablike Imbracings, stab to the heart their poor and silly patients, ere they be aware or once suspect such uncouth Treachery. [135]

The anti-quack writers worked themselves into a lather of righteous indignation over their enemies' disrespect for medical theory. While they usually admitted that experience and observation of disease was desirable, they maintained that such experience and observation could not be understood without theory, and that to cure a disease one must understand its almost invariably invisible cause. [136] The physician E. D. wrote in 1606:

> What though they can judge of the gout, the palsy and the dropsy? So can simple women do: but to judge rightly of the causes and differences of these diseases . . . , that requireth Art, which is not in any Empiric. [137]

The sixteenth-century writer, John Halle, illustrated the learned surgeon's regard for academic theory in his examination of the travelling shoemaker, mentioned above, who 'pretended to be very cunning in curing diseases of the eyes'.

> Then I asked him whether he were a surgeon, or a physician: And he answered, no, he was a shoemaker, but he could heal all manner of sore eyes.

I asked him where he learned that: he said that was no matter.
Well, said I, seeing that you can heal sore eyes, what is an eye?
whereof is it made? of what members or parts is it composed?
And he said he knew not.[138]

Halle also indignantly described the ignorance of one
Valentine, who arrived in Maidstone in 1560 claiming to be
able to cure all diseases, as follows:

> The truth was so: he had no learning in the world, nor could read
> English (and, as I suppose, knew not a letter, or a b from a
> battledore), as it was well proved, yet made he the people believe
> that he could speak Latin, Greek and Hebrew.[139]

This crime made Halle angrier than Valentine's use of magical
methods or the fact that he had three wives living in three
different towns.

The anti-quack writers warned of the dangers of powerful
medicines in the hands of ignorant healers. John Cotta wrote,
'Worse are the bad after-consequences of ill-applied medicines,
than diseases themselves'.[140] He also fulminated against the
claims of some empirics that a single preparation could cure all
diseases.[141]

Even worse, perhaps, than the remedies of unlearned
practitioners of physic, were the attentions of unskilful
surgeons. Thomas Gale, then Master of the Company of
Barbersurgeons, wrote in 1564, in his preface to a general
work on surgery,

> thou mayest easily judge that the rabble of these rude Empirics
> (and dross of the earth which when they cannot otherwise live
> chip straight ways into the art of Chirurgery) be no chirurgeons:
> but mankillers, murderers, and robbers of the people: such are
> some hosiers, tailors, fletchers, minstrels, souters, horseleeches,
> jugglers, witches, sorcerers, bawds, and a rabble of that sect:
> which would by laws be driven from so divine an art, the exercise
> of which for want of knowledge, bringeth sometime loss of
> member, sometime of life, and sometime both of limb and life.[142]

The anti-quack authors agreed that a basic understanding of
medical theory was desirable for the surgeon, despite the fact
that surgery was a mechanical operation. The sixteenth-
century physician, John Securis, wrote:

> There be many surgeons in this our time, that practise surgery,
> more by blind experience than by any science, who in using many

things appertaining to their art, know almost the virtue and operation of nothing that they do use.[143]

The self-advertisement and boasting of unlearned practitioners irritated their learned competitors almost past bearing. Licensed physicians felt insecure about their own ability to produce cures. Hearing unauthorised healers vaunting their successes – and realising that prospective patients believed their claims – added insult to injury. The fact that 'quacks' did sometimes succeed where learned practitioners had failed did not help matters. The learned defended their position by claiming that success on the part of licensed healers was due to art, while apparent success on the part of unlicensed healers was due to chance.[144] The physician James Hart wrote in 1624:

Neither let this suffice, that some of their proctors plead for them a number of happy and successful events; since that thus we may often magnify the most vile wizard, and most ignorant old wife in the country: this argument taken from issue and event being a mere Paralogism, a fallacy and deceit, taking that often for a true cause which is no cause indeed.[145]

Dr E. D. pointed out that patients often consulted licensed practitioners only in cases of extremity after all other sources of medical care had been tried. He wrote:

Here, if the sick person dies, all the fault will be laid by those that favour these Empirics, upon the last Physician, that they cannot see but that more die under the hand of the learned physician than under others, that they have no good luck, because they often times die to whom they come.[146]

Although the anti-quack writers attacked all unlicensed (and some licensed) providers of medical care, they were particularly virulent in their treatment of five popular types of healer – piss prophets, itinerant practitioners, women who practised medicine, magical healers, and ministers who treated bodies as well as souls.

The attack on piss prophets reflects a change in conventional medical treatment in the course of the sixteenth and early seventeenth centuries. In the Middle Ages diagnosis based on examination of urine had been so common that the distinctively shaped urinal flask had been the physician's symbol. In the early sixteenth century a number of handbooks designed to teach medical practitioners and laymen how to diagnose from urine samples appeared, and apparently sold well, judging by the number of editions printed in the mid–1520s.[147] By the seventeenth century, although physicians still examined urine, the Royal College of Physicians frowned on the practice. It was recognised that the colour and consistency of a urine sample was not necessarily the best guide to the patient's condition. Conversation with the patient and observation of symptoms, combined with other techniques such as pulse-taking, were by that time considered better aids in diagnosis.[148] However, as indicated above, there remained practitioners who offered to diagnose illness and pregnancy, to foretell the sex of an unborn child, and to predict whether a patient would recover or die on the basis of a urine sample, often brought to them by someone other than the patient.

Thomas Brain's description of piss prophets has been discussed above.[149] His tone was light and amused. The same cannot be said about the anti-quack writers' attacks on piss prophets.[150] These authors never assumed that the piss prophet might really believe in his own methods; to them, he was always fully aware of his treachery, deliberately deluding his patients in order to rob them of their money. Petrus Forestus spoke for all of the anti-quack writers in 1623:

> This scum and off-scouring of people, without conscience and honesty, yet seeking by all craft and cunning as well to attain to some credit and reputation amongst the people, as to convey unto themselves some part of their wealth and riches and that under some fair counterfeit colour of skill in the Profession of Physic, being withall conscious to themselves of their own insufficiency, and ignorant of the signs, causes, and consequently of the right cure of disease, to the attaining of which the most learned Physicians bestow no small labour and pains, then have they recourse to the sanctuary of unlearned fools, to wit, the judgement or rather imposture by Urines.[151]

No better than the piss prophets were itinerant healers. The most lengthy account of their activities was written by the surgeon John Halle and published as an appendix to Halle's translation of Lanfranc of Milan's *A Most Excellent and Learned Work of Chirurgerie* . . . in 1565.[152] This work, entitled 'An Historical Expostulation also against the Beastly Abusers, both of Chirurgery and Physic in Our Time', is a detailed description of some travelling practitioners who showed up in Kent in the years between 1555 and 1562. Their 'crimes' ranged from ignorant herbalism to sorcery; their patients, usually warned by Halle of the dangers of consulting such healers, ended up unhappy, disappointed or dead. Halle was concerned that so many of the inhabitants of Maidstone consulted unlicensed healers, despite the presence of seven learned physicians and a number of licensed surgeons in the town. He strongly advocated learning in both physicians and surgeons, and also pointed out the virtue of a healer maintaining a stable residence:

> It cannot be without suspicion therefore, either of the lack of cunning, or of a deceivable false conscience, that a chirurgeon, or physician, shall refuse to fix himself constantly in some dwelling place, and to become a wandering fugitive, as there were and are, of whom I have written.[153]

The situation had obviously not changed by 1612. John Cotta wrote disparagingly of

> they who in towns and villages hang up their banners and triumphant flags in fields of broken arms, rotted legs, and half faces, and haply also timber for new, displaying at large before the ignorant multitude.[154]

He admitted that travel was desirable in a physician, 'not as any part of his essence, but as an ornament'.[155] However, he distinguished between the well-travelled learned physician and the itinerant healer, saying of the latter,

> It is usual with these men, moving their wandering and uncertain steps from place to place and from town to town, by fair deluding promises and pollicitations to draw the lives of simple credulous men, for their own gain, into their own hands; and after they have by their common desperate courses provoked and drawn forth unwilling death (when they see him coming) to run away, and to leave the miserable beguiled innocent in his angry jaws, to answer their rash and needless challenge.[156]

Unlearned male practitioners were bad enough; unlearned female healers incensed the anti-quack writers by their femaleness as well as their ignorance. All of these authors castigated a wide variety of women, from the loving but misguided wife or mother who refused to follow the physician's instructions, to the unskilful midwife, to the female charlatan, to the witch. These healers, like their male counterparts, were considered unfit to practise medicine because of their ignorance and dishonesty. However, the anti-quack writers took the argument one step further, maintaining that women were unfit to practise because of their sex.

We cannot but acknowledge and with honour mention the graces of womanhood, wherein by their property, they are right and true sovereigns of affection: but yet, seeing their authority in learned knowledge cannot be authentical, neither hath God and nature made them commissioners in the sessions of learned reason and understanding . . . it is rash cruelty in them even there to do well, where unto the not judiciously foreseeing, that well might have proved ill, and that ill is no less than death.[157]

Women who wished to practise medicine were faced with a no-win situation. If they practised without training, they were attacked for their ignorance. However, many educational resources, such as university educations, were closed to them. Although women could and did become barbersurgeons, full participation in the activities of occupational organisations was denied them, and they were not encouraged to seek apprenticeship.[158] In a world in which men were considered the rational, strong, creative half of humanity and women the irrational, weak, destructive half, it is not surprising that learned upper- and middle-class male medical practitioners were contemptuous of the female healers who had the temerity to compete with them.[159] However, it is ironic that male practitioners happily accepted medical recipes and devoted nursing care from the women of their acquaintance who had the good sense not to charge for their services.

The most common sort of female practitioner in sixteenth- and seventeenth-century England was undoubtedly the midwife. While midwives were attacked for ignorance and butchery, as were unlicensed healers, the evidence regarding such attacks is ambiguous. It is notable that in the earlier period, male writers on the subject of midwifery agreed that female midwives performed a great service. The surgeon Jacob Rueff wrote in 1637:

It is observable that in all ages of the world and throughout all countries in the world, that the help of grave and modest women (with us termed midwives) hath ever been useful for relief and succour of all the daughters of Eve, whom God hath appointed to bear children into this world.[160]

However, he felt that women were unlearned and should be educated by skilful physicians and surgeons.[161] Later in the century, the man-midwife Percival Willughby, although generally well disposed toward midwives, criticised them for ignorance and for being over eager in their efforts to help women deliver.

> I leave all women to their liberty to make choice of their Midwife, yet I will not be forward to persuade them to take such a midwife as will bind them, perforce, in their chairs against their wills, or, that will pull, stretch, or hale their bodies, or use any violence to enforce the womb in hopes of a speedier delivery.[162]

By the same token, he warned against midwives being too hasty about sending for 'a young chirurgeon', who might injure both mother and baby in his efforts to extract the child.[163] Willughby never treated patients before having been summoned by the midwife. And he had to abide by the constraints placed on his activities by female modesty. He recorded details of a case where the midwife in charge was his daughter.

> About seven a clock that night labour approached. At my daughter's request, unknown to the lady, I crept into the chamber upon my hands and knees, and returned, and it was not perceived by the lady.[164]

He completed his examination in a partially darkened room, with his patient entirely covered with her own and the bedclothes.

By the eighteenth century male *accoucheurs*, having gained in both confidence and popularity, were ready to drive midwives from the birth chamber altogether. The physician William Smellie created a pedigree for man-midwives, calling Hippocrates the Father of Midwifery, unearthing a worthy called Paulus Aegineta (a fourth-century Greek medical writer who claimed to have been an *accoucheur*), and denying the existence of such ancient female physicians as the semi-legendary Trotula.[165] He and other writers again accused midwives of ignorance, but refused to instruct midwives in the use of instruments, including the midwifery forceps which were introduced in the 1730s. They also exaggerated the dangers of childbirth, which encouraged those with sufficient means to consult more learned and higher-status male practitioners. Fashion also came to the aid of the man-midwives, ladies with upward mobility aspirations summoning them rather than lower-status females in times of need. Thus, despite the chorus objecting to the invasion of the birth chamber by male practitioners, by the end of the century men had virtually taken over the practice of midwifery among all but the lower classes in society.[166]

Although midwives were not usually included in the list of

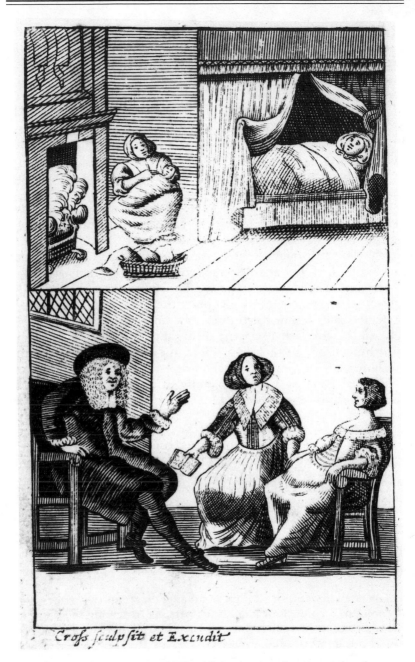

Cros̃ sculpsit et Excudit

Man-midwives were consulted with increasing frequency by the beginning of the eighteenth century. However, pregnancy, birth and the care of infants remained in female hands among the majority of the population. (J. Wolveridge, *Speculum Matricis*, London, 1671, frontispiece.)

healers they chose to censure, the anti-quack writers devoted a good deal of venom to attacking another sort of healer who was likely to be female – the magical practitioner. Not all such healers were female. Indeed, the most notorious of them all, Dr Simon Forman and Dr John Lambe, for instance, were men. However, many magical healers were women. The mid-seventeenth-century licentiate in physic and surgery, Edward Poeton, included as the first item in a list of the characteristics of white witches, 'weak and unlearned women'.[167] Female or not, no unauthorised healer was viewed with more abhorrence than the magical practitioner.

As indicated above, there was a large variety of magical healers for prospective patients to choose from, ranging from the high-status astrological physician to the lowly white witch. The anti-quack writers, unsure of the support of other learned healers, left astrologers alone, confining their attention to the unlearned magic practised by cunning- and wise-folk, white witches and itinerant practitioners. This target was perfectly safe, for in their attack the anti-quack writers could rely on the combined support of organised medicine, the state and the church. In this way, these authors contributed to the escalation of the English witchcraze.

Magical healers, like other unlicensed practitioners, were condemned for their lack of learning. Oberndoerffer wrote in 1602,

> Others, that they may colourably and cunningly hide their gross ignorance, when they know not the cause of the Disease, refer it unto charms, witchcraft, magnifical incantations, and sorcery, vainly and with a brazen forehead, affirming that there is no way to help them but by characters, circles, figure-castings, exorcisms, conjurations, and other impious and godless means.[168]

In addition, despite the loyalty of many patients, the anti-quack writers felt such healers were evil. Forestus wrote,

> The devil likewise being a most cunning craftsmaster, makes choice of such unclean and wicked persons, receiving them into his service, to the end he may by their means more easily deceive and entrap others.[169]

The Essex clergyman George Gifford maintained that consultation of white witches endangered the patient's soul. He wrote,

> A man is sick, his sickness doth linger upon him, some do put

into his head that he is bewitched, he is counselled to send unto a cunning woman, she says he is forespoken indeed, she prescribes what to use, there must be charms and sorcery used. The party finds ease, he is a glad man, he takes it that this is a common thing and well tried by experience, that many in great distress have been relieved by sending unto such wisemen or wisewomen. . . . Yet, now they cannot say that the Lord is their health and salvation, but their physician is the Devil.[170]

The anti-quack writers were obviously ambivalent about the talents of magical healers. They tended to believe that magic could heal. However, they were certain that such healers were both evil and dangerous. Cures produced by learned medical practitioners came from God: those produced by magical healers came from Satan.

Unfortunately the same could not be said about the medical activities of ministers. The anti-quack writers worried considerably about this source of competition. Ministers could not be accused of being either unlearned or evil. The worst the anti-quack writers could say about them was that it was unlikely that a clergyman could give proper attention to both the souls and the bodies of his parishioners. Cotta wrote of the

Ecclesiastical persons, Vicars and Parsons, who now overflow this kingdom with this alienation of their own proper offices and duties and usurpation of others, making their holy calling a linsey wolsey, too narrow for their minds, and therefore making themselves room in others affairs, under pretence of love and mercy.[171]

Of course it was precisely the ministers' apparent usurpation of the practices – and financial rewards – of the physicians which made the anti-quack writers angry. They resented clergymen earning money by practising physic. Cotta himself admitted that he had no objection to ministers giving 'their medicinal advice with incorrupt hands free from implication of private gains'.[172] He wished only to attack ministers who set up 'in their houses apothecaries' shops' and travelled 'up and down to spoil the proper labour of his hire'.[173]

The complaint that their practices robbed licensed practitioners of both prospective patients and income was at the heart of all the anti-quack writers' attacks on unlicensed healers. It might be argued, of course, that learned physicians and surgeons were equally motivated by altruistic concern about the public welfare. However, the learned were, if anything, more upset by the successes than they were by the failures of their competitors. Success bred reputation which, in turn, bred an increase in clientele. One writer warned that if this situation were allowed to continue, 'verily it will greatly discourage men of learning hereafter to apply themselves to the study of physic'.[174] The remedy which the learned and licensed sought was new legislation to confine the practice of medicine to themselves, and increased help from the government in enforcing already existing legislation.[175]

Unlearned healers had their defenders. The renegade healer and author Nicholas Culpeper wrote,

> Who are they that cry out against Empericks? Who? The College of Physicians; And why do they do so? They kill Men for want of judgement; And who is the cause of this? Themselves forsooth; for if they taught men the true rules of Physick, is any Man so mad as to practise false ones?[176]

He accused physicians of keeping medical knowledge from the people in order to keep a financial monopoly over treatment. The midwife, Jane Sharp, went even further. She derided the physicians' academic approach to her craft. Although she advocated the training of midwives in anatomy and the mechanical operations they must perform, she wrote,

> It is not hard words that perform the work, as if none understood the Art that cannot understand Greek. Words are but the shell that we ofttimes break our teeth with them to come at the kernel. . . . It is commendable for men to employ their spare time in some things of deeper speculation than is required of the female sex: but the art of midwifery chiefly concerns us, which even the best learned man will grant, yielding something of their own to us when they are forced to borrow from us the very name they practise by, and to call themselves man-midwives.[177]

A sixteenth-century writer ridiculed academic education, which he felt prepared the physician for practice as much as reading books on navigation prepared a man to be a sea captain.[178] However, the principal defenders of unlearned and unlicensed healers were the loyal patients themselves who voted with both their feet and their purses.

Patients consulted unlicensed healers partly because they generally charged less than did licensed practitioners. This fact was recognised by the physician E. D., who wrote that patients consulted unlearned healers 'and magnify them above the learned Physician . . . because they can employ them for less reward'.[179] One obvious solution to the problem would have been for licensed practitioners to reduce their fees. However, learned healers valued both their high incomes and their relatively high social status. They knew as well as any modern social scientist that status was, to a certain extent, a reflection of how much clients were willing to pay them. Physicians and surgeons could not reduce their fees without reducing their worth in the public eye.

Unable to provide their services cheaply, unable to prove that they were the only healers able to cure diseases and heal wounds, licensed practitioners were forced to rely upon social and political clout and the powers of the pen in their competition with unlicensed practitioners. Both weapons eventually proved effective. However, the battle was a long one and had by no means been won by the end of the seventeenth century. Further, the eventual incarnation of the structure of professional medicine, which placed the consultant surgeon at the top of the hierarchy, drastically reduced the classical academic components in the physician's education in favour of empirical observation, and created of the apothecary the general practitioner, would have pleased neither the anti-quack writers nor their opponents.

Authorities on the subject of professionalisation concentrate on the activities of occupational organisations. They are most interested in the efforts of such organisations to control the services members provide and to govern themselves without outside interference.[180] While the growth of occupational organisations and their support by the state were important to the development of a medical profession in Britain, these elements were not the only necessary ones. Despite the fact that for most of the seventeenth century the medical and surgical monopolies had already been in existence for a hundred years or more, sick or injured people could not be forced to consult licensed physicians and surgeons. Nor could they be coerced into deserting unlicensed healers. The sociologist Eliot Freidson admits this fact, but does not shed much light upon the mechanisms by which people were encouraged to change their loyalties and their behaviour.[181]

The answer to this question lies outside the scope of this study. However, it is obvious that some explanation of lay public compliance with the goals of members of occupational groups aspiring to 'professionalise' should be included in professionalisation theory. If we cannot answer the question here, perhaps we can pose it fully. Why did people eventually accept physicians and surgeons at their own valuations? Surely the answer cannot be that the general public was impressed by a demonstrable superiority of licensed medical services over unlicensed ones. The record of medical success, usually kept by interested parties, was too confused to yield any sort of conclusive evidence about the value of various practitioners. General claims of success were balanced by general attacks for failure.

Is it not possible that the advertising campaign fought by licensed healers, partly in the form of the anti-quack literature, helped convince people that licensed medicine was the only true and safe medicine? The attack on quacks combined with the appeal to sufferers to protect themselves and their loved ones from the fearsome depradations of disease and injury by consulting healers who, if not perfect, were still the best available, must have seemed wellnigh irresistible to some. Certainly something occurred to shift popular opinion from the ambivalence it displayed throughout the seventeenth century.

This chapter has concentrated on the attitudes and behaviour of those staffing the teeming seventeenth-century medical marketplace. It has drawn little, however, on the evidence which exists about the day-to-day practices of individual healers. It is difficult to generalise about the activities of medical and surgical practitioners in the period. Their behaviour depended on where they practised, the expectations of their patients, the disorders they treated and their own social, economic and educational backgrounds. For instance, it is as easy to find an example of a seventeenth-century physician using magical methods as it is to find another physician who used no magic at all. None the less, examination and comparison of several of the surviving medical and surgical casebooks of the period will illuminate some of the methods and experiences of seventeenth-century healers and their patients. Thus, the next two chapters will consider in turn the casebook of a London surgeon and those kept by three provincial physicians. While these discussions will not provide an overall picture of seventeenth-century surgery and medicine, they will indicate the possibilities of conventional therapeutics in that period and will also explore the historical uses of such casebooks.

3

A LONDON SURGEON'S CAREER: JOSEPH BINNS

Although this study is chiefly concerned with the experiences and choices of seventeenth-century patients, it would be incomplete without reference to the records left by those who spent their occupational lives with people in their roles as patients – the medical practitioners. Numerous medical and surgical casebooks have survived the last three centuries. Although often neglected by medical historians, one, like that of the early-seventeenth-century physician Richard Napier, occasionally surfaces, providing scholars with the opportunity of examining the day-to-day activities of a medical practitioner.[1] Such casebooks yield information about a wide variety of subjects, ranging from the disorders treated and the therapy provided to the names, social status, addresses and (occasionally) personal idiosyncrasies of the patients. Casebooks vary, both in the kind of information recorded and in their value to historians. Some are simply lists of patients treated or prescriptions dispensed. Some are account books. A few are made up of detailed descriptions of each case the practitioner undertook.[2] Such a casebook is the one kept by the London surgeon Joseph Binns in the years between 1633 and 1663.[3]

It is difficult to find out much about Joseph Binns. In his own time he was respectable, but unremarkable. Histories of the Barbersurgeons' Company and St Bartholomew's Hospital, to which he was attached, mention his name. Two copies of his will are housed in the Public Record Office. His casebook, bound with other medical manuscripts in the Sloane manuscript collection, is the richest source of information about him, yet it reveals nothing about his personal or social life. However, this very anonymity gives the casebook some value. Unlike the records left by such medical luminaries as Sir Theodore Turquet de Mayerne or Sir Edmund King, Binns's casebook gives us an insight into the work of an 'ordinary' practitioner (if such a thing can be said to exist).[4]

Joseph Binns was born in Derbyshire. He was made free of

the Company of Barbersurgeons by apprenticeship to the London surgeon Joseph Fenton on 28 March 1637, and thought so highly of Fenton that he named his eldest son Fenton Binns. Binns was elected as one of the three surgeons to St Bartholomew's Hospital on 12 November 1647. He was paid £30 a year by the hospital and occupied his position there until his death on 18 May 1664. In addition to his work at St Bartholomew's, Binns had an active private practice. He finished his career as a warden of the Barbersurgeons' Company in 1662 and 1663.[5]

Joseph Binns married Mary Holland whose father, Master Richard Holland, was named as one of the executors of Binns's will.[6] The wedding probably took place in the late 1640s, when Binns was a well-established surgeon. At the time of Binns's death he had at least three living children, none of whom had reached the age of 21. During his working life Binns leased a house on Butchers Hall Lane in the parish of Christchurch. Numerous relatives of Joseph and Mary Binns are mentioned in both the casebook and the wills. Many of them appear to have lived close enough to Binns to consult him in times of sickness. Binns was survived by a sister, Jane Risson. He also left bequests to two aunts, five brothers-in-law and their wives, three cousins and four godchildren. Other relatives mentioned in the casebook apparently died before Binns did.

At the time of his death, Binns was in an enviably solid financial position. He was receiving income from properties in Berkshire, Oxfordshire and Middlesex. In 1664 he had loaned an Oxfordshire gentleman, Sir Bulstrode Whitelocke, £800, and a Middlesex property-owner £500. He left his eldest son Fenton £100 in cash, and his daughter Mary £125 set out in East India Company shares. He left £5 apiece to the poor of the parish of Christchurch and the Barbersurgeons' Company. He left £10 apiece to his executors. His will provides for mourning clothes for his two executors, the minister who was to preach his funeral sermon, his wife and children, his sister and brother-in-law, and his servants. In addition, he bequeathed between 10s. and 40s. apiece to seventeen friends and relations, to be used to purchase rings.[7]

Binns had wide contacts within the London medical establishment. His cousin and executor, Joseph Colston, was a physician. Binns's casebook mentions approximately forty names of physicians and surgeons with whom he had dealings with one kind or another. Some, like the surgeon John Woodall and the physician Charles Scarborough, are well known to medical historians. Most have been as totally forgotten as Binns himself. Binns apparently had a regular arrangement with at least one physician, Dr John Bathurst, whose patients he treated at the physician's house.

Joseph Binns was a dedicated surgeon. His casebook records his patience in the face of conditions which stubbornly refused to heal, and his flexibility regarding therapy. Unlike some healers, he was not so wedded to a pet theory or nostrum that he could not change treatments when the situation so required. He was not 'knife-happy'; out of approximately 671 cases, many of which concerned badly infected extremities, Binns recorded performing only three amputations.[8] He clearly loved his craft, and hoped that his sons would become surgeons. His will provided dressing cases and silver instruments for the first two of his sons to follow in their father's footsteps.[9]

His eldest son Fenton did indeed become a surgeon. In December 1690 Fenton was accused by the Royal College of Physicians of prescribing internal medicines. The Court of the Barbersurgeons' Company ordered that if Fenton Binns were arrested, he should be defended at the cost of the Company.[10]

Like other licensed medical practitioners, Joseph Binns displayed some contempt for unlearned unlicensed healers. According to the casebook, patients in Binns's practice who had consulted such healers before consulting Binns were the lucky ones; they got better. Those consulting unlicensed healers after Binns treated them died. In a case of breast cancer which Binns had been treating for a month, the patient moved to Shoreditch to be near 'one Poleman a Chemist who makes no doubt but to cure her, for he hath cured those that have been 10 times worse'. Poleman exhibited the characteristics thought usual of an empiric; not only did he promise a cure he could not produce, but also he used a 'secret preparation out of antimony and mercury fixed so he can command it at pleasure'. The patient died ten days after her move. Binns did not claim that if the patient had remained under his care she would have lived. He merely ridiculed the chemist for his ignorance and attempts to defraud his patients.[11]

More remarkable than his disparaging remarks about some unlicensed practitioners is his failure to criticise others. He was most likely to give a single value-free statement about any other healer the patient had consulted, whether licensed or unlicensed. For instance, a patient whom Binns treated for syphilis had earlier had 'his pains eased by the use of a cataplasm from one Bonorenige'.[12]

However, he felt free to criticise even licensed members of his own craft. In one case he expressed disapproval of the surgeon Edward Moollins for behaviour similar to that of Poleman the chemist. Both Moollins and Binns were working on the case of a lawyer who had mouth cancer. Binns left the case because 'Ed Moollins pretended he could do him good (though he said to me he did not desire to deal with it for no good could be done in it) but did not for he died in 14 days after'.[13]

Binns also had unpleasant contact with another member of the Moollins family, Will.

> 6 June 1643 7 o'clock at night on the backside of the Red Lion in Holborne one Samuel Ward, an old Gardener near 80 years of age, asking an alms of one Sergeant Major Jenkins, he refused to give, the old man replied some words, Jenkins drew his sword and thrust him into the belly . . . with a broad sword. I put my finger as I conceive into the cavity, the wound went somewhat upward toward the Liver. He had a puncture behind close to the left shoulder, bruised about the head and arm, dressed him up to stay blood, next morn his pulse high and he hot . . . 4th day, some digestion & they [sic] friends of Jenkins desired that Will: Moollins might join with me he goes with them next day (without me) and reports the patient afore the Justice to be past danger, so Major Jenkins was discharged out of prison upon bail. Next day Moollins dresses the patient without me, and leaves word that I must meddle no further.[14]

This case notwithstanding, Binns apparently got on reasonably well with both his colleagues and the opposition. He was occasionally called upon to consult on other practitioners' cases. In at least 30 out of the 671 cases recorded, Binns acted as a consultant rather than as the initial or the sole healer involved. This figure appears small unless it is recognised that the seventeenth-century pattern of treatment and consultation was very different from the one in operation today. Patients chose healers according to their symptoms, their pocketbooks and their opinions about the merits of various types of practitioners. Thus, surgeons competed with each other for the opportunity to treat the self-selected group of patients who chose to consult surgeons. Their incomes and reputations were based on the size of their practices, the social status of their patients and reports of their success in curing. Consultations were resorted to either in very unusual or difficult cases where the practitioner in charge wanted to make sure he was doing everything possible for the patient, or in cases where the patient had a high social status. In addition, a consultation involving senior members of the Barbersurgeons' Company was required in cases where the patient seemed likely to die. Failure to present such cases to the Master and Wardens of the Company could result in either a fine or the loss of the right to practise surgery.[15] Consultants of choice were those who could give expert advice and, at the same time, be relied upon not to try to steal the patient. Binns's colleagues must have both respected his skill and trusted his honour to have consulted with him as often as they did.

Joseph Binns's casebook mentioned approximately 671 patients. This number is necessarily approximate because some casenotes are incomplete, some illegible and some duplicates. Out of the total, only 616 are detailed enough to make any sort of analysis possible. Binns's casebook reveals a good deal about his patients. In addition to the descriptions of their illnesses and the therapeutic regimens they underwent, there is information about their social class origins, sex, addresses and the duration of their treatment by Binns. Such information is useful, both in attempting to sketch a fairly complete picture of the career of a mid-seventeenth-century London surgeon, and in trying to reconstruct the experience of being a seventeenth-century patient.

The traditional view of medical historians has been that in the sixteenth and seventeenth centuries few licensed medical practitioners existed, and that those few served the needs only of members of the upper classes who could afford them. This assumption has been successfully challenged in the work of Margaret Pelling, who has found that the numerous seventeenth-century London barbersurgeons lived in all parts of the metropolis, catering to all social classes.[16]

Binns's casebook supports these findings. Again, the numerical breakdown can only be approximate. Unless a title or occupation was specified, social class could be determined only on the basis of a mode of address (Mrs Jones seeming higher in the social register than Goodwife White or Jack Barker), or by other information about the patient given in a casenote. For instance, hospital patients were invariably poor. Hospitals were, after all, founded as charitable institutions. People with means were expected to pay for their own medical care.

Binns's casebook indicates that some 29 of his patients were upper class, 181 middle class, 50 artisans, 71 servants and 74 simply lower class (their occupations being unidentified). The social class of 266 of his patients is unknown; 300 patients were men and 220 were women [see Table 3.1].

Table 3.1 *Social Position and Sex of Joseph Binns's Patients*

	Upper	Middling	Artisan	Servant	Lower	Unknown
Female	7	64	12	34	33	70
Male	22	117	38	37	41	141
Unknown						55

However approximate these numbers may be, they indicate clearly that Binns treated members of all social classes. Perhaps his most famous patient was Archbishop Laud, whom Binns treated for a scurvy rash on his leg in 1644, during Laud's imprisonment in the Tower.[17] However, Binns's patients were predominantly middle class and below, finding the money to pay for his services because he seemed the most appropriate of the variety of healers available to deal with their problems.

Of Binns's patients, 249 were Londoners, and of these, 41 were in St Bartholomew's Hospital. Thirty patients came from outside London. Some of these had obviously met with an accident while visiting London.[18] Others had made a special trip to the metropolis in order to obtain expert medical or surgical help.[19] Of the many patients whose addresses are unidentified, most probably lived in London. Binns's practice was largely local [see Table 3.2]. Although information is sparse, it seems that he visited those patients he treated for any length of time, rather than expecting them to visit him. He very often visited a patient once or twice a day.

Table 3.2 *Geographical Origins of Joseph Binns's Patients*

London	208
St Bartholomew's Hospital	41
Outside London	30

Table 3.3 *Duration of Binns's Treatment*

One week to one month	211
One month to six months	164
Six months to one year	28
One year or more	13

Not all of Binns's patients required long-term care; 184 of them consulted him during a period of less than a week, many simply obtaining a prescription or two. Most, however, needed personal treatment. Binns treated 211 patients for between one week and one month, 164 patients for between one and six months, 28 patients for between six months and one year, and 13 patients for over a year [see Table 3.3].

As the descriptions of disorders and therapies given below will indicate, seventeenth-century illnesses and injuries lasted a long time and required a good deal of day-to-day supervision by the surgeon in charge [see Table 3.4]. Prescriptions and dressings were altered depending on the patient's response to the treatment given. Such decisions could be made only by the healer consulted. The responsibility for the outcome of the treatment was his or hers. If a patient became dissatisfied, he or she was free to consult another healer. By the same token, if the patient or the patient's 'friends' refused to follow the healer's instructions, the healer was at liberty to refuse further treatment.[20]

Table 3.4 *Frequency of Binns's Visits*

One consultation	81
One to five visits	99
More than five visits	227
Daily visits at any time	111

Table 3.5 *Joseph Binns's Cases*

Disorder	Female	Male	Unknown
Gonorrhoea		27	
Syphilis	29	74	2
Ague	4	3	
Pain in side	1		
Nausea		1	
Insomnia		1	
Stopping of urine		3	
Preventative medicine	1	1	
General illness		1	
Back pain	1	2	
Spitting blood	1	1	
Cough	1	1	
Fits like fits of the mother	2		
Asthma	1		
Scurvy	1	1	
New fever		1	
Looseness	2	2	
Cachexia	4		
Catarrh	1		
Colic		1	
Headache	3	2	
Stomachache	3	1	
Clanula	1		
Sore throat	5	1	
Epilepsy		1	
Burns	3	3	
Dog bite		2	1
Human bite		3	
Head wound	12	9	1
Gored by a bull		1	
Viper bite		1	
Sprained ankle		1	1
Fractures	18	24	2
Dislocation	2	12	
Gunshot wound		9	
Stab wound	1	11	
Wounds (misc.)	3	14	1
Knee wound		1	
Cut throat		2	
Wrist wound		1	
Bruises	4	8	
Sprains	3	1	
Leg wound		1	
Apostem	26	37	3

Table 3.5 *continued*

Disorder	Female	Male	Unknown
Hernia		10	
Hernia Aquosa		8	
Fistula	6	15	
Anal Fistula		4	
Ulcers	3	2	1
Ulcer on hand	1		
Ulcer and tumour in tongue	1	2	
Mouth ulcer	1		1
Ulcer on arm		1	
Ulcer on leg	6	1	
Ulcer on lip		1	
Ulcer on chin		1	
Ulcer on face		1	
Tumours	5	14	3
Tumour on arm		2	
Tumour on back		1	
Tumour on forehead		1	
Wen in armpit	1		
Corns		1	
Polyps in nose	1		
Swellings on back		1	
Scorbutical swelling	1		
Swollen legs	2	2	
Itch		2	
Skin rash	4		
Shingles	1		
Scald head	1		
Wry neck		1	
Scrofula	4	1	
Plague bubo			1
Gangrene	1	2	1
Hydrocephaly			3
Carious bones	2	4	
Amputation		1	
Haemorrhoids	1	1	
Nose problem		1	
Swollen testicle		1	
Arthritis		1	
Leg ailment			1
Aneurism		2	
Displaced artery	1		
Pain in leg	1	1	
Problem with gums	1	4	1
Shoulder pain	3	2	

Table 3.5 *continued*

Disorder	Female	Male	Unknown
Swollen knee	2	1	
Pain in hip	1	1	
Bad teeth	1		
Lip problem	1		
Eye problem	7	2	
Breast infection	5		
Whites	3		
Menstrual problems	10		
Eye cancer		1	
Breast cancer	6		
Cancer in yard (penis)		1	

Binns identified nearly 100 symptoms or disorders which patients brought to him for treatment [see Table 3.5]. For most of these (often quite specific, such as 'lip ulcer' or 'gored by a bull') he treated very few people: in most cases, fewer than five in the course of his thirty-year career. In more general categories, of course, the numbers are larger. Binns treated at least sixty-six cases of apostems. However, a numerical breakdown of his cases reveals that Binns had a minor speciality in the treatment of venereal diseases: 196 of his patients complained of gonorrhoea, whites or a combination of syphilis symptoms. In addition, he treated numerous cases of hernia and urinary retention in men. Although he did not cut for the stone, he acted as an early modern urologist, and patients apparently sought him out for this kind of treatment.

Most of the disorders Binns treated would have been considered specifically surgical problems in his own time. These included wounds, fractures, ulcers, fistulae, herniae, apostems (infected swellings), tumours, skin rashes and venereal diseases. However, sixty-one of Binns's casenotes refer to 'medical' problems such as ague, stomachache, headache, insomnia, diarrhoea, and epilepsy. Some of these patients, including two who were apparently given prophylactic purges, were Binns's relatives who may have chosen to consult him rather than a more expensive physician. In one case, Binns treated himself for ague. However, Binns gave internal medicines to non-relatives as well. These medical cases show that to some extent Binns was operating as a general practitioner, despite the monopoly granted to the

Royal College of Physicians over the prescribing of internal remedies.

Indeed, the distinction between internal and external preparations was one which the most scrupulous of surgeons would have had difficulty in making and applying to his own practice. Regardless of the multitude of medical theories available in the mid-seventeenth century, therapy depended upon the humoral principles of maintaining or restoring the body's internal balance through evacuation. Thus, even if the disorder treated were a wound or fracture of an extremity, happening to an initially healthy body, treatment invariably included purges and clysters (enemas) to keep the body 'soluble'. Surgeons also prescribed diets which were expected to prevent or reduce infection and help in the healing process.

Binns's therapeutic routine was based on humoral conventions. Regardless of the patient's disorder, a careful record was kept of the number, and sometimes the consistency, of his or her daily and nightly bowel movements. These were controlled by laxatives, enemas and suppositories. The prescription given depended upon the patient's age and his or her 'habit of body' (general health), as well as upon his or her ailment. The 80-year-old gardener, mentioned above, who had been stabbed, was given clysters and suppositories rather than laxatives because he was elderly and weak.[21] Binns tended to begin any sort of treatment by prescribing a laxative. This might be given on its own or as one ingredient in a general-purpose 'diet drink' or 'bolus'.

Like any medical practitioner, Binns had favourite preparations which he prescribed again and again, some of which he probably made himself. His 'pill fortis', one of the medicines most frequently mentioned in the casenotes, must indeed have been strong; in the case of a carpenter whom Binns treated for a knee injury, two pills each morning produced eight stools a day for at least six days.[22] Binns even treated 'looseness' (diarrhoea) with laxatives. A woman who complained of having had this condition for three or four years, giving her between four and ten stools a day, was prescribed three pills fortis six days after her diarrhoea had improved. The dose produced six stools, after which the woman was well.[23] Pill fortis was also used in a case which may be an early report of induced abortion. A maid who complained that she 'wanted her menses' was given, as part of her treatment, a dose of the laxative which produced twelve stools.[24]

Binns never bothered to write down the recipe for pill fortis; perhaps he wished to keep it secret. However, he did give details for other purges he used. Rhubarb and senna, commonly used laxatives, appeared frequently in his prescriptions. Binns also used mercury in both internal and external applications for many illnesses. In his employment of both herbal and metallic remedies he was typical of the surgeons, who were quicker to adopt the new Paracelsian remedies than were the physicians.[25]

In addition, and sometimes in preference to purges, Binns prescribed emetics or 'vomits'. Most frequently used ingredients were cream of tartar and antimony. These were used for prophylactic as well as curative purposes. Traditionally the English thought it good to take physic at least once a year, usually in the spring, whether they were ill or not. In one instance, Binns prescribed vomits, purges and 'stomach pills' to five members of his cousin Edward Griffing's family, including Griffing, his wife, his daughter, his maid and the maid's mother.[26] Vomits were also used as the preferred treatment for agues. In one case, Binns prescribed a vomit for a maid-servant with ague; the preparation produced fifteen or sixteen vomits! There is no record of whether or not the maid recovered.[27] Like laxatives, emetics were used to prepare patients for further treatment. Before operating on two cases of hernia aquosa (collections of fluid in the scrotum), Binns prescribed vomits.[28]

While laxatives and emetics were the common currency of all medical practitioners, other means of evacuation were performed chiefly by surgeons. Letting blood, cupping, scarifying, blistering and making issues or setons (artificially produced ulcers which were not allowed to heal), were specifically surgical methods used to help the body void unnecessary or evil humours.

Blood-letting, like vomiting and purging, could be either curative or prophylactic. It is interesting that Binns did not record a single case of prophylactic phlebotomy. Perhaps he left such matters to lower-status barbersurgeons or barbers. Indeed, despite the bloodthirsty reputation of pre-modern medical practitioners, Binns was remarkably sparing in his use of this procedure. He tended to use it under very specific circumstances. He routinely let blood in cases of head injuries and, indeed, criticised the St Bartholomew's Hospital staff for not letting blood in the case of one patient who died of a head wound.[29] He also let blood in cases where other sorts of wounds appeared to be becoming infected.[30] He drew blood for headaches.[31] And he let blood in cases where humoral tradition specifically required such treatment, such as the case of amenorrhoea mentioned above, where Binns drew blood from the saphena vein in the foot in order to draw the menses downward.[32]

Binns also used phlebotomy when the circumstances seemed to warrant it, even though he did not normally let blood for the condition being treated. He occasionally bled his syphilis patients.[33] In one desperate case of a gunshot wound which had bled much initially, Binns let the patient's blood after his wound was dressed, and again the next day. Unfortunately the patient died that evening.[34] In the case of an infected swelling of the arm which had been caused by unskilful phlebotomy, Binns opened a vein in the patient's foot as part of his treatment.[35]

Cupping or using boxing glasses was another means Binns infrequently used to bleed patients (through suction rather than incision). He employed this method for head and eye ailments, and appeared to prefer it when counter-irritation was called for. In one case of an ulceration in the eye he applied cupping glasses, blistered the patient's neck and made an issue in her arm, all on the first day of treatment. He repeated the blistering and applied boxing glasses every day for about six weeks thereafter.[36] Cupping was sometimes combined with scarification. This increased the flow of blood through a number of shallow incisions. Such treatment was usually applied to the shoulders or neck.[37] Binns also used scarification on its own. In the case of a syphilis patient whose foreskin was becoming gangrenous, Binns cut away the mortified flesh and scarified the remaining foreskin.[38]

Blistering and the making of issues were the methods of counter-irritation Binns used most frequently. These were expected to provide alternative means of evacuation for the surplus humours causing the patient's discomfort. They were also expected to draw such humours away from the primary location of the disorder, thus giving relief. Patients themselves requested issues. In one case, that of a serving-maid who had burned the left side of her face, the patient did not feel completely well until Binns had made an issue in her left arm.[39] In the case of another patient who was suffering from leg ulcers, Binns removed and cured an issue which was not helping the patient, and then made a new issue in her arm three months later. The patient recovered.[40]

Like his colleagues, Binns mainly named and treated symptoms. This is not surprising, since according to humoral theory it was quite possible for collections of symptoms to alter, becoming more or less serious depending upon the individual sufferer's 'complection'. Thus, when the diarist John Evelyn had smallpox in 1646, his physician believed that if he had not been let blood, the disorder 'would have prov'd the Plague or spotted fever' because Evelyn's blood was 'so burnt and vitious'.[41] Thus, although healers identified specific diseases as well as symptoms, the symptoms were the main targets for treatment.

While Binns occasionally identified diseases, such as lues venerea and 'fits of the mother', his casebook is a modern diagnostician's nightmare. For those interested in what Binns's patients 'really' had, his descriptions are not only confusing, but also misleading. For instance, for Binns gonorrhoea was a symptom rather than a disease; he used the term to refer to a discharge from the penis, combined with discomfort during urination. He either treated the symptom separately with preparations specific for its cure, or treated the patient with his usual remedies for syphilis if other symptoms were present. Conversely his treatment of apostems was essentially the same whether the infected swelling was the result of a wound or the manifestation of some disease. However, for the purposes of this study, modern diagnoses of Binns's patients are irrelevant. We are solely concerned with Binns's point of view and that of his patients.

Binns's cases may be divided into three major groups: conditions resulting from injuries, those brought about by disease states, and those requiring repair work, such as herniae. There are, of course, overlaps in this categorisation. For instance, apostems, ulcers and fistulae were produced by both injury and disease, and were, as indicated above, given the same treatment regardless of the cause. But, by necessity, most injuries were dealt with differently from most diseases and will be discussed separately. This study will examine first the injuries Binns treated, then his handling of cases requiring repair techniques, and third his treatment of a variety of diseases, concentrating upon his speciality, venereal disease.

I INJURIES

> In the sixteenth and seventeenth centuries tempers were short and weapons to hand. The behaviour of the propertied classes, like that of the poor, was characterised by the ferocity, childishness, and lack of self-control of the Homeric age. . . . Their nerves seem to have been perpetually on edge, possibly because they were nearly always ill. The poor were victims of chronic malnutrition, the rich of chronic dyspepsia from over-

indulgence in an ill-balanced diet: neither condition is conducive to calm and good humour. Moreover, a gentleman carried a weapon at all times, and did not hesitate to use it.[42]

The sorts of injuries brought to a medical practitioner's consulting room or a hospital ward at any time can yield a good deal of information about the quality and risks of life for people living in that time and place. Binns's thirty years of practice spanned a particularly violent and dangerous period of English history, including as they did the years of the Civil War. Indeed, a number of Binns's cases – possibly as many as fifteen – dealt with patients wounded in battle. However, the casebook shows that London streets, shops and taverns were as dangerous as battlefields. While fourteen of Binns's patients were hurt in the course of their occupations and nineteen hurt by horses or coaches, some forty-one were wounded by violence.

Weapons varied. Binns treated nine gunshot wounds. Twelve people were injured with such instruments as rapiers, broadswords and a pack-needle.[43] One husband broke his wife's nose with his fist.[44] Several head and face injuries were dealt with pint pots.[45] And Binns treated three wounds caused by human bites. (He also treated three cases of dog-bite.)[46]

Often these violent injuries were crimes of passion, perpetrated when one or both of the participants were drunk. For example, on 25 February 1638 at 9 pm,

> One Mr. Robert Peyton of Donnington received a wound (by one Captain Nayle) with a pottle pot intercilium from the right eyebrow to the left, upon the very edge of the os frontis, the which fractured the cranium and depressed the lower part. . . . He was much in drink. With to do I dressed up the wound and stayed the bleeding & forced to hold on the medicines all night otherwise he would have plucked all off.[47]

In a similar case

> 7 June 1640 at night one Ellis Morgan a soldier received 4 several punctures (by his fellow soldier & kinsman in drink both) one in the middle of the sternum, one in the upper side of the left breast . . . , one near to the left shoulder . . . , one a little above the right arm pit going toward the end of the clavicle.[48]

Certainly passion, with or without the aid of alcohol, provoked the following assault:

> May 10 1643 at night Mr. Ashberry (a lutanist) was bitten by
> Gottier the French lutanist in Covent Garden had a piece of his
> cheek bitten out the breadth of an inch & longer on the left side
> from the corner of his mouth & neither lip down to the lower
> parts of his jaw, and as much tore up toward his cheek.[49]

Then as now, drunkenness and passion helped to explain, if
they did not excuse, violent acts. But a number of the injuries
Binns treated are harder to understand. It would be interesting
to know why Mrs Chayre, the butcher's wife, was stabbed in
the belly with a pack-needle by the porter.[50] And an almost
modern impression of anonymous urban violence is given in
the case of a servant of the trunk-maker who 'was shot in the
shoulderblade through the bone with a pistol out of Pauls
through 2 thick deals & he standing in the shop at work'.[51]
The man died two days later, presumably without ever having
seen or identified his murderer.

Social and economic tensions strained relationships between
people. Husbands and wives, parents and children, masters
and servants and apprentices abused each other.[52] A recent
explanation for the increase in the number of witchcraft
accusations in the Tudor–Stuart period cites as a reason for
accusations and executions the annoyance and guilt produced
by indigent old women who begged for alms or goods, and
when refused, cursed the reluctant donor.[53] An echo of this
situation appears in the case quoted above where Sergeant
Major Jenkins stabbed 80-year-old Samuel Warde when the
old gardener begged for alms and then 'replied some words'
when refused.[54]

Even those whose duty it was to keep order were not
immune from the violence they sought to control. On Boxing
Day 1643 Mr Oram, 'a cook in Holborn' who was also
serving as constable, 'was wounded over the head, cut over
the first three fingers of the right hand to the joint next the
hand, cut obliquely over the same elbow on the outside,
incising the process of the' elbow joint.[55]

Wounds dealt in battle had a better reputation than others,
imputing neither stupidity nor malice to either the giver or the
receiver. Binns treated three soldiers wounded at the battle of
Newbury fought on 20 September 1643. One, Captain
Broomfield, was 'shot . . . with a brace of bullets', one
passing through the left shoulder, the other entering the same
armpit and lodging in the scapula.[56] Major Manwaring was
more fortunate, merely having been 'shot through his gorget
[a piece of armour protecting the throat] & so did but bruise

his neck where the bullet lay'.[57] Binns's cousin, Edward Green, who served under the major, had both bones of his right arm broken just above the wrist by a splinter.[58]

Binns's tone in reporting all symptoms, whether caused by violence or disease, was that of detached objectivity. He displayed emotion very rarely, and this only in cases where patients refused to follow instructions or, in one case, where a patient neglected to pay a sizeable bill for his services.[59] Thus, it is impossible to obtain from Binns's casebook any attitude regarding the violence which surrounded him. Perhaps, then as now, it was so common as to be unworthy of comment.

Binns described eleven cases where patients were injured in the course of their occupations. The most dangerous trades he came into contact with were associated with construction. A carpenter, Mr Day, was injured on 23 October 1646, when in the course of 'breaking a board upon his right knee [he] struck a nail to the top of the rotula [kneecap]'.[60] Fifteen years later, Mr Day's man 'had [his] left arm hurt so with a crane that the minor fossil came through the flesh in the joint of the wrist the head of the fossil came all out we had much ado to reduce it'.[61] One Thomas Johnson, a joiner, fell off a ladder breaking both bones of his left leg below the knee, one of which 'broke through the flesh in the inside . . . w/wound of a finger's length'.[62] On 13 September 1653 the glazier, Launcelott Derrick, fell two storeys into a courtyard, breaking his left leg.[63] A bricklayer called Myllis was either unlucky or clumsy. On 27 November 1639 he

> had a severe fall near upon 3 storeys in the inside of a new building from the timber of one floor to another taken up speechless but within an hour spoke but not sensibly no hurt about him but his left clavicle broken close to the sternum & a little place contused in the occiput or pole behind his head.[64]

Binns reported laconically, 'Afterwards was killed in the same work, none knows how, found under a great window'.

Of course, other occupations had their hazards as well. Perhaps the most dramatic occupational injury Binns treated was the case of a young butcher on Saffron Hill who was gored in the left thigh by a bull. In a less dramatic case, a cutler in Holborn 'struck his first finger of his right hand against the hot tongue of an old knife which wounded him in the third joint which wounded the tendon in the inside'.[65] By the time Binns saw the wound, the tendon had 'rotted'. The man injured himself in May, but was not well until the end of July.

A number of Binns's patients were injured by horses or horse-drawn vehicles. One groom had his left leg broken 'by a blow of his horse heel'.[66] Others less occupationally qualified were hurt in similar ways. A woman 'had her left leg broke by a coach wheel'.[67] 'Mr. Payne broke his left collarbone . . . falling off a horse.'[68] A young man 'fell from a horseback & put his right arm out of joint in the elbow'.[69] Regardless of these cases, however, horses appear remarkably safe compared to the hazards of the age of the automobile.

The work of housewives and maid-servants was also dangerous. Mrs Carie, a goldsmith's wife, was treated for a badly infected hand and arm after pricking her finger with a needle.[70] Elizabeth Bemis, Mrs Brewer's maid, was 'burned with fire upon the left temple close to the eyelid and under the eye'.[71]

And the home itself was full of hazards. Children were particularly at risk. On 14 November 1648, 'Mrs. Swallow her daughter by the maid's carelessness warming the bed the girl being in bed, she burnt her left leg in the innerside in the small & the right leg her outer ankle'.[72] In another bed accident, 'A porter's child fell out of the bed and broke the left thigh bone'.[73] A 2-year-old, who tumbled even further, fell 'out at a window a storey high & bruised all the top of the head'.[74] Adults also hurt themselves at home. One Mr Balsom fell 'down the stone stairs in his garden upon a paving stone yard', bruising his left shoulder and suffering a compound fracture of his left forearm.[75] Indeed, it is remarkable that the casebook contains so few examples of accidents happening in the home, considering that in the seventeenth century open fires were the rule, building regulations were non-existent and tools conformed to no standard except the maker's own. To survive, one had to be careful.

Of course, even vigilance could not prevent some accidents. One poor woman, a servant at Gray's Inn, died after receiving a head injury 'being in a boat upon the Thames by a stick thrown from another boat'.[76] Another woman was wounded on the forehead by a tile, which presumably slipped off a roof.[77]

Binns did not describe the circumstances which produced many of the injuries he treated. Most of these were simple dislocations, fractures and cuts which he dealt with for very short periods of time. Typical of his commentary on such cases was the following: 'A girl in Shoe Lane put her right elbow out. Put it in. Well'.[78]

Joseph Binns was successful in treating most of the injuries he came across. What follows is a general description of his therapeutic approach to wounds, fractures, dislocations and bruises. Only brief mention will be made of the preparations Binns applied to the injured part. This study is only tangentially concerned with the seventeenth-century pharma-copoeia and whether or not it 'worked'. It will concentrate, rather, on Binns's routines which reveal both the results most important to the surgeon and the procedures patients willingly underwent.

In cases of stab wounds Binns first attempted to stop the bleeding with dressings which he called boulsters, pleagetts or rowlers. Sometimes he searched the wound with either a finger or a probe before dressing it, but he usually delayed this procedure for a day or two, presumably to avoid exacerbating the bleeding. He then usually prescribed a laxative or a clyster, to keep the body soluble, and a cordial to support the patient's strength and spirits. He also generally prescribed a light diet, often consisting exclusively of liquids such as broth and posset-ale. After the initial bleeding had stopped, Binns attempted to prevent infection by keeping the wound open. This he did by means of a tent (a roll of dressing or other material) inserted into the mouth of the wound to keep open a drainage tract.[79] If the wound were so small a puncture that it could not be easily searched, Binns might dilate it with an instrument he called a root before inserting the tent. Binns also occasionally injected medicines into puncture wounds.

Binns treated cuts or lacerations similarly to stab wounds, except that he usually stitched up the wound immediately after stopping the bleeding. In the case of a tailor in Postern Lane who cut his own throat, Binns sewed up the wound which did well for twelve days. At this point, it 'began to apostemate', so Binns reopened the wound and changed the ointment on the dressings. The patient recovered in spite of himself.[80]

Gunshot wounds presented special difficulties. Occasionally the bullet lodged in the body and had to be cut out. Sometimes there were powder burns to contend with. In one case part of the lining of the injured man's doublet was projected into the wound by the bullet and was removed three days after the man was shot.[81] Compared to most puncture wounds and lacerations, gunshot wounds were dirty, yielding 'a dirty black matter' for the first few days of treatment. They could also be foul smelling.[82] Some cases Binns treated similarly to his puncture wounds, keeping the wounds open with flamulae (fabric strips or strings) or tents moistened with medicines. Sometimes he used injections, as with puncture wounds; other gunshot wounds he simply dressed at the skin surface. Despite their difference from other sorts of wounds, Binns used no special medications for gunshot wounds. Once the bleeding had been stopped and foreign bodies removed from the wound, he adhered to his usual routine of frequent dressings, laxatives, clysters and occasional phlebotomy, watching for the signs of infection, and trying to prevent it if possible. It should be noted that Binns's definition of infection included swelling, the build-up of fluid, local heat or fever, and sometimes mortification. A moderate discharge from the wound was regarded as normal and healthy.

Binns used numerous preparations, both to bathe and annoint wounds and upon the different parts of his dressings. He expected wounds to heal in a certain fashion, and prescribed different preparations to aid in each stage of the healing process. If a wound were unusually painful, he applied a cataplasm (medicated poultice) to ease the patient's discomfort. He was then most concerned to bring the wound to 'digestion', that is to cause or facilitate the production of healthy discharge. If, in the process, 'proud' or 'spongy' flesh formed in the wound, Binns attacked it with spirit of wine or other preparations designed to remove it. Next Binns wished the wound to 'incarnate'. This involved a reduction of discharge from the wound and a generally healthy appearance of it. The final step was to cicatrise or close the wound. Binns was careful not to allow wounds to close until either the threat of apostemation had passed or, in the cases of compound fractures and incised bones, splinters of bone had emerged from the wound.

Of course, wounds very often did become infected. When they did, they were treated in the same way as other sorts of apostemations and fistulae. This treatment will be described below. Binns dealt with many infected wounds – cases so extreme that tendons and bones had become 'corrupt' or 'foul' and extremities threatened to become gangrenous. However, in only three cases did he resort to amputation.[83] One can only speculate about the reasons for Binns's reluctance to perform an operation which his colleagues certainly used more often than he did. The surgeon John Woodall, who had preceded Binns on the staff at St Bartholomew's and won a certain amount of lasting recognition for his publication of a handbook for naval surgeons, had written a detailed description of the procedure he used to amputate limbs, both gangrenous and otherwise.[84] Perhaps Binns did not consider himself to be sufficiently skilled in amputation to attempt the procedure even in desperate cases. Perhaps he considered the risks of amputation to be greater than those of the ills which might suggest it as a therapy. However, it is most likely that Binns's confidence in his ability to deal with infection made amputation seem unnecessary.

His success rate proves such confidence to have been justified. Out of seventy-nine injuries which involved open wounds, the casenotes report eight deaths, twenty-one unknown results and fifty cures. These injuries range from the most desperate, such as that of the servant of the trunk-maker, mentioned above, whose gunshot wound killed him within two days, to the most minor, such as that of the goldsmith's wife who pricked her finger with a needle.[85] These figures do not include all of Binns's patients who might have undergone amputation in the hands of another surgeon. Many of the apostemations of extremities Binns treated were very serious, possibly life-threatening, but were not the result of injuries. Indeed, the above figures do not include the case of one patient who did undergo amputation, because his disorder was caused, not by a wound, but by an aneurism in his arm which had developed after he had been let blood by an unskilful surgeon.[86] The figures also do not include the case of Binns's only patient who died of gangrene. This was Thomas Caswell, who on 25 June developed a little redness and pain in his toe. By 29 July his foot and lower leg were gangrenous. On 6 August he died. Binns apparently did not consider amputation.[87] None the less, the figures demonstrate that Binns was more than competent to handle the wounds which came his way.

Binns treated fifty-eight cases of fractures and dislocations, exclusive of head wounds.[88] In his treatment of these patients, his greatest concerns were to prevent or cure infection and fever, and to restore the use of the limb. He was not as interested in whether broken bones were properly set. Thus, in one case of a fractured leg where the bones refused to knit, 'the greater fossil being broken obliquely there start up a small corner of the bone towards the inner ankle so as it caused pain so I broke off the sharp point with my nail & applied mixt. ung. after which he had no pain'.[89] He did, of course, set bones, using splints, various sorts of plasters, rollers, laced stocking and pillows to immobilise the injured part. His approach varied from case to case. Concerning one leg fracture, where the initially applied splints caused much pain, Binns took the splints off and used linen and cotton ligatures with cotton 'stupes', tying the leg 'up close in a pillow'.[90]

The XXVI Table.

Of the extending of the Thigh broken into divers parts, and the setting of it; of the reducing of the knee that is disjointed; and of setting the whole foot in a mean posture.

FIG. I. represents the thigh broken extended by bands, when it cannot be extended with the hands, and *Hippocrates* his Form is not at hand: Let the Sick be laied on a common Form, with his face upwards; let the band be tied under his arm-pits, and put another band in the space that is between his privities and his fundament: Lastly, another band must be bound above his knee, and his ankle; these bands must be drawn by strong servants, the uppermost upward A, the undermost downward, till the Chyrurgian hath set the fracture. In the setting of the knee out of joint, when extension cannot be made with the hands, let the upper bands be bound alike, and the undermost above the ankles.

Fig. II and III. shews the mean figure of the members and muscles of the arm and the whole foot; which is necessary in the extension, setting, binding and placing of a part either broken or dislocated. But I therefore caused the figure of this configuration to be printed here, that young Chyrurgians, when it shall be often pointed at underneath, may at first sight learn it, and may imitate the same in their practice.

TABVLA XXVI.

Fig. I.

Surgeons were usually trained by apprenticeship. However, growing numbers of books on the craft were directed at young surgeons in the seventeenth century with the intention of improving their knowledge and skill. (J. Scultetus, *The Chyrurgeon's Store-house*, London, 1674.)

Binns regarded broken bones – particularly in the legs – as serious injuries, treating patients for months, applying plaster after plaster, and checking limbs for strength.[91] People who broke their legs spent a long time in bed. Mr Fisher, the innkeeper at the Star in Holborn, had his left tibia close to the ankle broken by a coach wheel in March 1640. It was a compound fracture and Binns feared gangrene, so he dressed it twice a day for the first two weeks. Mr Fisher was completely bedridden well into May, being laid on a pallet every two or three days while his bed was being made. Binns was still applying new plasters in August, when the casenote ended, incomplete.[92] Mrs Lynsie, whose leg was also broken by a coach wheel, was out of her bed only three times in the first twenty-one days after her injury.[93] Mrs Cromwell, who suffered a compound fracture of the tibia on 19 January 1645, was confined to bed for two months. She suffered so much pain in the first two days after her injury that Binns prescribed a sleeping draught – a very rare event in his practice.[94]

Less serious were broken arms, clavicles, ribs and noses. These Binns set, usually delaying application of the long-lasting 'restringent' plaster for a few days until the swelling had gone down.[95] He applied warm dressings to ease pain and reduce swelling. As in other injuries, he occasionally let blood, prescribed clysters or laxatives, and recommended a light diet.

Dislocations were usually regarded as less serious than fractures, except when they were accompanied by a wound.[96] Binns reduced the dislocation, then immobilised the limb. His treatment of the following patient is quite typical.

> Jonathan's son the carman fell from a horseback & put his right arm out of joint in the elbow so I put it in, myself with little extension by pulling the cubitus & withall bending it inward & thrusting up the eminence of the advitorium all at once & so it slipped in. It slipped out again by putting his arm out at length: it went in again as it did before.[97]

After some twenty days of treatment, during which two plasters were applied, the patient found his joint a little stiff so he could not straighten it, but 'by carrying it out & motion it came again, all praised be God'.

Head wounds – particularly those involving fractures – were among the most serious disorders Binns treated. Of the thirteen cases for which we have some details, four patients died, five got well and four casenotes were incomplete, so the outcome is unknown. The four patients who died experienced a similar pattern of symptoms. Each seemed reasonably well after the initial dressing of the wound and remained well for at least a week. After between nine and fourteen days each patient developed symptoms – vomiting, fever and/or paralysis – which became increasingly severe until the patient's death between thirteen and twenty-five days after injury.[98] In three cases Binns and the other surgeons consulted laid the cranium bare in order to determine whether the skull had been fractured.[99] In two cases the trepan was applied.[100] This procedure was obviously reserved for the most desperate cases, when the patient was expected to die in any event. Both of Binns's patients who underwent trepanning died within twenty-four hours after the operation.

Not all patients suffering skull fractures died. In August 1649,

> Frank the drawer at the Castle Tavern in Paternoster Row . . . received a blow with a pint pot upon the frons near the edge of the left temporal muscle, which made a little depression with a fracture round the depression and a piece of the depressed bone carried away to the side of the wound.[101]

Binns gave Frank the treatment he routinely used for head injuries. He opened a vein and gave Frank a suppository. He dressed the wound, using warm medications and bandages. He then prescribed a suppository every other day, changed the medicines used on the dressings as healing progressed, rolled the bandages loosely and watched Frank's daily progress. Frank recovered quickly.

Binns regarded this treatment regimen as necessary. In the case of Will Evims, a patient who died thirteen days after receiving a knife wound on the left side of his forehead, Binns, who merely consulted, criticised the attending surgeon for 'neither [having] given him clyster nor opened vein nor applied anything to his wound more than pleagetts coplaster'.[102] Binns was, however, flexible enough to learn from what he perceived as his own mistakes. In the case of a boy who died twenty-five days after having been kicked in the head by a horse, Binns apparently felt he was partly to blame for the patient's death, for he wrote, 'Let it be your care not to roll the head too hard'.[103]

In addition to the serious injuries described above, Binns treated a number of patients for sprains, bruises and relatively minor burns. One sprained ankle yielded quickly to several days of hot ointments and soaking, combined with a stiff

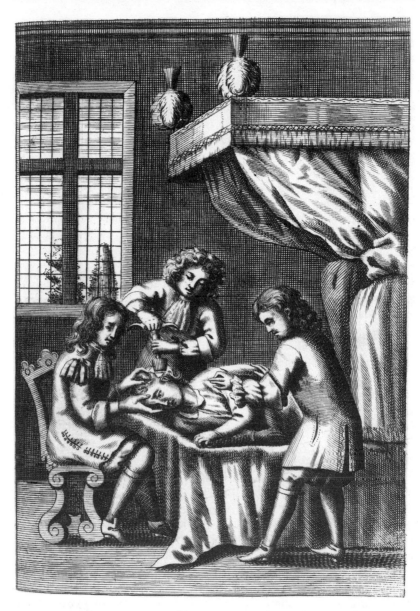

Engraving of a surgeon trephining a patient's cranium, 1678.
(Anon., Wellcome Library)

plaster.[104] A more stubborn case of a repeatedly sprained ankle resisted a long and varied course of treatment which included fomentations, purges, plasters, a laced stocking and a trip to Bath. The patient remained uncured.[105]

Bruises usually responded after several applications of oils and plasters.[106] However, some bruises became infected. These Binns treated similarly to apostems, which will be discussed below. The most remarkable case of bruising Binns treated, however, was that of Mr Lower, 'an ancient gentleman [who] fell & bruised his arm & shoulder' in January 1647. Binns and his assistant treated Mr Lower with a series of hot applications and soaking, plasters, fomentations, an ox's belly and a diet drink, until April. They were never paid for their trouble.[107] Lower owed them 30s. for plasters, oils and fomentations, and £5 'for my pains and my man's constant pains for 3 months'. This case is remarkable only because it was one of the few appearing in the casebook where Binns lost the cool objective style which characterises the bulk of his entries. His outrage at being denied his fee is apparent.

In the course of his long career, Binns recorded treating only five patients for burns. In each case the patient recovered.[108] In only one instance was Binns called immediately after the injury occurred. In this case, that of a maid-servant who scalded her arms in June 1651, Binns produced a cure within three weeks by the use of warm unguent applied with a feather and lawn (fine linen or cotton) rags kept wet with another ointment laid over the burn.[109] In two other cases Binns began treating burn victims only when other efforts had failed. When he 'began cure of Elizabeth Bemis Mrs. Brewer's maid', the burn on her left temple near her eyelid had caused an ulcer so deep it was 'almost to the cranium'. During his first visit Binns opened a vein, applied cupping glasses, ordered a clyster and fomented the ulcer with whey. After several of these fomentations, he applied an unguent until the burn had healed. However, after healing had taken place, 'her eyelid began to draw up within a month . . . so that the inside was turned out, it became very painful and swelled like a bladder'. This the patient treated by stroking her eyelid 'with a dead hand', thereupon finding relief. (Binns did not comment upon this therapy.) However, 'she had not perfect ease till she had an issue in her arm on the same side'.[110]

In the less serious case quoted above, Binns was called in a week after Mrs Swallow's daughter had received leg burns as a result of the maid attempting to warm a bed while the girl was lying in it. Mrs Swallow had been treating the child herself, and called in the surgeon only after a yellow salve she had applied had made the 'leg rise all in little blisters red and itching'. She treated the blisters with a red balsam she had obtained 'formerly' from a Dr Wright to treat a similar condition caused by a 'plaster of burgundy pitch'. Binns decided to continue using the balsam, adding two other ointments and a barley water application to the treatment. Within two weeks, the patient was cured.[111]

In the case of a young man who had burnt his face and hands with gunpowder, Binns appears to have been called in by 'young Mr. Plummer', the patient's surgeon, because the case might have proven to be serious.[112] Treatment, including blood-letting, a clyster, unguents and milk fomentations, was uneventful, however, the burns being nearly healed within ten days.[113]

The above discussion has shown that Binns's treatment of injuries followed predictable patterns and was quite successful. The following sections will turn to what might be referred to as repair jobs (such as his treatment of hydrocephaly, herniae, tumours, apostems and fistulae), and his approach to illnesses.

II SURGICAL REPAIRS

A significant part of Joseph Binns's practice was concerned with the surgical repair of such conditions as ulcers, herniae, apostems, fistulae and tumours, in addition to an assortment of less commonly encountered ills, such as hydrocephaly. Again, difficulties exist with regard to terminology. For instance, an apostemation, or infected swelling, might also be described as a tumour, since Binns used the word 'tumour' to refer to any swelling. Also, apostems frequently developed into fistulae. Equally, after opening, they might become ulcers. Thus, any figures mentioned in connection with these terms must be approximate. However, a rough breakdown of Binns's own references to these conditions indicates that he treated thirty-one patients for ulcers (excluding those caused by syphilis), sixty-six for apostems, twenty-five for fistulae, eighteen for herniae, thirty-five for tumours and nineteen for other disorders requiring repair.

These patients came to Binns hoping to obtain relief from pain and disability. Many also hoped to have their appearances improved. Consider the case of Mrs Storye, a coachman's wife, who had a 'tumour varicosus in the right cheek & coming out at her mouth, in her neck to her shoulder, no bigger than a cherry when she was born but increased as she did grow'.[114] The tumour was only occasionally painful: from time to time it apostemated and required surgical intervention. However, Mrs Storye must also have been concerned about the disfigurement it caused. When Binns saw her, the tumour 'was apostemated from behind her ear to the temple very big'. He was able to cure the apostem and leave 'the tumour less than it used to be, praised be God'. Another woman, 'one Goodwife Lewis', had 'a wen on the inside of the right arm in the armpit & so along the arm for almost a hand's length fastened up to the muscles of that side the scapula where it was rooted & hanging down as big as a child's head'.[115] Binns was able to remove the growth. Still another patient, 'One William White . . . had been troubled with hernia carnosa in his left stone . . . the whole body of the testicle dilated & grown the bigness of a mushmelon'.[116] This casenote was incomplete, so we never learn whether this poor man found relief.

These three sufferers must surely have worried about the unsightliness, as well as the pain, of their disorders. Despite the ubiquitous hazards of smallpox, syphilis, rickets and other diseases which disfigured those they did not kill, seventeenth-century Englishmen and women valued a good appearance. They bought or coveted luxurious fabrics and extravagant styles of dress. They used elaborate wigs and coiffures. Both men and women applied make-up. Thus, it should be remembered that surgeons, then as now, were required to repair the appearance as well as the function of the body.[117]

In any case, surgical repairs were more often required by people who were in pain and who, often justifiably, feared the possibly fatal consequences of allowing a condition to continue. Many such patients sought a return to their previously stable state, rather than a complete cure. For instance, Mr Arthur Rudle had worn a steel truss to control his rupture for many years. When, after having taken cold, he found he could not replace the rupture in the truss, he first called for the truss-maker, Mr Bostocke, and later for Joseph Binns to help him. Binns, through a series of clysters and warm applications to the rupture, was finally able to replace the rupture in the truss twenty-six days after he was first consulted. Mr Rudle was satisfied.[118] He was also fortunate. Mr Sadler was not so lucky. He bruised his old rupture, and all the efforts to replace the rupture in his truss made by Binns and the patient's friends were useless. Sadler died five days after he was injured.[119]

Some patients and their families were in the unenviable

position of deciding to alter a reasonably stable condition in the hope of getting permanently rid of a disorder. Consider the sense of guilt and responsibility which must have burdened Mrs Wilson. When her baby was born,

> it had a little knot or tumour soft in the nape of the neck upon the skull. This grew bigger every month so that in September 1648 it was as big as one's fist, I was satisfied that it was water, the child's head was larger much than children of that age usually are (it was then some 8 months old) I perceived there was a perforation in the skull. I was fearful to open it because of the accidents which might follow [,] but being earnestly desired of the mother of the child, she being well resolved concerning the child, the 15th of September, 1648, I opened this tumour by incision.[120]

There followed a month during which Binns repeatedly opened the baby's head. The child was feverish and sick most of the time. On 16 October it died.[121]

Not all surgical repairs of congenital disorders were so dangerous. Binns reported that 'Mr. Webster of Chesterfield his son was cut of a wry neck the 19 June 1640. It was skinned in 5 days. (Mr. Harris his way of cutting)'.[122] Binns made no suggestion that such an operation was either dangerous or unusual. However, Mr Webster was concerned enough to travel a long way in search of expert surgical help. He was not alone. London was used as a medical centre for the whole of England, and Binns's patients had often travelled long distances to consult him.[123]

Another sort of condition Binns was occasionally called upon to repair was the disorders caused by unskilful or unlucky surgery (not necessarily performed by a trained surgeon). Binns treated at least eight patients for iatrogenic illnesses ranging from an aneurism caused by blood-letting, which eventually led to the amputation of the affected arm, to an apostem in the anus caused by the passing of a clyster pipe 'through the skin close to the verge of the anus, and so through the gut into the rectum'.[124] These problems illustrate the hazards of prophylactic medicine. Seventeenth-century preventative health care required, in addition to a moderate diet and good sleep and exercise habits, regular use of purges, clysters and phlebotomy. Binns did not indicate how many of the eight patients mentioned above had been well before they had undergone the procedures which made them consult him. However, they had certainly been willing participants in operations which they expected to do nothing but good.[125]

Since Binns treated their problems in the same way as he treated other apostems, fistulae and skin irritations, we will not discuss them further here.

The repair job Binns most frequently undertook was the treatment of apostems and fistulae. As indicated above, these ailments resulted from various causes. Sometimes wounds apostemated.[126] Sometimes patients developed apostems and fistulae as complications of conditions such as haemorrhoids, tooth-decay, childbirth, breast-feeding and ague.[127] Anal fistulae were very common.[128] Sometimes these were complications of haemorrhoids. Sometimes they resulted from apostems in the pelvic region. Another frequent location of apostems and fistulae was the mouth. Rotten teeth usually caused these.[129]

Whatever the cause or location, Binns's approach was either to open and drain the infected swelling, making certain that all infected matter had issued before he allowed the orifice(s) to close, or to open the fistula (a hollowness left by earlier infection), cleanse the area, and make sure the flesh as it grew again was sound. His usual method of opening both apostems and fistulae was to apply 'the caustic stone' for several hours, which either opened the affected place on its own or made it easier for Binns to open it by incision. A typical case was that of

One Mr. Francis Tilney of Grays Inn [who] had a large apostem under his chin, of 10 days collection, the 7 Feb [1642] I laid on the caustic stone & opened it an hour after, there came out much matter, there remained a hollowness some days after being cut . . . & not likely to join. I laid the caustic stone upon it for one hour so it cast all & became an open sore, which healed in 10 days, but the siccatrix girte down his chin.[130]

Binns also used 'suppurative cataplasms' which occasionally opened apostems on their own.[131] Very rarely he opened apostems by incision alone.[132] And sometimes apostems obligingly opened spontaneously.[133]

Once an apostem was open, Binns assisted drainage of matter by inserting a tent into the opening. If the orifice was not large enough, he dilated it with a root. He then assisted drainage by the use of various medicines, either applying them to dressings, bathing the affected area or injecting them into the orifice.

In cases of fistulae where Binns could find two orifices, he sometimes drew a 'frenum' or string through both openings and tied the string progressively tighter. After several days he was usually able to open the fistula by incision quite easily.[134] After opening a fistula, he used similar preparations to those he used for apostems to cleanse the hollowness of matter, scar tissue and spongy flesh, before assisting healing.

The cure of apostems and fistulae was often a long, frustrating business. Just when it seemed that healing was about to occur, a new swelling would develop, or a new hollowness be found, and the whole process of treatment would begin all over again. In May 1645, after suffering from an ague, John the carman's son developed an apostem in his right calf. Binns opened and treated it in his usual manner, but John developed a fistula which became reinfected (that is 'full of matter') at least four times before it finally healed in April 1646.[135] He was unusually fortunate. Mrs Hodge's youngest son, who developed an apostem in his hip and buttock in December 1650, two years after having been kicked by a horse, was treated for his gradually deteriorating condition until he died in October of the following year, 'a very skeleton'.[136] Such patients required frequent visits for dressing changes, assessment of the healing process (often requiring alterations in prescriptions), and monitoring of the general physical state, including pain, sleep, appetite and bowel movements. Many of the working hours of Binns and his assistants or apprentices must have been occupied by visits to apostem and fistula sufferers.[137]

This section would be incomplete without mention of the most remarkable case of fistula Binns treated. A servant, Elizabeth Woodward, was admitted to St Bartholomew's Hospital in July 1650, suffering from a fistula which opened three fingers below her sternum and voided material from her stomach. She recovered enough to leave hospital in April 1651, but was admitted again in November of that year. She died in March 1652.[138]

From apostems and fistulae we will now turn our attention to ulcers. Binns treated many sorts of ulcers. Some, as indicated above, came about in the course of treating apostems and fistulae. Many (which will be discussed elsewhere) resulted from syphilis. Some were cancerous. Some were symptoms of scurvy. Some were complications of other disorders, such as tumours and corns. And still others appeared spontaneously on their own.

Binns kept a number of medications which he used mainly for the treatment of ulcers. He had his own 'ulcer water' and 'unguent mixt'. He also touched ulcers with strong preparations composed of such substances as mercury, antimony and vitriol. His aim was first to cleanse the ulcer of 'escars', discharge and unhealthy spongy flesh, then to promote healing.

His success in healing ulcers varied. Although he tried a number of different preparations on Mrs Lightfool's facial ulcers between May and July 1633, each new ointment caused much pain, but did no good.[139] Some ulcers, such as the apthas Mr Hutchinson's girl Sarah had on her gums and tongue, would almost certainly have disappeared on their own. (Sarah was well in ten days.)[140] Others of Binns's cures seem almost miraculous. On 4 April 1655 a 14-day-old infant developed an ulcer on the navel after the umbilical cord had fallen off. Despite the efforts of Binns and the physician Dr Bathurst, the ulcer grew until 'it spread as broad as a xx piece'. At this point Binns used his unguent with an antimony preparation, and reported 'good digestion'. The ulcer healed by 20 April, 'Laus soli deo'.[141]

Although Binns treated a number of ulcers he described as cancerous, he never approached them with much hope of success. Indeed, he reported a cure in only one case of cancer. This was that of Goodwife White of St Giles in the Fields. Binns removed her cancerous breast in St Bartholomew's Hospital on 3 February 1648. She was alive and well in 1653.[142] Binns attempted another breast removal seven months later. This patient was also in St Bartholomew's Hospital. Binns

> used a double ligature upon the woman's breast the 9 August at morn 1648. Tied it harder the 11th at morn & the 12, & the 14th it had gained much – the 16th & the 18 – the 22nd the lower string was through the bigness of a finger, the upper one near to an inch . . . so with string cut it off in the ligature. It bled pretty freely. Died a week after.[143]

Thereafter, Binns treated breast cancers more cautiously, dealing with the tumours and ulcers as he did non-cancerous ones. In addition to breast cancers, he treated cancerous mouth and tongue ulcers. Regardless of the therapy applied, patients with cancer usually died.[144]

Binns also treated several leg ulcers which had been caused by scurvy. These began with swelling and spots in the affected leg. The spots turned to pustules or blisters, and these eventually became ulcers. Binns treated such patients with juice of scurvy grass, purges and a variety of ointments (depending on what had the best result).[145]

Despite his lack of optical equipment, Binns was able to diagnose and successfully treat three cases of ulcers in the eye. In one case he described the affected eye in detail:

> I found her eye much inflamed [,] upon the pupilla a little whitish dint in the outward coat of cornea like the pressure of a pin's head with little towes from it as if it had been a little piece of flock of wool, which seemed to be an ulcer. Her pain was great pricking & burning.

Binns characteristically treated the woman's whole system, blistering her neck, purging her with pills, applying plasters to her temples and dropping medicines into her eye. The ulcers got worse at first, so Binns changed the eye medications (including woman's milk in the second preparation) and cupped and scarified the patient's shoulders. After this the eye improved. The woman was relieved of her pain and left with 'some weak sight' in her eye.[146]

Perhaps more clearly than with other types of disorder, Binns's approach to ulcers illustrated both the seventeenth-century surgeon's empiricism and his willingness to try his hand at any sort of problem which was brought to him, however frustrating. If one medicine failed to produce the desired effect, Binns tried another. If cancerous ulcers appeared hopeless of cure, he attacked them anyway. Despite both surgeons' and physicians' understandable unwillingness to accept 'incurable' cases, Binns and his colleagues did take them on, applying their skills as best they could. This perseverance reflects not only the surgeons' patience and dedication, but also the patients' demands. It is not surprising that the barbersurgeons were the most numerous among full-time medical personnel in seventeenth-century London.[147]

Binns's practice included the treatment of many tumours. As indicated above, he used the word 'tumour' to describe any swelling, rather as the modern practitioner might use the word 'oedema'. However, he also used the term more specifically, referring to growths which were not apostemated swellings. He also used other terms, such as 'wen', 'polyp', 'ficus' and 'ascites' to refer to such growths.

Some tumours were easier to treat than others. Polyps in the nose, for instance, were not difficult to remove, but tended to recur. Binns wrote in 1650,

> I extracted a pollipus out of Mrs. Cooper's daughter's nostril & made her an issue in her left arm. I had extracted it out of both nostrils 2 years afore this . . . (I expected it again in 1654). They

are in both nostrils like a bunch of grapes, injected after a restringent medicine.[148]

Likewise, Binns had no difficulty treating a 'ficus' in the anus of one Mr Lucas. On 2 February he 'made ligature' upon the tumour. He reported that 'it looked deadish the next day and flaccid, it came off going to stool the 6 February at morn'.[149]

However, other sorts of tumours were harder to deal with, and Binns approached them with caution. Indeed, Binns's casebook reveals nothing more clearly than this surgeon's reluctance to use the knife. Even when opening the flesh was necessary, Binns preferred gradual (and hopefully bloodless) means, such as the caustic stone and ligature. One can only speculate about the reasons for this reluctance. Perhaps Binns feared infection. Perhaps he feared making a bad condition worse.

The following case illustrates his caution. On 16 March 1661 he and the surgeon Mr Arris were called to see a Mr Chilsonne who had

> a great tumour on the inside of his right thigh very large in length from the middle of the thigh to the knee in thickness from the forepart of the thigh so to the underside of the thigh to the outside.

They judged that 'it was a schirrus cancerosus' and ordered a cataplasm to be applied. Their prescriptions were used for some two weeks. At this point, a Dr Williams was called in. He was in favour of opening the tumour by means of a 'sympathetic specific medicine' of his own composition. This was first applied on 8 April. On 10 April incision was tried, but 'there came blood trickling out pretty fast, so clapt on a dosell [dressing] . . . and bound it up till the 11 April, cut a little deeper till blood came', dressed it again, and continued this pattern of treatment until the physician could insert a probe two inches into the incision. At this point the patient died (16 April). The next day the tumour was opened. Binns reported 'there was nothing in it but coagulated blood & a substance like rotten liver, & but little thin blood, & a hollowness from it up to the groin full of black grumous blood'.[150] Binns obviously felt the patient would have been better off without the physician's radical help.

Binns attempted to remove only certain sorts of tumours. These were not always small. In a case mentioned above, Binns removed a wen from a woman's shoulder-blade which was 'hanging down as big as a child's head'.[151] In a less successful case he 'incised' a cancerous tumour on a man's thigh on 12 February 1652. He then treated the resulting ulcer and a new tumour which developed on the patient's ribs until 29 August, when the man died. Despite this sad outcome, Binns reported 'his thigh is even cicatrised'.[152] He obviously felt that his course of treatment was appropriate.

Other sorts of tumours Binns dealt with by using surface applications and internal medicines. In a case of scrofulous tumours of the neck, for instance, Binns prescribed a course of vomits, purges, salves and plasters. This patient was under his care on and off for four years. Her condition did not heal permanently, so she left Binns and looked elsewhere for a cure. Binns noted laconically, 'She was after touched by the King'.[153]

Most of the tumours Binns treated were easily visible, occurring on the extremities or the neck and head. Tumours of the abdomen and chest were more difficult, both to identify and to treat. Many patients with such internal growths must have taken them to physicians, since surgical excision of them would not have been possible and, in any case, the formal division between surgery and medicine would have placed such ills within the physician's sphere. Binns did undertake treatment of an 'ascites' tumour of the belly. He opened this swelling on 24 June 1655, releasing a gallon of fluid the first day and a similar amount on the two following days. The fourth day he released three quarts and the patient felt better, but was very restless. He died that evening.[154] As in the case of hydrocephaly discussed above, and one of another infant who was born with an 'aqueous tumour on the small of the back', Binns was able to drain the swelling, but could not stop production of the fluid.[155]

The last major type of repair job Binns undertook was the treatment of hernia. He treated eighteen male patients for hernia. Eight of these suffered from 'hernia aquosa', a condition during which one testicle filled with a watery fluid. Ten patients had other sorts of herniae.

Binns's treatment of hernia aquosa followed a routine which was usually successful. The day before surgery, the patient was prescribed a vomit. The next day the swelling was opened by incision. The following case was typical.

> 1652. Dr. Bennet hath had a hernia aquosa 12 months in his testicle [.]. I opened it the 8th of April in the afternoon the stone lay to the seam in the middle of the scrotum, & I made incision on

the outside towards the thigh an inch from the stone, and toward the bottom of the tumour. There came out of clear water three parts of a pint, I used a restringent & warm fomentation for 5 or six days, morn & night, with a hot stupe.

The patient recovered.[156]

The problem with hernia aquosa was that it tended to recur. Poor Mr Samuel Davison had had a hernia aquosa opened by the surgeon, Mr Will Moollins, in the spring of 1653. After the operation, Moollins had given him a diet drink and pills which made his mouth and throat sore. Mr Davison developed a fever. His hernia grew again. This time he consulted Binns, who opened the hernia 24 October 1653; half a pint of fluid issued. Binns prescribed a purge and a new diet drink. However, the hernia grew again.[157]

Binns treated other sorts of hernia with surface applications and trusses. Mrs Benfield's son, who had had an inguinal hernia as a baby, developed an intestinal hernia as a young man. Binns treated it with purges and the application of hot ointments and dressings. The patient was cured in two weeks.[158] Mr Robinson's old intestinal hernia fell down so that it filled the scrotum. Binns and two surgical colleagues, Mr King and Mr Heath, tried to reduce it without success. They treated the patient with clysters, fomentations and cataplasms, but the patient died seven days after he became ill.[159]

In his treatment of hernia, as in his other repairs, Binns's very mechanical approach to disorder can be clearly observed. He treated symptoms. Although he prescribed purges, clysters, issues and phlebotomy, these procedures were designed to keep or produce a humoral balance in the body, rather than to attack primary causes of disease, about which Binns seems not to have speculated. He aimed merely to get rid of an unwelcome manifestation of disease or to return the patient to a bearable stable condition. He frequently succeeded. Of the approximately 194 repair jobs he undertook, 92 left the patient well, 22 resulted in improvement of the condition, and only seven left the sufferer no better than before. In forty-four cases the outcome is unknown, and thirty-one patients died.

In reporting the outcome of an attempt at surgical repair, Binns's casenotes frequently ended with the statement, 'Well laus deo'. Yet his personal definition of the word 'well' seems limited at best. Patients were well when they could function more or less independently. Thus, people who could walk on their broken legs when the legs were still in plaster were well. Hernia aquosa sufferers were well as long as their recurring ailments did not inconvenience them. Binns's surgical repairs were, therefore, conservative measures. His was no miracle surgery which could restore lost beauty or promise permanent cures. Rather he attacked the immediate problem, hoping to produce stability in the patient's condition.

III DISEASE STATES

Joseph Binns treated many ailments which were produced by disease states. Some conditions, like the spots, ulcers and swellings which appeared on the legs of scurvy sufferers, fell properly within the surgeon's sphere of operation. Others, such as diarrhoea, sore throat, agues and coughs, might more appropriately have been taken to a physician.[160] Binns treated internal problems with purges and vomits, sometimes adding a typically surgical remedy, such as an issue, to the course of treatment. His general approach to illness has been more fully discussed above, and need not concern us here. What we will investigate at length is his handling of venereal disease, which called upon all of his medical and surgical abilities at once.

Binns was consulted in 133 cases of gonorrhoea or syphilis.[161] In addition, twenty women brought to him problems which might be called 'female disorders', including whites (copious and unpleasant vaginal discharge), suppression of the menses, inordinate menstruation, and 'fits of the mother' (seizures produced by a wandering womb). Some of these patients may have had syphilis.[162] Several men called upon him to treat urinary retention which may or may not have been caused by venereal disease.[163]

Syphilis marked its victims both physically and morally. The disease was a chameleon, changing its manifestations during its course, and becoming dormant for years at a time, reappearing when its unsuspecting host had thought him- or herself long since cured. Dr Thomas Sydenham described the progress of syphilis as follows:

> The patient is affected with an unusual pain in the genitals . . . a spot, about the size and colour of a measle, appears on some part of the glans. . . . A discharge appears from the urethra . . . the aforesaid pustule becomes an ulcer. . . . Great pain during erections pathognomic of the disease. . . . Ardor urinae. . . . Bubos in the groin. . . . Pain in the head, arms and ankles. . . . Crusts and scabs appear on the skin. . . . The bones of the skull, the shin-bones, and the arm-bones, are raised into hard tubers. . . . The bone becomes carious and putrescent. . . .

Phagadaenic ulcers destroy the cartilege of the nose. This they eat away; so that the bridge sinks in and the nose flattens. . . . At length, limb by limb perishing away, the lacerated body, a burden to earth, finds ease only in the grave.[164]

Symptoms of advanced syphilis were well known, and even lampooned by the dramatists of the time. In the sad tale of a man who fell first into the arms of a harlot and then into the hands of a radical surgeon, the sufferer complains,

I am a knight, Sir Pock-hole is my name,
And by birth I am a Londoner,
Free by my copy, but my ancestors
Were Frenchmen all, and riding hard this way,
Upon a trotting horse my bones did ache
And I faint knight to ease my weary limbs,
Light at this cave, when straight this furious fiend,
With sharpest instrument of purest steel,
Did cut the gristle of my nose away,
And in the place this velvet plaster stands,
Relieve me gentle knight out of his hands.[165]

However, the 'saddle-noses' and pain-racked limbs were no joke to the victims of the pox, whose only hope was in a course of treatment nearly as savage as the disease itself.

Binns adapted the remedies he prescribed to the severity and types of symptoms presented, the sufferer's previous experience of 'cures' and the patient's reactions to the means tried. The first manifestation of the disease which Binns saw most frequently was gonorrhoea, which involved discharge from the penis, 'smarting' during urination, and uncontrollable erection or 'standing'. Binns routinely began treatment with a dose of 'pill Barbarosa', which purged the patient, and an injection into the urethra of his 'green water'.[166] To this he often added a diet drink which contained the purging herb senna. If the condition continued, he moved on to one or both of the two courses of treatment favoured at the time – a month's prescription of either guaiacum or mercury. The guaiacum cure was considerably more pleasant for the patient. Sometimes it apparently succeeded.[167] However, Binns used mercury far more often.

The mercury treatment of syphilis involved taking mercury internally, applying it in ointments to rashes, scabs and ulcers, and in 'waters' injecting it into apostems, noses and genitalia. Side effects of treatment were a sore mouth and throat, sometimes involving ulceration, spitting great quantities,

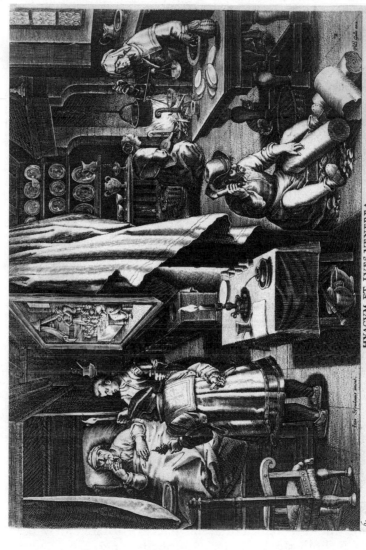

The preparation and use of guaiacum in cases of syphilis. Guaiacum and mercury were the preferred medicines for venereal disease in seventeenth-century England. (Philip Galle c. 1600, after J. van der Straet, Wellcome Library)

occasional nausea and frequent bowel movements. In the hands of an unskilled or unscrupulous practitioner, the cure could be worse than the disease. On 8 May 1639 Binns first saw Joan Carter,

> who hath the lower mandible corrupt (& the teeth fallen forth) all the chin from the one cheek to the other, her cheeks & chin much swollen & hard, she was fluxed by Kixton the Quack 3 years ago, & she continued spitting at times ever since, & at that time where her cheeks were ulcerated for want of looking to they grew so hard cicatrised that she could not well open her jaws so he cut them & after that she had a contraction of some branches of sinews down her neck, that she could neither open well her mouth nor lift up her head much.[168]

By October he could report that 'she [was] very well praised be God, & no great blemish, only her chin a little shrunk in'.

Binns himself was very careful about mercury doses and patients' reactions to them. If the patient had too extreme a reaction, he either reduced the dose or withdrew the mercury for a time. By the same token, if doses did not seem to be working, he increased them.[169]

Binns apparently experimented with different mercury doses and preparations. His 'guinea pigs' were patients in St Bartholomew's Hospital. During one February he gave three men the same number of 'precipitate pills' on three successive days and compared their reactions. On the first day, five grains gave one man four stools and the others two stools apiece, with no vomits. Eight grains on the second day produced two, five and four stools respectively. On the third day, sixteen grains gave the patients two stools, four stools and two vomits, and six stools respectively. One man had begun to spit at this point.[170] The mercury preparation Binns used most frequently was called manna mineralis. However, he also experimented with a recipe which included mithridate and one called Sampson's Turbith.[171]

In addition to careful monitoring of mercury doses, Binns treated the symptoms which the mercury produced. Mr Thomas Mazeine had first consulted Binns in May 1635, at which time 'the diet' removed all his pains. In March 1637 he had nodes in both shins. Binns prescribed a mercury course which relieved the pain in his legs, but caused ulceration of his tongue and cheeks 'with white sloughs'. Binns treated this problem with 'lotion of barley, althea roots, licorice and violet leaves which cleansed the ulcers in the 7th or 8th day'.[172]

Characteristically Binns combined a mercury flux with

other prescriptions designed to improve the patient's general health. He almost always prescribed a diet drink, and recommended healthy eating habits. He blamed a repeat patient, Mr John Malett or Merett, for the fact that his ulcerated forehead was slow to heal, writing 'but sometimes it would be all cicatrised, & he keeping no good diet, but disordered, so it would ulcerate by places & some little pieces of bones cast out'. Several months later the patient 'took pills, & became temperate so, he grew fat & in very good health & all his forehead healed save a little moisture came out above his nose, very well in April 1655'.[173] Binns also prescribed sweating for syphilis patients, as did other practitioners.

The nature of the disease required the healers who treated syphilis to apply their skills to particular immediate problems as well as to the disease as a whole. Most distressing to both sufferer and practitioner were the ulcers on the foreskin which rapidly became gangrenous and caused patients to lose all or part of the penis.[174] In one case Binns applied 'a strong cataplasm to revocate the spirits and hinder putrification', and twice scarified the foreskin. When these measures did not work, Binns cut away the mortified flesh.[175]

Another manifestation of syphilis which was particularly difficult to treat was its invasion of bones which caused tumours and the eventual rotting away of the bone itself. In 1645 Mr Fotiley was cured 'of a pain in his left leg nocturnal a little tumour upon the bone' by a Mr Sase. 'In 1651 he had pain again. The bone foul which Quince [another surgeon] took off with a mallett and chisel & the diet. Took away his pains'. Binns first saw the patient in April 1659, when the bone was 'like a rotten post'. Binns applied dressings to the bone itself and gave mercury internally. In August Mr Fotiley went down stairs 'and coming up again he turned a little awry & broke the rotten part of the maior tibia in sunder so keeps his bed wholly'. By October he was feeling a bit better, but still had to return home to Berkshire in a horse litter.[176]

Other symptoms of syphilis which Binns treated separately were ulcerated throats, palates, noses and lips, bubos in the groin, obstructions in the urethra, nodes in the shins and the skull and various pains in the joints and the head. His treatment was remarkably successful. Of the 133 patients he treated for gonorrhoea or syphilis, 60 recovered and 15 got better. He left only ten uncured. Two patients died. In forty-six cases the outcome is unknown.

These figures indicate that Binns knew what he was doing, but they do not tell the whole story. Some patients, disheartened by long and inconclusive courses of treatment decided to consult other practitioners.[177] Some who had apparently been cured became ill again years later. Binns's casebook contains references to quite a few repeat patients who consulted him along with other practitioners in their interminable efforts to rid themselves of the pox. The most faithful of these sufferers was one Mr Brooks who underwent some seven courses of treatment in four years.[178] Thus the number of 'cures' indicated above is probably an overestimate of the patients who were permanently healed, and the small number of deaths recorded is probably an underestimate.

Binns and his patients were clearly convinced that syphilis was sexually transmitted. Mr Baker, a bookseller's man, developed pustules upon the glans 'by dealing with a pocky woman'.[179] Mr Henry Richards 'the 20 July in the night suffered much pain bet. glans & praeputaion having lain with a wench some 5 or 6 days afore'.[180] Indeed, Binns was puzzled about the possible origins of Mr Millbank's 'Fistula in Scroto', writing

> these two years past we can understand no venereal cause, but, nocturnal pollutions & sometimes a forcing of his seed to flow & so caused some disorder & caused the flux at first & so from an ill habit in the parts & so communicated to the whole habit.[181]

This suggestion that masturbation could cause syphilis is surely novel.

Because of its associations with unclean sexuality, syphilis affected people's attitudes and behaviour concerning marriage. Mr Baker was aghast when his syphilis re-emerged shortly after his marriage in the summer of 1655. He had thought he had been cured five years earlier.[182] Mr Egas apparently felt he had been unfairly treated by the pox when the disease returned after four years' dormancy. He protested 'that he had not dealt with any but his wife who was then very well & had been for long time'.[183]

None the less, people with syphilis married and had children. William Bemis and his wife were not the only husband and wife that Binns treated as a couple for syphilis.[184] And Mrs Rud, who was 'troubled with the whites . . . , ulcer in pudenda & tumours in labias pudenda' and had 'much smart in making her water' was treated with pill Barbarosa, the green injection and other local applications until she had stopped breast-feeding her baby girl. Thereafter her symptoms were cured with mercury prescriptions. She had no trouble until she developed nodes in her shins three years later, having recently married again.[185] One wonders what her first husband died of.

As the above discussion has amply indicated, syphilis was a loathsome disease. It disfigured its victims and lasted a dreadfully long time. A severe case of the pox could impoverish the sufferer. In one year of treatment, Mr John Merett or Malett ran up a £35 bill at the apothecary's. And, due to its associations with sexual vice, it was also an unrespectable disease. While a person suffering from smallpox or scrofula (also disfiguring ailments) was an object of pity, a pox-ridden sufferer was more likely to be ridiculed – and avoided.[186]

Therefore it is not surprising that many of the people Binns treated for syphilis complained of more innocent-sounding individual symptoms, such as chronic headache or sore throat. 'My cousin Spooner's sister' consulted Binns for 'extreme pain in her head . . . it being all her head over & as much by day as night but somewhat worse in the night'.[187] Several days later she developed nodes on her forehead and pains in her shoulders. Binns prescribed a mercury flux. Considering such attempts at concealment, it is possible that more of Binns's patients were syphilitic than the numbers quoted above indicate.

Certainly the women who consulted Binns for amenorrhoea, too small an amount of menstruation and the whites may have had the pox. Mrs Elin Barker, who complained of amenorrhoea, 'sloughs & stench', falls within this category.[188] The unfortunate 5-year-old girl who had the whites in very great quantity was another possible victim. Binns wrote 'it was feared [that] one that had the gonorrhoea spent his sperm betwixt the child's legs upon her pudenda, but this was not certainly proved'.[189]

There was, of course, another possible explanation for amenorrhoea. On 20 July Binns treated 'Mary at Mr. Barham's' who 'wants her menses' with laxatives and emetics. He also let blood from the saphena vein in the foot – a treatment for this complaint which was used in classical times. Nine days later her menses 'came down very well'.[190] This sounds very like induced abortion.

Binns also treated other 'female problems', such as inordinate menses, fits of the mother and swelling in the hand and arm which occurred after childbirth. For all of these conditions he prescribed laxatives and/or emetics which usually produced the desired result.[191] One interesting case of 'fits like fits of the mother' may shed some light on this now-archaic disease. Binns treated 'My sister Gray's sister' for such fits with the usual emetics until, nearly a month after beginning treatment, she voided a worm. He then prescribed one dose of the mercury preparation manna mineralis, after which the patient was well.[192]

Binns's treatment of syphilis and other genito-urinary disorders was mechanical and conventional. His choice of this area as a speciality, if choice it was, was also conventional. Surgeons had been undertaking the cure of venereal diseases since the early sixteenth century at least. Binns left related areas of surgery alone. He did not cut for the stone. Neither did he act as a man-midwife. He apparently found his own area of expertise sufficiently demanding and rewarding. Indeed, his regular syphilis patients alone must have provided him with a good living. For services and medications for the year 1658, Mr Edward Carothorne paid him £29 9s.[193] St Bartholomew's Hospital paid him only £30 a year for acting as a staff surgeon. Binns's therapeutic methods did not change over the entire thirty years covered by the casebook. Venereal disease provided him with an arena where his own special talents – patience, caution, conscientiousness and persistence – paid off.

IV CONCLUSIONS

There is much Joseph Binns's casebook does not tell us, both about his own practice and about the ordinary practice of surgery in seventeenth-century England. Only tantalising hints are given about Binns's 'man' – the servant, apprentice or assistant who is occasionally mentioned in a casenote. Since surgical training was invariably by apprenticeship, and since Binns was an active member of London's surgical community, it is more than likely that he kept a series of apprentices in the course of his career. It is equally likely that, as a well-to-do man, he employed one or more servants. However, the casebook deals almost exclusively with Binns's own contacts with patients; the identity, function and status of his 'man' must remain a mystery.

In addition, the casebook provides little information about the prices Binns charged for his services. Money due or received is mentioned only under unusual circumstances. Thus we know nothing about the surgeon's ordinary rates, or whether he charged on a sliding scale, according to the patient's ability to pay.

It is more than likely that Binns did not record details of every case he dealt with during his thirty-year career. Even considering this factor, the number of patients Binns treated was small, compared to the thousands who consulted the astrological physician, Richard Napier, during forty years of practice.[194] How accurate a picture of seventeenth–century surgical practice does Binns's casebook provide, considering the size of the sample?

It seems probable that Binns was far more typical of surgeons than Napier was of physicians. Because Napier provided a very specialised service, sufferers travelled for many miles to consult him in his own home. His national reputation inflated his clientele. Furthermore, Napier dealt with his patients' problems in the course of fairly brief conversations; thus he was able to treat as many as fifteen patients a day.[195]

Binns, on the other hand, visited his patients in hospital or in their own chambers. His duties often involved time-consuming procedures, and usually required repeated visits – sometimes more than one a day. Thus, the demands on his time prevented him from treating large numbers of patients at any one time. Furthermore, although he was respectable, Binns did not command a national reputation. His reputation was closely tied to that of the Company of Barbersurgeons and London surgeons generally.

Although Binns's casebook was intended simply as a record of treatment given and reactions achieved, a great deal can be inferred from it about what being a seventeenth–century surgical patient was like. It was anything but pleasant. In reading Binns's matter-of-fact observations, it is easy to lose sight of the fact that all of his operations were performed without anaesthetic, that the ulcers produced by his mercury cures were painful, and that the desired reactions to purges and emetics were unpleasant. People did not expect to feel good while undergoing medical and surgical treatment.

Why did they seek out such torture? Part of the answer lies in popular ideas about illness. The more suffering illness caused, the stronger were the measures needed to combat it. Thus, the sufferer in the midst of a mercury cure could take comfort in the very discomfort he or she felt. At least something was being done. Surgeons were so frequently consulted because the service they provided was highly specialised. While lay-people often made and prescribed medicines and advised therapeutic regimens, they less frequently used surgical instruments.

In addition, if Binns's casebook is an accurate indicator, surgeons frequently succeeded in relieving their patients. In those cases for which information is available, 265 patients emerged well from Binns's treatment and 62 got better. Twenty-two patients failed to improve and fifty-three died. This was an impressive achievement. Most of his patients did not consult Binns until they had spent some time treating themselves or receiving treatment from friends and/or relatives. Thus, by the time he undertook their cases, their conditions had already become acute.

It must be reiterated that Joseph Binns was in no way unique. He did not obtain unusual wealth or fame in the course of his career. Neither was he ever censured by his own Company or the Royal College of Physicians for irregular practice. He published nothing. His casenotes indicate that he was cautious and very conventional. His career very probably paralleled the careers of many of his colleagues. Thus, his casebook testifies to the great service provided by seventeenth-century surgeons. Modern medical historians have underrated them because of what they could not do, ignoring the value of what they did.

4

THE PHYSICIAN'S TALE

Seventeenth-century medicine has received more attention from historians than has seventeenth-century surgery. Biographies of great physicians form the backbone of traditional medical history. Studies focusing on the day-to-day practices of physicians are rare, but they do exist. Michael MacDonald's recent *Mystical Bedlam: Madness, Anxiety and Healing in Seventeenth-Century England* is based on the voluminous casebook of the astrological physician Richard Napier.[1] MacDonald's work provides an excellent example of the kinds of information such sources can yield. Napier's life, thought, techniques and clientele are investigated in great detail and related to the more general question of mental illness in the period.

However, useful as it is, MacDonald's study tells us little about the practice and experience of physic in seventeenth-century England. His focus upon madness leaves the vast territory of 'physical' illness, even within Napier's practice, unexplored. And Napier was himself obviously untypical. MacDonald calls him 'one of the last Renaissance magi' who attracted patients, one suspects, partly because the service he provided was relatively hard to find elsewhere.[2] Napier, as an astrological physician, was a specialist. Although astrology was used as a diagnostic and therapeutic tool by many seventeenth-century healers, it was secondary to other methods.

At present, no studies comparable to MacDonald's exist of 'conventional' seventeenth-century physicians. Having examined Joseph Binns's surgical practice, therefore, we will take a briefer look at some physicians' casebooks in order to provide a basis for comparison of the experience of physicians and their patients with those of Binns and his clientele. As indicated above, a number of physicians' casebooks are available.[3] For example, the great mid-century physician, Sir Theodore Turquet de Mayerne, who served the Court and

Doctor in Medicina Togâ ordinàriâ Indutus, cui per omnia conformis est ea quâ uluntur Doctores in Iure Ciuili

The seventeenth-century physician's gown was the same as that worn by the practitioner of Civil Law. (Wellcome Library)

numerous upper-status families, left extensive records, beautifully written and bound.[4] However, analysis of Mayerne's casebooks, interesting as it might be, would leave many questions unanswered and might, indeed, prejudice our viewpoint by supporting old stereotypes. For instance, it is generally assumed that physicians' services were more expensive than those of other healers and that physicians were therefore patronised only by the well-to-do. Neither Mayerne's casebook nor that of the late-seventeenth-century London physician, Sir Edmund King, could yield fair evidence regarding this issue.

The casebooks of less-well-known physicians, then, provide more suitable source material for this study. As indicated above, extensive 'physical' casebooks, such as Napier's, do exist. However, for purposes of comparison, three shorter casebooks kept during different periods have been selected for study. We will examine the casebook of Dr Barker of Shrewsbury for the years 1595 to 1605, that of a physician probably practising in Cambridge between 1619 and 1622, and the notes and correspondence of John Symcotts for the years between 1633 and 1660. Through comparison of these records kept by provincial healers, both among themselves and with those kept by the urban healer Binns, some conclusions may be drawn about occupational healing in seventeenth-century England.

I JOHN SYMCOTTS

The records kept by the physician John Symcotts are particularly appropriate for our purposes.[5] Symcotts was an almost exact contemporary of Joseph Binns. Born c. 1592 and dying in 1662, his practice spanned the same period as Binns's. Because Symcotts was a rural practitioner, his casebook will allow us to compare rural with urban circumstances. It will also allow us to identify similarities and differences in the practice of medicine and surgery in the same period.

Inevitably Symcotts's casebook differs from that of Binns. It is by no means as rich a source, giving information about only 83 patients in contrast to the 671 whom Binns mentioned. Further, unlike Binns, Symcotts noted only sporadically the outcome of the treatment he prescribed. However, the Symcotts papers include a collection of correspondence which reveals much about his relationships with his patients – an element notably lacking in our knowledge about Binns. In addition, due to the efforts of F. N. L. Poynter and W. J.

Bishop, who edited the Symcotts papers, we know far more about Symcotts's biography than will ever be known about Binns's.

John Symcotts was one of seven children born to John and Elizabeth Symcotts, who settled in Sutton, Bedfordshire. Not much is known about the Symcotts' economic and social status. However, the physician's brothers George and Thomas became London merchants, his twin, Robert, a minister, and John himself undertook a long course of study at Cambridge at about the age of 16, information which suggests that the family was reasonably well-to-do. John Symcotts was admitted as a pensioner at Queens' College, Cambridge, in 1608, matriculated in 1610, received his BA in 1615 and his MD in 1636, after he had already been practising medicine for many years.[6]

After leaving university, Symcotts settled in Huntingdon where he lived until his death in 1662. His medical practice extended over Huntingdonshire, Bedfordshire and Cambridgeshire. He worked closely with Gervase Fullwood the elder, who was most likely his assistant. Fullwood himself kept a 'man', Edward Johnson, who collected fees and carried on some correspondence for the practice.

During the Civil War Symcotts's sympathies lay with the parliamentarians. Indeed, Oliver Cromwell was the most famous of his patients.[7] Although he apparently never joined the army, Commonwealth and Protectorate governments frequently called upon Symcotts to serve on commissions for the regulation of financial, military and other civic affairs in Huntingdonshire.[8]

Poynter and Bishop write of Symcotts's appearance and medical history:

> His brother Thomas refers to his lean and spare body. In early life the doctor suffered from headaches, which he eventually cured with a diet drink. On his own statement he had three attacks of smallpox, and he was, during the last ten years of his life, a martyr to gout.[9]

He never married. Since his brothers predeceased him, the bulk of his property was bequeathed to his nephew, Dr William Symcotts, only son of his brother Robert.

Notwithstanding Poynter and Bishop's judgment that 'His fortune was not large, considering his "painful indeavours" during forty or more years of practice', John Symcotts became prosperous, if not wealthy, as a result of his exertions.[10] His will indicates that he left nearly £200 in cash to friends and relations. He also left property in Huntingdonshire, Cambridgeshire and London, which included arable land, meadow, an inn, six houses, a dovecot yard and an adjoining hog-yard.[11] Symcotts, like Binns, did well in the medical marketplace, although he certainly never charged fees on the scale of those commanded by well-known London physicians.[12]

His casenotes, few as they are, indicate that Symcotts was truly a general practitioner. Although he treated more cases of consumption than any other disorder, sixteen cases out of a total of eighty-two do not demonstrate a speciality. Indeed, one suspects that Symcotts kept his casebook, not as a record of all the cases he dealt with, but as a way of noting the sorts of treatment he applied to various kinds of ailments, perhaps for future reference.

Symcotts's records demonstrate that the conventional division between surgery and medicine applied as little to provincial medical practice as it did to London surgical practice. He treated many ailments which might more appropriately have been dealt with by a surgeon, including apostems, sore eyes, haemorrhoids, itching, skin rashes, tumours, urinary retention and disorders resulting from issues.[13] He also treated menstrual problems and disorders related to childbirth which might equally well have been treated by a surgeon or midwife.[14]

However, his approach to such ailments was sometimes different from that of a surgeon. For instance, in November 1641 he was summoned by the midwife Mistress Willis to the bedside of Mistress Lewis of London who was in labour. The child had died, and the midwife sought medication which would hasten its delivery. Symcotts prescribed and then went home. After twenty-four hours, when the patient was nearly at the end of her strength, Symcotts prescribed again and the woman was delivered, 'Deo soli laus sit'.[15] A surgeon would very likely have tried to deliver the child by the use of instruments, which almost certainly would have mutilated it.[16] Perhaps the midwife consulted Symcotts for this very reason.

Sometimes Symcotts approved typically surgical treatment, although he did not perform most surgical procedures himself. For instance,

> 1652. Mr. Cater of Kempson, having an issue in his left arm, and purged too little, had a hard glandulous tumour in his left armhole very painful, attended with a feverish distemper. Then was

applied poultices ex apio and other emplasters as friends advised. It grew worse and worse, would not be dissolved, but tended to maturation, to which at length it came. I forced out at a little orifice much purulency, and it was laid open by a London surgeon and healed by him.[17]

He was also interested in surgical problems which he may not have treated himself. For instance, he reported successful treatment of two cases of gaping navels. In the first,

Mr. Corbet's child of Huntingdon (a girl), by the unskilful cutting of her navel string, her navel gaped and would not come together, seemed an omphacele, and so continued for three years at least. The mother found a receipt in an old English physic book which she adventured with success.[18]

Symcotts then repeated the 'receipt'. In the second case,

1651. Mery Herby his son of Thurleigh had a gaping navel for a year and more. Mistress Child (the musician's wife) applied to it parsley (and (she) (Mistress Herby) thinks some knotgrass and plantain withal) stamped and made into a plaster with butter and so applied it. The child voided great store of urine and thereupon the navel closed perfectly.[19]

None the less, the majority of Symcotts's patients suffered from problems which were, by definition, medical. The list of their ailments includes gout, cachexy (defined by the *Oxford English Dictionary* as 'a depraved condition of the body in which nutrition is everywhere defective'), asthma, worms, ague, fits (including fits of the Mother), jaundice, palsy, apoplexy, mania, constipation, looseness (or diarrhoea) and a variety of aches and pains. Symcotts also saw a single case of bubonic plague.[20] One wonders if he would have attended this patient had he and the other healers consulted known beforehand what they were dealing with.

Often, neither the patient nor Symcotts appear to have put a single name to the disorder from which the patient suffered. Rather, Symcotts listed symptoms in his casenotes as his patients described them. The following report is typical.

Mistress Christian Tenum of Cambridge, fifty years of age, could sleep so little that for fifteen years she had scarcely two and only rarely three hours sleep each night. For twenty years she had a pulsing of the arteries and when she first lay down to rest many images of things passed before her eyes. Ringing in the ears. She felt as if a heavy burden or weight was continually pressing down upon the top of her head. She had a feeling of intense heat at the back of the head. She was usually delirius once a day. Pain in the left abdomen. In colic a concentration of wind. Weakness of the back. During her menses (which had stopped five years earlier) her face had swollen, and it was followed by several stools. Three years ago she was stricken with paralysis and from this she still has a numbness of the head.

This patient consulted several other healers before seeing Symcotts. He prescribed a regimen of diet drinks, a vomit, purges and diuretics. About a year after he began treating her, Mistress Tenum 'made much bloody water and voided many stones which she dreamt not of before, and so was cured'.[21] In this case, although Symcotts prescribed diuretics, he obviously did so as a matter of routine. It is notable that both Symcotts and his patient appear to have been surprised when she passed stones with her urine.

In other cases both Symcotts and his patient determined that a collection of symptoms belonged to a single condition. For example, under the heading 'De Asthmate 1637' he wrote:

> Goodwife Usher of Dunton was extreme short winded, oft times wheezed, was much fallen away and in a consumptive state of body, insomuch that her mother and others feared she could not hold out one month at most, being in likelihood to be choked of a sudden for want of breath.[22]

Of course, like all healers, Symcotts found that he was occasionally wrong about a diagnosis. In one case a young girl exhibited the following symptoms:

> There seemed a great compression of a sudden of the midriff and spirital parts which made her cry lamentably and struggle with hands and feet for breath and pain. At last, fetching a large breath, she came to herself again; then she fell into another, and so into a third and fourth or more; then, upon a little rest, she would be as well as ever, eat heartily and walk strongly.

Although he noted that 'It of all diseases most resembled the Mother' (that is fits or suffocation of the Mother or womb), he 'conceived it to be from worms'. He treated the girl with remedies specific for worms, but she grew no better. Then, 'upon application of black soap (taught by Sir Rowland St. John's lady as the best remedy for fits of the mother) to the soles of her feet, the fits went off'.[23]

Like Binns, Symcotts's therapeutic techniques were based upon humoral theory. To restore the body's humoral balance, he purged, sweat and vomited his patients. He also frequently ordered bleeding, clysters and issues – procedures often requiring consultation with a surgeon. Sometimes the courses of treatment he ordered were quite radical, as we shall see. However, they were never irresponsible. Symcotts believed firmly in the 'means' he used. In one case of sore eyes he wrote, 'Nothing prevailed till an issue was made in both arms, by which means she stands perfectly cured'.[24] In another case a patient died because he unwisely had an issue healed.

> Sir Thomas Nevill of Holt, having had an issue in his leg which ran much, he would need have it healed by a surgeon about Michaelmass 1635. About Christmas following he found his stomach ill and all parts out of order. He had a vomit and purgatives but nothing availed. After, he fell into asthmatical fits, and was hectical, grew weaker, his urine utterly confused, and so continued for 11 or 12 days. . . . At last after a great draught of ale (upon which he was at first refreshed) he fell into a great quivering and within seven hours after died. The only cure had been the opening his issue in time.[25]

Symcotts routinely ordered his patients to be bled. However, he did not resort to this treatment 'in almost every case of disease or injury', despite Poynter and Bishop's observation.[26] Like Binns, he used blood-letting sparingly, ordering it in only twenty-two out of eighty-three cases. Sometimes he apparently considered phlebotomy a last resort. In the case of Larance Gunnill, who suffered from a painful skin eruption, he prescribed several inward and outward preparations from which the patient 'presently' found ease. Symcotts noted, 'If not I had opened a vein'.[27]

Regardless of his caution, however, Symcotts let blood plentifully when he felt it was necessary. When Mr Egerton, youngest son of Lord Bridgwater, lay unconscious 'in an apoplexy' in 1648, Symcotts first 'cupped his shoulders and head without scarification'. Later the patient was 'cupped again and scarified on the shoulders and crown, where, by deep scarification, a vein bled as it had been from the arm'. At the same time, 'leeches were set to the fundament'. All in vain, for the patient died shortly afterwards. Even in this case, the physician was cautious. He commented, 'I omitted opening of a vein in his arm, lest it might have been blamed as the cause of his death, and so also the bleeding of the jugulars, for want of skill in the surgeon'.[28]

Symcotts's papers, like Binns's casebook, make clear that the conventional treatments of the time were powerful. Even good treatments must be properly applied. Symcotts warned against 'too much confidence in issues alone without due purgatives'.[29] He noted that

> Colonel Herby of Thurleigh, trusting to his issue in his arm (made at London) neglected the taking such usual course of physic (as his rheumatic and nephritic case required) this last fall of the leaf, and thereby a tumour arose under his armhole, induced much pain, but brake within 9 or 10 days after poulticing.[30]

In another case, Symcotts had prescribed a seton as part of his treatment for severe pain in the lower back.

> At last, wearied with her complaints, I caused a large seton to be made in the ham of the same leg, with a skein of silk (drawn through by the eye of the great long needle that was red hot at the little end), wetted in oil of elder to fetch out the fire. This in a fortnight's space gave her admirable ease; her sleep and appetite returned. By unskilfulness she lost the seton, and thereof made a fontanella by putting in a piece which was not of that efficacy that the former was, and so about a quarter of a year after died.[31]

Even properly applied treatments sometimes proved too powerful. Two of Symcotts's patients died after taking the vomits he had prescribed.[32] In such cases, where the patient was very weak, the physician took a calculated risk in prescribing the remedies he felt were necessary.

Symcotts preferred herbal remedies above all others. In only one recorded case did he use mercury.[33] He used herbal preparations internally, usually as purgatives, diuretics and emetics. He also applied them outwardly on poultices, plasters and in baths.

He obtained recipes from many sources. Thanks to Poynter and Bishop's careful reading of the Symcotts papers housed in the Wellcome Library (not included in their edition of Symcotts's records), some information is available about the physician's reading. As one might expect, he made no reference to popular medical and surgical works, but he did consult

> recognised medical authorities of the time. Among them are Riviere, Joel, Croll, Guillemeau, Garencieres, and Forest. The first three were prominent spagyric or chemical physicians, followers of Paracelsus (1493–1541).

Thus, Symcotts's reading was in advance of his practices.[34]

Symcotts also obtained medical recipes and advice from English physicians, although these were imparted, not from published writings, but by correspondence and word of mouth. Several letters from other physicians to Symcotts are printed in Poynter and Bishop's edition. In one, apparently written by a William Vylan, Symcotts received information about bubonic plague. Symcotts had asked four questions: first, whether a patient with plague should be purged regardless of his or her general physical condition; second, 'whether a pestilent botch [bubo] can wholly go back without any mark or hardness left in for guide'; third, 'that a man dying of the plague having no botch or rising appear, is he not apt to have spots appear, being rubbed, laid by the fire, etc.'; and fourth, 'that if a man die of the plague and lie two days and two nights, whether that body will retain the natural stiffness as others of common diseases'.[35] This letter is particularly interesting, for it reveals Symcotts's belief or suspicion that plague was a disease different from all others – a feeling he shared with his contemporaries, both healers and lay-people.

Again like his contemporaries, Symcotts collected medical recipes from non-medical sources. While most of his informants were relatives and friends, he was receptive to almost any account of a cure. For instance, he noted the following treatment:

> My Lady Cotton, being about 13 or 14 years old, had so great a bleeding at nose that nothing would stay it. She being brought into a desperate condition, Sir John and her mother having gone from her that they might not see her die, the cook-maid boldly took a cloth wet in cold water (vinegar it may be had been better) and made her sit upon it, and so her bleeding was stayed.[36]

A similar report concerned

> Goodwife Viccar of Sutton, being stricken with a palsy all one side, after the taking of a purge or two and some other small remedies, a woman gave her counsel to lie close covered with two large sheep-skins new taken off for 24 hours together. She endured 17 hours of her task, sweating exceedingly all that time, and so was recovered.[37]

Symcotts cited such examples, not as curiosities, but in a respectful uncritical manner.

He frequently noted recipes given to him by gentlewomen.

Thus, he recorded directions for the making of a 'spleen plaster' given him by Lady Pickering and 'Mrs. Rolt of Pertenhall's Medicine for the Ague'.[38] Indeed, he apparently respected such amateur female healers as colleagues, noting in one case that an ointment had 'been proved singular good by the Lady Frances Somerset for fourteen several infirmities'.[39] Sometimes he shared his patients with such ladies. For instance, when Goodwife Finsam of Eyworth three weeks after childbirth developed 'great swellings in her hands, feet and other parts about her', complicated by a feeling of numbness in those parts, 'Mistress Anderson gave her first diascordium, then bezoar'. Only when a swelling in one of her breasts 'brought her to extremity of pain night and day' was Symcotts called. He was not in the least critical of Mrs Anderson's treatment. Indeed, the first poultice he himself recommended did no good. However, the second poultice he prescribed caused the apostemation to break, 'and all her pains ceased'.[40] The physician apparently felt quite comfortable with this informal system of referral, as is demonstrated in the case cited above where a midwife summoned him when she was unable to hasten the delivery of a dead baby.

In some cases medically knowledgeable gentlewomen were also Symcotts's patients. His correspondence with Mrs Anna Carr provides a good example of the mutual respect such a relationship could generate. Mrs Carr wrote to the physician, thanking him for his 'choice receipts which I highly esteem of'. She went on to send Symcotts her recipe for a poultice for a bruise, writing about it,

> If it were for my life I would not use anything else, for with this only I have cured those that carts have gone over, whose water was been gore blood; one that a loaded cart pressed in that sort that blood issued out at all passable places; an old man that was by a bull tossed up, and by the fall lighting on his head and back, and both made and spat blood.

She also sent Symcotts a calcined toad which he had requested, asking him 'what powder of toads calcined is good for. I only use it to staunch blood, but then I do not calcine them'. In addition, she sent word to Mr Fullwood that she had received three dozen vial glasses and two dozen pots which she had requested. Symcotts apparently wrote to her, saying that calcined toad stopped bleeding 'by holding it in the party's hand, so smelling to it; or else hanging it against the pit of the stomach'.[41] More will be said below about Symcotts's relationships with both patients and other healers.

As the above examples make clear, Symcotts used some medicinal substances which fell outside the categories of herbal or chemical remedies. One can only guess at the mechanism by which calcined toad stopped bleeding. The same can be said about the bullet he directed to be swallowed as part of his treatment for fits of vomiting.[42] More familiar, but equally mysterious, was his application of 'pigeons sprinkled with salt' to the feet of a man who was dying of apoplexy.[43] Obviously, although Symcotts had no respect for unlearned healers, he approved of some techniques borrowed from traditional medicine. Indeed, this physician demonstrates why rigid demarcations between academic, popular and magical healing techniques are anachronistic in a discussion of seventeenth-century English medicine.

Symcotts also used diagnostic techniques which were becoming old fashioned even in his own day. The Royal College of Physicians disapproved of uroscopy and many of its members frowned upon astrological medicine.[44] Symcotts used both, although he was sceptical about astrology. For instance, he wrote to his patient Mr Powers, who dabbled in that science,

> I am sorry for your bearing an unnecessary pain by forbearing the use of the plaster, which might have been safely laid on today, notwithstanding your skill in the passage of the sign, which (for anything I know) is nowhere else to be found, but only in the Almanack. The ancient co[nceit] of it is but a fancy, and the ominous events thereof either lies or false positions.[45]

Although he sounds sceptical, warranting Poynter and Bishop's observation that the physician 'scorns such beliefs', he either belied his scepticism or humoured the patient when, in later correspondence, he wrote that 'this season is not propitious to eradicate physic'.[46] Symcotts also examined urine. A patient, John Williams, sent the physician a urine sample, together with a description of his symptoms. Symcotts himself wrote that he was concerned about a patient who subsequently died because the patient's 'water was thick and yellow which intimated the great oppression of the stomach and heat of the liver which had made so much choler'.[47]

None the less, neither of these techniques are mentioned frequently in Symcotts's notes. More important were the patient's appearance and description of his or her sensations.

Also significant was Symcotts's own knowledge of the patient's medical history. For instance, he prescribed for a lady who was not his patient, excusing his breach of occupational ethics in the following way:

> without any derogation from that knowing man, your present physician . . . , but for my long experience I have had of your constitution from your childhood.[48]

Symcotts's methods were rewarded. Of the cases for which the outcome is known, thirty-five patients recovered, seven improved and only thirteen died.

Symcotts's relations with other physicians were, on balance, harmonious. Certainly he was much respected by his assistant or partner, Gervase Fullwood the elder. As Poynter and Bishop say, nothing is known about Fullwood's qualifications. 'That he was named with Symcotts on commissions between 1647 and 1660 indicates that he was of good family and position.'[49] Fullwood deferred to Symcotts's judgment in the correspondence the two healers carried on with Mr Powers, which will be discussed below. His letters to that difficult patient frequently state that the prescriptions sent were directed by 'the doctor'.[50] The impression given by this correspondence is that Symcotts was the senior member in the practice.

Symcotts was sometimes critical of other physicians. Edward Adye, who received a Cambridge MA in 1628 and was an extralicentiate of the Royal College of Physicians, was Symcotts's contemporary and competitor. The two physicians shared at least two patients.[51] Symcotts disapproved of Adye's therapeutic and diagnostic techniques. Concerning Adye's views on smallpox, he wrote 'Therefore in these cases [of the disease in strong adults] in which Mr. Adye by urine gives a warrant of security, he may be deceived'.[52] Symcotts was more outspoken in a letter to Mr Powers dated 19 February 1641.

> For Adye's conceit of bleeding at the beginning, you have it commonly in any case, sex or age whatever [unless] these do contraindicate. That noddy little thinks what an adventure it is to take blood from an old withered man, whose fountains of blood-making may be justly suspected of weakness and some unsoundness.[53]

More frequently Symcotts mentioned the successes of other

healers and adopted their methods. Thus, when Mr Taylor of Clapham was cured of haemorrhoids by a surgeon who advised him to take tobacco, Symcotts 'upon this example' prescribed the same treatment for Mr Boner of Hail Weston.[54] He also approved a course of treatment prescribed by Mayerne.[55]

As indicated above, Symcotts consulted with his colleagues by mail. This correspondence reveals that he gave advice in addition to soliciting it. In a letter addressed to a Mr Templer from Lawrence Wright (1590–1657), physician in ordinary to Oliver Cromwell during the 1650s, it is clear that Wright's interpretation of a particular case is partially based upon information given him by Symcotts and Dr George Bowles, another provincial physician.[56]

Symcotts was a self-consciously respectable physician who recognised the importance of having a good reputation. In one case he actively defended his own by mail. He wrote to a Dr Francis of London in order to give his version of the death of one of his patients, Mr Elms.[57] It is, perhaps, significant that this case was also known to Mr Powers.[58] Mr Elms died after having taken a vomit prescribed by Symcotts. The physician's defence of his methods says much about his feelings about his medical colleagues, his concern about his reputation in the lay community and his contempt for unlearned healers. Thus, his letter to Francis will be quoted at some length.

D. Francis. Your verdict of Mr. Elms his death, I believe much wrested from your own meaning, is still kept up by two empirics (they who lived on each hand of Lilford) to render me odious to that side of the country and raise their own credits by blasting mine. For them, as the testimony of my conscience bears me above their malice, so do I contemn to give accounts unto them (for their sakes) or make an apology for myself. My desire is to satisfy you or be satisfied by you.

They report you to say Mr. Elms had not a pleurisy, that the cupping glasses were improper for drawing humours to the place affected, that bleeding did more hurt than good.

In my description of the cause, symptoms, and remedies applied, which was sent up to London, I set down . . . with all fidelity what was applied and in what order. The second day after he was clearly sick, I gave a vomit which, though it wrought fully, yet the night following he slept soundly and awakened comfortably, and sent me word he was very well, but thirsty and desired beer, whereof (drinking plentifully) taking a great draught and cold, contrary to my directions, within two hours after he felt a sharp pain at his left breast which, increasing quickly to an insufferable height, I first laboured to mitigate with useful fomentation.

Symcotts then applied cupping glasses to the patient's chest – a treatment he continued to feel was warranted. Later, to ease the pain, he applied hot bread with mithridate. Notwithstanding these measures, the patient died.

Symcotts felt that Mr Elms was partly to blame for his own death. Unbeknownst to the physician, Elms had been 'tampering' with mercury sublimate six weeks before his final illness, which had caused inflammation of his mouth. When he became ill, he spent an entire day 'setting his house in order, disquieting himself all the day long . . . and infinitely weakening his spirits thereby'. Another contributing factor was Elms's general condition. Symcotts wrote that

> a strong disease fell upon weak principles. He had a dry cough for
> three months before; his flesh was wasted almost to skin and
> bones . . . his eyes sunk, his face more than ordinary swarthy,
> and the vivid colour of his lips decayed.

Finally Symcotts maintained that another practitioner had interrupted his own course of treatment, to Elms's disadvantage:

> I might justly allege Mr. Resburrow with his apothecaries
> constant interrupting for near three days together (in my absence)
> the course I had prescribed, though upon those remedies they saw
> his pains abated.

Such an interruption was clearly in violation of Symcotts's understanding of proper medical ethics.

Although the physician's feelings about his licensed colleagues varied depending upon the circumstances, his disapproval of unlearned healers never altered. He wrote of one such practitioner who had been treating Powers, 'For your doctor his advice, I like it not; such roweling, drawing and slabbering smells too much of his barber's shop from whence he went out Dr.'.[59] In a later letter he wrote

> I hear your Dr. there is much offended with me for inveighing
> against him. I pray stop the rumour. I assure you I have been ever
> silent in the censure of wandering practitioners, and so of him,
> but for a few words I inserted into a letter to you. I suffer such to
> weary out themselves. I think him worthy of contempt, not of

opposition, which would make the world think there were something good in him that might disadvantage me. Let him therefore not think of me, as I do not of him, being neither sorry for his stay nor glad for his removal.[60]

Symcotts's contempt for his unlearned competitors echoes that expressed by the anti-quack writers.[61] He also singled out unlearned barbers, empirics and wandering practitioners as particularly harmful. However, his ire, like that of the anti-quack writers, rarely extended to amateurs who dabbled in medicine. For instance, one of the physician's patients, Mistress Cosens of Croxton, 'being seven months with child, had a severe haemorrhage for two days together'. Symcotts 'ordered that her legs should be rubbed and bound . . . that a cupping glass should be placed on the region of the liver and a plaster of vinegar and true bole on her forehead'. He also prescribed a 'julep . . . of plantain water, oil of vitriol and syrup of violets'. These measures helped, but did not totally check the patient's blood loss. Then, 'a beggar woman told the patient that she would recover if she took shepherd's purse in her broth'. Symcotts ordered a broth with this herb in it, and the patient was cured.[62] Indeed, the remedy worked so well that he prescribed it for a girl with excessive menstrual flow shortly afterwards.[63] Perhaps Symcotts, like the anti-quack writers, only felt threatened by other healers if they charged for their services.

The basis of any healer's success or failure is his or her clientele — how large it is, the prices it can afford, and its opinion of the healer's services. Because we become acquainted with relatively few of Symcotts's patients (surely only a fraction of those he actually treated) we know rather less about his clientele as a whole than we know about that of Binns. The physician treated forty-seven female and thirty-three male patients. The sex of three patients is unknown. There is no obvious explanation for the slight predominance of females in his practice as there is for the predominance of males in that of Binns. Like Binns, Symcotts treated people in every social class except royalty. Of the eighty-three patients whose cases were recorded, twenty-seven were upper status, forty-one of middling status and thirteen of lower status origins. Again, as in our analysis of Binns's clientele, these figures can be only approximate. Categories for each patient were determined either on the basis of information provided by Poynter and Bishop or according to Symcotts's own mode of address. As a general rule, a title such as 'Lord' or 'Sir' suggested upper status, 'Mistress' or 'Mister', middling status, and 'Goodwife', 'Goodman' or a name without any prefix, lower status.

Comparison with Binns's clientele reveals that, while the great majority of his patients were middling status or below, the majority of Symcotts's patients were middling status or above.[64] Such an observation provokes a number of questions. Is it possible that relatively few lower status people consulted Symcotts because his services were too expensive? This seems unlikely. For instance, Symcotts's patient Mr Powers paid only £1.2s.8d. for two months of treatment in 1641. Even considering the effects of inflation, the £29.9s. one of Binns's patients paid for a year's treatment in 1658 suggests that urban surgeons could command fees as high as, or higher than, those charged by provincial physicians.[65] While one could, with little probable profit, debate the relative spending power of poor people in rural and urban settings, perhaps another line of inquiry would be more appropriate.

In Chapter 2 the different statuses of physicians and surgeons were discussed. These differences were perceived by both healers and their patients. Despite the fact that the status of physicians was not as high as they could have wished, they were well educated and certainly at home with 'high culture'.[66] The skill physicians sold in the medical marketplace was authority based upon familiarity with the theories encapsulated in medical writings, both published and unpublished. Surgeons, on the other hand, were more akin to expert craftsmen. No one else could provide their service as well as they did, but they used their hands rather than their mouths.

Physicians' patients could receive not only a prescription, but also a humoral explanation of their ailments. Physicians gave these explanations with the same seriousness and conviction ministers of the time gave to sermons on sin. Perhaps this very seriousness and the verbal aspect of their occupation made physicians easy to mock.[67] In any case, one suspects that patients must have had to be of a certain social and educational level fully to avail themselves of the physician's services. For instance, Symcotts wrote to Mr Powers:

Your high coloured urine is an apparent sign of inflammation of blood and multitude of choleric humours, which (nature not rightly disburthened of by the common ways) are carried upwards, fixed in the bordering parts of the brain, cause that pain, noise and impostumous matter which you complain of.[68]

Mr Powers suffered from headache and sore eyes.

Those who most appreciated the physician's academic attainments were people of backgrounds similar to, and more elevated than, the physician's own. While the anti-quack writers accused unlearned healers of talking pretentious gobbledegook in order to impress ignorant patients, better educated people would have known the difference. In consulting physicians, they hoped for a cure, but expected knowledge. Thus, Symcotts's patients reflected elevated social statuses disproportionate to their presence in the population at large.[69]

As indicated above, Symcotts's patients were drawn from a wide area. The map of patients' residences shown below, drawn from the casenotes, demonstrates that virtually all of Symcotts's clients lived within a twenty-mile radius of Huntingdon, with the exception of the patients who came from London. Although the physician and his assistants did travel to visit clients, much of the practice's business was

The geographical distribution of Symcotts's patients.

conducted by correspondence, regardless of how far from Huntingdon the patient lived.

The correspondence printed in Poynter and Bishop's edition of Symcotts's papers provides an excellent opportunity for us to explore the physician's relationships with his patients. The Powers correspondence is particularly useful, spanning as it does nearly ten years of treatment. There can be no doubt that Symcotts got on well with his patients. Their trust in him is reflected in the fact that although Mr Elms died during the summer of 1641, his wife consulted the physician when her young daughter was suffering from fits in September 1642. Obviously Mrs Elms did not believe that the vomit Symcotts had prescribed had killed her husband.[70]

None the less, the correspondence makes clear that Symcotts's patients were demanding and by no means uncritical of the treatment they were given. They also had sufficient confidence in their own medical judgment to suggest possible treatments to the physician. Thus, John Cotton wrote,

> Mr. Doctor,
>   It being now three weeks since my wife was delivered I think it now convenient for her to use some abstersive physic, for though she finds herself very well, yet I think after such a time it will not be amiss to use evacuation. Pray consider what you think may be most proper for her, and, if you think it convenient, we shall be very glad to see you here.[71]

Cotton's tone is similar to that taken by John Evelyn in his relations with physicians.[72] Both gentlemen consulted with physicians on more or less equal terms. Less arrogant, but perhaps even better informed is the letter quoted above from Anna Carr. Indeed, she made no mention at all of any illness for which Symcotts was treating her. Her letter reads less like that of a patient consulting an expert physician, and more like a note from one colleague to another.[73]

The physician's letters to his patients reveal both his respect for their knowledge about medicine and their own bodies and his concern that they accept his judgment. Thus, he explained the reasons for the therapy he advised in addition to sending prescriptions and directions for their application. To Mistress Halford he wrote a long epistle which, although it does not tell the modern reader what specific symptoms the patient suffered from, it does illuminate Symcotts's diagnostic methods and his determination that Mistress Halford understand the rationale behind her treatment. He proposed to heal her:

> first, by a gentle purgative way to abate such serous and waterish humours which must necessarily abound in the first region by your sedentary life and are the antecedent matter of those which (abounding in the (liver) veins and other inward parts and likewise in the whole habit of the body) have now by long custom found an irregular vent for themselves. . . .
>
> In the second place, I should prescribe bleeding (necessary indeed to the cure, if the opinion of impropriety of the season did not reclaim) in regard of the hotter temper of your liver, the fountain of redounding choler which, insinuating into the veins, sharpens the blood and humours thereof and causeth by turns that inflammatory humour of your eyelids, moradicty of urine, and those small eruptions on your nails and suchlike . . . symptoms, all which are dulled if not quite removed by this remedy. . . .
>
> After this, I shall proceed to things rather of a drying than astringent nature, as the disease requires. . . .
>
> Last of all, for the absolution of the cure, much and great exercise by degrees is requisite. . . .[74]

The casenotes indicate that Symcotts at one point treated this patient for 'fits of vomiting, great pains in her stomach and the whole abdomen, which sometimes together, sometimes successively, followed the pains of her back; which being all most incessant, soon wasted both her flesh and spirits'.[75] It is not clear whether the above letter concerned this illness.

As his letter to Mistress Halford indicates, Symcotts, in true humoral fashion, treated whole patients, not merely diseases. He took into account the sufferer's age, mental state, body type and general physical condition, in addition to the specific complaints the patient made. Nowhere are these concerns more obvious than in the Powers correspondence.

Mr Richard Powers kept a shop in Ramsey, which was about ten miles from Huntingdon. He is referred to as 'an old and withered body', who was about 60 years old in 1633, when the surviving correspondence began. He suffered from a multitude of disagreeable symptoms, chief among them gout. Symcotts and Fullwood were not the only healers he consulted. As indicated above, he was treated by Dr Adye and a wandering practitioner to whom Symcotts took exception. In addition, he talked to friends about his ailments. In an early letter the physician defended his own prescriptions against 'whatever your neighbours talk against physic'.[76] In another letter he wrote, 'Your friends that tell you this will not cure you full little know what your case had been by this time if you had not taken this course you have done'.[77] Regardless of Symcotts's impatience with the ignorant medical advice Powers received, however, he did not wholly dismiss it. In one letter he wrote, 'The counsel of your two friends I approve of, to be careful of that pain in your neck'.[78]

Repeatedly the physician reassured Powers that the course of treatment he advised was the best possible. In answer to Powers's worries that the therapy he received was too violent, considering his age and weakness, Symcotts wrote,

> Considering the symptoms laid down before my eyes I found some proper to the scurvy, others peculiar to the old gouty humour which whirls about and if you look not to it may fall upon some inward part as the stomach, guts, sides, etc., or unto your foot, as very lately upon my old father (before that as healthful a man as lived) and that so suddenly that in three days it corrupted so his foot to the bone that daily flesh deaded and putrified parts of bones were taken out. I spared not his age, 77, but advised bleeding and purging above 40 times in less than seven weeks space, or he had been in his grave.[79]

On a later occasion, Powers had been told by an acquaintance that his illness would kill him. Symcotts wrote,

> The Londoner spake like a pothecary, or himself, to determine such an event. I have seen it oft cured in as old as you, especially in two but last year; the one was old goodman Church of our town, the other Mr. Chessam of Brampton, who was all over like a dried leather skin, his legs as black as the stock and as sore and lame as a cripple. It was within the compass of my skill and God his blessing to help these.[80]

Despite the physician's long-suffering patience with Powers's complaints and doubts, he occasionally showed annoyance. When in 1633 Powers had been reading a popular medical work by Sir William Vaughan, *Natural and Artificial Directions for Health* (1600), he wrote to Symcotts, citing Vaughan in his criticism of the treatment he was receiving. Symcotts replied,

> The crick of your neck, the pain of your toe, the swelling of your knees and the trembling of your joints which you call the palsy are all from one and the same cause.

He went on to explain the humoral origins of these symptoms for which, 'I have . . . prescribed you a regular course which, if you follow, I make no question but your author Vaughan his prognostic vain and frivolous'.[81]

Regardless of Powers's incessant queries and criticisms of Symcotts, he grew very dependent upon his physician. Indeed, he consulted Symcotts about each detail of his personal life, becoming unable to make the smallest decisions without worrying about their possible medical consequences. In the autumn of 1642 Symcotts advised him

> to keep your chamber . . . and there to maintain a constant warm air day and night. . . . For the [question?] of keeping your chamber whether all or part of the winter I cannot determine. That will be longer or shorter as you get strength and the disease weakens.

Powers must have asked if it was safe for him to go to church, for the physician wrote, 'You need not take care for going to church. God in this case will have mercy and not sacrifice'.[82]

Powers obviously preferred Symcotts to Fullwood. In one instance he complained bitterly about a remedy Fullwood had prescribed: 'This physic put me to intolerable pain and gripings in my breast, back, stomach and sides'. He suffered with this medicine for three days.

> Then the doctor [Symcotts] must amend Fullwood's stuff and he sent me three pills which I took in hope the pills would take away the [evil?] of Fullwood's physic, and so I hope it did for it wrought very well and gently; but for Fullwood I had neither ease nor sleep . . . in three days and three nights, but lay in miserable torments.[83]

A likely reason for Powers's dislike of Fullwood was Fullwood's obvious impatience with Powers. Fullwood apparently handled the financial business of the practice. Characteristically Powers quibbled over paying in full several of the bills he was sent. In June 1639 Fullwood wrote indignantly,

> Mr. Powers,
> I thank you I have received the 13s.3d. by Mr. Peacock and have given him acquittance in full. But I much wonder you should yet so much question the dueness of the 4s.8d.. I thought I had satisfied you about it when you was to Huntingdon and we spoke about it last; but for the most part of it you deceive yourself in this present letter, for that drink which you say Mistress Willis brought you was certainly made with the plantain water and juice

of barberries and mirabilons etc., by your description of it to me. That you took it was not my fault, nor is it good reason why I should bear the loss. Directions for the use of them was also sent with them, howsoever it miscarried. For the glass, you say right: it's most like we had charged it, for we could not send the water without a glass. For the lenitive electuary and ointment, I know not what became of them afterwards, but I am sure your messenger had them all from me; and all were sent, not by my freeness or forwardness, but by direction from Dr. Symcotts for you, as he himself can yet remember, and will tell you if you will believe him.[84]

Neither Fullwood nor Edward Johnson, Fullwood's 'man', had much sympathy for the cantankerous old man. Compare with Symcotts's tone of patient reassurance Johnson's remark, 'You need not wonder that your cure is no further on foot, you may rather wonder that you was not in your grave long before this'.[85] Indeed, it is quite possible that Fullwood and Johnson actually had more contact with Powers than did the physician. Many of the 'physic directions' for Powers's use came from Fullwood, and he and Johnson had the unpleasant duty of collecting Powers's fees. It might follow that Powers actually blamed Fullwood and Johnson for the medical bills he paid. Certainly Powers resented these bills. On a wrapper he used to enclose his papers was written, 'Dr. Symcotts' letters, physic [directions] and apothecaries' bills; from which God deliver us'.[86]

The financial dealings between Powers and Symcotts's practice leave no doubt that the administration of physic was charged for in a way similar to that of surgery. The major difference between the bills of Binns and Symcotts was that Binns named a specific fee for his own labour and that of his man. It may be that this was one way physicians sought to demonstrate their claims to professional status. By charging only for medications, physicians could demonstrate their disdain for the 'trade' connotations of charging for services rendered. One can only speculate about whether prices for remedies were padded in order to include an unspecified fee for expert advice. In their introduction Poynter and Bishop mention that 'there is a record of a purge being rewarded with £65' – a princely sum in the seventeenth century.[87] While Symcotts never charged such enormous prices, he managed to prosper on the basis of the fees he received, which suggests that there was a healthy profit margin attached to the remedies he prescribed. It is also likely that patients offered him payments after consultations which were not noted in the practice's records.

How typical was Symcotts of seventeenth-century provincial physicians? For purposes of comparison, we will take a brief look at two other 'physical' casebooks from the period.

II TWO PROVINCIAL HEALERS

Little is known about Dr Barker of Shrewsbury. The local record office has no specific record of him, but suggests that he might have come from London. As indicated above, his casenotes are drawn from the period 1595 to 1605. Thus, his is the earliest healer's practice examined for the purposes of this study.[88] There can be little doubt that Barker was, indeed, a physician, although his qualifications are unknown. Many of his case-descriptions and most of his prescriptions were written in Latin. Like Symcotts and Binns, his orientation towards diagnosis and therapy was humoral.

Barker's casebook refers to some 145 patients, of whom 70 were men and 75 women. Less can be inferred about the social status of his patients than is the case with the practices of Binns and Symcotts. This is true for several reasons. Barker's is a difficult hand to read. Thus, the deciphering of names and titles is more difficult for his casebook than for the others considered. We are also without the sort of background information provided by Poynter and Bishop for the Symcotts papers. As far as can be determined, Barker's clientele came largely from middling and lower status backgrounds. Only five of his patients were titled; eighty-three were designated Mr or Mrs; fifty were called Goodwife or Goodman, or simply named with no prefix.

Like Symcotts, Barker was a general practitioner, treating a large variety of ailments. Some disorders were named, as was the case with vertigo, arthritis, ague, dropsy, green sickness, epilepsy, apoplexy, melancholy, lues venerea, asthma and gout. However, as with Symcotts, Barker usually began his notes by giving a list of the patient's symptoms. Thus, Mr Bownes had a cold brain, pain in the left side of his head and neck, a disturbance in the bottom of his stomach and a feeling as if cold water were in the region of his left 'stone'. He spat much phlegm, and had weak joints and 'windiness' of the stomach.[89]

Like Symcotts, Barker dealt with a number of problems which might have been treated by a surgeon or midwife. He was consulted for the stone, bruising, purulent bloody flux from the uterus, menstrual problems, pimples, itching, syphilis, ulcers, fistulae and complications of childbirth. Indeed, 29 out of 145 cases might properly be considered 'non-medical'. Barker treated such ailments by using internal remedies to purge the patient. He also applied medication to the skin in the form of ointments. However, he did not use surgical instruments. Thus, he treated a fistula by ordering the patient to be bled, and treated an apostem by purging, then rubbing, washing and anointing the affected place.[90] One suspects that Binns would have had little time for such methods.

Unlike Symcotts, Barker treated several patients for emotional illnesses. In the seventeenth century no rigid demarcation was made between physical and mental ailments. Thus, patients with emotional problems were usually treated for physical symptoms as well. For instance, Mr Aron the younger was given a purge for wind in the genital region, 'nocturnal pollutions' and impotence.[91] Mr Clyve was also purged. He was

> Very melancholic delighting in solitariness. He thinketh that he speaketh foolishly and vain. And imagineth that he is weak and that his legs and body is worn away. When he is worst he is gotten to be most heaving and lumbering. . . . He eateth and sleepeth well. His skin is rough and is dry, stiff and cleaveth to his flesh.[92]

Barker treated nine patients for melancholy. He also dealt with one phantom pregnancy and one case of 'disturbance of reason often speaking vain things and idle' associated with 'convulsive pains within her body, left arm and that side of her head and neck'.[93] In the latter case the physician obviously suspected true lunacy, for he noted the moon signs throughout the long description of this patient's case.

Indeed, it should be noted that Barker was more serious about astrology than any of the other healers whose casebooks have been consulted for the purposes of this study. His notes are dotted with astrological signs which aided him in both diagnosis and treatment.[94] Barker also routinely examined his patient's urine.[95] This is not surprising, considering that the Royal College of Physicians did not officially disapprove of this practice until 1601 and, as we have seen, many respectable physicians employed uroscopy well after it became controversial.[96]

Unlike the other healers whose casebooks are consulted,

Barker was interested in the prophylaxis of plague. He visited one Mathew Warrow in Turk's Hill on 20 August 1603. There he prescribed preventative treatment for Mathew which consisted of purging, sweating and weekly 'pestilent pills'. He also prescribed the pills for Mathew's wife. In addition, on the same day he prescribed pestilent pills for Owen Meredith's wife, his servant and three maids.[97] Barker also treated several who had survived plague but suffered from secondary effects. One patient was left with a sore knee.[98] P. Yonge's wife, 'being recovered of the pest and the apostem being not well cleansed and . . . healed, after three months a humour fell into her hips and knees . . . with stiffness . . . and weakness of stomach'.[99] There is no record of the physician treating an active case of plague.

Because Barker treated a number of women who suffered from menstrual disorders and other 'female' problems, this area of his practice is worth some consideration. In keeping with the humoral orientation which considered the body's general condition before determining treatment, an adult female's menstrual history was frequently mentioned by seventeenth-century healers, regardless of the symptoms the patient presented to the healer. For instance, Dr Symcotts treated Lady Howard for symptoms including a dry cough, which had lasted for ten or twelve years, griping in her body, weakness and thinness. In his description of her condition he noted that her menses had been suppressed for many years.[100] Barker made similar notes. For instance, he treated one woman for headache, fever, backache, pain in the side, melancholy and 'trembling of the heart'. He also mentioned that she had inordinate menses.[101]

However, Barker treated a number of patients whose chief complaint was gynaecological. He dealt with a 'purulent flux from the uterus', retention or suppression of the menses, green sickness, irregular menstruation, inordinate menstruation and 'whites'.[102] In these cases, he invariably prescribed an herbal purge, frequently containing betony.[103] He occasionally ordered other remedies. For instance, for green sickness he anointed the patient's side, purged her, ordered that she sit in a bath for three days, then purged her again.[104] Although several of his gynaecological patients may have been suffering from syphilis, actually named in only two cases, there is no record of Barker prescribing mercury. In only one case did he order guaiacum. For Mrs Berk he prescribed a purge, then a diet drink of guaiacum, sweating every fifth day and a vapour bath. He also ordered cloths moistened in honey and guaiacum water to be applied to Mrs Berk's body.[105]

Little can be inferred from Barker's casenotes about his relationships with his patients. That the Pilstor family, for instance, consulted him on several occasions suggests that he had a loyal clientele.[106] As was the case with other healers, Barker's patients sometimes helped to determine their own treatment. Mrs Coderington received treatment for a mysterious quartan ague which kept returning about the time of her menstrual period. She told the physician that all hot medicines offended her.[107]

Equally little is known about Barker's relations with other healers. One example suggests that he consulted amicably with his colleagues:

> Dr. Turner sayeth that before Mr. Cole fell into . . . [that disorder] he had a troublesome cough through a distillation and I know he had divers . . . fits through tartarous matter and once after a clyster by P. Pena his counsel he avoided many stones.[108]

However, in a case of phantom pregnancy, he implied criticism of the physician Dr Davis, who prescribed 'a strong vomit . . . which made her weak and a fortnight after she fell into a grievous and continual vomiting'.[109]

Considering his casebook as a whole, Dr Barker appears to have been a conventional physician of his time. He used astrology, examined urine and prescribed quantities of herbal remedies. While it is possible that his clientele came from a relatively lower social status than did that of other physicians, it is equally possible that his patients were higher status than this reading of his casenotes suggests.

The third 'physical' casebook which will be examined in this chapter was kept by a healer who probably practised in Cambridge during the years between 1619 and 1622.[110] It is assumed that he was a physician, because of the kinds of cases he undertook and the therapeutic methods he used. However, it is possible that he was an empiric. Some of his prescriptions were unorthodox, as we shall see. His hand, although easy to read, seems relatively uneducated. None the less, his prescriptions were routinely written in Latin, which suggests that this healer had at least a basic medical education. He noted treatment of eighty-two patients: forty-eight male, twenty-seven female and seven whose sex is unknown. Thirteen of his patients were titled, forty-one of middling status and twenty-four of lower status. The social status of four of his patients could not be identified. A large number of his patients resided in Cambridge colleges. This may account for the relatively large number of males in his clientele.

His casebook, like those of the other physicians, is not as detailed as that of Binns. Often, he merely noted the name of the patient and the symptoms complained of. Never did he indicate the outcome of the treatment he applied. Like Symcotts and Barker, he treated numerous 'surgical' cases including bruising, the stone, itching and haemorrhoids.[111] He treated these with internal remedies combined with phlebotomy and clysters. He also dealt with five cases of gonorrhoea in men, for which he sometimes prescribed 'pillulae chimica' (a mercury preparation?) and guaiacum in addition to other remedies.[112] Considering that the total number of his casenotes is relatively small, it is possible that this healer treated gonorrhoea as a minor speciality.

Like Symcotts and Barker, this healer most often described symptoms rather than naming a single disease. Even when a disease was named, the healer was himself cautious about diagnosis, implying that the patient had suggested it. The following casenote is typical:

> The young lady Maynard
> Her liver obstructed. Her stomach clogged with phlegm. Her body waterish. Subject to toothache. Her eyes swollen or puffed up. She hath had fluxum menstruam abundant but now little. But often and waterish. She fears most a consumption, or dropsy.[113]

Occasionally his diagnosis was more definite. Specific diseases named are gonorrhoea, the stone, jaundice, worms, frensy, palsy, dropsy, haemorrhoids, 'The Mother' (that is fits or suffocation of the mother or uterus) and epilepsy.

This healer mentions using neither astrology nor uroscopy. He was fonder than was Barker of phlebotomy and leeches. He rarely prescribed a clyster. He is unique among the healers we have examined for having ordered a course of treatment at a spa. His directions for Mr Samuel Cutler of Ipswich include nine prescriptions of internal remedies, a special diet, liniment to be applied by a barber to the neck, arm and hand, and instructions for the use of 'the Cross Bath'.[114] Presumably Mr Cutler was going to Bath to find relief. The detailed directions he was given included the following warning:

> The weather growing cold use the King's Bath but beware of that

I told you. As you find good, use it. In any case, never go into the bath but after a stool either naturally or by a suppository.

We are not told Mr Cutler's symptoms.

The area in which this physician most differed from the other healers examined was his marked attraction to remedies and ingredients which were neither herbal nor chemical, but which were either animal or exotic in nature. To Mr Standish, who suffered from the stone, he gave numerous directions including the following:

> To make a powder for yourself, take a young male hare quick.
> Kill it and save all the blood in a dish. Pull all the hair off the skin.
> Mix it with the blood. And dry it in an oven. Beat it to fine
> powder and sear it. Take of this the weight of [illegible] in like
> order as the former powder.[115]

Goodman Kettle, who suffered from nosebleeds, was told to take 'his own blood, dried between two tiles, beat to fine powder and often blowed into his nose'. He was also directed to 'make a tent of cobweb and fresh hog's dung to put into your nose' – presumably in order to drive the blood away from the evil smell. In addition, to draw the blood inward and downward, Kettle was advised to eat calves' feet, neates' feet and sheep's feet.[116] This healer suggested that

> for preserving your sight, take of woman's milk that bore and
> nurseth a man child in spoonfuls: of the urine of the same child iiii
> spoonfuls, beaten with a new-laid egg with some camphor added.
> Set to steep all night in a closed glass in a warm oven. Soak little
> linen cloths in the mixture and apply them to the eyes all night.
> This to be done three nights running four times a year. Also the
> eyes are to be washed in the morning with white wine.[117]

In three cases he prescribed the eagle stone for women in labour. This object, a round or egg-shaped stone, hollow in the middle, which rattled when shaken, was attached to the mother's thigh in order to hasten delivery. So powerful was it that midwives were warned not to leave it in place once the child was born for fear that it might cause prolapse of the uterus.[118]

It is obvious that occasionally this healer dabbled in sympathetic magic. Apparently he did not use other magical methods, such as incantations, spells or amulets. However, his techniques would certainly have been frowned upon by the more conventional healers Binns, Symcotts and Barker. These healers also avoided the use of such exotic substances as mummy and unicorn's horn, prescribed by the Cambridge practitioner.[119]

This healer used some methods which reflected classical medical traditions. No case provides a better example of this than his treatment of 'the Mother'. Rather than prescribing the standard purges and vomits, he returned to the classical notion of the wandering womb which must be lured back to its proper place. Thus, he had the 'Gentlewoman, Mr. More's friend' use sweet applications on her genitals and introduce foul smells to the nose: 'Let her smell to partridge feathers burnt: smell to asafoetida'. He also ordered her to sneeze in order to drive the rising womb downwards.[120]

We know little about this practitioner's relationships with other healers. In one case he apparently consulted with two other 'doctors', Goslin and Forthow.[121] However, these are the only colleagues mentioned in his casebook. Equally little is known about his relationships with patients. The Maynard family consulted him on at least three occasions.[122] That his university patients resided in six colleges suggests that his reputation among the scholars there was reasonably good. Neither he nor Barker made any reference to the charging and payment of fees.

III COMPARISON AND CONCLUSIONS

Comparison of the physicians' casebooks examined here reveals a number of similarities. All three practised outside London. Although each healer was based in a relatively populous town, the patients of each were drawn from a large rural area surrounding the town. The physicians were all general practitioners. They all subscribed to humoral theory. They prescribed herbal remedies, in the main, although the Cambridge physician also used animal and exotic ingredients. Their prescriptions were usually written in Latin, though case descriptions were usually in English. Although they used some surface applications in the form of ointments and baths, they largely depended upon internal medicines. Some of these remedies were sent to patients already prepared; occasionally patients were expected to follow the physician's instructions in preparing the remedies themselves. While the physicians prescribed such measures as blood-letting, issues, blisters and clysters, they did not perform these procedures themselves.

Each of the physicians used some relatively old-fashioned techniques. As indicated above, it is not surprising that

Barker, the earliest physician studied, routinely employed uroscopy and astrology. Appropriately Symcotts had less frequent recourse to these methods. Indeed, the correspondence he received suggests that he occasionally examined urine and paid attention to astrological indications at the patient's request.[123] The Cambridge physician used neither uroscopy nor astrology, but dabbled in natural magic. His was the only casebook encountered which reveals strong links with traditional medicine.

These findings confirm the suspicion that the anti-quack writers attempted to create the impression that there was a more definite line of demarcation between reputable physicians and 'quacks' than really existed. A combination of personal interest and patients' demands could make a 'piss prophet' of the respectable Symcotts. Physicians were by no means inflexible in their adherence to academic authorities and the guidelines laid down by the Royal College of Physicians. Again, Symcotts's papers indicate that even a conventional physician was willing to try unconventional methods if such methods seemed likely to produce a cure.

How did the physicians studied differ? The records kept by our nameless Cambridge healer are of the utmost help here, for they permit us to see the tremendous similarity between Barker and Symcotts. Barker and Symcotts were the earlier and later sides of the same conventional coin. Their responses to the symptoms presented were predictable. They took the patient's medical history, then prescribed several herbal preparations designed to produce evacuation. Rarely did they record either the outcome of the treatment prescribed or the necessity of a return visit by the patient.

Barker's use of uroscopy and astrology was relatively insignificant. He was neither a 'piss prophet', depending totally upon signs in urine for prescription and prognosis, nor an astrological physician, relating all diagnosis and treatment to signs found in the sky. The differences between his practices and those of Symcotts reflect the changes in conventional medical treatment in the first half of the seventeenth century.

The Cambridge healer's notes do not conform to the pattern followed by Barker and Symcotts. He was lavish in his prescriptions, apparently ordering remedies in proportion to the patient's wealth. For instance, Sir William Maynard was directed to take some twenty medicines for gonorrhoea. Sir Oly of Clare College received only four prescriptions for the same disorder.[124] Often the remedies he prescribed were unconventional. And the traditional notions which underlie these remedies offered him an alternative to the manipulation of humours produced by conventional techniques. His use of the eagle stone, for instance, provides a direct contrast with Symcotts's use of internal remedies to provoke delivery. It also served as an alternative to consultation of a surgeon with his instruments.

It is tempting to see this healer as a minor medical renegade, operating dangerously near to the territory of unlearned healers. Yet his use of Latin, his upper status and university patients and his apparently amicable relations with at least two local 'doctors' suggest that he was also reasonably respectable. Although his qualifications are unknown, it is quite possible that he himself had pursued a course of university study. Thus, while he does not quite fit the pattern of the conventional physician of his time, his practices demonstrate the spectrum of medical care available within the fold of respectable medical practitioners.

Comparison of the physicians' casebooks with that kept by the surgeon Binns adds to our knowledge of this spectrum. Binns's therapeutic routines were similar to those followed by Barker and Symcotts. Like them, he depended upon purges, emetics and diuretics to promote evacuation, thus keeping the patient's body in a 'soluble' state. Like them, he used surgical procedures such as blood-letting and issues responsibly and sparingly.

With hindsight, it is possible to see Binns as the most modern of these three very conventional healers. He did not use uroscopy and astrology at all. His prescriptions reveal a wide knowledge of the relatively new chemical remedies popularised by the disciples of Paracelsus. Unlike Barker and Symcotts, he applied all of the treatments he prescribed himself, not depending upon additional lesser healers to act according to his orders.[125] And, unlike Symcotts, he charged both for remedies provided and services rendered, thus directly recognising his place in the medical marketplace.

In addition, because of the sorts of problems Binns treated, he dealt more with specific disorders than did the physicians. While the surgeon used evacuative medicine to treat the whole patient, he focused his attention on localised symptoms in a way the physicians rarely did.

What did physicians and surgeons think of each other? Judging by the casebooks analysed here, there was much tolerance and little prejudice on both sides of the occupational divide. Binns apparently respected physicians generally, although he recorded one case in which he disagreed with a physician's judgment.[126] Correspondingly Symcotts respected surgeons, although he felt a surgeon was unskilful in one instance.[127] None the less, there can be no doubt that physicians regarded surgeons as subordinate to themselves, and surgical procedures as essentially menial. On the other hand, no impression is given in Binns's casebook that the surgeon felt inferior to any other practitioner. He took independent charge of his patients, worked with physicians as colleagues, and saw himself as rendering an expert service.

It is not possible to compare Binns's success rate with that of the physicians. While the surgeon conscientiously noted the outcome of his treatment, the physicians did so only erratically. Symcotts reported the outcome in only fifty-five cases. According to this meagre sample, he did well; thirty-five patients recovered, seven improved and only thirteen died. Barker and the Cambridge practitioner reported the outcome of a case so rarely that consideration of their success rate is impossible. Thus, one cannot make an informed statement about the relative efficacy of 'physic' and surgery in seventeenth-century England. In this area, as in many others, the perceptions and preconceptions of sufferers and patients were more important than any demonstrable expertise. As we shall see below, at least one patient, Samuel Pepys, had greater regard for surgeons than he had for physicians.[128] One can only speculate about how general this feeling was.

Concerning relations between healers and patients, certain generalisations are possible. Symcotts's correspondence and the diaries of lay-people confirm that seventeenth-century sufferers knew a good deal about their own ailments and took a large amount of responsibility in their courses of treatment.[129] Very often, people attempted to cure themselves and sought medical advice from relatives and friends before consulting healers. Symcotts and Binns each had many patients who had come to them as a last resort. The remedies prepared by lay-people – particularly women – were valued by people beyond their own social circle. As indicated above, Symcotts knew a number of gentlewomen who acted as amateur healers with his entire approval and respect. Further, their medical recipes were collected by lay-people and healers alike. Robert Hooke's collection will be discussed below.[130] Symcotts's has already been mentioned.

Whether or not they acted as healers, lay-people were often required by healers to make or apply their own remedies. Ingredients frequently came from their own larders, cellars and gardens. For instance, Symcotts's 'restorative water for any that is in weakness' contained the following:

> Take 3 pints of new milk, 1 pint of red wine, 24 yolks of new laid eggs. Beat all these together, then put to it as much fine white manchett [bread roll] as will soak up the aforesaid milk and wine. Distill it with a soft fire.
>   Take a spoonful in any spoon meat you eat and in each draught of drink. This hath recovered one wasted to skin and bone in a month's time.[131]

Patients and their servants also performed minor surgical tasks such as applying leeches, giving clysters and making up medicinal baths and fumes. Sometimes physicians' prescriptions were made up by people other than either the patient, the physician or an apothecary. For instance, Mistress Willis, a midwife, brewed a diet drink for Symcotts's patient, Mr Powers.[132] Thus, patients and many lay-people surrounding them were intimately involved with illness and medicine.

Patients and their families sometimes asked healers for particular services and remedies. This was usual in the case of prophylactic physic, often taken once a year, when an individual would purchase a purge or ask a surgeon to let blood. Equally usual was the preventative medicine aimed against a specific disease. We have seen that Barker on one occasion provided 'pestilent pills' for two families and their servants. However, medical and surgical services were often specified for other disorders. Mr Cotton asked Symcotts for a purge for his wife after she had given birth.[133]

Further, patients felt free to consult more than one healer. As we have seen, Mr Powers, loyal old nuisance though he was, sought treatment from at least two other practitioners during the course of his relationship with Symcotts. In this, he was quite typical. Each of the casebooks examined makes references to patients who had consulted other healers before coming to the one writing the notes.

Thus healers, competing in the open market, had to justify treatments prescribed, hoping to be vindicated by success. Symcotts's correspondence is full of letters from him to patients, explaining the advice he has given in terms of the patient's own needs. For instance, to Mr Powers he wrote, 'I am in haste yet I will not grudge to give you a short account of my intention in the late prescribed course'.[134] This was followed by a full page concerning his prescription of a purge. Such letters show great respect for the patient's understanding.

Surfeyte, age, and sickenes, are enemyes all to health,
Medicines to mende the body excell all worldly wealth:
Pisicke shall florishe, and in daunger will giue cure,
Till death vnknit the liuelj knot no longer wee endure.

This sixteenth-century woodcut both praises physic and reminds the reader that no physic can prevent death. (W. Bullein, *Bulleins bulwarke of defence against all sickness . . .*, London, 1562.)

They also show the healer's concern that his methods appear to be correct, regardless of the outcome.

Herein lies the core of the physician's problem. Unlike other learned authorities, such as ministers and lawyers, the physician was expected to demonstrate his knowledge in a concrete way by curing people. Whether the patient recovered or died, however, the physician wished his knowledge and expertise to be recognised and trusted. Indeed, to some extent, actual curing was regarded by the physician as irrelevant, since the medical knowledge he possessed was felt to be of intrinsic value. This knowledge was the commodity he offered the community.

In terms of economic and social success, physicians as a group achieved neither the rewards they coveted nor the failure their worst enemies, the empirics, might have wished them. Physicians like Symcotts were prosperous members of the community, living satisfying lives and helping their patients through a variety of crises. However, they did not have a monopoly over the provision of internal medicine in seventeenth-century England.

5

SUFFERERS AND PATIENTS: THE DISEASES OF THE PEOPLE

In 1651 Thomas Hobbes wrote that 'the life of man is solitary, poor, nasty, brutish and short'.[1] While this statement was inaccurate for many living in his own time, it does reflect a comparative truth which historians and demographers have been eager to enlarge upon. Dietary, sanitary and housing conditions have been held accountable for a great deal of misery, including disease.[2] High infant and child mortality, and a relatively short expectation of life at birth have been meticulously determined and duly regretted.[3] However, it must be remembered that, while the seventeenth-century English criticised the conditions they lived with, they had not the standard of comparison which blesses (or curses) late-twentieth-century scholars. This study is concerned with seventeenth-century perceptions and expectations. Thus, it will try to avoid implicit (and self-congratulatory) comparisons between then and now.

No attempt will be made below to make causal associations between living conditions and illness. Such associations necessarily refer to the hypotheses and discoveries of modern science, and are thus irrelevant for the understanding of seventeenth-century experience. The same objection applies to efforts made to diagnose the diseases seventeenth-century sufferers 'really' had. They *knew* what they had. Our presumptuous diagnosis of the green sickness as chlorosis, for instance, has nothing to do with their understanding and treatment of the disorder – nor with our understanding of their behaviour. Neither will any assessment be made of whether or not the treatments people underwent 'worked'. In this area, as in others, the sufferer will speak for him- or herself.

People suffered from a multitude of discomforts and disorders in seventeenth-century England. Some scholars maintain that most people felt unwell most of the time.[4] None the less, historians, demographers and epidemiologists have

· concentrated their attention on epidemic diseases, particularly plague.[5] While this concentration is understandable in view of the tremendous mortality and social dislocation caused by epidemics, it distorts our perception of the diseases people suffered and died from in the period.

In the sixteenth and seventeenth centuries London underwent six major outbreaks of plague. These occurred in the years 1563, 1593, 1603, 1625, 1636 and 1665. These outbreaks were sometimes, but not always, reflected in provincial epidemics. For instance, Bristol suffered severely from plague in 1563 and 1603, but not in 1625 and 1636.[6] And, it must be remembered, most people lived in villages or hamlets in the countryside: areas much less susceptible to plague infestation. Gregory King, the pioneer demographer, calculated that nearly 80 per cent of the population was rural.[7] Thus, although dread of the plague was certainly a part of general seventeenth-century English mental furniture, it was quite possible for an individual – particularly someone living outside London – to live out a long lifetime without ever personally experiencing a plague epidemic. Thus, other diseases, although not carrying the dramatic impact possessed by the very word 'plague', were as or more significant in the lives and deaths of members of the general public.

One way of estimating the incidence of serious diseases in a population is to obtain a numerical breakdown of the causes of death. This method has its faults, which will be discussed below. However, it is such a good indicator of both the disorders people died from and contemporary popular diagnoses of symptoms that it cannot be ignored.

Perhaps unfortunately, the following discussion is based largely on London records. It is widely repeated that the London experience was untypical. London was many times larger than any other seventeenth-century English city and contemporaries and historians agree that it was an unusually unhealthy place to live.[8] However, the medical casebooks and lay diaries which are cited elsewhere in our discussion support the conviction that both diagnostic categories and individual experience of endemic diseases were similar throughout the country. The Josselin family, living in deepest Essex, and the Hobys, living in remote Yorkshire, suffered from conditions which were all too familiar to Londoners.

The two best seventeenth-century sources giving causes of death are the London Bills of Mortality and those parish burial records which record the disease the newly deceased was suffering from.[9] A superb work which serves both as a provider of new information and as a guide to the London Bills of Mortality is John Graunt's *Natural and Political Observations Made upon the Bills of Mortality* (1662). On the basis of these sources, a profile of killing diseases can be drawn over a long period of time.

As suggested above, the widest fluctuation is seen in the incidence of epidemic diseases. For instance, in 1625 the plague killed 35,417 people in London. In 1648 it killed 611. In 1629, 1633 and 1635 no plague deaths were reported at all.[10] A similar, though less dramatic, fluctuation appears in the incidence of death from other diseases recognised as infectious. For instance, smallpox killed some people every year in seventeenth-century London. However, it was worse some years than others. In 1659 smallpox killed 1,523 people, while in 1660 it killed 354.[11] Even non-infectious killers exhibit fluctuations which are more difficult to account for. For example, in 1648 only 106 London women died in childbirth; in 1652 the number had jumped to 213.[12] Even allowing for population growth, that increase is extreme, particularly considering that only 194 women died in childbirth in 1660.

Despite the fluctuations observable in the incidence of all the disorders recorded, however, it is possible to identify the diseases which had the most significant impact on the population. From this information one can make inferences about some of the disorders which disrupted the lives of the survivors, as well as those of the deceased. Among the most consistent killers were unspecified 'fevers', consumption and the simple experience of being born, usually labelled as 'chrisoms' or 'infants'. In a comparison of the Bills of Mortality for 1632, a non-plague year, and the plague year, 1665, over 1,000 people died in each of these categories. Other major killers were smallpox, abortion and stillbirth, 'teeth' and old age, which claimed between 450 and 1,000 deaths in each year.

Certain changes can be observed over a period of years in the incidence of a number of non-infectious disorders. These changes can be viewed either as alterations in diagnoses of conditions which had always been present, or as indications of the advent of new diseases. John Graunt wrote about both of these alternatives. For instance, he felt that deaths in infancy had been reported differently early in the century than they were later, writing,

Of convulsions there appeared very few, *viz.* but 52 in the year 1629, which in 1636 grew to 709, keeping about that stay, till

1659, though sometimes rising to about 1000.

It is to be noted, that from 1629 to 1636, when the convulsions were but few, the number of chrysoms and Infants was greater: for in 1629, there was of Chrysoms, and Infants 2596, and of the Convulsion 52, *viz.* of both 2648. And in 1636 there was of Infants 1895, and of the Convulsions 709, in both 2604, by which it appears, that this difference is likely to be only a confusion in the accounts.[13]

He goes on to say that deaths put down to teeth and worms are also interchanged with the categories Infants, Chrysoms and Convulsions, which further confuses matters. The indication of convulsions as the cause of death became increasingly common in the course of the century, judging by the burial records of St Vedast parish, London. For the years 1674–83, convulsions was the single most frequent cause of death, followed closely by consumption, fever and gripes. Although the ages of those dying of convulsions is not usually given, the burial register often indicates that the deceased were children by identifying them as 'son' or 'daughter' of certain parents.[14]

One disease which is generally regarded by both historians and contemporaries as new in the seventeenth century is rickets. Graunt pointed out that rickets is not mentioned in the Bills of Mortality until 1634. However, he was undecided whether rickets was a new disease, or whether it was simply a new way of reporting deaths from the conditions 'livergrown' and 'spleen'. None the less, he leaned toward the judgment that rickets was a new disease, since the numbers dying from it steadily increased, while the numbers of those dying livergrown remained constant.[15] He made the same decision about another apparently new disease, the stopping of the stomach, which was first mentioned in the Bills in 1636.[16] While he did not view scurvy as a new disease, he observed that it was rapidly increasing in incidence, having killed but twelve in 1629 and twenty-five in 1660.[17]

Determination of the cause of death was made by the searchers. Graunt described the procedure as follows:

When any one dies, then, either by tolling, or ringing of a Bell, or by bespeaking of a Grave of the Sexton, the same is known to the Searchers, corresponding with the said Sexton.

The Searchers hereupon (who are ancient Matrons, sworn to their Office) repair to the place, where the dead Corps lies, and by view of the same, and by other enquiries, they examine by what Disease or Casualty the Corps died. Hereupon they make their report to the Parish-Clerk.[18]

Graunt, who was, after all, himself a haberdasher by trade, was not unduly concerned about the medical ignorance of the searchers, maintaining that most determinations of the cause of death were simply matters of 'sense', and that underlying causes for conditions such as old age (affecting persons who died at ages above 60) baffled even learned physicians.[19] For example, he wrote,

> As for Consumptions, if the Searchers do but truly Report (as they may) whether the dead Corps were very lean, and worn away, it matters not to many of our purposes [that is those of the Statisticians], whether the Disease were exactly the same, as Physicians define it in their Books. Moreover, in case a man of seventy five years old died of a Cough (of which had he been free he might have possibly lived to ninety) I esteem it little error (as to many of our purposes) if this person be, in the Table of Casualties, reckoned among the Aged, and not placed under the Title of Coughs.[20]

However, he mentioned one disease, the diagnosis of which the searchers often deliberately falsified. This was syphilis. About the pox he wrote,

> Forasmuch as by the ordinary discourse of the world it seems a great part of men have, at one time or other, had some species of this disease, I wondering why so few died of it, especially because I could not take that to be so harmless, whereof so many complained very fiercely; upon inquiry I found that those who died of it out of the Hospitals . . . were returned of Ulcers and Sores. And in brief I found, that all mentioned to die of the French Pox were returned by the Clerks of Saint Giles's, and Saint Martin's in the Fields only; in which place I understood that most of the vilest, and most miserable houses of uncleanness were: from whence I concluded, that only *hated* persons, and such, whose very Noses were eaten off, were reported by the Searchers to have died of this too frequent malady.[21]

Graunt observed that most who died of syphilis died 'emaciated and lean'. Thus, the searchers, 'after the mist of a cup of ale and the bribe of a two-groat fee', were nearly justified in reporting as the cause of death consumption, hectic-fever, atrophy or infection of the 'Spermatick parts'.[22]

It is, perhaps, more significant for the purposes of this study than it was for Graunt that the searchers were lay-women. Although they were occasionally told the cause of death by the attending physician, more often they made the determination themselves, aided by the family and friends of the deceased. The diseases or 'casualties' noted in the Bills of Mortality and parish records thus reflect popular categories for diseases.

A consistent killer with strong associations with humoral medical theory was surfeit, which killed between 63 and 371 people in each year between 1629 and 1660. Still another consistent killer was dropsy or timpany, which killed between 185 and 931 people a year in the same period. Apoplexy and 'sudden death' was far less deadly, in some years killing no one at all and at most, in 1658, claiming but 138 deaths.

Disorders which might be viewed as mental rather than physical in origin also killed. A condition identified simply as grief accounted for the deaths of between seven and twenty-two people a year in the period 1629–60. Suicide, under the heading 'Hanged, and made away themselves', was the cause of the deaths of between three and thirty-six people in each year of this period except one, 1633. Lunacy killed between two and eighteen people a year.

It is interesting that, in a time period renowned for both aggressive behaviour and dangerous living conditions, more people did not die as the result of violence or accidents. Between 1629 and 1660 there were three years in which no murders were reported – 1629, 1630 and 1633. And in only two years were there more than ten murders in all of the parishes contributing information to the Bills of Mortality. One wonders what was going on in 1660, when twenty were murdered, and in 1659 when seventy died by violence. These numbers do not include criminals who were executed; between seven and twenty-nine people died in this way from 1629 to 1660. More people died from accidental injuries than were killed by other people. These accidental deaths are reported under two headings – 'killed by several accidents' and 'sores, ulcers, broken and bruised limbs'. In only two years, 1650 and 1659, were more than a hundred people killed accidentally.

While the Bills of Mortality are an unrivalled source of information about the diseases people died of, this study is more concerned about the disorders people lived with. In this area as well, John Graunt is of some help. His comments about syphilis, quoted above, indicate that the pox either was or was thought to be a more common disease than the Bills of Mortality would lead one to believe. He also explained that gout, from which many people suffered, did not show up very frequently in the Bills because 'those that have the Gout are said to be Long-livers, and therefore, when such die, they are returned as Aged'.[23] Indeed, both Graunt's book and the Bills of Mortality can be seen as of unique value because the information they give cuts across class lines. Unlike medical casebooks and other sorts of private papers, parish records report the diseases of rich and poor alike.

This is not to say that the rich died of the same diseases as the poor did. Those reported as having been 'found dead in the streets' are unlikely to have been members of the upper classes. The same holds true for the few who were diagnosed as 'starved' in each year 1648–60. By the same token, a poor man or woman might have been considered fortunate to die of surfeit. Regardless of these observations, the Bills of Mortality provide a helpful insight into seventeenth-century interpretations of the always-democratic activities of the Grim Reaper.

More useful information about the ailments middle- and upper-class people suffered on a day-to-day basis can be obtained from the many diaries which have survived the last 300 years. These diaries are a veritable gold mine of evidence, not only about illnesses, but also about what the writers thought and did about them.

Inevitably diarists provide a one-sided view of the disorders people suffered from. Samuel Pepys, because of his personal experience, was very interested in bladder and kidney ailments, reporting not only his own sensations, but also those of acquaintances and relatives, as well as lectures and conversations with medical experts on the subject.[24] The Essex vicar, Ralph Josselin, greatly feared smallpox, and reported any local outbreaks of the disease, even though no one in his immediate family suffered very acutely from it.[25] The ever-ailing Robert Hooke's life revolved around how well or ill he slept.[26] None the less, the diaries and collections of correspondence available for the period can be examined and compared for indications of both commonly experienced ailments and disorders which could seriously affect an individual's life, whether or not a sizeable percentage of the population died of it.

Then as now, the most ubiquitous ailment was the common cold. All of the writers consulted had colds. However, while today this disorder is usually confined to the head and the chest, for seventeenth-century sufferers the term 'cold' retained more of its original humoral connotation and the ailment could attack any part of the body. Thus, Pepys often described his recurring pain during urination as being due to cold. Hooke complained of catching cold in his 'pole'.[27]

Colds were usually dismissed as minor ailments, treated, if at all, with casual remedies.[28] For instance, on one occasion Pepys asked Lady Batten for a spoonful of honey for his cold while dining at her home.[29] The sufferer, although inconvenienced, usually did not take up a sick role. However, sometimes colds were taken more seriously. In April 1649 Ralph Josselin took both mithridate and a stybium vomit for a cold.[30] John Evelyn was cupped and scarified for a cold he picked up in Italy.[31] And it was recognised that any illness, however minor, could suddenly become fatal. Mr Clerke, a solicitor of Pepys's acquaintance, died of a cold, having been ill for only two days.[32] In addition, colds in children were far more worrying than in adults.[33]

Nearly as common as colds were eye problems. Many diarists, including Pepys, Josselin, Evelyn and Hooke, suffered from either eyestrain or rheum in the eye or both. Indeed, Pepys gave up writing his diary for fear of exacerbating the eyestrain he worried might eventually blind him.[34] Eye problems, like colds, tended to be treated as minor annoyances – inconvenient, but not life-threatening.

Only in Pepys's case did the problem become serious enough for the sufferer to seek out a specialist. Pepys eventually consulted Dr Daubigny Turberville, who was 'the most successful practising oculist of his day', according to the editors of Pepys's diaries.[35] He also used a preparation advised by a fellow-sufferer, one Mr Cooling, and had his eyes dressed by his belt-maker's wife, 'an oldish woman in a hat'.[36] John Evelyn, who apparently favoured phlebotomy, was bled four times for his sore eyes in May 1647.[37] The other diarists simply waited out their eye ailments, which eventually passed.[38]

More serious than either colds or eye problems were the agues or intermittent fevers which afflicted many of the diarists and their relatives and friends. The Josselins' experiences with ague will be discussed below.[39] They, like others, found ague worrying and debilitating, but not fatal. The exception to this general observation is Dorothy Osborne's father who never really recovered from a severe attack of ague. Even after the fits ceased, he remained in his chamber. His attentive daughter wrote, 'I cannot say that he is at all sick but has so general a weakness upon him that I . . . do extremely apprehend how the winter may work upon him'.[40] Her fears were justified, for her father died soon after. Dorothy's brother, who came home to recover from an ague during her father's illness, was more fortunate. He eventually recovered, as did Dorothy herself, who had a relatively mild attack in April 1653 while her brother was recuperating. She wrote of her own illness, 'I have gotten an ague that with two fits has made me so very weak that I doubted extremely yesterday whether I should be able to sit up today to write to you'.[41] The following month she, her brother and her father had finally 'lost' their fits, 'but we all look like people risen from the dead'.[42]

Ague afflicted children as well as adults; like other diseases, it was more worrying in children. Lady Anne Clifford's daughter, Lady Margaret (at that time referred to only as 'The Child') had an ague during the February and March of 1617, when she was a toddler.[43] Lady Anne, who seems to have spent little time with her baby before the illness, reported spending 'most of her time . . . in going up and down to see the Child'.[44] Lady Margaret recovered. John Evelyn's first-born son, Richard, was not so lucky. He died of ague at age 5 years and 3 days.[45]

The cold and hot fits of ague were very unpleasant. And the intermittent character of these fits made agues particularly frustrating, since the sufferer felt fairly well between fits and could convince him- or herself that the illness had passed off. For instance, when Samuel Pepys's patron, Lord Sandwich, had an ague in January 1663, Pepys described a visit during which he found Sandwich 'not sick, but expecting his fit tonight of an ague'.[46] Later in the same illness, Lord Sandwich 'missed his fit' and hoped he was well.[47] His hopes were groundless, for the ague returned nearly a month later.[48]

In addition to agues, the diarists and their family members suffered from toothache. Elizabeth Pepys and Jane Josselin were particularly plagued with that painful disorder. In November 1661 Elizabeth Pepys had her teeth 'scaled' by Peter de la Roche, the operator for the teeth to the Royal household, in an attempt to improve her appearance and prevent further attacks.[49] However, as a preventative measure the operation did not succeed, for Elizabeth had yet another tooth drawn in May of that year.[50] Jane Josselin treated herself for toothache with tobacco.[51] She also suffered from pain in her gums.[52] However, like colds and eye problems, toothache, even when it ended in extraction, was regarded as being of minor significance.

Another widespread type of disorder were the various digestive ailments which attacked almost everyone at one time or another. Responses to these usually brief illnesses were mixed. Generally speaking, constipation was regarded as being more serious than either vomiting or diarrhoea (usually described as looseness or scouring). In the autumn of 1663 Pepys suffered from a disorder he described variously as wind, colic and being costive. It seemed very ominous to him that he could neither break wind nor produce bowel movements as 'naturally' and frequently as he would have liked.[53] While he complained of 'great pain' and took an enormous amount of purging medication for this problem, his main concern stemmed from the conviction that a constipated state was unnatural and fundamentally unhealthy.

Pepys's attitude was quite consistent with the humoral view of disease which regarded evacuation and a 'soluble' state of the body as beneficial. It was reflected in Hooke's relief upon vomiting after eating pullet and cheesecakes and Josselin's belief that the diarrhoea he suffered from in December 1648 had done him much good.[54] Such responses are certainly understandable, considering that most of the medicines people took were expected to cause evacuation of one kind or another. Natural vomiting, diarrhoea, sweating, expulsions of phlegm and even bleeding (from the nose, or in menstruation) may often have seemed merely the body's attempts to cure itself.[55] Thus, despite the evidence given by the London Bills of Mortality that, although no one died of constipation *per se* (although some died of surfeit), and many died each year of flux and scouring, the prevailing preference was for vomiting and diarrhoea as opposed to constipation.

Colds and disorders of the eyes, teeth and digestive tracts appeared in all of the diaries examined. Other conditions, although less ubiquitous, made frequent appearances. Not all the women who wrote or figured in the diaries consulted underwent pregnancy and childbirth. Lady Margaret Hoby and Elizabeth Pepys were childless. Dorothy Osborne was unmarried at the time she wrote her famous letters to William Temple, whom she later wed. However, Lady Anne Clifford had two pregnancies during the period in which she wrote her diary, and Mary Evelyn, Jane Josselin, and Alice Thornton were exceptionally productive, Mary having eight live births, Jane, ten and Alice, nine. Mary miscarried three times and Jane approximately five.

Of the fertile women mentioned above, only Lady Anne Clifford and Alice Thornton described their own experiences. Thornton's childbearing will be discussed below. Lady Anne did not describe her first pregnancy and the birth of Lady Margaret Sackville (born 1615). She did mention her second pregnancy, during and after which she was ill. She reported feeling herself quick with child in August 1619. In mid-October she wrote that she 'began to be ill'. From about this time she stayed in her chamber until the end of March 1620. The only specific symptom she reported was on 8 November 1619, feeling 'so ill that I fell into a swoon which was the first time I ever swooned'.[56] The child, Thomas, died soon after birth.

The experiences of Jane Josselin and Mary Evelyn were reported by their husbands. Jane's childbearing will be discussed below at some length.[57] Suffice it to say that her pregnancies were uncomfortable and her deliveries straightforward. Although she dreaded her labours for months before they occurred, she apparently accepted her frequent pregnancies as her natural lot and took an interest in them which is revealed in the predictions that she made early in at least five of her pregnancies about the sex of the unborn child.[58]

Mary Evelyn's pregnancies and deliveries were reported in far less detail than Jane Josselin's. The overwhelming impression given by her husband was that her fertility was desirable (indeed, expected) because of dynastic considerations. For this reason, too long a gap between babies was deplored.[59] Partly for this reason, her miscarriages were regretted.[60] John Evelyn did not indicate whether his wife's pregnancies were comfortable or uncomfortable. Nor did he describe her deliveries.

Mary's childbearing life was long. Married at 12, she miscarried at age 16, having been given a dose of physic which she took, unaware that she was pregnant.[61] Thereafter, she was more careful. She had five sons, born in 1652, 1653, 1655, 1657 and 1664, and three daughters, born in 1665, 1667 and 1669. She miscarried in October 1660, after falling from a stool.[62] Her last miscarrage occurred in April 1666, only six months after her daughter Mary was born.[63]

Unlike Jane Josselin, Mary Evelyn breast-fed none of her own children. This was undoubtedly due to the class difference. The Josselins were middle class by any definition of that inexact term; the Evelyns belonged to the landed gentry. While breast-feeding was increasingly acceptable and practised among the middle classes in seventeenth-century England, upper-class mothers did not usually feed their own babies.[64] John Evelyn had himself been put out to nurse immediately after birth and did not return home, weaned, until he was 15 months old.[65] His own children were also fed by wet-nurse. Jane Josselin almost certainly fed all of her babies herself. Comparison of the experiences of the Josselins and Evelyns make unavoidable the conclusion that the Evelyns suffered the consequences of wet-nursing. Of their five sons, three died within the first three months of life – one possibly having been overlain by the nurse.[66] The Josselins lost only one baby immediately after birth. That child died, aged 10 days, of a condition which could not possibly have been related to the care taken of him.[67]

Both Jane and Mary were comparatively fortunate in their childbearing. Although Jane complained of many more ailments during her childbearing years than she did in the twenty years after those years ended, she sustained no permanent handicap or illness through carrying and bearing children.[68] She lived to be at least 66 years old. Mary Evelyn died aged 74. Although her husband's account of her medical history must be regarded as sketchy at best, she apparently lived a remarkably healthy life, suffering hardly any illness at all until she was over age 50.

Both the Bills of Mortality and the diaries indicate that their contemporaries were not always as lucky as Jane and Mary. Many women did die in childbirth. In 1646 two neighbour women of the Josselins died giving birth.[69] John Evelyn's sister died at age 20 as the result of giving birth to a baby six months before.[70] Miscarrying caused problems as well. Pepys's Aunt Wight became very ill after a miscarriage in March 1662; his Cousin Scott died as the result of a miscarriage in February 1664.

Gynaecological disorders appear less frequently in the diaries than do conditions relating to pregnancy and childbirth. It is probable that this paucity of evidence reflects female modesty and male ignorance and disgust more than it does as actual absence of such disorders. Fortunately Samuel Pepys was interested in and sympathetic with his wife's 'female problems', and described them in some detail. Elizabeth Pepys had three distinct gynaecological disorders. She suffered from painful menstruation; according to her husband, she was infertile; and, most serious of all, she had recurring abcesses and eventually a fistula in her external genitalia.

The very first page of Pepys's diary referred to the couple's disappointed hopes of having a child. He wrote in January 1660,

> My wife, after the absence of her terms for seven weeks, gave me hopes of her being with child, but on the last day of the year she hath them again.[71]

By 1664 he was obviously more than resigned to their childless state, writing that Elizabeth thought she was pregnant, 'but I neither believe nor desire it'.[72] The fact that she had not borne a baby did not bar Elizabeth from helping out at the confinements of women of her acquaintance. Samuel reported that she was summoned to their labours; in one case he wrote that 'the midwife and she alone have delivered poor Betty of a pretty girl'.[73]

It is an open question whether the Pepys' married life would have been happier had they had children. Possibly Elizabeth would not have felt as isolated and bored as she increasingly did. And Samuel might have demanded less of her artistic and musical talents had she been busy with a young family. However, their childlessness gave them opportunities for companionship and communication denied to partners in more fruitful marriages. Pepys took a great interest in his wife's appearance and her artistic endeavours. And although they argued frequently, they also depended on each other for support. For example, in March 1668 Samuel's mind was troubled because of office business. Unable to sleep, he asked Elizabeth to talk to him 'to comfort him'. This she did; it eased him somewhat.[74] Thus, despite their spats and Samuel's infidelity, the Pepys marriage might be viewed as having been more 'companionate' than some modern scholars have maintained.[75]

Elizabeth's dependence on Samuel is certainly reflected in his description of her recurring bouts of pain in her external genitalia. Pepys first mentioned this problem on 2 August 1660. He wrote,

> When I came home, I find my wife not very well of her old pain in the lip of her *chose*, which she had when we were first married.[76]

This bout lasted only until 8 August, when Elizabeth was well enough for the couple to have sexual intercourse. However, the pain returned. By 21 October Elizabeth was complaining of boils in the 'old place'. She improved after using remedies sent by Dr Williams, the physician who had treated her before for this ailment.[77] This time she remained fairly well until May 1661, when the swelling returned. On 12 May it broke spontaneously and Samuel 'put in a tent (which Dr Williams sent me yesterday) into the hole, to keep it open till all the matter be come out – and so I question not but she will soon be well again'.[78]

After this episode, Elizabeth's 'old pain' mercifully stayed away for nearly three years. However, she was apparently not cured, for on 16 November 1663, Pepys wrote,

> and in the evening Mr. Holliard [a surgeon and friend] came, and he and I about our great work to look upon my wife's malady in her secrets; which he did, and it seems her great conflux of humours heretofore, that used to swell there, did in breaking leave a hollow, which hath since gone in further and further, till it is near three inches deep.[79]

Holliard decided to open the fistula by incision the following night. He arrived, prepared to operate, but found Elizabeth

> so fearful, and the thing will be somewhat painful in the tending, which I [Pepys] shall not be able to look after but must require a nurse and people about her; so that upon second thoughts, he believes that a fomentation will do as well.[80]

This decision relieved both Samuel and Elizabeth. Elizabeth had begged Samuel to stay with her and see the operation done, partly for moral support, partly because she refused to allow anyone else to 'see it done; no, not her own maids; and therefore I must do it, poor wretch, for her'.[81] Samuel was pleased that surgery was unnecessary, 'for I confess I should have been troubled to have had my wife cut before my face – I could not have borne to have seen it'.[82] The painless fomentation Holliard prescribed could be administered by Elizabeth's maid without the maid 'knowing directly what it is for, but only that it may be for the piles – for though it be nothing but what is very honest, yet my wife is loath to give occasion of discourse concerning it'.[83] Thus, Elizabeth's worries about both impending pain and the shame of having her malady generally discussed were dispelled. The fomentation was apparently a success, because Elizabeth never again complained of her 'old pain'.

She did complain of menstrual cramps which sometimes sent her to bed for a few days. These were frequently very bad indeed. On the occasion of the death of Samuel's brother, Tom, Elizabeth stayed at Tom's house to see the deceased laid out; her menstrual period arrived, causing her such discomfort that she had to be taken home and put to bed.[84] Despite the pain, however, Elizabeth seems to have had a fairly regular menstrual cycle. It should also be remarked that her period was not always painful. In no year from 1660 to 1669 did menstruation send her to bed more than four times.

Pepys's diary provides unique documentation of one woman's menstrual history over a long period of time. Samuel did not note Elizabeth's menstruation each time it occurred. He seems to have reported it only when it caused her discomfort. For instance, 1666 must have been a reasonably good year for her, since Samuel made no mention of her menstrual periods at all. None the less, Pepys's diary was the only one located which regularly referred to menstruation at all. It even provides somewhat conflicting information about sexual behaviour during menstruation. On 25 May 1668 Samuel and Elizabeth 'lay long making love', despite the fact that she was ill enough with her menstrual period to have stayed in bed the previous day.[85] However, Pepys was unable to talk Mrs Daniel into a little sexual play at the office the following summer because she was menstruating.[86] Pepys's diary is also informative about some of the terms used to refer to menstruation in mid-seventeenth-century London. He called it Elizabeth's '*mois*' or 'months', '*ceux la*' or simply 'those'.

The exclusively female experiences of pregnancy, childbirth and menstruation were the only subjects relating to health and illness about which the seventeenth-century diarists and correspondents were at all reticent. Certainly these writers were not as inhibited about male genito-urinary troubles. Ralph Josselin suffered for a week in 1647 with swellings in both sides of his groin.[87] As indicated above, Robert Hooke complained of having caught cold in his 'pole'.[88] And, more seriously, Samuel Pepys's father had an old rupture (of at least twenty years' standing) which occasionally escaped the truss which supported it, and caused him intolerable pain. Samuel described one horrifying occasion when he and his father had spent the day together away from home. When he returned after a brief absence from the room, he found his

> father unexpectedly in great pain and desiring for God sake to get him a bed to lie upon; which I did, and . . . I stayed by him, in so great pain as I never saw, poor wretch, and with that patience, crying only: 'Terrible: terrible pain: God help me, God help me' – with that mournful voice, that made my heart ache.

After a time, Samuel got him into a coach and drove home, stopping only once, in 'Paul's Churchyard . . . the jogging and pain making my father vomit – which it never had done before'.[89] Fortunately, after a half hour's rest in bed at home, the sufferer's 'bowels went up again into his belly, being got

forth into his cod, as it seems is usual with very many men –
after which he was at good ease and so continued'.

Perhaps more common than ruptures, and certainly more
deadly, were the kidney and bladder stones which plagued
both women and men. Women both suffered and died from
this disorder. Pepys's mother had a fit of the stone late in
1660.[90] And his Aunt James died of the stone in 1666.[91]
However, if the (largely male) diarists are to be credited, most
of those who had this disorder were male.

John Evelyn's brother Richard died of 'the stone in the
bladder' after having suffered increasing agony for well over a
year, refusing surgical intervention.[92] John described his pain
as 'such exceeding torture . . . that he now began to fall into
convulsion fits'.[93] John Evelyn himself suffered from kidney
stones toward the end of his life. He first reported pain in his
kidneys in March 1682.[94] By March 1692 he 'feared gravel in
my kidneys'.[95] In July 1705, seven months before his death, he
reported 'I had this night a very severe fit of [cold] trembling
& heat after, with very great pai[ne in my] sides & back & all
over my body, all symptoms of the stone'.[96] And by late
December, in addition to his pain he was making 'bloody
water'.[97] It should be remembered that he was 85 years old at
this time.

Robert Hooke visited Sir Christopher Wren when he lay ill
of the stone.[98] Pepys mentioned the death from the stone of
the Lord Treasurer in May 1667.[99] He also marvelled at the
size of the stone cut from the body of Sir Thomas Adam
during the autopsy performed on his body. The stone was

> very large indeed, bigger I think than my fist, and weighs above
> 25 ounces – and which is very miraculous, never in all his life had
> any fit of it, but lived to a great age without pain, and died at last
> of something else, without any sense of this in all his life.[100]

By contrast, Robert Hooke described the death of the Bishop
of Chester. Everyone had assumed the bishop had the stone,
which had caused the urinary retention which finally killed
him. However, the account of the autopsy given by Dr
Needham indicated that the bishop had had

> no stoppage in his ureters nor defect in his kidneys. There was
> only found 2 small stones in one kidney and some little gravel in
> one ureter but neither big enough to stop the water. Twas
> believed his opiates and some other medicines killed him, there
> being no visible cause of his death.[101]

Without a doubt, the most famous sufferer from the stone of all time was Samuel Pepys himself. He was successfully cut for the stone by the surgeon Thomas Holliard on 26 March 1658. Thereafter, he held an annual celebration to commemorate the event. He maintained a special interest in genito–urinary problems, conversing with medical specialists on the subject and at one point attending a lecture about it at the Surgeon's Hall.[102]

He also made of himself a minor celebrity among his wide acquaintance on the basis of his recovery from the 'disease of the stone'. He visited people who were suffering from that disorder, urging them to undergo surgery, and displaying the stone which had been removed from his own body as an inducement. John Evelyn took Pepys to visit his brother Richard nine months before Richard's death. He wrote that Pepys 'carried the stone (which was as big as a tennis–ball) to shew him [Richard], and encourage his resolution to go through the operation'.[103]

It should be said that Pepys's enthusiasm for the operation had a sound basis, not only in his personal experience, but also in the evidence given by the London Bills of Mortality. In most years many more people died of the disease than died of the operation. The exceptions were, ironically, 1659 and 1660 when more people died of the operation.

Although surgery possibly saved Pepys's life and certainly spared him a good deal of pain, he was not entirely free of problems stemming from either the original disorder or the operation which had been performed to cure it. For the entire period covered by his diary, 1660–9, Pepys complained of a variety of related ills, ranging from pain and swelling of his 'cods', to difficulty in urination, to the actual passage of two stones in March 1665.[104] However, probably because of his fear of the pain he obviously had suffered before his operation, Pepys was unwilling to attribute any later symptoms to his earlier disease. Recurring tenderness and swelling of his testicles, combined with pain and difficulty in urination, he almost always attributed either to bruising or to taking cold.[105] Even when he actually passed two stones, he wrote 'I could feel them, and caused my water to be looked into, but without any pain to me in going out – which makes me think that it was not a fit of the stone at all'.[106] The following day he wrote 'I hope my disease of the stone may not return to me, but void itself in pissing'.[107]

This hope and the fear which accompanied it were never far from Pepys's mind. Indeed, he was even loath to use the words, 'the stone', instead referring to that disorder by implication. Thus, when he suffered from constant backache in June 1664, he wrote that he feared 'the worst'.[108] He was even apparently relieved, though mystified, when, in the following month, the physician Dr Burnett diagnosed an ulcer either in the kidneys or bladder.[109] He must have felt even better when in August Mr Holliard disagreed with this diagnosis, saying that the pain Pepys was suffering was 'nothing but cold in my legs breeding wind, and got only by my using to wear a gown'.[110]

Pepys suffered from another disorder which was probably unrelated to his urinary problems. This was the recurring colic, wind and constipation mentioned above. Although he complained of this disorder on and off throughout the 1660s, he suffered most acutely from it from September to December 1663. It gave him pain in his back and abdomen, and made it difficult for him to produce natural bowel movements. He also complained of pain in his cods and yard which resulted from 'straining to stool'.[111] As was the case with his urinary problems, Pepys worried a lot about this disorder, writing in October 1663, 'In no great pain, but do not think myself likely to be well till I have a freedom of stool and wind'.[112] Four days later he was able to report with pleasure that he had had his first natural bowel movement for five or six days.[113] Needless to say, he attributed none of his discomfort to the massive amount of physic he took during this illness.

Pepys had another relatively minor, though recurring, ailment. This was the swelling, redness and itching which attacked his whole body, mainly in cold weather. He first suffered from it in February 1663.[114] It not only made him feel ill, but also made him 'ashamed of myself to see myself so changed in my countenance'. Fortunately, on the first occasion, the 'itching and pimples' passed in two days. By the last time he experienced these symptoms, January 1665, Pepys was not particularly worried about them, writing 'and I find myself, as heretofore in cold weather, to begin to burn within and pimple and prick all over my body, my pores with cold being shut up'.[115]

Other diarists had illness profiles of their own, of course. Ralph Josselin's, Margaret Hoby's and Alice Thornton's will be discussed at length below. Some descriptions of symptoms are too brief and vague to be of use in compiling a medical biography. Other sources, like Dorothy Osborne's letters, Lady Margaret Clifford's diary and Roger Lowe's diary, are either too short, too intermittent, or too much devoted to other matters to yield much medical evidence.[116] Some diarists, such as John Evelyn, were remarkably healthy, suffering mainly from relatively minor common ailments.

Robert Hooke, whose physic-taking will be discussed at greater length below, presents a somewhat confusing picture. His multitudinous ailments can hardly be attributed to hypochondria. He was a chronically ailing child who, in his first seven years, ate only diary products and fruit, 'no flesh in the least agreeing with his weak constitution'.[117] As a teenager, Hooke was apprenticed to the portrait painter, Peter Lely, but had to leave this study because he could not stand the smell of paint.[118] Waller's description of his appearance as an adult suggests some form of physical illness or disability:

> As to his person he was but despicable, being very crooked, tho' I have heard from himself, and others, that he was straight till about 16 years of Age when he first grew awry, but frequent practicing, turning with a Turn-Lath, and the like incurvating Exercises, being but of a thin weak habit of body, which increased as he grew older, so as to be very remarkable at last: This made him but low of stature, tho' by his limbs he should have been moderately tall. He was always very pale and lean, and latterly nothing but skin and bone.[119]

However, Hooke almost never complained of specific illnesses, except for colds and minor stomach upsets. His most distressing symptoms were giddiness and sleeplessness, for which he dosed himself radically and experimented with various changes in diet. Indeed, one almost could argue that Hooke used his own body and its reactions as a kind of laboratory, testing a multitude of substances for their properties and the characteristics of his own responses to them over time. Thus, Hooke's contribution to this study will be very much in his role as patient rather than in his role as sufferer, although one cannot deny that he did suffer.[120]

Otherwise, Hooke's diary and the other sources consulted yield a good deal of miscellaneous information about the illness experiences of both the writers and the people who surrounded them. This information tends to support the evidence yielded by the London Bills of Mortality. For instance, the diarists mentioned a number of children who died young. Both John Evelyn and Sir Christopher Wren lost infants to convulsion fits.[121] Evelyn lost a 7-week-old baby to teeth and dropsy.[122] And both Evelyn and Ralph Josselin had children who were livergrown. Evelyn gave a useful description of this condition as it was diagnosed during an autopsy performed on the body of 5-year-old Richard:

> Being opened they found a membranous substance growing to the cavous part of the liver, somewhat near the edge of it for the compass of 3 inches, which ought not to be; for the liver is fixed only by three strong ligaments, all far distant from that part, insomuch as it could not move in that part; on which they confidently affirmed, the child was (as tis vulgarly called) liver-grown & thence that sickness & so frequent complaint of his side: & indeed both liver & spleen were exceedingly large.[123]

The spleen was apparently a disease most common among women and children.[124] The evidence of the diaries and correspondence consulted supports this observation. Lady Anne Clifford and Dorothy Osborne suffered from the spleen.[125] Lady Anne described her symptoms as a pain in her side; Dorothy Osborne's seem to have been mainly emotional and temperamental. Ralph Josselin's daughter Jane suffered from the same ailment.[126]

Only two of the diarists gave a personal account of undergoing a contagious disease. Alice Thornton and her family suffered multiple attacks of smallpox. John Evelyn contracted the disease while travelling in Switzerland in 1646.[127] His was a mild case, producing few spots and confining him to his chamber for only five weeks. However, it was both frightening and expensive. Evelyn paid his host forty-five pistoles of gold for lodging and nursing, his physician five pistoles for advice and medication.[128]

Although the other diarists escaped smallpox, at least during the periods in which they kept diaries, everyone knew someone who had had the disease. Several of Ralph Josselin's children caught it as teenagers, after becoming servants or apprentices in London.[129] And Hooke and Pepys frequently commented on the smallpox victims among their acquaintance.

Hooke's experience of the disease, although not personal, was intimate. A servant of his, Tom Gyles, died of smallpox after only three days of suffering.[130] Tom's attack was very acute. The day before he died he was both 'pissing blood' and bleeding at the nose and mouth — symptoms which his physicians interpreted as mortal.[131] Hooke's niece Grace also had a severe bout of smallpox while she was keeping house for him. She was ill for nearly three months during the summer of 1679.[132]

Although none of the diarists and correspondents or their

immediate family members suffered from plague, Samuel Pepys and John Evelyn wrote fascinating descriptions of plague-ridden London. These, along with Ralph Josselin's reflections on plague, will be incorporated into our discussion of ideas and attitudes regarding disease. The same use will be made of the diarists' references to syphilis. These diseases were powerful in name as well as in experience, affecting those they spared as well as those they attacked.

6

SUFFERERS AND PATIENTS: APPROACHES TO ILLNESS

The seventeenth-century English had two main approaches to illness, which, for the purposes of this study, will be called religious and secular. A subsidiary approach to illness, the magical approach, related to both secular and religious orientations, and will be described below. At the outset of this chapter, it should be emphasised that these three categories are employed largely because they provide a useful structure for discussion. Although they can be identified in seventeenth-century writing and behaviour, the categories are themselves somewhat anachronistic.

Secular and religious approaches to illness existed side by side. It was rare, if not unheard of, for any individual to be characterised by one approach to the exclusion of the other. The most secular people, Samuel Pepys for example, thanked God for their escapes from disease. Indeed, to divorce the divine from any aspect of human experience would have been an admission of atheism, a virtually incomprehensible position in seventeenth-century England. The pragmatic surgeon, Joseph Binns, whose career has been described above, acknowledged his debt to God by concluding the notes for a successful case with the words 'laus deo' or 'laus soli deo'.

By the same token, even the very religious, such as the Reverend Ralph Josselin, employed secular explanations and therapies in times of illness. Not to have done so would have been to disregard the gifts of God to mankind – to look a gift horse in the mouth, so to speak. None the less, the religious and secular approaches to illness can be distinguished in both the private papers (diaries and correspondence) and the published literature consulted. Medical behaviour depended to some extent upon the spiritual orientation of the sufferer.

The secular and religious approaches to illness did not necessarily operate in opposition to one another. For instance, it was generally agreed that God had the power both to inflict and to cure disease. It was also piously assumed that God had created certain medicinal substances and appointed certain healers (usually physicians) to help human beings battle illness.[1] This having been said, however, it should also be observed that the religious approach to illness favoured passive prayer and trust in God, while the secular approach was characterised by as active an attack as possible on the symptoms and causes of the illness.

Exemplifying the religious approach were the numerous books and pamphlets which might be called the literature of moral medicine. These works were intended for the use of laymen, who read them for both entertainment and instruction. Typical was Bishop Lancelot Andrewes's *A Sermon of the Pestilence*, which, although first preached in 1603, was published in 1636. While he paid lip-service to the knowledge and expertise of physicians, Andrewes argued that if the primary cause of illness – the wrath of God – be not dealt with, the other methods of dealing with it were bound to fail. In his own words,

> And as the Balm of Gilead, and the Physician there, may yield us help, when God's wrath is removed: so if it be not, no balm, no medicine will serve. Let us with the Woman in the Gospel [Mark 5, 26] spend all upon Physicians, we shall be never the better, till we come to Christ, and he cures us of our sins who is the only Physician of the diseases of the soul.

Andrewes's argument is well stated by the earlier secular writer, William Bullein, in his *A Dialogue against the Fever Pestilence*, published in 1578.[2] In this popular work the well-to-do Civis, after trying various remedies for his illness, realises he is dying. He says to his wife,

> Now my body is past cure, no Physic can prevail. . . . From henceforth . . . I shall be turned into a stinking carrion for worm's delight, dust, clay, rotten, most vile, forsaken of all men, poor without substance, naked without clothing, sown in dishonour, forgotten of my posterity, not known henceforth, vanish like a shadow, wither like a leaf, and fade as a flower.[3]

His wife wants to send for the physician, but Civis says,

> Help me into some house, whereas I might send for some man of God to be my heavenly Physician, teaching me the way to the Kingdom of Christ.[4]

Even works which were intended mainly to provide secular

information address quite seriously the religious issues involved. The well-known *The Anatomy of Melancholy*, by Robert Burton, first published in 1621, is one such book. Burton wrote that the general causes of illness were either supernatural or natural.

> Supernatural are from God and his angels, or, by God's permission, from the devil and his ministers. That God himself is a cause, for the punishment of sin, and satisfaction of his justice, many examples & testimonies of holy Scriptures make evident unto us.[5]

Although he advocated the consultation of physicians in cases of melancholy, Burton cautiously reminded readers that 'From Jove is our origin; we must first begin with prayer, and then use physick; not one without the other, but both together'.[6] He even suggested that physick might not work without prayer.[7]

The belief that God sent diseases in order to punish or educate human beings was pervasive. The many fast-days proclaimed by seventeenth-century parliaments were directed at propitiating divine wrath. God was capable of inflicting any sort of disaster. For instance, in January 1662 Pepys reported that Parliament had ordered a fast-day

> to pray for more seasonable weather – it having hitherto been some summer weather, that it is, both as to warmth and every other thing, just as if it were the middle of May or June, which doth threaten a plague (as all men think) to follow; for so it was almost the last winter, and the whole year after hath been a very sickly time, to this day.[8]

Any event out of the ordinary could be interpreted as an indication of divine displeasure. However, the most universally recognised weapon God employed was the plague.

It was generally agreed that plague was the result of human sin. Thus, the many pamphlets published during or immediately after plague years blamed mankind rather than God for the misery the epidemics produced. For instance, a pamphlet published in 1593 was entitled *An Approved Medicine Against the Deserved Plague*.[9] Its author wrote,

> And now my beloved, and important charge, I beseech you by the mercies of God, remember with me, there is no plague but for sin, and the Lion roareth not without his prey. We are now under this growing plague with others, let us repent effectually as others

which truly seek the Lord, cast our sins from us, and draw the Lord's mercy to us.[10]

The tone of such writers did not change in the course of the following century. Richard Alleine's book, published in 1667, rejoiced in the lengthy title, *The Best of Remedies for the Worst of Maladies: or Spiritual Receipts and Antidotes for the Preservation of a Plague-Sick Sinfull Soul. Wherein is shown, sin is the Cause, and Repentence the Cure of the Pestilence. Seasonably published by a Lover of Peace and Truth: and one that desireth that all would (though the Lord's hand seems to be withdrawn, as to the late universally raging Pestilential Disease) forsake those Provoking sins, which call for Vengeance and Judgements on the Sons of Men.*

It is certainly not surprising that plague was identified as the Lord's preferred method of punishing collective sin. Although a great many remedies and preventatives existed for plague, nothing really helped. The disease was devastating in both the speed of its attack and the effects it produced. Not only did it kill, but also it completely disrupted social, economic and political life. The wealthy, including many in positions of authority and responsibility, fled before it. This group included both medical personnel and clergymen who might have been most useful in comforting and helping those who had to remain within striking distance of the plague. Shops were shut, church services forbidden, Parliament suspended.

Samuel Pepys wrote such excellent descriptions of plague-ridden London that they are worth quoting at length. In June 1665 he wrote,

> This day, much against my will, I did in Drury Lane see two or three houses marked with a red cross upon the doors and 'Lord have mercy upon us' writ there – which was a sad sight to me, being the first of that kind that to my remembrance I ever saw. It put me into an ill conception of myself and my smell, so that I was forced to buy some roll tobacco to smell to and chaw – which took away the apprehension.[11]

By early August he reported, 'The streets mighty empty all the way now, even in London, which is a sad sight'.[12] On 22 August he wrote,

> I went away and walked to Greenwich, in my way seeing a coffin with a dead body therein, dead of the plague, lying in an open close . . . which was carried out last night and the parish hath not appointed anybody to bury it – but only set a watch there day and night, that nobody should go thither or come thence, which is a

most cruel thing – this disease making us more cruel to one
another then we are [to] dogs.[13]

On 20 September:

But Lord, what a sad time it is, to see no boats upon the River –
and grass grow all up and down Whitehall-Court – and nobody
but poor wretches in the streets.[14]

And finally, on 16 October:

But Lord, how empty the streets are, and melancholy, so many
poor sick people in the streets, full of sores, and so many sad
stories overheard as I walk, everybody talking of this dead, and
that man sick, and so many in this place, and so many in that.
And they tell me that in Westminster there is never a physician,
and but one apothecary left, all being dead – but that there are
great hopes of a great decrease this week: God send it.[15]

The plague did not actually abate until mid-winter.

Pepys was unusual for one of his class and wide social
contacts in that he stayed in London throughout the period of
the epidemic. He sent his wife and servants to Woolwich,
however, to put them beyond reach of contagion. Evelyn sent
his family to Wotton to his brother's home. Like Pepys, he
spent some time in London on official business, but did not
concern himself as much as Pepys did with the havoc the
plague was causing in the city. He seems mainly to have
observed the misery when it was thrust upon him, writing in
October 1665,

I returned to London: I went through the whole City, having
occasion to alight out of the Coach in several places about
business of money, when I was environed with multitudes of
poor pestiferous creatures, begging alms; the shops universally
shut up, a dreadful prospect.[16]

Both Pepys and Evelyn obviously felt that the plague
epidemic was a lottery. Both knew of people in high places
who had died of the disease, and by no means felt confident
about escaping it themselves. Evelyn reported that he had a
fainting fit while dining with his brother, 'which much
alarmed the family, as well it might, I coming so lately from
infected places, but I bless God it went off'.[17] Pepys took
several preventatives, including the tobacco mentioned above,
Venice Treacle and plague water given him by Lady Carteret,

hoping to ward off infection.[18] When his servant Will had to take to his bed with a headache, Pepys was in 'extraordinary fear'.[19]

However much Pepys and Evelyn feared the plague, others feared it more. Pepys's surgeon, Mr Holliard, and his minister, Mr Mills, both left London. Mr Mills had apparently left 'the parish before anybody went and now [stayed] till all are come home'.[20] Pepys's physician, Dr Burnett, might have gone as well, but Burnett was confined to his house early in the epidemic because one of his servants contracted plague. The physician died of the disease in August, shortly after his house was reopened.[21] London physicians left the city in great numbers and felt defensive about their behaviour later. Pepys reported that, at the first meeting of the Royal Society after the worst of the epidemic had ended, Dr Goddard (Robert Hooke's physician) defended the physicians' actions, 'saying that their particular patients were most gone out of town, and they left at liberty − and a great deal more, etc'.[22]

Fear of the 1665 plague was not confined to London and its vicinity. Ralph Josselin, although living in the relatively safe village of Earls Colne, Essex, was terrified of the plague. His fear, which will be discussed at length in another chapter, arose from his conviction that the plague was God's supreme punishment for sin.[23] Such collective punishment resulted from collective sin. To appease God's anger, collective repentance was required. Josselin felt that his village was very sinful, and that the total repentance both he and the Lord required was not forthcoming. He was amazed that, with the exception of one or two cases, the village was spared.[24]

Josselin's might be said to exemplify the religious approach to illness. Although he used conventional remedies for his many ailments, he almost never consulted healers. The only medicine he really trusted was prayer. Perhaps the reason he was less frightened of non-epidemic than he was of epidemic disorders was that he believed his prayers and those of his family would act as spiritual preventative medicine. Most certainly he believed that the illnesses and deaths of members of his family directly resulted from specific sins − usually his own. And even when 'secular' causes of ailments could be identified − cold weather producing a cold, for instance − Josselin might well have asked who sent the cold weather? The answer is obvious.

Josselin's faith supported him through long illnesses. These he could regard either as God's punishment or God's test of his faith. Even at one point in his life when he felt a bit out of touch with his heavenly Father – a feeling he described as .a spiritual deadness – he never felt that re-establishment of contact was impossible. He simply continued to pray. His faith also helped him in times of bereavement. When his well-beloved daughter Mary lay dying at the age of 8, Josselin was able to write 'fear came on my heart very much, but she is not mine, but the Lord's'.[25] And even when a sick child did not die, Josselin frequently resigned him or her to God. He also saw the manifestations of certain diseases as symptomatic of the human spiritual condition, writing when his son Tom had smallpox, 'Tom's pox came out after a treacle posset. At night they began to run, oh that the inward filth and corruption of our heart might be drawn out'.[26]

For Josselin, all events were related to the providence of God. He wrote in 1658, 'One Dorothy Layer, being got with child by a weaver, afterwards was married to him, and delivered before her time, and died. God make such things to be warning to us'.[27] And in 1657 he wrote, rather smugly, 'it was no small mercy in my eyes that when agues and fevers as formerly the smallpox stepped in at many doors God preserved me and mine'.[28]

Josselin's viewpoint and medical behaviour certainly was reflected elsewhere in the population. The Lancashire mercer, Roger Lowe, was frequently called upon to pray with ailing neighbours who, like himself, were Presbyterians.[29] However, Josselin's dependence on prayer as the best physic was not typical even of other very religious people. The pious Lady Margaret Hoby, whose diary was written essentially as a spiritual record for the years 1599–1605, took physic, consulted healers, and even acted as an unlicensed general practitioner for people living in her remote area of Yorkshire. And Josselin's contemporary, the Reverend John Ward, served as both minister and physician in Stratford-upon-Avon from 1662 to 1681.[30] Thus, it must be emphasised that it is impossible to generalise about medical behaviour in the period, or even to assume a certain type of behaviour on the basis of knowledge of an individual's religious and occupational profile. Individual character, or humour, was, one suspects, a major factor determining behaviour in times of illness.

Distinctions made between 'religious' and 'superstitious' approaches to illness are invidious. Other terms must be found. None the less, since people living in seventeenth-century England themselves distinguished between 'lawful' religious practices and 'unlawful' practices smacking of witchcraft, demonianism, heresy or 'popishness', it would be improper to omit these practices, as they related to medicine, from our discussion.

None of the lay diaries or collections of correspondence examined in the course of this study described personal consultations of magical healers. However, these sources do yield evidence of practices at least related to magical beliefs. For instance, Samuel Pepys felt that his 'very perfect good health' in March 1665 was due to a combination of keeping his back cool, taking a turpentine pill every morning and carrying a hare's foot.[31] He also described the apparently usual practice of putting pigeons to the feet of a dying person.[32] Robert Hooke recorded numerous successful cures produced by unorthodox means. Perhaps most remarkable was the case in which Sir Christopher Wren cured his wife of a thrush 'by hanging a bag of live boglice around her neck'.[33] A patient of the London surgeon, Joseph Binns, did not find ease from a facial burn until she had stroked her scarred eyelid with 'a dead hand'.[34] And the physician Francis Herring wrote *A Modest Defence of the Caveat Given to the Wearers of impoisoned Amulets as preservatives from the plague* (1604), in which he advanced no objection to the wearing of amulets, provided that wearers did not neglect internal preventative medicines.

Certain medicinal substances routinely sold by apothecaries were valuable partly because of their inherent magical properties. One such substance was mummy – literally bits or powder of mummified human bodies. Pepys reported having seen a mummy in a merchant's warehouse:

> all the middle of the man or woman's body black and hard; I never saw any before, and therefore pleased me much, though an ill sight; and he did give me a little bit, and a bone of an arm I suppose.[35]

Another frequently used substance was human or animal excrement. The man–midwife Percival Willughby believed 'that an ass's hoof, or dung, put on coals, and the fume received under the labouring woman's clothes, will draw forth the child'.[36]

Such remedies, along with many others, were used by magical healers, in conjunction with rituals designed to relieve the sufferer.[37] Although not as frequently resorted to as the remedies themselves, these healers were apparently widely consulted. John Cotta, whose anti-quack writings have been referred to above, was thinking of magical practitioners in addition to other unauthorised healers when he maintained,

> So many and so infinitely do the numbers of barberous and
> unlearned counsellors of health at this time overspread all corners
> of this Kingdom, that their confused swarms do not only
> everywhere cover and eclipse the sun-shine of all true learning &
> understanding but generally darken and extinguish the very light
> of common sense and reason.[38]

And the licentiate in physic and surgery, Edward Poeton,
wrote,

> So then, . . . it is not to be held a thing to be either new or
> strange that white witches should find so many friends and
> favourers (as now they do) in this last corrupt age of the world, in
> the which most men mind earthly things.[39]

Those who attacked magical healers did not usually argue that
magical methods could not cure. Indeed, reserving their
scepticism for those who knowingly pretended magical
powers, most writers assumed that magic *could* cure. Robert
Burton argued,

> Many famous cures are daily done in this kind, the Devil is an
> expert Physician . . . and God permits oftentimes these Witches
> and Magicians to produce such effects. . . . Such cures may be
> done, and, as Paracelsus stiffly maintains, they cannot otherwise
> be cured but by spells, seals, and spiritual physick.[40]

And Burton went on to state the case:

> It being assumed that they can effect such cures, the main question
> is whether it be lawful in a desperate case to crave their help, or a
> Wizard's advice. 'Tis a common practice of some men to go first
> to a witch, and then to a Physician; if one cannot, the other shall;
> if they cannot bend Heaven, they will try Hell. It matters not,
> saith Paracelsus, whether it be God or the Devil, Angels of
> unclean Spirits cure him, so that he be eased.[41]

However, regardless of the relief magical healers can bring,

> *Evil is not to be done that good may come of it.* Much better it were
> for such patients, that are so troubled, to endure a little misery in
> this life than to hazard their soul's health for ever, and . . . much
> better to die than be so cured.[42]

The belief that magic could cure was crucial. On the basis of this belief it was possible for people to consult and praise the white witch, wise-man or -woman, and cunning-man or -woman, while condemning the activities of witches practising harmful black magic. Thus, Poeton's character Gregory, speaking for all of 'the giddy headed vulgar', argues that, as cunning-folk get their skill from God, it is no sin to consult them.[43] Gregory and his living counterparts were willing to risk divine displeasure (if, as they doubted, God actually disapproved of white magic) in order to obtain cures.

In discussing 'magical' cures, it must not be forgotten that seventeenth-century sufferers made no artificial distinction between such remedies and the supposedly rational remedies listed in the *London Pharmacopoeia*.[44] As Keith Thomas points out, 'From the patient's point of view . . . , all medical prescriptions beyond his comprehension were in a sense magical, since they worked by occult means'.[45] Indeed, the same holds true today. How many in our 'enlightened' age can give a rational explanation of how aspirin relieves headaches? Thus, this categorisation of 'religious', 'magical' and 'secular' approaches to illness is employed merely for the sake of convenience. At best, it overemphasises a reality which existed; at worst, it gives a false impression by anachronistically exaggerating elements of belief and behaviour.

Virtually everyone in seventeenth-century England had a humoral view of the human body, health and illness. This generalisation covers those who employed magical healing techniques, those with an essentially religious approach to the causes and cures of illness, those adhering to academic orthodox medical theories and those espousing relatively new schools of medical thought, such as Paracelsians, Van Helmontians, iatro-chemists and iatro-mechanists.[46] Popular humoralism showed itself in many ways. It acted as a basis for describing physical appearance and behaviour. For instance, John Evelyn described his father as

> of a sanguine complexion, mix'd with a dash of choler. . . . He was for his life so exact and temperate, that I have heard he had never in all his life been surprised by excess, being ascetic and sparing.[47]

Humoralism was also evident in prophylactic and remedial therapeutics, which were directed at producing evacuation, whatever the intellectual orientations of the prescriber and the patient. Regardless of whether treatment actually cured disease, its importance cannot be underrated. Proper application of therapy might, for instance, prevent a relatively minor disorder from becoming worse. For instance, Evelyn was bled in the early stages of smallpox – a procedure usually not advised under those conditions. Evelyn's physician excused himself later by telling Evelyn that his blood 'was so burnt and vitious, as it would have proved the plague or spotted fever, had he proceeded by any other method'.[48]

Popular humoralism dovetailed nicely with popular astrology, which helped to explain variations in health and illness phenomena from person to person and time to time. Evelyn, for instance, was referring to his astrological profile when he noted the exact time of his birth – twenty past two a.m., Tuesday, 21 October 1620.[49] Astrology also was used to establish medical routines. It determined when medical herbs should be planted, harvested and prescribed. It also determined when particular individuals should undergo various types of treatment.[50] For example, astrology was responsible for the tradition of taking prophylactic physic in the spring.[51]

The humoral/astrological approach provided a satisfactory basis for the explanation and treatment of illness which was not successfully challenged on the popular level until the nineteenth century. It related the individual to the natural universe as well as co-ordinating the multitudinous parts of the human body into a comprehensive whole. It also opted out of religious controversy by allowing for the existence of the soul at the individual end of the spectrum and God as prime-mover at the universal end.

Thus, seventeenth-century sufferers could be far more confident about explaining their ailments than can their twentieth-century descendants. Pepys, for example, always knew the causes of his various aches and pains. More often than not, the culprit was cold. Thus, in November 1662 he developed 'some pain in making water, having taken cold this morning in staying too long barelegged to pare my corns'.[52] In September 1665, while visiting his wife in lodgings in Woolwich, where she was staying in order to avoid the plague, Pepys reported

> And so I to bed, and in the night was mightily troubled with a looseness (I suppose from some fresh damp Linen that I put on this night); and feeling for a chamber pot, there was none . . . ; so I was forced in this strange house to rise and shit in the chimney twice.[53]

According to Pepys, he was nearly always responsible for his own disorders. One might suppose that this gave rise to a good deal of guilt. However, it also allowed the hope that proper behaviour would produce health. In October 1663, when Pepys was recovering from a period of constipation and colic, he resolved upon a 'regiment of health' which he was sure would prevent recurrence:

1. To begin to keep myself warm as I can.
2. Strain as little as ever I can backwards, remembering that my pain [in penis and testicles] will come by and by, though in the very straining I do not feel it.
3. Either by physic forward or by clyster backward, or both ways, to get an easy and plentiful going to stool and breaking of wind.
4. To begin to suspect my health immediately when I begin to become costive and bound, and by all means to keep my body loose, and that to obtain presently after I find myself going to the contrary.[54]

This was but one of Pepys's good resolutions, taken to maintain or improve his health. He frequently vowed to give up drinking wine, to stop going to plays and, when his eyes began to fail, to stop reading by candle-light. However, Pepys was one of the best intentioned, but worst disciplined of men. Temptation always mastered him.

Robert Hooke also was confident about the causes of his own symptoms. For instance, he caught cold in August 1676 by wearing a new velvet coat and cloth breeches.[55] In December 1672 he complained of giddiness resulting partly from 'drinking milk and posset drink at night and partly from coldness of peruke'.[56] Like Pepys, Hooke made many resolutions designed to improve his health. His resolutions usually took the form of either deciding to take or give up a certain substance, such as chocolate, whey or tobacco, or resolving to give up all other employments in order to concentrate on his health.

The confidence Pepys, Hooke and other diarists displayed about the diagnoses and explanation of their own ailments resulted in the conviction that they, as individuals, were responsible for their illnesses in all senses of the word. In this they were quite typical. Seventeenth-century English men and women owned their own disorders. Even when they consulted healers, they reserved the option to accept, dictate or reject the therapies offered.

Their confidence was sometimes supported by the reading

of medical works. Indeed, much of the vernacular medical literature was specifically directed at lay-men. Many home-medicine and first aid handbooks were designed to help those who lived in remote areas or could not afford the services of physicians and surgeons.[57] Equally important were the many 'regiments of health', designed to help the reader prevent disease by establishing healthy living habits.[58] Other works, such as almanacks, cookbooks and gardening manuals, gave medical advice and recipes in addition to other information.

As Paul Slack points out in a recent article, one must be cautious in making assumptions about the extent to which these books were read or their ideas disseminated. He writes, 'Such works can scarcely have reached the illiterate poor, and the extent of the diffusion even among the literate may well be questioned'.[59] None the less, the hundreds of works giving medical information which were published in English make possible the tentative assumptions that there was a market for this sort of literature and that the ideas so vended influenced medical behaviour.

Certainly seventeenth-century diarists confirm this assumption. It is no surprise that Robert Hooke, who took an MD in 1691, read a number of medical works.[60] Lady Margaret Hoby had read Turner's *Herbal* and Bartholomew Vigo as part of her general education.[61] Grace Sherrington, born in 1552, read daily from her 'Herball and books of physick'.[62] And Ralph Josselin read two medical books in the year 1649.[63]

Seventeenth-century plays reveal both a considerable amount of medical knowledge and the assumption that their medical allusions and metaphors would be appreciated by their audiences. For instance, Beaumont and Fletcher lampooned both the practice of uroscopy and physicians who used it. Three physicians made three diagnoses from one flask of urine, thus:

1 Physician.	A plurisie, I see it.
2 Physician.	I rather hold it
	For tumour cordis.
3 Physician.	Do you mark the faeces?
	'Tis a most pestilent contagious fever,
	A surfeit, a plaguey surfeit; he must bleed.
1 Physician.	By no means.
3 Physician.	I say bleed.
1 Physician.	I say 'tis dangerous;
	The person being spent so much before-hand,

<table>
<tr><td></td><td>And nature drawn so low, clysters, cool clysters.</td></tr>
<tr><td>2 Physician.</td><td>Now with your favours I should think a vomit:
For take away the cause, and the effect must
follow,
The stomach's foul and fur'd, the pot's unflam'd
yet.</td></tr>
<tr><td>3 Physician.</td><td>No, no, we'll rectifie that part by mild means,
Nature so sunk must find no violence.[64]</td></tr>
</table>

People used the medical knowledge they gathered from their reading and from oral tradition to treat themselves, their family members, and their friends and acquaintances. Self-treatment was surely the most common type of medical therapy in seventeenth-century England. The diaries and collections of correspondence consulted are replete with examples of self-diagnosis. For instance, although most physicians no longer used uroscopy for the purposes of diagnosis by the mid-seventeenth century, many lay-men examined their own urine. Josselin, Pepys and Hooke all described characteristics of their 'water' in times of illness.[65]

People also prescribed for themselves. The remedies used were sometimes purchased at apothecaries' shops which, of course, laboured under no restrictions regarding prescription versus non-prescription drugs. In addition, many people, particularly women, made their own medicines. Dorothy Osborne dosed both herself and William Temple for colds with an unspecified medicine she had prepared herself:

'tis like the rest of my medicines, if it do no good 'twill be sure to do no harm, and 'twill be no great trouble to you to eat a little on't now and then, for the taste, as it is not Excellent, so 'tis not very ill.[66]

And Samuel Pepys usually tried to cure himself before consulting a healer. For instance, when he suffered from a combination of wind and difficulty in urination in July 1666, he took a clyster of sack and a coach ride, hoping to find relief.[67]

Undoubtedly Robert Hooke was the great seventeenth-century medicine-taker. Indeed, his diary gives the impression that Hooke considered many types of human activity, including eating, drinking, sleeping, dressing, exercise and orgasm, almost entirely in the light of their medical effects.

Thus, in examining his diary, it is difficult to determine where medicine-taking stopped and simple dining or snacking, for instance, began. As indicated above, aside from occasional colds, Hooke suffered from few of what his contemporaries would have recognised as diseases. Rather, he complained of recurring symptoms, including sleeplessness, indigestion, giddiness, loss of sense of smell, a noise in his head, an evil taste in his mouth and headaches. To prevent and cure these symptoms, he took a massive amount of medicine. Indeed, it is tempting to suggest, rather snidely, that most of his ailments were caused by Hooke's efforts to find health.

Hooke tended to give each new remedy a trial period. When he started writing his diary in August 1672, he had been drinking an iron and mercury preparation for a while. He then moved on to a steel drink. After that for a time he depended almost entirely on Dulwich water, taken from a natural spring at that location which was, 'at that time a pleasant hamlet 5 miles from London . . . , famous for its medicinal waters'.[68] He also used a preparation called Andrew's cordial for a long time, took Dr Goddard's tincture of centaury, swallowed Aldersgate cordial, drank senna and jalap in various liquids, took sal tartari and sal amoniac, and used a Mexican jalap called mechoacan. All of these remedies were expected to purge him. In addition, he took a variety of emetics. When these did not produce the desired vomits, he employed either a feather or a whalebone. To help him sleep, he took opiates. He bathed an aching shoulder with aqua vitae. He also was blistered, cupped and scarified by the healers he consulted.

In addition to taking medicine, Hooke deliberately experimented with substances not universally considered medicinal. For long periods he drank great quantities of chocolate, coffee, tea, whey, burnt claret and 'malago' wine. He smoked tobacco on and off. He ate stewed prunes and cherries. He also drank a diet drink recommended by a friend's wife, which he called 'Tillotson's ale'.

Hooke recorded the effects of both the measures he took to obtain health and the incidental behaviour which produced results. He frequently reported whether the food he ate digested well. Indeed, both the food he ate and the conditions under which he ate it were significant. Thus, on 19 March 1677, when his dinner digested well, Hooke wrote:

> I judge somewhat to be attributed to change of air, partly to a pleasant small beer, possibly to the warmer weather, possibly to my drinking ale with toast and cheese in the morning.[69]

Indeed, he was supremely confident in his interpretations of how various foods affected him. For instance, on one occasion rice pudding caused him to sleep badly.[70] Another time, he drank 'malago', which made him sick, then drank chocolate, which 'cleared his stomach'.[71]

Hooke was equally certain about the effects of the remedies he took. Most often, they 'wrought well'. Sometimes, they did not produce the desired purge or vomit and, by remaining in his stomach, caused discomfort. For instance, on 20 July 1673 he 'drank Dulwich', then 'slept ill, the water lying still in my belly, not so well next morning as last week'.[72]

Hooke's certainty about which substances caused which reactions gave rise to some complicated record-keeping. One powerful substance could produce many results. On 27 April 1674 Hooke 'took Dr. Thomson's vomit. It vomited twice. Purged 10 or 12 times. . . . Made me sleep ill, and made my arms paralytic with a great noise in my head. I had also some gnawing at the bottom of my belly'.[73] By the same token, several substances produced contrary results. On 16 February 1673 Hooke took Andrew's cordial, which purged him and

> brought much slime out of the guts and made me cheerful. Eat Dinner with good stomach and pannado at night but drinking posset upon it put me into a feverish sweat which made me sleep very unquiet and much disturbed my head and stomach. Taking sneezing tobacco about 3 in the morn clear my head much and made me cheerful afterwards I slept about 2 hours, but my head was disturbed when I waked.[74]

As one might expect, Hooke occasionally became infatuated with a new remedy. In midsummer 1675 he began to take spirit of sal amoniac. On 31 July he reported, 'In a new world with new medicine'.[75] The following day he wrote, 'This is certainly a great Discovery in physic. I hope that this will dissolve that viscous slime that hath so much tormented me in my stomach and guts'.[76] None the less, Hooke stopped taking 'SSA' soon thereafter, perhaps having discovered an unpleasant effect which he failed to record.

It is apparent that all of the medicines Hooke took failed to make him a healthy man. However, this failure did not cause Hooke to lose his faith in medicine. Indeed, the question of whether or not a remedy 'worked' was understood very differently by Hooke and his contemporaries than it would be by a twentieth-century sufferer. The seventeenth-century medicine-taker expected a preparation to show its strength by producing an immediate result – usually in the form of multiple bowel movements or vomits. Thus, the fact that a remedy 'wrought well' had nothing to do with whether or not it cured the sufferer's symptoms. Indeed, prophylactic medicine was expected to 'work' in the absence of illness.

In addition, medicine was not expected to make the taker feel good. While Hooke occasionally reported feeling relief after vomiting, for instance, the reader is reminded of the dubious pleasure of hitting yourself over the head with a hammer because it is so nice when you stop. Physic-taking confined the sufferer to his or her chamber until the effects of the physic had passed. Woe to the individual who left home prematurely; the public lavatory had yet to be invented. For instance, Samuel Pepys reported taking Lady Paulina Montagu, his patron's daughter, to a play in April 1662.

> In the middle of the play, my Lady Paulina, who had taken physic this morning, had need to go forth; and so I took the poor lady out and carried her to the Grange [a nearby inn], and there sent the maid of the house into a room to her, and she did what she had a mind to. And so back again to the play.[77]

In addition, most medicines tasted foul. Dorothy Osborne commented on the popular 'steel drink',

> I drink your [William Temple's] health every morning in a drench that would poison a horse, I believe, and 'tis the only way I have to persuade myself to take it, 'tis the infusion of steel, and makes me so horridly sick that every day at ten o'clock I am making my will, and taking leave of all my friends.[78]

Indeed, physic-taking could produce a worse effect than minor inconvenience. Ralph Josselin's only living children, Thomas and Jane, became 'sick even to death' when given prophylactic medicine in June 1650.[79]

None the less, the seventeenth-century English were enthusiastic medicine-takers. They patronised the shops of apothecaries, who grew prosperous and powerful because of their enthusiasm. They made their own remedies. They imported exotic substances from newly explored continents. And they eagerly took the products distilled by those relative newcomers to the medical scene, the chemists.

People also drank and bathed in the waters of the many natural springs around which fashionable spas had grown up. Hooke drank Dulwich and Epsom waters. The pleasure-loving Pepys visited Epsom and Bath, partly to take the waters and partly to amuse himself.[80] About one visit to Epsom, he wrote,

> I met many that I knew; and we drunk each of us two pots and so walked away – it being very pleasant to see how everybody turns up his tail, here one and there another, in a bush, and the Women in their Quarters the like.[81]

Mary Evelyn, Dorothy Osborne and Ralph Josselin also visited such spas.[82]

In addition to taking internal medicines, people underwent surgical procedures for both prophylactic and curative purposes. Phlebotomy was common, although some sufferers apparently thought more highly of it than others. John Evelyn was frequently let blood. For instance, in June 1651 he was let ten ounces of blood for a sore throat; in July of the same year he was let blood for haemorrhoids; in March 1652 he was let nine ounces of blood for 'a swelling in my throat and neck, which fore-ran the piles'.[83] Samuel Pepys was less attracted to phlebotomy, but occasionally underwent the procedure. In July 1668, for instance, he was let fourteen ounces of blood, 'towards curing my eyes'.[84]

Phlebotomy, like medicine-taking, was at best an unpleasant business. After Pepys was let sixteen ounces of blood in April 1662, his arm became so sore that he had to stay home from work the next day. At worst, blood-letting could be very dangerous. Joseph Binns reported several cases of phlebotomy which went disastrously wrong. At least two patients developed gangrene after being let blood from the arm.[85]

Other routine procedures could also be dangerous. Pepys and Hooke took many clysters without suffering any harm. However, Binns reported a case where the unskilful manoeuvring of a clyster pipe resulted in a patient's death.[86] Issues became infected, blisters burned.

Although many surgical procedures required a skilled hand, it should be emphasised that the patient (or consumer of medical services) was often in control of what sort of procedure was done and when it was administered. For instance, John Evelyn 'caused' an issue to be made in the neck of his 1-month-old son when the baby was suffering from convulsions.[87] Pepys sought out the surgeon, Mr Holliard, when he felt he should be let blood.[88] In this respect, surgeons and their assistants were in much the same category as the barbers whom people paid to draw aching teeth. Instead of acting as authorities, they were often employed as skilled craftsmen.

Medical decisions, then, were often made by the sufferer him- or herself. They were also made by parents for their children. We will discuss the Josselins' approach to childhood disorders below. Perhaps one reason for parental decisiveness in times of illness or accident was that no one else could be counted on for help. This was certainly the case when John Evelyn helped extract a bone from his 2-year-old son Richard's throat. The boy had choked while eating broth. The maid who had been looking after the child had fainted. There was 'no chirurgeon near'. Evelyn held 'its head down, incite[d] it to vomit. . . . It pleased God, that on the sudden effort & as it were struggling his last for life, he cast forth a bone . . . I gave the child some Lucotellus Balsame, for his throat was much excoriated'.[89]

In addition to self-treatment, people sought medical help from relatives, friends and neighbours. As indicated above, Lady Margaret Hoby acted as an informal, unpaid general practitioner for her neighbours and friends. Her midwifery and surgical skills were most frequently required. She attended the confinements of neighbours and relatives and dressed wounds. Indeed, in the year 1600, she made thirty-two references to 'dressing patients'. She sometimes had more than one patient at a time. For example, on 10 February 1600 she 'dressed her patients' in the morning, then 'dressed other poor folks' in the afternoon.[90]

Although most gentlewomen had neither the interest nor the time Lady Hoby expended on medical pursuits, proficiency in medical matters was expected of them. Lady Anne Clifford's mother had been 'a distiller of medicinal waters, a dabbler in alchemy, an expert in the properties of plants, flowers and herbs'.[91] Ralph Josselin's neighbour, Lady Honeywood, frequently offered medical advice and help to members of the Josselin family.[92] Jane Josselin returned the favour on one occasion by helping with the Honeywoods' sick child.[93] More frequently she treated the ailments of family members and attended the confinements of her daughters and neighbours.[94]

Samuel Pepys occasionally followed the medical advice given him by friends and other lay-people. When he suffered from itching, swelling and burning in February 1663, Sir J. Mennes

would not have me take anything from the apothecary, but from him, his Venice Treakle being better than the others; which I did consent to and did anon take and fell into a great sweat; and about 10 or 11 o'clock came out of it, and shifted myself and slept pretty well . . . and in the morning, most of my disease, that is, itching and pimples, was gone.[95]

When Pepys had a bad attack of colic and wind in October 1663, Mennes and another colleague, Sir W. Batten, advised him to take juniper water, 'and Sir W. Batten sent to his lady for some for me'.[96]

Experience of a certain ailment gave the sufferer a certain expertise in it. For instance, when Dorothy Osborne had ague in April 1653, she wrote

it is impossible I should keep it long for here is my eldest brother and my Cousin Molle and two or three more of them that have great understanding in Agues as People that have been long acquainted with them and they do so tutor and govern me that I am neither to eat drink nor sleep without their leave, and sure my obedience deserves they should cure me or else they are great tyrants to very little purpose.[97]

However, a person need not have suffered a disorder to be interested in its treatment.

Robert Hooke seems to have collected bits of medical advice and recipes the way some people collect stamps. Some of the advice was obviously not intended for him. For instance, he recorded one Mr Middleton's remedy for rattlesnake bite.[98] However, more often the advice concerned ailments Hooke suffered from himself. For instance, Mrs Tillotson gave him the recipe for a 'physic ale' which he drank with apparently good results for quite a while.[99] He did not try the recipe told him by a woman who cured vertigo with 'stone horse dung'.[100]

In addition to self-treatment and treatment given by friends and acquaintances, the diarists consulted healers. Some of these were unlicensed. Hooke, for instance, drank 'Mountebank's drink', presumably purchased from a mountebank.[101] Most of the healers referred to, however, were recognised physicians and surgeons.

Ralph Josselin consulted physicians and surgeons most rarely of all the diarists referred to in this study.[102] He summoned a physician to a child's death-bed only once.[103] He consulted physicians and surgeons fewer than ten times during the forty-year period covered by his diary.

Samuel Pepys, John Evelyn and Robert Hooke, on the other hand, routinely consulted physicians and surgeons. However, their medical behaviour was not necessarily as 'modern' as it appears to be. Evelyn seems to have used the services of healers rather as he employed servants. He praised the good ones he consulted and despised those who were apparently more inept. He very often directed the activities of his medical attendants and does not seem to have paid them very well.[104] Beginning in the late 1650s, most of his physicians were acquaintances of his; after 1660, fellow members of the Royal Society. However, Evelyn still consulted *with* them, possibly considering his own medical judgment to be as reliable as theirs.

His confidence and superiority stemmed partly from his university education and elevated socio–economic status, partly from his own medical interests and observations. During his travels on the continent in the 1640s, Evelyn visited several hospitals, herb gardens and medical schools.[105] In the 'Hospital of the Charity' in Paris, he saw five people cut for the stone on the same day.[106] And in 1672 he observed the amputation of a sailor's gangrened leg.[107] He apparently also watched the autopsy which was performed on his 5-year-old son.[108]

Like Evelyn, both Pepys and Hooke had interest in and knowledge of medical subjects which ranged beyond those of their contemporaries. As indicated above, Pepys attended lectures at Surgeon's Hall and Hooke eventually took an MD. Both men numbered many surgeons and physicians among their acquaintance. The medical men they consulted were also friends of theirs.[109] Thus, their consultation of licensed healers may be viewed as being similar to their uncritical acceptance of medical advice from 'lay' friends. Only once did Pepys refer to his own attitude toward his medical attendants. This was at least partly in fun. When in September 1665 he drank some 'strong drink', he wrote that he was

> fain to allow myself [this pleasure], by advice of all and not contrary to my oath, my physician being dead and chyrurgeon out of the way whose advice I am obliged to take.[110]

Indeed, on the one occasion when Pepys consulted both his physician, Dr Burnett, and his surgeon, Mr Holliard, about the same condition, his healers disagreed about the diagnosis. Burnett felt that Pepys's back pain and difficulty in urination was due to an ulcer in his bladder or kidneys.[111] Holliard first diagnosed it as a return of Pepys's old complaint of the stone.[112] However, later he decided that it was merely wind, and that Pepys had no ulcers.[113]

A similar, but more disturbing, disagreement occurred when Pepys's brother Tom lay dying. Tom's 'doctor, Mr. Powell' diagnosed the pox. Samuel called another physician, Dr Wiverly, who denied that Tom had syphilis. To relieve his own mind, Samuel and Dr Wiverly 'searched my brother again at his privities, where he was as clean as ever he was born'. Wiverly told Powell that 'he should cease to report any such thing', and Samuel Pepys 'threatened him that I would have satisfaction if I heard any more such discourse'.[114] Such was the evil reputation attached to syphilis that Samuel wrote, 'The shame of this very thing, I confess, troubles me as much as anything'.[115]

It is not surprising that Pepys, Hooke and others 'shopped around' for medical advice. The quality of medical care varied. Pepys was fortunate in coming into contact with two skilful practitioners – Mr Holliard, who had removed his bladder stone in 1658 and was still treating him eleven years later; and Dr Williams, who twice successfully treated Elizabeth Pepys for her genital abscesses.[116] Pepys's experience with Dr Burnett was less rewarding. Perhaps it is significant that he did not consult another physician in the four years between Burnett's death and the close of his diary. His respect for physicians was certainly not increased by his observation of their behaviour during the 1665 plague.

Although Hooke consulted the physicians, Goddard and Cox, and the surgeon, Gidly, he seems mainly to have patronised apothecaries' shops. He compared the products of various apothecaries and made his own evaluations of them. For instance, on 30 May 1674 he bought two vomits, one each from the apothecaries Witchcot and Child.[117] Child's vomit, taken 31 May, 'wrought well' at the time, but did him 'much harm' the following day. Witchcot's vomit, taken 5 August, made him worse.[118] Hooke attached no more weight to the medicines prescribed by his physicians than he did to remedies recommended by acquaintances or purchased from apothecaries' shops. His approach to medication was truly Baconian.

Indeed, one can say about both Hooke and Pepys that each was essentially empirical about medical treatment. A good result was more important than fashion or the dictates of medical authorities. It is not possible to make the same observation about the other diarists and correspondents. As we have seen, Dorothy Osborne carried on taking the steel drink, upon the advice of her physician, even though it tasted nasty and made her sick. She hoped it would do her good. And Lady Margaret Hoby mainly took prophylactic physic, which made her feel unwell.[119] The remedies she took when ill did not usually do her much good. The young mercer, Roger Lowe, was rarely ill. When he did develop an ailment, it is unclear whether he ever consulted healers or took medicine.[120]

It is difficult to obtain much information about seventeenth-century attitudes towards healers from diaries and correspondence. A better source is the large body of popular literature referring to medicine, published during the period. A few of these works were semi-serious prose attacks on the medical status quo. A few were poems.[121] The majority were plays, performed and published to entertain. While it is hard to know how seriously to take the opinions expressed in such literature, examination of it is valuable because it helps to balance what the healers said about themselves.[122] Medical historians have always been too eager to accept licensed physicians and surgeons of the past at their own valuation.[123]

How representative were the attitudes expressed in popular literature? Some authors, Gideon Harvey for example, were eccentrics whose opinions reflected only their own bitter experiences with the medical establishment. However, there do appear to have been both serious criticism of various types of medical practitioners and the mirror image of these attacks – stereotyped caricatures of healers. Whatever may have been the individual opinions of the laymen to whom healers tried to sell their services, the images of these healers as portrayed by dramatists and the popular press were as much a part of general mental furniture as are the 'doctor jokes' current today.

The physician was frequently attacked. His academic education and Latin conversation were beyond the understanding of most prospective patients. His rich dress and haughty manners were resented. The relatively high fees he charged were disapproved of. Disagreements between physicians were pointed to as evidence of the basic inexactness of their art and the amount of hocus–pocus that found its way into diagnosis and treatment. In the 1680s Gideon Harvey made fun of the physicians'

> great learning, vast skill, gravity, formality, conceited caps, valpony gowns, anatomical theatre, circulation library, coach and horses.[124]

One hundred years earlier, Pedro Mexia had criticised medical theories, writing that it was more important to know the cure than the cause of a disease:

> And why should I more believe Hippocrates (who affirmeth the substance of the matter to be in the spirits) than Erisistratus, who attributed it to the turning backward of the blood and the arteries. And why should I credit more these than others, who assigned other principles?[125]

Mexia also accused physicians of using increasingly complicated and exotic medicines in order 'to give a more comely visage to their new science that none may know the secrets thereof' and 'to deceive and bewitch the people'.[126] He even suggested that physicians used these means to murder their patients.

Gideon Harvey was still more savage about therapeutic techniques used by all licensed healers, writing that the patient

> is falsely convicted of this or that Felony on himself; and, most commonly, if his crime or Disease be great, is sentenced to die, and to be executed by tying a Halter about his arm, and afterward to be stabbed in it with a Lancet, to draw off so much blood, until he be Herring-dead. Another way of execution they use, is to impale the sufferer with a machine of Box or ivory, being in nothing different from a clyster-pipe; and this to be used so oft, until it comes out at his mouth; or, if this fails, to order such la Voisine drenches to be poured down his throat, which may do them the good service to stifle the sufferer's . . . vital flame in a few days.[127]

However, it should be recalled that these procedures and prescriptions were actually demanded by sufferers and sometimes used without the sanction of a healer. Thus, Harvey was criticising the approach of lay-men to illness as well as the approach of healers.

The dramatists, like the writers of polemics, disagreed about the value of physicians and physic. Shakespeare tended to favour academically trained physicians. Concerning Gerard de Narbon, he wrote that his

> skill was almost as great as his honesty; had it stretched so far, would have made nature immortal, and death should have play for lack of work. Would, for the King's sake, he were living! I think it would be the death of the King's disease.[128]

Most other dramatists thought less highly of physicians. Ben Jonson wrote:

> Mosca He has no faith in physic: he does think
> Most of your doctors are the greater danger
> And worse diseases, to escape. I often have
> Heard him protest, that your physicians
> Should never be his heir
>
> . . . .
>
> No, sir, not their fees
> He cannot brook: he says they flay a man,
> Before they kill him. [129]

And Beaumont and Fletcher lampooned the many remedies physicians prescribed. In this case, the sufferer had insomnia.

> 1. Courtier. What cures has he?
> Bawdber.   Armies of those we call physicians, some with
> glisters,
> Some with lettice-caps, some posset drinks some
> pills,
> Twenty consulting here about a drench,
> As many here to blood him.
> Then comes a Don of Spaine, and he prescribes
> More cooling opium than would kill a Turke,
> Or quench a whore ith dogdayes: after him . . .
> An English doctor, with a bunch of pot herbs;
> And he cries out endiffe and suckory,
> With a few mallow roots and butter milk,
> And talks of oil made of a churchmans charity,
> Yet still he wakes. [130]

The endless controversy over medical theories was also ridiculed.

> 1. Doctor. Why I, for if he be a chemist, his opinion and ours
> must needs differ, and consequently not agree in
> consultation.
> 2. Doctor. I am, sir, of your opinion, for I think it infra
> dignitatem to hold consultation with
> mountebanks. . . .
> 3. Doctor. Pardon me gentlemen, I have known some chemical
> physicians learned and rational men; and though not
> strict adherers to the Galenical method, produced with
> great reason, and good success, which, I take it,
> answers all we can say or do.
> 2. Doctor. I profess I think it as bad as murder to cure out of the
> methodical way. Oh what satisfaction 'tis to have a
> patient die according to all the rules of art. [131]

The dramatists were gentler with surgeons, mainly lampooning their connection with syphilis. George Chapman wrote:

Pock: My name is Pock sir; a practitioner in surgery.
Darioto: Pock the surgeon, y're welcome sir, I know a doctor of
              your name master Pock.
Pock: My name has made many doctors sir.
Rinaldo: Indeed tis a worshipful name.
Valerio: Mary is it, and of an ancient descent.
Pock: Faith sir I could fetch my pedigree far, if I were so
              disposed.
Rinaldo: Out of France at least.
Pock: And if I stood on my arms as others do.
Darioto: No do not Pock, let others stand on their arms, and
              thou a thy legs as long as thou canst.
Pock: Though I live by my bare practice, yet I could show
              good cards for my gentility.[132]

Apothecaries were mentioned chiefly as the servants and henchmen of physicians. When they were ridiculed, it was for avarice and for the plethora of harmful and useless remedies they sold.

Unauthorised healers were even more vulnerable to attack than were the physicians. We have dealt with the serious criticisms of them launched by the anti-quack writers above. Needless to say, dramatists found them irresistible. Thomas Heywood's *Wise Woman of Hogsdon* has been quoted above.[133] Shakespeare's weird sisters were more interested in black magic than in white, although their concoction sounds like many of the medical recipes current at the time.[134] However, the character Pinch – described in *The Comedy of Errors* – was a caricature of the travelling mountebank.

Antipholus of Ephesus: Along with them
They brought one Pinch, a hungry, lean-fac'd villain,
A mere anatomy, a mountebank,
A threadbare juggler, and a fortune-teller,
A needy, hollow-ey'd, sharp-looking wretch,
A living dead man. This pernicious slave,
Forsooth, took on him as a conjurer,
And gazing in mine eyes, feeling my pulse,
And with no face, as 'twere, outfacing me,
Cries out I was possess'd.[135]

A lighter treatment of the same theme was presented in *The Skilful Mountebank . . .* published in 1638. Similar in form to the do-it-yourself medical works popular during the period, it offered humorous cures for a number of disorders. For instance, for melancholy, it prescribed a joke and a warm bed with a virgin in it, along with the following cordial:

> The stones of a goat, the guts of crabs, the brains of sparrows, monkey's marrow, pith of oxens, with the yolks of 5 new layd eggs, laid by an hen of the Game.

The book ends with a song sung by the mountebank himself:

> Are any fools that would be wise?
> Are any falling that would rise?
> Is any such that would be poore,
> Ile purge his substance in an hour:
> Is any bound that would be free?
> Ile do 't, let him repair to me.
> I come to cure what e'er you feel,
> Within, without, from head to heel.

Like authorised healers, unlicensed practitioners had their defenders. Pedro Mexia took a leaf from the physicians' own book when he created a pedigree for unlearned practice, writing that early men

> cured one another for charity, and not for interest, and they cured with herbs and vertuous simples experimented, and not with venemous compositions that now are used, which you know not what they be.[136]

Mexia favoured experience over theory. However, he hedged a bit, saying that there were good physicians as well as bad, and that the good should be allowed to get on with their work.

The portrait painted of healers and medicine by seventeenth-century popular writers is both detailed and confusing. It indicates the great extent to which both writers and their audiences were familiar with medical matters. It also shows the diversity of opinion on medical topics. It indicates, for instance, that the physicians were justified in feeling insecure about the trust and support they received from the general public. It also suggests that although people took a lot of medicine, they were cynical about the salutary results the medicine would produce. In addition, the popular literature reinforces the notion that the seventeenth-century medical marketplace was perceived as such by both healers and sufferers. Sufferers came, willing to buy, but suspicious of being cheated. Healers came, anxious to sell, eager to convince potential buyers of their worth.

The above discussion has concentrated upon seventeenth-century medical variety. It has described the disorders people suffered from and the ways they dealt with these disorders. It has indicated the diversity of approaches to illness which existed. At this point in our study, then, it is appropriate to turn to an in-depth analysis of the medical experiences of one seventeenth-century family – to move discussion from the general to the particular.

7

IN SICKNESS AND IN HEALTH: THE JOSSELINS' EXPERIENCE

I INTRODUCTION

The extent to which diaries reflect general experience is frequently, and deservedly, questioned. The seventeenth-century diarists whose writings have survived were members of the middle and upper classes. Furthermore, diarists and autobiographers are unusual in any age, feeling a need most people never feel to commit thoughts and experiences to paper. Their attitudes and behaviour can be taken as representative, neither of general experience, nor of the experience of others at their social level.

None the less, such records of unique, personal experience are invaluable to the historians, providing, as they literally do, a voice from the grave which can make the past live as no other source can. And the fact that the experiences they describe may not be representative is, perhaps, insignificant, since each individual's experience is, to a large extent, unique, whether or not he or she describes it in a diary. One cannot quantify pain, fear, grief, confidence or comfort.

In any case, this chapter is not concerned with general experience. It will concentrate on the health and illness of one family, seen through the eyes of the head of that family, Reverend Ralph Josselin. Josselin was born 25 January 1616, and died in August 1683. His diary, preceded by a brief autobiography and annual notes, covers the period between the autumn of 1643 and July 1683.[1]

From late 1640 until his death, Josselin was the vicar of Earls Colne in Essex. In the course of his life there, he became a prosperous landowner, one of the ten wealthiest men in his village.[2] He and his wife, born Jane Constable, produced ten live-born children, five of whom were living at the time of Josselin's death. Although the Josselins were middle class by any definition of that vague term, they socialised with people of higher status living in the vicinity, including two gentry

182

families, the Harlakendens and the Honeywoods. They kept one maid-servant to help with the housework, hired nurses for short periods after childbirth and, in later years, employed a man-servant.

Ralph Josselin's diary is an unusually good source of information on medical matters. He was interested enough in medicine and disease to have read at least two works on the subject.[3] In addition to his intellectual interest, he appears to have been unusually preoccupied by his own ailments, describing symptoms of both major and minor disorders in loving detail, always fearing the worst. Fortunately for the historian, he was also concerned about the ailments of his wife, children, servants, friends, neighbours, relations and colleagues. Thus, the diary provides medical information about quite a large number of people, something which is not equally true about otherwise 'rich' diaries of the period. The length of the Josselin diary is also an advantage. Unlike some diarists, Josselin was consistently conscientious about making his entries. Thus we have a nearly daily record of the family's illnesses, accidents and childbearing during a period of approximately forty years.

The Josselins underwent a variety of disorders during this time. These will be discussed within three major categories: the discomforts and dangers relating to childbearing, children's accidents and diseases, and adult disorders, including Ralph Josselin's own. Needless to say, there are overlaps between categories. All of the members of the family suffered from some ailments, such as colds, the 'scab' and stomach upsets. Josselin and some of his children seem to have been particularly prone to eye disorders. And he and at least three of his children suffered from worms. Thus, something should be said to justify this categorisation.

The first heading, dealing with pregnancy and childbirth, needs no explanation. Neither, perhaps, does the last, which will cover adult ailments, excluding those discussed within the first category. A separate category has been set aside for the diseases and accidents of children, because of the high level of infant and child mortality, both within the Josselin family and within the seventeenth-century English population at large.[4] Diseases which provoked minor upsets in adults might kill a child. With good reason, the first two years of life were regarded as particularly dangerous by Josselin and his contem-poraries.[5] Certain ailments, such as those associated with teething, mainly affected children in that age group. Weaning, which in the case of the Josselin children occurred between 12 and 19 months, was regarded as a perilous process.[6] Children were also particularly endangered by accidents. The Josselin children fell downstairs and into fires, set their clothing and household linen afire, and were kicked by horses.[7] For all of these reasons, their disorders deserve separate discussion.

II DISORDERS

Pregnancy and Childbirth

Jane and Ralph Josselin took seriously the biblical injunction to be fruitful and multiply. They married relatively young; Jane was just under and Ralph just over 20 years old. In their first twenty-two years of marriage, Jane had at least fifteen pregnancies producing ten live-born children and at least five miscarriages. She probably breast-fed all of her children.[8]

The Josselins were delighted when they felt certain of Jane's first pregnancy, some ten months after their wedding. Ralph's diary entry for July 1641 attests to their 'great joy and comfort' concerning her condition. He was not as communicative about the news of her subsequent pregnancies, although he was never happy about her miscarriages, regardless of the size of his family. On one occasion in June 1656, when four of the seven children which by then had been born to the couple were living, he wrote, 'This morning my wife thought she miscarried, lord a miscarrying womb is a sad affliction'.[9]

Jane's feelings when anticipating yet another pregnancy were not recorded, but they certainly must have been mixed. She did not carry her babies easily. She was sick and uncomfortable throughout her pregnancies, and dreaded her deliveries for months before the baby was due. She suffered from nausea, faintness, weakness and pain in her back, false labour, after-pains and pain in her breasts, in addition to sometimes long, usually painful, and always frightening deliveries.[10] Indeed, Ralph recognised his wife's unusually uncomfortable pregnancies, writing on 30 October 1653, 'My poor wife very ill, she breedeth with difficulty,' and later in the same pregnancy, on 11 December, 'my wife very ill, and weakly in her childing'.[11] Surely Jane must have echoed his prayer at the beginning of that pregnancy, 'the lord bear up her head under the difficulties of her condition'.[12]

None the less, Jane apparently accepted her obstetrical fate with equanimity and interest. She had, for example, a considerable degree of success in predicting the sex of her unborn children very early in her pregnancies. Ralph reported her predictions for five babies. The first four were accurate. The fifth guess she muddled by changing her mind: on 15 May 1657 she reported being pregnant with a girl. By 31 May she was sure she carried a boy. Mary was born on 14 January 1658. Jane should have stood by her first hunch. None the less, Ralph was right when, in recording her prediction of the sex of their third child, he wrote, 'She useth not to be mistaken'.[13]

Jane's fears about her deliveries were understandable and, probably, very common. The hazards of childbirth in seventeenth-century England were immense. Complications, such as an unusual presentation of the baby, or the mother's inability to expel the child once it was in the birth canal, were often fatal to both mother and child. Even normal deliveries were fraught with danger. Haemorrhages could not be stopped. Infection after birth was common. Tears could not be effectually repaired. Neither midwives nor the occasionally called surgeons could do much to help the labouring women who came into their hands. Both could hurt a great deal – the midwives with well-meant but ill-judged interference intended to speed up labour and delivery; the surgeons with their clumsy instruments used, mainly, to extract dead children when all other means of delivering them had failed.[14]

Jane Josselin's fears had been shared and written about in the 1620s by a woman with the oddly coincidental name of Elizabeth Joceline. Elizabeth was so convinced that childbirth would kill her that 'when she first felt herself quick with child (as then travelling with death itself) she secretly took order for the buying of a new winding sheet'.[15] Elizabeth was certain she was carrying a girl. She wrote her book in order to provide religious instruction for the child, doomed to grow up without a mother. All of Elizabeth's predictions came true. She died of fever nine days after giving birth to a daughter. Her book found a sympathetic readership. It was first published in 1624, two years after the author's death, and was republished six times between 1684 and 1894.

Like Elizabeth, Jane Josselin took her fears to God. On one occasion she prayed with neighbour women when she felt the child quicken.[16] On another, she and Ralph prayed together the night before her labour began, because Jane 'was oppressed with fears that she should not do well on this child'.[17] With the next pregnancy as well Jane was 'under great fears she shall not do well of this child'.[18] It is not surprising that Jane should have been particularly frightened during this pregnancy. In the preceding year, 1646, two neighbour women had died in childbed, one after an excruciating labour lasting for two weeks.[19]

Even years of fortunate experience did not lay Jane's fears to rest. When in August 1661 she thought she might be pregnant, Ralph wrote, 'I see she apprehends a breeding again with fear, the blessing of a fruitful womb is by weakness of nature her fear'.[20]

Childbirth in seventeenth-century England was a social occasion. Indeed, the church required that at least two or three 'honest women' in addition to the midwife be present to witness the birth for legal reasons. The invitation of several 'gossips' to a birth was also required by social convention. Acquaintances who did not receive an expected invitation might justifiably take offence.[21] When Jane was delivered of her third child at nearly midnight on 25 November 1645, the midwife and 'almost all' of the women Ralph had summoned were present.[22] When her fourth child was born, the midwife was not there, and she was attended by 'only' five neighbour women.[23] In her turn, Jane attended the confinements of her neighbours and her daughters.[24] In one case, Ralph reported that she saved the life of a labouring woman.[25]

Jane Josselin was fortunate in that all of her labours and deliveries appear to have been quite straightforward. This is not to say that they were easy. Ralph reported Jane's experience of 'sharp pains' or unusually long difficult labours during the births of their third, eighth, ninth and tenth children.[26] In two cases she gave birth without a midwife present.[27] Even when a midwife was there, her presence was not always regarded as an unmixed blessing. After the birth of her eighth child, Jane criticised the midwife for not having done 'her part'. Not only was this labour unusually 'sharp', but also the baby appeared to be dead at birth. Josselin attributed its revival to the intervention of God.[28]

After the birth was over, the mother's health was a subject of special concern for a few weeks at least. The risks of fever and breast infections were very real indeed. Jane was again fortunate. She suffered from sore breasts after the birth of her first child, which were healed 'with use of means'.[29] When her fourth child died at 10 days old, Jane became 'weak and faint with the turning of her milk'.[30] Otherwise, there was no apparent cause for concern. Jane left her bed within three weeks, and left the house between one and two months after her deliveries.

Because Ralph Josselin was so conscientious about recording details of the symptoms and illnesses of the members of his family, it is possible to compare Jane's health during her childbearing years (1642–63) and during the last twenty years of her marriage (1663–83). During the first twenty-one years of their married life, Ralph reported 131 instances of Jane being unwell. Of these, seventy-three cases were clearly related to pregnancy and childbirth. Fifty-eight cases recorded a plethora of symptoms ranging from toothache, to ague, to being 'sickly with toiling over' a dying child.[31] Some of these miscellaneous disorders may have actually arisen from gynaecological or obstetrical problems. For instance, in July 1656 Jane suffered from symptoms which she first diagnosed as the 'falling down of the mother' (prolapse of the uterus) and later, with relief, as piles.[32] This episode occurred a month after she thought she miscarried.[33]

Once Jane's reproductive years were over, she apparently became much healthier. In the last twenty years of the Josselins' marriage (1663 to Ralph's death in 1683), Ralph reported that Jane was unwell only seventeen times. This significant improvement might be explained in a number of ways. It is possible that for a short period of time Ralph lost interest in recording his family's symptoms. Certainly the years between 1665 and 1672 are remarkably poor in their references to illness. However, it is more likely that the Josselins were fairly healthy during those years. It is also possible that after November 1672, when Ralph was first troubled with the leg ailment which probably killed him, he ceased to mention any but the most dramatic illnesses of family members, concentrating, as the elderly and sick may be excused for doing, on his own problems.[34] However, this is also unlikely, for he did mention a cold Jane had in November 1680.[35] Indeed, Jane's health was of great concern to Ralph for purely selfish reasons. He frequently echoed the prayer he made when she was ill with a pregnancy in 1648, 'Blessed be God, oh continue her a comfort to me and mine'.[36] The prospect of being left alone to care for a large house and family would have been grim indeed. Thus it seems that Jane's health did improve considerably once she finished childbearing. Certainly she outlived her husband and was apparently healthy at the time of his death.

Children's Accidents and Diseases

In seventeenth-century England, as in most 'developing' societies, childhood was an especially dangerous period of life. As we have seen, the London Bills of Mortality included special categories for infants and 'chrisom' children – infancy seeming to be in itself a sufficient explanation of the cause of death.[37] Certain illnesses, such as being livergrown, ailments associated with teething, and rickets were peculiar to the early years. Other ailments, like 'the scab' and worms, although they affected adults as well, were most common and dangerous among children.

Of the five Josselin children who died before their father, three were under the age of 8. One baby, the first Ralph, died at 10 days. The second Ralph died at 13 months. Mary, the first-born, died aged 8 years, 1 month. Each of the three died under circumstances which would have been tragically familiar to Ralph Josselin's peers.

The first baby Ralph was born on 11 February 1648. He was the Josselin's fourth child; the elder three were living when he was born. Josselin himself was very ill with ague at the time of his birth. He first mentioned the baby's illness on 17 February, when he wrote that the child 'was ill, full of phlegm', and that they sent for the physician. This was, quite remarkably, the only occasion when Josselin mentioned having summoned a physician to the bedside of any member of his family! At this point Jane Josselin had already 'persuaded herself that it would die[,] it was a very sick child indeed', and Ralph himself 'took my leave of it at night, not much expecting to see it alive'.[38] On 20 February Ralph wrote

> This night again my son very ill, he did not cry so much as the night before, whether the cause was want of strength I know not: he had a little froth in his mouth continually, in the morning there came some red mattery stuff out of his mouth, which made us apprehend his throat might be sore.[39]

By this time the baby was being fed breast-milk, and had been dosed with syrup of roses.[40] He died on the 21st, the Josselins having 'looked on it as a dying child, 3 or 4 days'.[41]

The second baby Ralph and Mary died within six days of each other. Indeed, the late May and early June of 1650 was a disastrous period for the Josselins, since they lost a close friend, Mrs Mary Church, the same day that baby Ralph died.

The second Ralph was born 5 May 1649. His father mentioned that he was treated for wind on 13 May. He was reasonably well thereafter until the end of November when his father wrote that he was ill, 'but I hope it was only breeding teeth'.[42] On 1 December the baby 'pined and grew very tedious these cold nights to his poor mother'.[43] On 21

December Jane took the child to Lady Honeywood's, who 'fears he is in a consumption, but indeed he is troubled with the rickets'.[44] The lady suggested that the boy be treated with an issue, but Jane decided against this therapy. On 27 January 1650 the baby was still ill. On 5 February he 'was very sick as if he would have died, he vomited, and something stirred in the bottom of his stomach, which he endeavoured to bring up but could not'.[45] On 18 February his eyes were 'wonderful ill as if he should be blind'.[46] By 10 March the child's eyes were better, but he had broken out 'in very many angry pimples and the rheum continues'.[47] On 27 March the child was still ill, and his parents resolved to wean him from the breast.[48] On 21 April 'My little boy continueth ill, and sore, and forward'.[49] By 7 May the Josselins had concluded that little Ralph was 'liver-grown, there is no passage between his short ribs, which is a sign thereof'.[50] By late May 8-year-old Mary was dying, so attention was somewhat diverted from the ever-ailing Ralph. However, on 26 May Josselin wrote that 'my little son in all peoples eyes is a dying child'; and die he did on 2 June, his father commenting that 'his life was continual sorrow and trouble, happy he who is at rest in the lord'.[51]

Mary Josselin was born 12 April 1642. Her first major illness was a severe cold she had at about the age of 3, during which she spat blood. She had ague at 5 and, along with her brother and sister, a skin disorder on her scalp at the age of 6. She had trouble with her eyes at the same time as her infant brother Ralph in early 1650. With these exceptions, she was an unusually healthy child until a month before her death. On 28 April her father mentioned that she was 'ill but not down sick'.[52] On 5 May she was still ill. By 12 May Ralph wrote, 'my dear Mary, very ill, she is heavy, and joyless as it were, god in mercy restore her and spare her life'.[53] On 21 May he wrote, 'the last night Mary talked idly, she began to sweat'.[54]

The Josselins suspected that she suffered from worms, and on 22 May Ralph went to the priory requesting a medicine for that disorder. Upon his return home he was told 'she had had a stool, and 3 great dead worms'. The same day they gave her a clyster which 'wrought very well'.[55] On 24 May Mary 'void six worms more'.[56] On the 25th Ralph had some hope that Mary would survive, but by the next morning 'all our hopes of Mary's life was gone, to the Lord I resigned her'.[57] She died on 27 May, and was buried the following day.

Although they mourned the losses of all three children, Jane and Ralph were especially grief-stricken over Mary's death. On 4 August, more than two months after Mary died, Jane was 'very faint and ill'. Ralph wrote, 'I apprehend she disquiets herself in grief for Mary as the occasion of it'.[58] While the two boys had been sickly infants, not expected to live, Mary had actually survived the perilous early years and showed great promise. Ralph wrote of her, 'She was a child of ten thousand, full of wisdom, woman-like gravity, knowledge, sweet expre[ssions of god, apt in her learning,] tender hearted and loving, an [obed]ient child'.[59]

The townspeople of Earls Colne reflected the different reactions of the parents. While 'many of my neighbours' attended the first baby Ralph's funeral, 'most of the town' came to Mary's, including the wives of two of the foremost citizens, Mrs Margaret Harlakenden (her husband was the richest man in town) and Mrs Mabel Elliston, who laid her in her grave.[60]

Of course, childhood illnesses and accidents were not always fatal. Many of the Josselin children were ill when they were cutting teeth.[61] They suffered from numerous skin ailments, ranging from pimples, to shingles, rashes on their scalps, the itch and boils.[62] They also were subject to worms. The first Mary had worms when she was nearly 3 and John was 'full of worms' at the age of 4.[63] Ralph senior and several of the children had the 'rheum' in their eyes, and other eye ailments.[64] The second Ralph and Jane were supposed to have had rickets which, in Jane's case, may have been associated with weaning.[65]

The children also suffered from ailments which today are commonly viewed as childhood diseases. In July 1649 one of Ralph's two sons (probably 5-year-old Thomas) developed 'great swellings' under both his ears – possibly mumps.[66] In March 1656 John, Jane and Ann developed 'colds nigh chincolds', Josselin describing their 'fierce and troublesome cough that is too hard for means that we can use'.[67] This sounds like whooping cough. In July 1658 4-year-old Ann and the Josselins' maid had the measles.[68] And in August 1652, when he was 18, Thomas also had the measles.[69]

Although Josselin and his wife apparently escaped the ravages of smallpox, their children were not so fortunate. Thomas, John, Ann and Elizabeth each caught the disease as teenagers, while living in London.[70] Only 15-year-old Thomas, who contracted smallpox only two weeks after being sent to London as an apprentice, returned home to be nursed. The others remained in London, sending word of their condition home to their anxious parents. Despite the seriousness of the disease and the fear it inspired, these adolescents survived it without any permanent handicap worthy of remark.

Like their father, the Josselin children suffered from frequent colds and occasional bouts of ague. On a number of occasions, the whole family came down with colds at the same time.[71] Colds were usually regarded as unpleasant but inevitable, worthy of comment but not of fear. However, in children they were sometimes regarded as dangerous. When 3-year-old Mary suffered from a 'great cold' during which she 'strained and spit much blood', her parents sought help for her from Lady Honeywood. Ralph was worried about her to the extent that he prayed that 'the Lord will preserve her'.[72] Colds were even more dangerous in infants. When 10-month-old Thomas developed a cold in the night which seemed 'ready even to stop him up', Jane Josselin was so frightened 'that she was even at death's door'.[73] Agues could be even more severe. The intermittent hot and cold fits were very unpleasant and the disease was very debilitating, often lasting for months. When she was only about 8 months old, Elizabeth picked up an ague which lasted from early February until mid-April.[74] None the less, Ralph Josselin apparently feared the consequences of an ague only once, and that, perhaps understandably, was when he suffered a bad case of it himself in February 1648.[75]

The Josselins and their friends were also involved in accidents. Like many of his contemporaries, Josselin recorded his family's brushes with disaster as marks of God's providence. Thus he wrote on 7 October 1644, 'I found god had graciously kept my daughter Mary who was struck with a Horse her apron rent off with his nails, and her handkerchief rent and yet she had no hurt'.[76] Mary was 2½ at the time. While adults also had accidents, children were most at risk because they were only beginning to learn how to deal with their environment.

Fire was particularly dangerous. The Josselin house had six hearths. In February 1648 Jane, then just over 2, fell into the fire without hurt. A year later she fell into a fire and hurt her hands.[77] The second Mary also burnt her hands in an open fire at just under 3 years of age.[78] On 27 October 1658 4-year-old Anne both fell into a 'great fire' and tumbled down the entry stairs. At the end of the day she was unhurt.[79] Candles were as hazardous as open fires. In January 1669 11-year-old Mary's neckcloth caught fire on a candle, 'and she blew it, which increased the flame, my maid damped it and I with both hands over it quenched it'.[80] On 27 September 1672 10-year-old

Becky 'fired a bed mat with a candle. My wife run up into chamber and quenched it'.[81]

Then as now, children frequently fell and hurt themselves. In July 1650 6-year-old Thomas fell down the school stairs and hurt his cheek.[82] In November 1653 2-year-old John broke a bone in his foot by falling at the street threshold.[83] The following year John fell down the school stairs (which must indeed have been dangerous!) but received no hurt.[84] In addition, children were injured by the adults looking after them. When the second Mary was 2½, her arm was pulled out of joint 'by a snatch of our maid Alice'.[85]

The Josselin children also endangered each other. In February 1648 2-year-old Jane 'dagged a pair of scissors in Thom: eyebrow', fortunately not much injuring him.[86] And in 1654 Jane, then nearly 9, dropped 2-month-old Ann into a bowl of milk. The baby was unhurt.[87] Equally the children saved each other from harm. In December 1644 2-year-old Mary held 1-year-old Thomas out of the fire, crying until their father came to help.[88] Indeed, in view of the dangers which surrounded them, the Josselin children were remarkably fortunate in escaping both accidental injury and death from epidemic diseases. This good fortune certainly supported Ralph Josselin's belief in the special providence of God towards him and his.

Adult Disorders

Although Ralph Josselin conscientiously reported the illnesses of his family, friends and neighbours, he was most interested in his own ailments. He was not a true hypochondriac; his illnesses cannot be regarded as 'imaginary'. However, he was unusually preoccupied with his symptoms, major and minor – so much so that his wife lost patience with him at one point. In January 1672 Josselin began to suffer from the pain, swelling and ulceration in his left leg which remained with him until his death over eleven years later. He wrote, at that time, 'I am sensible I bear my infirmities about me, but my wife taxes me for great impatience, when I fear there is a provoking carelessness in her etc. and impatience too much, that bears nothing but expects I must bear all'.[89] The reader of the diary cannot help but sympathise with both Ralph and Jane. Certainly Ralph spent most of his life handicapped by minor, annoying ailments. However, one imagines that his exhaustive (and exhausting) descriptions of his sensations found their way into breakfast-table conversation, as well as into the pages of his diary.

Ralph noted the state of his health in both daily entries and in weekly summaries, written on Sundays. In addition, he frequently made marginal notes which, as often as not, referred to an acute or chronic disorder.[90] Like his contemporaries, he was involved in determining the diagnoses and prognoses of his own illnesses, and helped decide the therapeutic 'means' to be used.

Josselin suffered from frequent, long-lasting colds which he described in great detail. He mentioned colds in the throat, poses (the term he used to refer to head colds), rheums, 'stuffing' and 'wheezing' (mostly at night), chest colds, 'stopping' in the chest and aguish colds.[91] Out of some 317 mentions of his own illnesses, 114 referred to colds. He also gave full descriptions of the onset and various stages of his colds. For instance, he wrote in June 1646, 'I was now in taking of cold sensible of it most in my throat, a roughness and kind of soreness at the upper part next my mouth and especially on the left side'.[92] During another cold in December 1646, he wrote 'my cold begun to thicken, and to stuff and wheeze exceedingly'.[93] His conjectures about why he 'caught' cold sound much like those we hear today. For instance, he came down with a pose and chest cold as a result of wearing thin stockings in October 1677.[94]

Although Josselin very occasionally took medicine for his colds, his attitude towards them was far more fatalistic than towards his other ailments.[95] For one thing, despite the discomfort they caused him, Josselin's colds never appeared to him to be very serious illnesses, unlike other ailments such as severe agues or the chronic leg problem (variously diagnosed as scurvy and dropsy) which tormented his final years. For another thing, Josselin's colds dragged on so long that to have allowed himself to take up a sick role during them would have been financially and professionally disastrous.

This is not to say that Josselin always regarded colds as minor ailments. As we have seen, children's colds sometimes concerned him greatly.[96] However, Ralph's own colds, though annoying, were considered minor problems and even served as rather gratifying tests of faith and fortitude. For instance, he wrote in September 1647, 'This week I was somewhat troubled with a pose, but though rheums and pose haunt me I praise God, they do not cast me down'.[97]

Josselin was prey to a host of minor symptoms which annoyed more than worried him. During his early years at Earls Colne he frequently mentioned rheums in his eyes.[98] He also developed a sore tongue, pain in his chest which he concluded was wind, and occasional soreness in his bones.[99] At one point he also developed swellings in both sides of his groin which mercifully abated within a week.[100] Some of the sensations he experienced were downright mysterious – for example, the 'coldness or moistness in the crown of his head' which he felt on 14 January 1649.[101] In addition to these problems, Josselin was a bad traveller. Frequently even short journeys left him feeling ill. Sometimes he experienced nausea and vomiting; sometimes he felt aguish and sore.[102] In one case, while returning from London, he was overcome with wind and had to be treated in the home of an acquaintance.[103]

Like their contemporaries, Josselin and his family were occasionally 'ill in their stomachs'. However, the humoral theory dominant in the period, which regarded evacuation as beneficial, helped them to bear their discomforts. For instance, when Ralph suffered from diarrhoea in April 1646, he 'conceived it a mercy'.[104] Again, in December 1648 he wrote, 'After above 30 hours illness in my stomach I fell into a great looseness which I conceive did me much good'.[105] When 5-year-old Ann had an 'each day ague' in August 1659, the fact that she vomited and sweat gave her parents hope.[106] In some cases the evacuation was indeed a blessing. This was true in August 1656, when Ralph suffered from worms, and in November 1672, when he vomited after a surfeit of oysters.[107]

Also in company with their contemporaries, the Josselins were plagued by toothache. In one case Ralph's gums began to swell in March 1655. He suffered through the month of April, and finally had the offending tooth drawn in May. The tooth itself 'was corrupted, and the flesh within it, most loath-some'.[108] Two days after the tooth was drawn, Josselin 'pulled out a piece of bone by the place where my tooth stood . . . it was firm, but I conceive begun to rot, it was putrified round about, it must needs have been dangerous if God had not directed me to draw my tooth'.[109] On 23 June another small piece of bone emerged from the tooth socket, after which Josselin's face finally healed.[110] On a number of other occasions he suffered from painfully swollen gums.[111] In July 1646 Jane had a toothache 'which brought her as it were to death's door'.[112] In this case, the pain went away, so the tooth was not pulled.

Almost every member of the Josselin family had ague at one time or another, in most cases more than once. These attacks ranged from single fits to life-threatening illnesses such as the ague Ralph had in February 1648. During this illness, Josselin wrote that his friends were very worried about him – despite the fact that his wife gave birth to a son who died during Ralph's convalescence. At one point, a week after his fits had begun, Josselin wrote a will.[113] His illness actually ended within fourteen days of its onset, but it frightened him considerably. Some attacks lasted a good deal longer than this. Jane Josselin (senior) developed a quartan ague in October 1668, which lasted until mid-March of the following year and was so serious that her adult daughter Jane was summoned home to look after her.[114]

In addition to the ailments mentioned above, Josselin suffered from two long-term illnesses worthy of mention. The first was an inflammation of his navel which troubled him between September 1648 and mid-April 1652.[115] This was a discouraging illness because his navel would appear to heal, then would become sore and moist all over again, despite the various treatments Ralph tried on it. Although never incapacitated by the discomfort his navel caused him, he was worried about it. In March 1649 he wrote that he had 'heard of one that after 2 years illness was killed with a rawness in his navel, but God shall heal me of this infirmity'.[116] However, as time passed, he grew less concerned, writing in August 1651, 'my navel was a little but not much ill, it hath not been dressed near a year'.[117]

The second long-term illness Josselin suffered from was the swelling and ulceration of his left leg which incapacitated and probably eventually killed him. The first hint of a problem came in November 1672, when Ralph had a 'sciatica pain' in his hip.[118] This passed by the end of the following month, when he reported being able 'to take many steps without stick or stay'.[119] However, by 27 February 1673, 'or sooner, some red spots appeared on my lame thigh, which they conceived the scurvy'.[120] From that time on, the diary is a catalogue of pain, swelling, different treatments applied, fears and disappointed hopes. As the old sores healed the swelling broke open in new places. By early 1683, after ten years of misery, Josselin was a very ill man indeed. His leg was swollen and painful. His belly also swelled. He was very short of breath. He developed a 'great and dangerous cough' and double vision.[121] Despite his infirmities, he continued to preach.[122] However, he must have feared that death was near, for he wrote on 1 June, 'I saw my countenance much changed . . . I did no[t think] I gathered strength nor lost any, but in the use of means continued in the same way. However I stay [myself] on my good god, that this sickness doth not issue in death, but in a trial to do me much good'.[123] This forlorn hope was never realised. Josselin died two months later, at the age of 67.

Josselin described his own last illness, and those of his children who died in childhood, in some detail. It is interesting that he does not give descriptions of the deaths of two adult children, Thomas and Ann, in the summer of 1673. Alan Macfarlane suggests that Thomas may have died of consumption.[124] However, Josselin himself wrote nothing to support this diagnosis, reporting only that 29-year-old Thomas had come home ill on 22 March 1673, and that he died on 15 June, having suffered very little.[125] We do not know when Ann returned to Earls Colne from London, but Josselin wrote that she was ill on 17 June.[126] On 20 July she was 'ill and deaf and thereby uncheerful'.[127] She died on 31 July, aged 19. Josselin wrote 'God hath taken 5 of 10. Lord let it be enough, and spare that we may recover strength'.[128]

As we have said, Ralph Josselin was most concerned about his own ailments and those of his family members. Josselin's 'family' included his servants. Since the smooth operation of his domestic life depended upon the labour of at least one maid-servant, the health of his servants was important to him.[129] Thus he reported the ill-health of servants in his diary, although he never went into much detail about their ailments. For instance, when his maid Jean went home to her mother's 'very sick, urina nigra', he prayed 'God restore her to her health'.[130] In another case, 'our maid wonderful out of quiet with a sore finger, so that she especially had little rest'.[131] The ill-health of a servant could certainly inconvenience the household. When Josselin's maid was very ill in March 1650, his wife was 'toiled above measure'.[132] A servant's illness could also endanger the family, as in January 1649, when Ralph feared that his maid had smallpox.[133] In turn, the family's ailments could endanger the servant, as in August 1658, when the Josselins' maid caught the measles from 4-year-old Ann, and had to return home.[134]

Josselin was less forthcoming about the illnesses of neighbours and friends. Although it was his duty as a clergyman to visit the sick, he did not report doing so very often. Sometimes he was summoned to sick-beds, as in the case of 'a sick man one Guy Penhache who was much troubled in mind upon his life: he had strong temptations from Satan'.[135] In other cases, the sick person was his friend, as when in June 1646 he visited Mr Thomas Harlakenden who was suddenly ill.[136] Jane Josselin was more involved with sick friends and neighbours, often taking the role of nurse in their illnesses and confinements.[137]

Although Ralph Josselin was not as active in visiting the sick as his sociable contemporary, Samuel Pepys, he was interested in the ills which beset others. He was particularly fascinated by the deaths of other ministers. On 1 September 1644 he reported that 'Mr. Pilgrim Minister of Wormingford fell down dead in his pulpit'.[138] He heard of the deaths of two ministers (including the apparent successor to Mr Pilgrim's living) on 28 August 1646.[139] And on 18 June 1657 he 'heard of Mr. Whiting's death minister of Lexden, who putting his finger into a man's mouth whose throat was ill with a squinsey, and non compos mentis, he bit it vehemently on which it gangrened, and killed him about 8 days after'.[140]

Perhaps similar to his interest in the calamities befalling other ministers was his preoccupation with the providence of God in afflicting those who broke heavenly rules. His satisfaction is apparent in his story of 'one John Chrismas a miller in our town whose parents were godly and one in a way of doing well, but his heart boding him to tipple and game, and his wife being sharp to him, he got what he could together, and left her, his brother brought him home, but about a week after he was sick of the pox and died, a warning not to go out of God's way'.[141] Josselin was even more smug in the following report: 'I observe a providence. A man I was hiring one Peakes son, declined me to go to a Quaker I know not his motives, there he fell sick of the small pox, and his mother keep[ing] him came home and died, the Lord watch over me and mine for good'.[142]

In addition to their physical ills, Josselin and his contemporaries were prey to a host of mental disorders. Some were essentially spiritual in nature. Josselin himself apparently suffered from a severe depression during the spring and summer of 1652, writing frequently of a deadness of heart which he felt powerless to combat.[143] However, in Josselin's world the distinction between mental and physical ills was cloudy at best. His friend, Mr R. H. (Richard Harlakenden?), had a spiritual crisis which Josselin felt should be treated with physical means. He wrote, 'Mr. R. H. in great agony of heart sent down for me, weeping, apprehending himself lost for ever. I feared his head most. Got a physician who let him blood, advised him to alter his course of diet[,] he promised it. I lay with him that night. God gave him rest, and I hope in time perfect health.'[144] Another Harlakenden, William, died in 1675, after suffering from madness for a time. His insanity was actually cured by a physical complaint. Josselin wrote, 'an illness in his feet from his running abroad brought the madness out of his head, but he recovered no great use of his reason spiritual or natural, only on discourse, he savoured of both'.[145] Unhealthy mental states brought on physical illness. When Josselin's daughter, Jane, had a relapse of ague, he wrote, 'my wife thinketh with fear and grief to see her mother so tormented as she was with a felon on her finger'.[146] And when Jane Josselin senior became faint and ill two months after the death of her daughter Mary, Ralph felt her disorder was caused by grief.[147]

Like their children, seventeenth-century adults were victims of accidents. The Josselins were fortunate in this respect. Although Ralph reports quite a few 'near misses', only a few of the accidents he and Jane were involved in resulted in injury. Thus on 27 October 1649, 'I was cutting wood the axe slipt and cut the leather at the toe of my shoe almost through without any hurt'.[148] In May 1651 Jane, who was pregnant at the time, fell from her horse, but was not hurt.[149] Sometimes they did hurt themselves, as when Ralph hurt his eye 'very dangerously' and when Jane fell and bruised her eye.[150] However, their neighbours fared much worse. Josselin reported a case where 'One Robert Davy of my town a butcher cutting out of meat, his son in law Kendall stood beside him, was stricken with the cleaver upon the forehead dangerously, beat out his eye etc'.[151] In another case, 'One Mr. Talbot [was] killed in our town by a fall down his stairs at new-house in Coln'.[152]

Despite these examples, the overall impression given by the Josselin diary is that people had less to fear from accidents in seventeenth-century rural England than they do in our gadget-ridden age, regardless of our supposed safety consciousness. A far greater threat posed by the environment was disease – both infectious and non-infectious. The above discussion has concentrated on the ills people suffered from. The next section will describe what Josselin and his social circle did about their ailments.

III 'MEANS' AND HEALERS

Although Ralph Josselin's diary is replete with details about symptoms (particularly Ralph's own), it is much less informative about the treatments used and healers consulted. Indeed, considering the seventeenth-century fondness for remedies (a predilection we share with the people of that time), the diary is tantalizing in what it does not say. In all, Josselin reported approximately 762 cases of illness or injury happening to himself, his family members, his friends, acquaintances and neighbours. In only seventy-nine cases did he mention the treatments applied. And in only twenty-one cases did he even suggest consultation of a healer. What do these numbers mean? It is possible, but unlikely, that most symptoms went untreated. It is more likely that Josselin simply did not always mention the treatments applied. Concerning the consultation of healers, the diary is probably a bit more reliable. Such consultations, except when they involved the midwife or the local bone-setter, required either a journey or formal correspondence. In either case, it would have been uncharacteristic of Josselin to fail to note an incident which cost him either effort or money or both.

Like many of his contemporaries, Josselin was fairly knowledgeable about medical matters. In 1649 he read two medical works – Leonard Lessius' *Hygiasticon, or the Right Course of Preserving Life and Health unto Extreme Old Age* (1634) and Daniel Sennertus' *Institutionum Medicinae* (many Latin and English editions). He routinely examined his own urine during times of illness, interpreting its characteristics in order to determine the prognosis of the disease. For instance, when recovering from a severe ague attack in early March 1648, he wrote, 'my water broke very ragged and a little red sediment[,] it argued as I conceive a remainder of ill humours in me and that nature was concocting and expelling them'.[153] His comment upon the maid Joan's 'urina nigra' mentioned above suggests that he may have examined the urine of other members of his household as well.[154] Josselin also commented upon other bodily excretions. As already indicated, he subscribed to the humoral view of the body and its processes. Thus when he took two ounces of syrup of roses during his 1648 ague, he wrote that it 'wrought very kindly with me, gave me 9 stools brought away much choler'.[155] When he suffered with a 'pose' in November 1646, he hoped it would 'purge out my rheumes', thus helping to end the cold he had had since August.[156]

Together with his wife, Ralph Josselin diagnosed the ailments of his children. They decided that their baby daughter Jane had rickets, that the second Ralph was livergrown, and that 6-year-old Jane had the spleen.[157] When Jane and Thomas were 'shrieking' in their sleep in October 1650, Ralph felt they probably had worms.[158] Having diagnosed a disease, Ralph and Jane treated it themselves or sought out treatment they felt would be appropriate, feeling free to reject both new diagnoses and suggested treatments. Thus, when Jane took 7-

month-old Ralph to Lady Honeywood's to consult with her about his problems, the diary reported the interview as follows:

> my lady fears he is in a consumption, but indeed he is troubled with the rickets, my lady adviseth an issue to which my wife hath no mind god in mercy bless other means that are used.[159]

Indeed, the main authority on medical matters in the Josselin household was not Ralph, but Jane. Ralph did not indicate whether or not she had read medical works, but he mentioned her role as nurse and medical consultant during many illnesses of family members, friends and neighbours. Jane made at least two of the medicines she used – a distillation of roses and hyssop syrup.[160] She dosed members of her family, acted as a surgeon when their burns, cuts and ulcers needed dressing, and helped out during her neighbours' and daughters' confinements.[161] She nursed her husband and children when they were ill, sometimes becoming ill herself in the process.[162] Indeed, nursing was so important a part of her expected role that Ralph was quite annoyed when she withheld this service, as was the case on 16 November 1676, when 'my wife on some discontent which I know not, would not assist me in dressing my poor leg'.[163] Jane was also summoned to the sickbeds of friends and neighbours. When her dear friend Mary Church hurt her leg in April 1647, Jane applied leeches to it.[164] When Lady Honeywood's child was ill in August 1648, Jane went to Markshall (the Honeywoods' home) to help out.[165] Jane also treated herself, dosing herself with 'pills' for wind and tobacco for toothache in one instance.[166]

The Josselins relied mainly on herbal remedies and 'simples', rather than the compound medicines favoured by apothecaries and physicians. When Ralph was stung by a bee in September 1644, he applied honey to the bite.[167] He used 'violet cake' for an aguish feeling in March 1645, syrup of roses for ague in February 1648, and a mixture of plantain water and loose sugar as a dressing for his sore navel in November 1648.[168] Similarly the Josselins dressed baby Ralph's sore eyes with rose ointment and plantain water, and treated Tom with treacle posset when he had the smallpox.[169]

Very occasionally more complex remedies were tried. In April 1649 Ralph treated a cold both with mithridate, which he must have purchased, and with a 'Stibium vomit prepared at Cogshall', presumably by an apothecary.[170] During his final illness, he took Daffy's elixir, Talbor's pills and a medicine prescribed by the London physician Dr Cox, with whom Josselin corresponded.[171] In an attempt to cure his leg, Josselin also made a trip to Tunbridge Wells, drinking the waters there between 13 July and 1 August 1675. He also had an 'issue made on me in order to the cure of my leg' in June 1675.[172] However, even during those last ten years of torment, Ralph relied mainly on simple, herbal remedies, both as dressings and as internal medicines. He poulticed his leg with red rose leaves and milk, with bread, with burdock leaves, clote leaves and green tobacco leaves.[173] He ate nutmeg, took hartshorn drops and drank 'Mrs. Spicer's ale'.[174]

A question which is often asked is 'did these remedies work?' Certainly modern herbalists and homeopaths rely on substances which would have been familiar to the Josselins. However, the purpose of this study is not to determine by controlled experiments whether herbal or 'old-fashioned' remedies actually ameliorate symptoms like those the Josselins suffered from, but to explore the Josselins' experiences as related in Ralph's diary. As indicated above, the question of whether or not a medicine 'worked' was understood differently by Ralph Josselin from the way it would be by a modern patient.[175] For him, a remedy could 'work' without curing the patient. This was the case when his daughter Mary, five days before her death, was given a clyster which 'wrought very well'.[176] Indeed, medicine was expected to make the patient feel sick. When Josselin's two children, Thomas and Jane, were given physic in June 1650 (presumably in a state of health), they 'were sick even to death, so that our hearts trembled, fearing the issue, but the lord in mercy to us quickly blew it over, and they revived and are now well'.[177]

Of course, the Josselins hoped that medicine taken during times of illness would help to produce a cure. In May 1683, when Ralph was desperate for relief from his multiple ailments, he wrote to Dr Cox in London for prescriptions. He reported, 'Cox sent me his old receits: the Apothecary made [me] pay dear'.[178] Several days later he wrote, 'I took my physic from Dr. Cox . . . my wife apprehends it doth me no good, but I cannot be fully of that mind'.[179] Some remedies were more definite in their effects. When Jane senior had wind and toothache in July 1646, pills 'wrought very kindly and carried the wind sensibly out of her side' while tobacco gave her 'much ease' from her toothache.[180] And when Ralph returned from travelling, aguish and sore, Jane's 'careful use of means', together with her tenderness and God's goodness, cured him.[181]

In most cases Ralph and Jane Josselin relied upon their own medical knowledge and skill to treat their own ailments and those of their children. However, they occasionally asked for the help of other people – friends, nurses, part-time healers and full-time medical 'professionals'. Lady Honeywood apparently acted as an informal general practitioner, advising the Josselins when their children were ill, and even looking after Ralph senior for over a month when his left leg first began to trouble him.[182] About this visit Ralph wrote on 27 January 1673, 'Went to Markshall. My L. Honeywood sent her coach for me. There I stayed to March 10 in which time my Lady was my nurse and physician and I hope for much good'.[183] As we have seen, Jane Josselin was able to return Lady Honeywood's favour, helping out at Markshall when a Honeywood child was ill. The Josselins also asked the Harlakendens at the priory for medical help, getting from them a medicine for worms during Mary's final illness.[184] Neighbours other than the local gentry also helped the Josselins during their illnesses. When Ralph suffered from a particularly severe ague fit on 13 February 1648, '2 hours before day . . . some neighbours came in'.[185] And when Jane became faint and ill with grief in August 1650, Ralph 'sent for neighbours'.[186]

In addition to this informal help from lay-people, the Josselins also consulted two local women who apparently acted as bone-setters. When John Josselin 'had a fall about the street threshold which made him limp', the 'shut-bone in his instep' was set by 'Spooner's wife'.[187] When the second Mary's arm was pulled out of joint by the maid, 'Mrs. Withers came and set it', splinting Jane senior's instep at the same time (for what injury we are not told).[188]

When Jane Josselin gave birth she was routinely attended by the midwife and a number of neighbour women. In at least one case a nurse was present. Twice Jane's labours were so quick that the midwife could not be summoned.[189] As Ralph wrote on one of these occasions, 'when god commands deliverance there is nothing hinders it'.[190]

In three recorded cases the Josselins hired a nurse to help out for the first few weeks after a baby was born, when Jane was still in bed. The nurse stayed for about a month after their third child was born, and stayed for five days after the death of the first Ralph.[191] She stayed only two weeks after the birth of their eighth child, but this was because she had promised her services to another woman.[192] Ralph thought no less of her for this, calling her 'an honest harmless quiet woman'. The nurse was apparently summoned about a week before the child was expected. For instance, although in the last mentioned case where the nurse left when the baby was 2 weeks old, Josselin indicated that she left on the twentieth day of her stay.

The Josselins almost never consulted physicians and surgeons. Despite the fact that five Josselin children died between February 1648 and July 1673, only once was a physician called to a child's death-bed. Oddly enough, this one occasion was four days before the death of the first Ralph, then only 6 days old.[193] One wonders whether the physician also saw Ralph senior, then ill of ague, since the baby was prescribed syrup of roses – the same medicine his father had taken three days earlier.

Otherwise the only member of the Josselin family to consult physicians, surgeons and apothecaries was, as far as we know, Ralph senior. This he did on only one recorded occasion in his early life, during a quotidian ague.[194] He did not see a physician thereafter until 1675, when he had already suffered with his swollen and ulcerated left leg for two years. During his long final illness, Josselin consulted the physicians Dr Talbor and Dr Cox.[195] He apparently visited Dr Talbor in person, while he merely corresponded with Dr Cox. During the same illness he also consulted two surgeons – the first unnamed, the second a Mrs Doughtie.[196] He also used the services of an apothecary to make up Dr Cox's prescriptions.[197]

It would be incorrect to suggest that Josselin 'did not believe in' physicians. In one case already cited, the instance when Mr R. H. suffered an emotional crisis, Josselin sent for a physician himself, feeling that medical intervention was necessary. Indeed, Josselin had a personal friend who was a physician. Dr and Mrs Colier and their daughter arrived from London on 1 August 1664, and stayed with the Josselins until 19 August. During their visit, John Josselin developed a violent fever: Josselin wrote, 'it was a great mercy Dr. Colier was with us'.[198] None the less, it seems obvious that the Josselins only rarely felt that the services of a physician were necessary, even in the most extreme cases. Since Ralph never wrote about his feelings about physicians, one can only speculate about the reasons for his behaviour.

Possibly the Josselins avoided licensed medical practitioners because of the expense involved in consulting them. Despite Ralph's comparatively high socio-economic standing in Earls Colne, he mentioned cash-flow problems on several occasions, and certainly as a man with a large family, he felt the need to be careful about expenditure.[199] Perhaps there were so few physicians and surgeons in the vicinity that the Josselins felt it impractical to rely upon them even during crises. However, the most likely explanation of the Josselins' behaviour is that neither healers nor remedies were of ultimate importance in determining the outcome of an illness. Whatever happened was God's will.

Josselin rarely mentioned health or illness without mentioning God. In this, as indicated above, he was a man of his time. It might be tempting to argue that Josselin, the vicar, was merely paying pious lip-service to convention. After all, he did resort to physical remedies as well as prayer. However, the diary leaves no doubt that Josselin's faith was real and, from his point of view, rewarded. For instance, when Josselin was troubled with an ague in 1643, his physician told him he would have one more harsh fit, 'but on Friday night seeking God for my health that if it pleased him I might go on in my calling, I was strangely persuaded I should have no more fits neither had I'.[200] As this example demonstrates, although Josselin occasionally consulted healers and used medicines, hoping that these would help, he placed far more confidence in the Divine Physician.

Josselin truly felt that the best remedy was prayer and the best preventative medicine was a sinless life. As Alan Macfarlane points out, Josselin held himself responsible for both his own ailments and those of his children.[201] This belief is taken to its logical extreme in Josselin's assumption that God had punished him for his fondness for playing chess by killing the infant Ralph.[202] Josselin's feelings of guilt and responsibility drove him to ever-stronger devotion to God: after all, his family and friends were, in effect, hostages for his good behaviour.

Fortunately for Josselin, the divine pendulum swung both ways. His preoccupation with providence as it affected himself and his neighbours has been mentioned above. Believing that evil-doers were surely and swiftly punished, he was often relieved and grateful when potential disasters failed to harm him and his. For instance, on 31 March 1648 on a trip to Colchester, 'my horse threw me as I returned home, but through the good providence of God, I had no hurt at all'.[203] However, only good behaviour and prayer could predispose God in Man's favour, and even those sometimes failed. Because of his limited capabilities, Man could not always know how he had sinned in order to bring calamity upon himself. Thus, when both his wife and daughter were ill, Josselin wrote, 'It's hard to find out the particular cause of our troubles, but what good we omit, or ill we do that is hinted to us, it's safe to reform, to thee oh . . . lord we come in Christ for thy healing in body and spirit'.[204] Therefore, Josselin and his family were perpetually at work to propitiate their stern heavenly father. They prayed as individuals, in family groups and with friends and neighbours to heal sickness, survive childbirth, avoid epidemics and, in one case, help a parishioner while he was being cut for the stone in London.[205]

Ralph Josselin's theological view of illness dovetailed nicely with his humoral orientation. Both approaches saw ill-health as a personal, particular manifestation stemming from divine displeasure, or an imbalance of the individual's humoral make-up. Thus, each individual's ailment was different from those of others, requiring individual understanding for its cure. Thus a cold could be caused either by the sufferer's sin or by his having had wet feet. In either case, it could be dealt with by a combination of physical 'means' and prayer. Without divine sanction, it could not be cured. In the case of epidemics, of course, collective sin and 'distempered and infected air' worked together to produce a calamity in the face of which humanity could only bow its collective head.[206] Perhaps this is why Josselin so feared epidemic diseases such as smallpox and plague. His own good behaviour and repentance might not be enough to save him and his family from such infections. Consider his reflections in August 1644, when the plague, 'that arrow of death', was at Colchester. 'What a mercy of God is it to respite our town Lord spare it, and let not our sins, our covetousness and pride of the poor in the plenty of their Dutch work cause thee to be angry with us'.[207] How fearful, to have to depend upon the relative virtue of all of one's fellow townspeople!

IV SICKNESS BEHAVIOUR AND ATTITUDES

Despite the numerous references to ill-health contained in the diary, neither Ralph Josselin nor members of his family often took up a 'sick' role. While they frequently complained and sometimes took medicines, their behaviour was analogous to that of modern people whose livelihoods would be threatened by too frequently 'calling in sick'. This is not surprising. When Ralph fell sick, he had either to find a local clergyman willing to preach to his congregation or to leave his flock without spiritual comfort. As noted above, even when he became a near invalid in his last years, he managed to preach on Sunday. Certainly his living was by no means so secure that he could afford to neglect his duties. Particularly after the

Restoration, Josselin remained in Earls Colne on sufferance.[208] A long illness might have helped to persuade the already suspicious authorities that the Nonconformist Josselin had to go.

Jane Josselin also could not afford to take to her bed when she felt unwell. Although she had a maid-servant to help with housework and childcare, her task was a heavy one. Her house was relatively large, her family at most times numbering seven or eight (including husband and servant as well as children). In addition to helping with the cooking, cleaning and farm-work she nursed her husband, children and servant when they were ill, and also helped friends and neighbours, as indicated above. She was needed. Thus, although her pregnancies were uncomfortable and she frequently complained of aches and pains when she was not pregnant, she neither took up a sick role nor was regarded as sick by her husband unless her illness actually incapacitated her.

The diary does not always indicate when one of the Josselins was confined to bed. Jane senior spent about three weeks in bed after each childbirth. Ralph was confined to bed for about two weeks with a severe ague attack in February 1648. Thomas spent at least two weeks in bed with smallpox in June 1659. Mary spent between two and three weeks in bed with her attack of worms before she died in May 1650.

During acute bouts of illness, the Josselins were treated differently from the way they were during periods of minor discomfort. They were visited by friends and neighbours, remedies were actively sought and, in at least Ralph senior's case, the sufferer's urine was examined. Family members took care of one another. We have already seen that Jane or her daughters were expected to dress Ralph's diseased leg. When Jane senior was seriously ill with a quartan ague in the autumn of 1668, her adult daughter Jane came home to tend her. And when Elizabeth was reported to be fatally ill in London in March 1682, Jane senior hurried to be with her.

The process of arising from a sick-bed was gradual and apparently conformed to certain expected conventions. Ralph reported when Thomas was able to sit up and when he first came downstairs during his recovery from the smallpox.[209] He mentioned when his wife arose from her bed and when she first left the house – usually to go to church – after giving birth.[210]

Conversely Josselin occasionally commented when an illness did not confine the sufferer to bed or keep him or her from daily employments. On 28 April 1650, in one of his many weekly reports of his family's health, he wrote, 'Mary, and my wife, ill but not down sick'.[211] And when Ralph had a cold, 'pose' and pain in the right side of his head in September 1646, he wrote 'yet praise be god I continued able to do my work'.[212]

Unfortunately the diary does not mention special food or clothing used during times of sickness. It says virtually nothing about the expected sick role and treatment of young children. Yet it certainly gives the impression that the Josselins had definite expectations of themselves and others during periods of acute illness. Sick people were expected to act sick – to stay in bed, be waited on and (possibly) take medicine. People well enough to be out of bed were entitled to complain about discomfort but were expected to carry on with their normal duties as far as possible. The major exception to this rule, then and now, was chronic illness. Although Ralph was able to preach during the last ten years of his life, he behaved in other respects like a sick person, trying many remedies, consulting several healers, and expecting special services and consideration from family members.

As we have seen, the Josselins suffered from and died of a variety of illnesses. However, the ailments they had, with minor exceptions, were not the ones Ralph most feared. For instance, although his daughter Mary died of worms, he did not appear to be particularly concerned when he or others of his children suffered from that complaint. After her death, he even mentioned his relief that her disease had not been infectious.[213] Yet he was terrified of epidemic diseases, particularly smallpox and plague. He mentioned his apprehension about smallpox no fewer than twenty-one times in the course of some thirty years. His fear remained even after several of his children had contracted the disease and recovered from it. Whenever smallpox was in Earls Colne, Josselin mentioned the fact, and often gave details of those who died from it.[214] Always nervous about it, his fear apparently reached a peak during a particularly virulent outbreak of the disease in 1651. When both Thomas and John developed rashes in early 1652, Josselin was certain they had the smallpox.

Although plague was a less frequent visitor to the vicinity, Josselin feared it terribly. During the great plague year 1665–6, he recorded figures from the London Bills of Mortality weekly. His comments on Earls Colne's virtual escape from infection ranged from the complacent 'God good in our preservation', to the frantic 'when will Colne lay it to heart', to the mystified 'and yet Colne, sinful Colne spared'.[215]

Josselin's fears were based on both medical and religious concerns. Plague and smallpox were particularly deadly diseases. Although there were many remedies which promised to prevent or cure the plague, it was generally regarded as incurable. And, while physicians argued the merits of 'hot' or 'cooling' regimens in the treatment of smallpox, the disease mutilated those it did not kill and was, therefore, particularly horrific.[216]

More frightening than the failure of medicine to deal with epidemics was their sudden and mysterious onset. Josselin was convinced that epidemics, like all other diseases and misfortunes, were God's punishment for sin. Seeing epidemics as a threat, Josselin yet felt he could do very little to keep them away. He could merely pray and watch their progress with horrified fascination. He also may have seen epidemics as possible heralds of the end of the world. For instance, he described the late summer of 1647 as a time

> of great sickness and illness, agues abounding more than in all my remembrance, last year and this also, fevers spotted rise in the county, whether it arise from a distempered and infected air I know not, but fruit rots on the trees as last year though more, and many cattle die of the murrain, this portends something.[217]

Whatever the reasons, epidemic diseases were for Ralph Josselin what cancer is for many modern Westerners. The mysterious terrors of their very names made the shivering and burning of ague fits seem desirable by comparison.

V CONCLUSIONS

The Josselins' experience of ill-health can by no means be assumed to be typical for mid-seventeenth-century England. For instance, Ralph Josselin's near contemporary, Samuel Pepys, was both more secular in his attitude toward disease, and more likely to consult a licensed physician or surgeon than was the vicar. The conclusions we can draw must therefore refer only to the Josselins themselves.

Ralph Josselin was unwell, or at least uncomfortable, most of the time. It is no wonder that he at one time reflected that 'this life is a bundle of sorrows'.[218] The nearly continual colds which plagued him and his family, their unpleasant eye and skin disorders, and the endless discomforts of Jane's pregnancies, surely encouraged the feeling that ill health was a normal state of affairs. Indeed, Josselin commented on good health whenever he could in his weekly reports, thus giving the impression that such a state of affairs was at least worthy of remark.[219]

Although the Josselins occasionally consulted healers and more frequently used medicines, they did not expect to be cured by such measures. Rather, they hoped for some help through them, but were not disappointed when remedies and healers failed. Their ultimate trust was in God, and they did not expect to feel completely well in any case.

For the Josselins, as for their contemporaries, death was familiar and expected. It could come at any time, as the result of any accident or illness. Thus, it was natural to think of death for oneself or one's loved ones in almost any situation. For instance, nine days after giving birth, Jane was 'very ill, as if she would have even died, [and] she uttered as formerly these words thou and I must part'.[220] When 2-month-old John became ill, his father expected death and 'cried to my God with tears for him and he heard presently he sweetly revived'.[221]

However, for Ralph Josselin the expectation of death did not reduce the value of the loved one. If anything, his wife and children were precious to him partly because his fear of losing them was quite real. Certainly Josselin did not fail to become emotionally attached to his children because of the likelihood that they would not survive. His grief for 8-year-old Mary produced the most moving passage in the diary, and his desolation is apparent in his reflections on the deaths of Thomas and Ann in the summer of 1675: 'god hath taken 5 of 10. lord let it be enough, and spare that we may recover strength'.[222]

And, in the same vein, despite Lawrence Stone's argument, naming a child after a deceased sibling did not, for the Josselin family, indicate 'a lack of sense that the child was a unique being, with its own name'.[223] There were probably two different reasons for the two examples of this practice in the Josselin family. In one case, two infants born within fifteen months of each other were named Ralph after their father. In this case the re-use of the name indicates, not disregard for the individuality of the first baby (though he died at only 10 days old), but a special value placed upon the name itself. In the second case, the Josselins' eighth child was named Mary nearly eight years after the death of her older sister of that name. In this case, it is fair to assume that the name was meant as a memorial to the deceased older child rather than as a negation of her individuality.

Despite expectation of death, the Josselins were relatively fortunate in surviving the hazards of their time. Ralph himself lived to be 67. His wife, only ten months younger than he, survived him, as did five of his children, the eldest of whom was nearly 38 and all of whom were over 19 at the time of his death. Considering Lawrence Stone's findings, that in 1650 40 per cent of squires and above left no son; that nearly 40 per cent of children born in 1650 died before the age of 15; and that peers born in 1625 could expect to live until only about 31, Ralph Josselin and his family did very well indeed.[224]

8

THE CHARACTER OF A GOOD WOMAN: WOMEN AND ILLNESS

I INTRODUCTION

In this chapter we will see the experience of sufferer and healer combined. Women, like men, endured the multifarious ills of seventeenth-century life. However, as indicated above, their traditional role demanded that they also act as healers. Such a demand was not unique to seventeenth-century England. One anthropological study states

> No matter how we may wish to interpret a prehistoric
> gynomorphic world and women's ritual roles in it, it is clear that
> feminine ritual domains and roles today usually centre on
> midwifery, participation in possession cults, and healing. Women
> participate in rituals of healing nearly everywhere, for in most
> cultures such ritual roles are both achieved and ascribed.[1]

The stereotypes of the female witch, midwife, nurse and traditional healer remain a familiar part of our own cultural heritage.

The evidence suggests that by the seventeenth century both the scope of activities of female healers and the respect generally accorded them was in decline. Muriel Joy Hughes's excellent study of *Women Healers in Medieval Life and Literature* gives details of both literary characters and female medical practitioners known in medieval Europe.[2] Her work shows that women acted as both amateur and paid healers and that some women received medical educations comparable to those of their male colleagues. Although few medical faculties opened their doors to women, those at Florence and Naples apparently did in this period.[3] Some medieval female healers were both respectable and famous.[4]

Alice Clark, whose *Working Life of Women in the Seventeenth Century* remains the standard authority on the subject, maintained that the gradual exclusion of women from many

A late sixteenth-century birth scene. While the midwife delivers the baby, the mother's friends comfort and encourage her, and the physician casts the new-born's horoscope. (J. Rueff, *De conceptu et generatione hominis*, 1580.)

paid occupations was an aspect of the growth of capitalism and industrialisation. She wrote,

> It has been shown that when social organisation rested upon the basis of the family, as it chiefly did up to the close of the Middle Ages, many of the services which are now ranked as professional were thought to be specially suited to the genius of women, and were accorded to them in the natural division of labour in the family.[5]

In the seventeenth century such services as school teaching and healing had established themselves in the marketplace. Removed from the domestic sphere, they became less and less appropriate for women.

Although many women did practise as paid healers in seventeenth-century England, their activities were frowned upon by male practitioners and most conventional avenues for medical and surgical education were closed to them. English universities would not admit them. Neither would the Royal College of Physicians. While the London Company of Barbersurgeons admitted women to the 'freedom', these practitioners were denied the privileges of full membership.[6] And the Charter of the Company of Barbersurgeons at Salisbury (1614) specifically excluded women.[7]

Such discrimination was directly related to commonly held views regarding the basic nature of women. These views were partly determined by theology. Judaic and Christian scholars saw women as the daughters of Eve, inherently sinful and evil. The only way a woman might possibly escape such categorisation was by denying her femaleness and becoming a nun. According to St Jerome,

> As long as a woman is for birth and children, she is different from man as body is from soul. But if she wishes to serve Christ more than the world, then she will cease to be a woman and will be called man.[8]

Classical and medieval theories of female physiology supported the theological line. Some writers, with Aristotle, saw women as inversions of men, imperfect and corrupt; the mere uncreative vessels of male seed. Some took Galen's slightly more positive view that women were unique in design, like men possessing the creative 'semen' necessary to produce a child.[9] However, none of the medical writers argued that women were equal to men. They assumed that women were peculiarly vulnerable to disease because of their physiology and often took a female patient's menstrual and childbearing history into account in diagnosing and treating her, regardless of the ailment she complained of. Menstruation, the common denominator of female experience and identity, while necessary to the mature woman's health, was also the mark of her inferiority. Menstrual blood itself was regarded as venomous, sometimes hurting women as it flowed, and posing danger to anything or anyone coming into contact with it.[10] Menstruating women soured wine and caused plants to die. A book published in 1506 warned that sexual intercourse during menstruation would be fatal to the man.[11]

In addition, women were viewed as sexually insatiable. Lack of orgasm, like amenorrhoea, could cause illness. The physician Nicolas Fontaine wrote in 1652, 'Wives are more healthful than widows or virgins, because they are refreshed with the man's seed, and ejaculate their own'.[12] For men, however, retention of semen increased physical and moral strength.[13] The man's sexual urge was controllable; the woman's was not.

Thus, female physiology reinforced the view that women were both inferior and dangerous. Such views permeated social life and were manifested in various ways. Perhaps the most extreme was in the scholarship concerning witchcraft. The *Malleus Maleficarum* (1486), for two centuries the chief handbook for witch-hunters, is imbued with male fears about female physiology and sexuality.[14] Although authorities on the subject agreed that men as well as women could be witches, the *Malleus* argued that 'Women are chiefly addicted to Evil Superstitions'.[15] Such women copulated with devils. They also came to innocent men as they slept and sexually assaulted them in a kind of demonic rape. Witches could make men impotent. They also performed a form of magical castration, working 'some Prestidigitory Illusion so that the Male Organ appears to be entirely removed and separate from the Body'.[16] Women deprived of normal sexual activities were most likely to become witches, partly because Satan offered himself to them as a sexual partner.

Witches, both male and female, were involved with the causing and curing of illness. Traditional healers, such as white witches, cunning-folk and wise-men and -women, were particularly vulnerable to the attacks of witch-hunters. Indeed, the feminists Ehrenreich and English see the European witchcraze as essentially a male conspiracy to remove women from their prominent place in the practice of medicine.[17] While this overstates the case, persecution of witches did much to discourage the open practice of traditional medicine.

Of course, most women were not witches. However, their bodies handicapped them both socially and morally. Medical writers took a cooler tone than did witch-hunters. None the less, in their works

> woman is considered to be inferior to man in that the physiological effects of her cold and moist humours throw doubt on her control of her emotions and her rationality; furthermore, her less robust physique predisposes her . . . to a more protected and less prominent role in the household and in society. Although apparently not bound by the authority of the divine institution of matrimony, doctors nonetheless produce a 'natural' justification for woman's relegation to the home and exclusion from public office, and provide thereby, as well as coherence with a central tenet of theology, an important foundation on which arguments in ethics, politics and law are based.[18]

Writers of sermons and works on household management conventionally advised husbands that it was their duty to control their wives. Man, as the rational half of creation, was required to direct and organise irrational woman.

None the less, women were felt to possess natural aptitudes which were basically good. Healing, if done within the proper sphere, was one of these. Timothy Rogers, whose handbook was published in 1697, wrote that the good woman was one who

> distributes among the indigent, money and books, and clothes and physick, as their several circumstances may require.

She relieved

> her poor neighbours in sudden distress, when a doctor is not at hand, or when they have no money to buy what may be necessary for them; and the charitableness of her physick is often attended by some cure or other that is remarkable. God gives a *peculiar blessing* to the practice of those women who have no other design in this matter, but the doing good: that neither prescribe where they may have the advice of the learned, nor at any time give or recommend any thing to try experiments, but what they are assured from former trials is safe and innocent; and if it do not help cannot hurt.[19]

Such a description of female duties obviously was intended for

women of middling and upper status. That many gentlewomen conformed to this ideal is evident. We have seen that
Lady Margaret Hoby, Lady Honeywood and Jane Josselin,
among others, gave medical treatment to relatives, friends and
neighbours. In addition, examples are cited of poor women
who cured and gave medical advice.[20] Along with household
duties, gardening, bearing and caring for children and looking
after men, healing was a natural manifestation of the feminine
duty to nurture and sympathise.

As an amateur activity, healing remained respectable. In the
early eighteenth century Cotton Mather wrote,

> It is time to fix my three elder daughters in the opficial and
> beneficial mysteries, wherein they should be well instructed; that
> they may do good unto others. . . . For Katy, I determine
> knowledge in physic and the preparation and dispensation of
> noble medicines. For Nibby and Nancy, I will consult their
> inclinations. . . . To accomplish my little daughters for
> housekeeping, I would have them at least once a week, to prepare
> some new thing, either for Diet or Medicine.[21]

More than a century earlier, Lady Mildmay, born Grace
Sherrington, wrote that the cousin who had brought her up
included medical studies in her general education:

> And when she did see me idly disposed she would set me to
> cypher with my pen, and to cast up and prove great sums and
> accounts, and sometimes to set me to write a supposed letter to
> this or that body concerning such and such things, and other
> times let me read in Dr. Turner's Herbal and Bartholomew Vigo,
> and other times set me to sing psalms, and other times set me to
> some curious [needle] work.[22]

This lady's daughter wrote of her that she 'spent a great part
of her days in the search and practice [of] man's body drugs,
preparations of medicines, and signs of disease'.[23]

Even the anti-quack writers, despite their doubts about
women's fitness for learned endeavours, were uncharacteris-
tically taciturn about the activities of gentlewoman healers.[24]
These women were not only respectable, but also necessary.
Even learned physicians accepted and used recipes culled from
gentlewomen of their acquaintance.[25] Such ladies continued to
heal long after the end of the seventeenth century.

Less generally respected, but certainly as useful, were the
women who acted as paid healers. Lowliest in status were
sick-nurses. Alice Clark reminds us that not all nurses were

amateurs. Hospitals employed them and expected them to conform to convent-like rules. Parish account books record payment of nurses who attended the poor. Private families also hired nurses.[26]

The archetypal female healer was the midwife.[27] However, women also became surgeons and apothecaries. This sometimes happened as the result of a family connection. For instance, the sister of the great seventeenth-century oculist, Dr Turberville, practised in London after his death. Sometimes the family connection is either unknown or non-existent, as is the case with the female bone-setters and surgeon consulted by Ralph Josselin.[28]

It should be emphasised here that the services performed by paid female medical practitioners were identical to those performed by amateurs. Women routinely prepared and administered medicines, delivered babies, gave enemas, applied leeches and dressed wounds. As long as they remained unpaid, the worst crime male healers accused them of was interference.

Thus, women were intimately involved with all the health incidents of humanity – illness, injury, childbearing, old age and death. Female bodies, with their recurring cycles of menstruation, pregnancy, childbirth, lactation and menopause, tied women both personally and socially to the physical processes of life. Their roles as sufferers and healers were interwoven; within the domestic sphere, women were the medical authorities of seventeenth-century England.

II CASE STUDIES

In order to give a personal dimension to our exploration of the female experience of illness, we will examine a diary and an autobiography written by seventeenth-century women. The same difficulties attend the use of these materials as are associated with the use of similar records kept by men. The writers are invariably of middling or upper social status. Thus, one cannot assume that their attitudes and experiences are representative of those of the general population. This is particularly true for women, since fewer women than men have left any sort of personal account. In addition, the search for information relating to medical matters inevitably distorts our perception of the writer's general preoccupations. None the less, this study has thus far concentrated upon the experiences, attitudes and behaviour of male healers and sufferers. It is time to hear from the ladies.

Diaries and autobiographies, although equally useful to the medical historian, yield different sorts of information about the writer's illness experience. Diaries tell us of the day-to-day ailments, major and minor, suffered by the writer and her social circle; they also reveal much about attitudes toward pain and disease. Autobiographies, on the other hand, may say little about daily aches and pains. However, because their subject matter is selected from the writer's past, they can indicate much about the importance matters of health and illness had for her. In this section we will explore and compare the medical experiences of two women, the diarist Lady Margaret Hoby, and the autobiographer Mrs Alice Thornton.

Lady Margaret Hoby

Margaret Dakins was born in Linton, Yorkshire, to the prosperous landowner Arthur and his wife Thomasine in February 1571.[29] As their only child and heir, Margaret's future prospects were taken seriously; she was educated in the 'sternly Puritan' household of Catherine, Countess of Huntingdon. There she met her first husband, Walter Devereux, second son of the Earl of Essex. She was married in 1589 at the age of 18. As her husband was only 20, one might have expected the marriage to last for many years. However, he was killed in 1591, while taking part in his brother Robert's mission to assist Henry IV of France in the siege of Rouen.[30] Margaret and her fortune were again eagerly sought after in the marriage market. Within two months of Devereux's death, she married Thomas Sidney, favourite nephew of the Countess of Huntingdon. However, this marriage did not last much longer than her first. Sidney died in July 1595, and Margaret was again a widow.

Within a week of her husband's death, Margaret was approached by Sir Thomas Posthumus Hoby who, with the help of his redoubtable mother, Lady Russell, had sought her hand after Walter Devereux's death.[31] Hoby, whose personal attractions were apparently not great, pressed his suit eagerly.[32] However, it seems that business, rather than love, won the lady for him. Hoby and his powerful connections helped Margaret in a law suit she was involved in concerning land which both she and the new Earl of Huntingdon claimed.[33] She became Lady Hoby in August 1596, and took up residence in Hackness, Yorkshire. There she lived during the years 1599–1605, when she wrote her diary. There she died in 1633 after a long and virtuous life.

Margaret Hoby was a very wealthy woman. Her property was worth £1,500 a year when she died. She had no children, but committed herself and her fortune to the conventional life-style of the Puritan gentry of her time and to a variety of good works. She was very religious. After her death, Sir Thomas acted upon her wishes by having a chapel built in Harewood Dale 'for divine service for the good of the souls and bodies of the inhabitants' dwelling in the vicinity.[34] However, her spiritual concerns certainly extended beyond death-bed bequests. During her life she spent much of her time in prayer and devotional reading and conversation. So important was religion to her that she intended her diary as a kind of spiritual account-book, giving details of her devotional exercises and her emotional responses to them.

Despite the fact that hers was a spiritual diary, much may be learned from it about Margaret's illnesses, her healing activities and her attitudes concerning medical matters. It is noteworthy, however, that her diary is relatively poor in details regarding symptoms and treatment. It also mentions few disease names. Thus, while Margaret and Thomas were frequently unwell, we are rarely told what ailed them.

Such vagueness and brevity does not indicate ignorance on the writer's part. As we have seen, Lady Hoby was an active amateur healer who practised both physic and surgery. She grew medicinal herbs, and made many remedies.[35] We know little about her medical education. However, some of it at least came from her reading. As part of her normal routine, she 'read of the herbal'.[36] By the age of 28 she had a reputation as a healer which attracted patients from a large area surrounding her home. Thus, her taciturnity about the ailments she suffered and dealt with requires another explanation.

Matters of health and illness were sufficiently important to Margaret to warrant frequent mentions in her diary. How-ever, they, along with other temporal matters, took a definite back seat to the spiritual concerns which dominated her life. Her entry for 13 January 1600 is quite typical:

> In the morning I, being not well, was driven, to the discomfort of my heart, with short prayer and preparation to go to church: after I came home I dined and, though I were not well, I went again to church where I heard a good sermon. . . . After, I passed the afternoon with little reading because of my sickness.[37]

Illness, as an obstacle to spiritual exercise, was to be either ignored or dealt with as quickly as possible. Intrinsically it was not of sufficient importance to warrant detailed description. Only as a sign of God's displeasure was it significant. Thus, in September 1599 she wrote,

> I was at public prayers very sick: the Lord pardon the sin for which I was so punished, it being the will of God often to punish one sin with another, for I had little profit by that prayer, by reason of my sickness.[38]

Illness was one of God's tools for educating and chastising humans. Only in this context was it truly worth mentioning in a spiritual diary.

A similar observation may be made about Margaret's healing activities. Entries are characteristically extremely brief. Most often she merely recorded having 'dressed' her 'patients'.[39] Even these single words tell us that she was rendering surgical services to people who viewed her as a healer and whom she viewed as clients. However, they tell us almost nothing about the disorders her patients suffered from. Surely her references to her healing activities were made because they redounded to her credit in the spiritual balance sheet she kept concerning herself and other people.

Like many of her contemporaries, including Ralph Josselin and Alice Thornton, Margaret Hoby believed in providence. Her God rewarded the good and punished the evil in this world as in the next. Illness and injury were never random. Thus, on 26 December 1601,

> Was young Farley slain by his father's man, one that the young man had before threatened to kill and, for that end, prosecuting him: the man, having a pike staff in his hand, run him into the eye and so into the brain: he never spoke after: this Judgment is worth noting, this young man being extraordinary prophane, as once causing a horse to be brought into the Church of God, and there christening him with a name, which horrible blasphemy the Lord did not leave unavenged, even in this world, for example t'others.[40]

Unlike Josselin, she rarely viewed her own ailments as punishment for specific sins. However, she credited God with both causing and curing them. Illness, like all other experience, was grist for her spiritual mill: she wrote after recovering from a pain in her shoulder, 'afflictions draw one nearer to God'.[41]

The personal medical history which can be extracted from Margaret's diary is brief, undetailed and undramatic. She was, after all, only 28 when she began writing it. She reported no major illness between 1599 and 1605. Indeed, she was blessed with comparatively good health, which she occasionally mentioned.[42] She did not suffer the repeated colds which tormented other diarists such as Josselin and Pepys. Neither did she report having had ague, although on one occasion Sir Thomas thought he was coming down with that disorder.[43] She noted no menstrual disorders; and, despite the fact that dynastic considerations probably made children desirable, she never mentioned her childlessness as either a physical or a spiritual problem.

This is not to say that she was never ill. Her repeated bouts of toothache sometimes made her so ill that she could not go to church.[44] She also suffered from two fits of the stone in 1601.[45] In addition, she complained of several colds, a cough, headache, pain in her spleen and pain in her shoulder.[46] However, usually she was simply 'unwell'. She reported feeling ill most frequently in the years 1600 and 1601, noting twenty-five complaints in 1600 and twenty in 1601. After that, her reporting of illness dropped dramatically. She mentioned being unwell only once in 1602 and 1603, three times in 1604 and twice in 1605. However, this was more likely the result of her gradual loss of interest in keeping a diary than a reflection of perfect health.

Although she was convinced that God caused illnesses, she did not expect Him to cure them without human aid. None the less, she believed that the hand of the healer was guided by the Lord. She wrote,

> I may truly conclude it is the Lord, and not the physician, who both ordains the medicine for our health and ordereth the ministering of it for the good of his children, closing and unclosing the judgements of men at his pleasure: therefore let everyone physician and patient call upon the Lord for a blessing.[47]

Like her contemporaries, Margaret dosed herself, was treated by friends and consulted healers. She rarely specified the kinds of remedies she took, reporting only the use of 'means'. Only infrequently did she note that a medicine had done her good. In September 1599 'means' cured her of a sickness. And in May 1605 she took 'something' which relieved a pain in her shoulder which came 'by reason of the cold'.[48] She reported only once that remedies had not helped. When she had a toothache on 28 February 1600, she 'was forced to use diverse medicines that did little profit'.[49] On other occasions we can only assume that the treatments applied had the effects she expected.

Both Margaret and Thomas Hoby took prophylactic physic. In April 1600 they travelled to York where they visited friends, heard sermons and consulted healers. Margaret saw two physicians, Dr Benet and Mr Lister, and was probably treated by a surgeon as well. It is likely that she was healthy at the time and that the trip was made primarily for medical reasons. She arrived in the city on 8 April, visited Dr Benet on the 10th, saw 'her physician' again on the 12th, took physic the 14th, 15th and 16th, was let blood on the 18th and took a clyster on the 19th. It is not surprising that she reported feeling unwell on the 20th and 21st.[50] Indeed, the physic she took on the 16th made her so ill she could not pray. Such a medical journey was quite typical for those of the Hobys' social status in the seventeenth century. Many people routinely took physic in the spring; and York, as the nearest population centre, provided a concentration of healers not available in the countryside.

During the period in which her diary was written, Margaret's physician was Mr Lister. She consulted him regularly after an initial interview in September 1599, when she noted that she had 'talked with a physician which, I hope, the Lord hath provided for me in stead of Dr. Brewer'.[51] Brewer had died suddenly about a month previously after having taken 'a medicine he ministered to himself to cause him to sleep'.[52] Lister became a friend of the family, visiting and dining with the Hobys in times of health as well as illness.[53] During a visit to York, when Sir Thomas was taking physic, Margaret 'talked awhile with Mr. Lister, and walked abroad and did see his lodgings' one morning. That evening Lister came to supper. The following morning, Margaret 'talked awhile with Mr. Lister of some of my griefs'.[54]

In addition to Mr Lister, Margaret consulted other healers, paying one, Stephen Tewble, a £7 fee.[55] She was also treated by lay-women of her acquaintance. When she suffered from a cold in London in December 1600, she took a medicine made by 'my lady of Limbrick'.[56]

Friends gave moral as well as medical support in times of illness. During the same cold mentioned above, Margaret stayed in her chamber and was 'visited by Mrs. Thornborow every day'.[57] Indeed, Margaret noted visits during illness and physic-taking as a matter of routine. When Thomas kept his chamber after taking physic in September 1600, he was 'visited by Mrs. Thornborow, Mrs. Blackcollor, and other[s]'.[58]

Margaret returned the favour, visiting the sick-rooms of relations and friends.[59]

However, Margaret's help to the ailing was more often medical than social. It is hard to tell whether her healing activities were more extensive or expert than those rendered by other gentlewomen of the time. None the less, it is certain that she viewed healing as an important duty. Between January and April 1600 she noted that she 'dressed' her 'patients' no fewer than thirty-two times. She appears to have held informal clinics in her home, to which those in need of her services came. For example, on 2 February 1600 she wrote, 'After I had prayed I dressed the sores that came to me'. In another entry she reported that she had 'dressed a poor boy's leg that came to me'.[60] Occasionally she attended her patients twice a day.[61]

She rarely described the problems she dealt with. Many appear to have been wounds. For instance, the serving-man Blakeborn cut his foot with a hatchet on 17 April 1600. Margaret dressed the wound that day and those following until at least the 27th.[62] She also dealt with other 'surgical' problems, giving a 'poor woman of Caton salve for her arm' on one occasion and making 'a salve for a sore breast' on another.[63] Her attempt to find a passage for the waste products of a baby born without an anus have been described above.[64]

In addition, Margaret prepared and prescribed internal remedies. She recorded having made an oil and having prepared a 'purgation for my cousin Ison's woman'.[65] She also attended confinements, although she never reported having delivered a baby herself.[66]

The great majority of her patients were nameless 'poor' people. Thus she provides an interesting contrast to Jane Josselin who treated friends and neighbours regardless of their economic and social circumstances. Margaret Hoby's healing activities smack of *noblesse oblige*. She gave medical treatment as charity – partly because she was skilful, partly because God approved. As a gentlewoman healer, she was conventional; as a Puritan, she aspired to salvation in all she did.

Margaret Hoby's experience of illness serves as a reminder of the dangers of basing historical generalisations on assumptions regarding the behaviour of people whose circumstances conform to predetermined categories. For instance, because she lived in the early years of the century in a remote rural area, was deeply religious and acted as an amateur healer, one might expect her to depend upon self-treatment and God's will in preference to the services of physicians. However, as we have seen, she regularly consulted physicians even when she was not ill, even making special journeys to York to do so. The previous chapter demonstrates that despite certain similarities, she and Ralph Josselin differed markedly in this respect. Both were intensely religious; both comparatively well educated. Both lived in rural communities. Both numbered physicians among their friends. Yet Margaret Hoby was routinely treated by physicians and Ralph Josselin was not. Perhaps the explanation lies in the differences in the circumstances of the two diarists. Josselin, although prosperous, was by no means wealthy. He had a large family to provide for. His village was his social world; he travelled little and lived on the fringes of gentry social circles very much as the neighbourhood vicar. On the other hand, Margaret Hoby was both wealthy and childless. She travelled often to York and London, a respected member of the gentry circuit of town and country houses. In consulting healers as she did, one suspects that she was simply acting in a conventional manner. Certainly her behaviour in this respect is similar to that of Alice Thornton and Lady Anne Halkett, despite their different religious views. Members of the gentry and nobility employed healers as they employed servants – to provide a specific service which they did not wish to do for themselves.

Alice Thornton

Alice Thornton's autobiography tells the tale of a gentlewoman whose status was in decline. She was born in February 1627, to Christopher and Alice Wandesford, wealthy landowners then residing in Kirklington near Ripon. Her father's cousin and patron was the Earl of Strafford. Due to that powerful connection, Christopher Wandesford became Lord Deputy to Ireland, 'acquiring a noble position and estate'.[67] Thus, Alice spent the years between 1632 and 1642 in Ireland, there living among the loyalist gentry and nobility. Her father died of a fever in 1640, and the family finally left Ireland after narrowly escaping harm in the Irish rebellion of 1641. The Wandesfords spent the years of the Civil War, at first wandering around England, then living at Hipswell, Alice's mother's jointure. Although her father's Irish property provided no income for them, enough was available of the English property to maintain their genteel life-style, despite the troubles and expenses inflicted on them by the war.[68]

In 1651 Alice married William Thornton of East Newton in Ryedale. According to the editor of her autobiography, the

Thornton family 'had occupied a fair position among the minor gentry of the North Riding of Yorkshire' for more than three centuries.[69] Greater matches had apparently been proposed to Alice. However, her mother favoured Thornton's suit, and his income (£600 a year) combined with Alice's portion (£500 from the English estate and £1,000 promised from the Irish) appeared to promise a 'handsome competency'.[70]

Alice was a dutiful rather than a joyful bride. She wrote of her engagement,

> Nor could I, without much reluctance, draw my thoughts to the change of my single life, knowing too much of the cares of this world sufficiently without the addition of such incident to the married estate.[71]

Some of her doubts concerned Thornton's religious convictions. His family had converted from Roman Catholicism to Presbyterianism in about 1600. Alice, having been 'educated in the faith of God, and the profession of the true protestant Church of England' could not bear to think of her children being brought up to be Presbyterians. However, Thornton assured her that he was 'for a moderated episcopacy, and kingly government' and that, if she would marry him their children might be educated as she wished.[72] This reservation having been satisfied, Alice accepted his proposal. However, her misgivings went with her to the altar. After the service, she became very ill with 'a great vomiting and sickness at my heart, which lasted eight hours'. This 'condition was extremely bewailed by my husband and mother and my friends, and looked upon as a sad omen to my future comfort'. Alice wrote with hindsight,

> Thus was the first entrance of my married life, which began in sickness, and continued in much afflictions, and ended in great sorrows and mournings. So that which was to others accounted the happiest estate were embittered to me at the first entrance, and was a caution of what trouble I might expect in it.[73]

Despite the bleakness with which she approached her marriage, Alice devoted herself to William Thornton until his death from palsy in 1668. Together they produced nine children, only three of whom survived infancy. None the less, her editor wrote that William was 'a weak, improvident man', who reduced rather than increased the income he had had at their marriage, eventually dying a bankrupt. In addition, Alice was 'unfortunate enough to be deprived of the greater part of her own inheritance'.[74] After her husband died, the widow lived on in the house the couple had had buily shortly after their marriage. She occupied herself with legal business concerning her property, fighting the slanders directed at her by enemies, and religious exercises. And, to record the events of her life and vindicate herself, she wrote her autobiography which she finished in 1669.

Because an autobiography is written from memories of the sometimes distant past, the process of selection involved in its composition reveals much about the general preoccupations of the writer. Alice Thornton was interested in the honour of her family (the Wandesfords), the events of the Irish Rebellion and Civil War, estate business and her own good name. In addition, she was concerned about matters of health and illness. She gave details of all of her own major illnesses and those of her husband and children. She described the last illnesses and death-bed scenes of a number of close relatives. She also recorded narrow escapes from injury and death as marks of the providence of God. Thus, her autobiography provides a wealth of information for the medical historian.[75] It is not as rich a source as diaries written to record the events of daily life, such as those kept by Ralph Josselin and Samuel Pepys. However, it is arguably as useful as the spiritual diary kept by Margaret Hoby because of its attention to detail. And, because it describes the writer's childhood ailments and those of other children in the household, it gives us information about more than one generation's experience of illness and healing.

Alice's preoccupation with the health incidents related to the bearing and rearing of children is understandable, considering her adult experience. She wrote that her own mother had 'brought me forth in great peril of her life, she being weak upon the birth of all her children, having had seven in all, four sons and three daughters'. Alice was 'both a strong and healthful child all along, never having had either the rickets or any other disease' – a fact which she attributed to having been nursed by the same healthy careful wet-nurse who had fed her elder brother.[76] This wet-nurse had 'fresh' milk for Alice, having 'had a child betwixt the nursing my brother and myself'. In this Alice was apparently more fortunate than were some of her own children.

Her daughter, Katherine, for instance, died aged 1 year, 6 months and 21 days, having 'been long in the rickets and consumption, gotten at first by an ague, and much gone in the rickets, which I conceive was caused by ill milk at two nurses'.[77] There is a suggestion that Alice's first living child also suffered from rickets.[78]

Alice's autobiography is a good source for information concerning breast-feeding. Her eldest child, Alice, was nearly overlain by her nurse when she was a new-born.

> One night my mother was writing pretty late, and she heard my dear child make a groaning troublesomely, and stepping immediately to nurse's bed side she saw the nurse fallen asleep, with her breast in the child's mouth, and lying over the child; at which she, being affrighted, pulled the nurse suddenly off from her, and so preserved my dear child from being smothered.[79]

Her experience of wet-nurses certainly suggested to Alice that she should breast-feed her children for their own good. She fed her son Robert until he was 3 years old.[80]

The most serious children's disorders Alice described were rickets, measles, convulsions and smallpox. When she was staying with her Aunt Norton, her father's sister, at about the age of 4,

> It pleased God to bring me into a very dangerous weakness and sickness, upon an accident of a surfeit, by eating some beef which was not well boiled; this causing an extreme vomiting, whose violence drove me into great fever, and that into the measles, and both brought me so low and weak that my aunt and . . . our maid almost despaired of my life.[81]

This description has been quoted at length because it demonstrates the common belief that one disorder could easily change into another, given the appropriate circumstances.[82]

Although the London Bills of Mortality indicate that convulsions claimed the lives of many children in the seventeenth century, in Alice Thornton's experience only one child suffered from this disorder. Her daughter Alice (or Naly, as she was called) had recurring seizures beginning when she was 1 year old. In the first instance, Naly

> being asleep in one cradle and the young infant [Katherine] in another, she fell into a most desperate fit, of the convulsions . . . her breath stopped, grew black in her face, which sore frighted her maid Jane Flower. She took her up immediately, and with the help of the midwife, Jane Rimer, to open her teeth and to bring her to life again. But still, afterwards, no sooner that she was out

of one fit but fell into another fit, and the remedies could be by
my dear mother and Aunt Norton could scarce keep her alive, she
having at least twenty fits; all friends expecting when she should
have died.[83]

In another instance, the 6-year-old Naly was taken to see a
procession celebrating the Restoration. Having 'never seen any
such things as soldiers, or guns, or drums, or noises, and
shouting', she became distraught and 'fell into most dreadful
fits of convulsions there, while she was at Richmond, in Mr.
Smithson's shop'.[84] Again, all feared she would die.

Smallpox, in Alice's experience, was most dangerous to
children. Like John Symcotts, Alice reported having had this
disease more than once. She and her brother Christopher
contracted smallpox in 1631 while living in London. Their
father sent them to Kent, presumably to rid his house of the
infection, and the two children, aged 4 and 6 respectively,
'lodged at one Mr. Baxter's, being kindly used with much care
in that house'. Alice's case was mild and she recovered
quickly.[85] Eleven years later, during their flight from Ireland,
the Wandesford children found themselves in the midst of a
smallpox epidemic. This time it was Alice's brother John who
became ill first, having 'taken them of one of my cousin
William Wandesford's sons'. John had a bad case which left
him 'very much disfigured, having been a very beautiful child,
and of a sweet complexion'. Alice's mother warned her to
stay away from John's sick-room, obviously not assuming
that previous experience of the disease would provide
immunity. Alice obeyed, but she sent messages to her ailing
brother tied around a little dog's neck,

> which, being taken into his bed, brought the infection of the
> disease upon myself, as also the sight of him after his recovery;
> being struck with fear seeing him so sadly used and all over very
> red, I immediately fell very ill, and from that time grew worse till
> I grew so dangerously ill and inwardly sick, that I was in much
> peril of my life, by their not coming well out but kept in at my
> heart.

She was treated by her mother, physicians and 'others', but
had no ease until God 'pleased to hear out petitions for my life
and to spare me in much mercy, and caused them to come
well forth'.[86] As we shall see in Alice's descriptions of her own
children's bouts with smallpox, the question of whether the
spots 'struck' in or out was of much moment in the prognosis
for any case.

Alice and John survived this epidemic. They were fortunate compared to Frank Kelly, a 9-year-old Irish boy whom their father had taken into his household 'for charity'. This child became very ill, was 'miserably sore and could not swallow; his sight was eaten out'. He died after fourteen days of torment, notwithstanding the efforts of Alice's mother, a 'doctor' and 'two watchers'. His death-bed conduct was exemplary, pious and selfless. Alice's account of it, like John Evelyn's descriptions of the deaths of his mother and 5-year-old son, create a picture of the ideal seventeenth-century English death. Alice wrote,

> All the time of this boy's sickness he was so full of sweet expressions and heavenly minded, with much acts of religion, that it was a great comfort to my mother, and all about him, with abundance of patience and gratitude to God and my mother for all they had done for him. . . . This poor boy . . . still prayed for me; when he heard I was in danger of death, desired with tears that God would be pleased to spare my life, and to bless me, that I might live to do much good to others, as to him, and that he might rather be taken away and I spared.

Such reports gave the dear departed the status of secular saints in the memories of those who survived them. They also enabled the healthy to make a much needed mental distinction between the beautiful spirit and disgusting body of one suffering from such a 'loathsome disease'.[87] In an age when the desperately ill were not segregated from the rest of the community, a 'good' death was doubly important to those being reminded of their own mortality.[88]

Alice's own children suffered from smallpox. One infant, William, died of the scourge at only 1 week old. In this drastic case the pocks 'struck in', taking the form generally recognised as the most deadly.[89] Indeed, the 'hot' regimen in treating smallpox favoured by most physicians, which included keeping the patient warm in bed and prescribing cordials, was specifically designed to force the spots outward. Another of Alice's new-borns, Christopher, may have died of the disease at 3 weeks.[90] Katherine had smallpox at the age of 10. Her illness began

> with a violent and extreme pain in the back and head, with such strikes and torments that she was deprived of reason, wanting sleep, nor could she eat anything.

After three days the spots appeared, but due to her

'unguidableness struck in again'. After medication, they came out again and 'she was all over her face in one scurf, they running into each other'. She was bedridden for a month, afterwards healing well, but she 'lost by this sickness her fair hair on her head, and that beautiful complexion God had given'. Two months later, 5-year-old Robert contracted the disease, running through the now familiar pattern of general illness, concern about whether the spots would strike inwards, loss of sight, then a crisis, after which recovery followed quickly. However, Naly came down with smallpox just as Robert was recovering. She had a hard time, like Katherine losing her hair and complexion.[91] The experience of the Wandesfords and Thorntons makes clear just how common and deadly smallpox was in the mid-seventeenth century. It also demonstrates that the scarring left by the disease was not a handicap in the marriage market. In that practical age, social status and economic circumstances were far more important than a pretty face.

The Thorntons, like the Josselin children, encountered numerous accidents as well as illnesses. Alice herself suffered two serious injuries in childhood. At the age of 3 she stumbled in a passageway and struck her forehead against a stone. The wound was so severe that 'the skin of the brain was seen'. This hurt was healed by her mother.[92] The other injury occurred when she was 11. Unlike the accidents befalling the Josselin children, this came as the result of a game. Young Alice, along with other ladies, was 'using the custom to swing by the arms for recreation', an exercise regarded as particularly healthful for children. Alice was being swung vigorously by a young French page and let go of his hands, falling on her face on the floor. She landed

> with such a violent force with all my weight on my chin-bone upward, that both the chin and chap-bones was almost broke in sunder, and put the bone out of its place, and did raise a great lump as big as an egg under my chin and throat, which suddenly astonished me, and took away my breath in so much as I was nigh death.

Again, her mother was able to cure her.[93] In another play injury, Alice's daughter Naly received a 'wound in her belly'.

> My two children was playing . . . in the parlor window and Kate [then 5] being full of sport and play did climb into the window, and leaping down fell upon her sister Alice and thrust her upon

the corner of the same with a great force and strength she had,
and her sister cried out with pain and soreness which had
grievously hurt the inner rind of her belly so sore till I was afraid
she had broken it.

With hindsight, Alice praised 'the name of my God for ever
that she was not wounded so as to break her bowels, it being
in so dangerous [a] place and hazard in her bearing of
children'.[94] For a girl with a reasonable marriage portion, such
a handicap might ruin her future.

Solitary play was dangerous as well. At the age of 3 Kate
'was playing with pins, and putting them in her mouth. . . .
At last she got a pin cross in her throat' which Alice removed
with her finger. However, the situation was quite extreme, for
Kate was 'as black as could be, and the blood set in her face
with it'.[95] We are reminded of John Evelyn's son choking on a
bone.[96] Kate, who was apparently a bit of a handful, while

playing with her cousins in Newton barn and swing cross by a
rope, she got so high a fall . . . that she was taken up dead, being
black and without breath for a long time . . . ; and it was half an
hour before any signs of life appeared. . . . [She] knew nothing of
the fall a long time; it had done her much harm in her head, with
great pains.[97]

Alice's descriptions of children's accidents make the reader
wonder whether the Josselin diary might not have contained
many more notes of the special providence of God regarding
children's narrow escapes from death or serious injury had it
been written by Jane, the main carctaker of the children, rather
than Ralph.

Of course, adults suffered injuries as well as children. Alice's
brother George drowned while attempting to cross a river on
horseback.[98] Alice nearly lost the sight in one eye when it was
pecked by a pet chicken.[99] She also tripped and fell when she
was six months pregnant and worried that she might
miscarry.[100] As it happened, the baby 'stayed in the birth, and
came cross with his feet first' – a problem which Alice
attributed to her fall. The infant died after less than an hour of
life. In addition, she fell downstairs when pregnant with her
son Robert, but the child was unharmed.[101]

The aspect of Alice Thornton's medical history which has
received most attention from historians is her experience of
childbirth and breast-feeding. Lawrence Stone was principally
interested in the Thornton family's high infant mortality and

Dorothy McLaren in that mortality as it related to breast-feeding and wet-nursing.[102] Alice was certainly less fortunate concerning the survival of the babies she bore than was Jane Josselin. Five of Jane's ten live-born infants survived, as opposed to three of Alice's nine.[103]

Alice's own experience motivated her to feed her later babies herself. Her first living child, Naly, was nearly overlain by her wet-nurse, as we have seen. She fed Elizabeth for a short time, but the child died at 18 months of rickets and consumption caused 'by ill milk at two nurses'.[104] It is unlikely that Alice fed her third daughter, Katherine, herself, since the next baby was born only eighteen months after Katherine's birth. That infant died only half an hour after birth, so his death could not have been the result of bad nursing. However, Alice resolved to take no chances with the next baby. She wrote of William that he was

> in good health, sucking his poor mother, to whom my good God had given the blessing of the breast as well as the womb, of that child to whom it was no little satisfaction, while I enjoyed his life; and the joy of it maked me recruit faster, for his sake, that I might do my duty to him as a mother.[105]

Alice found breast-feeding personally satisfying; however, it failed to save William, who died of smallpox aged 1 week. None the less, after this experience, Alice continued to nurse her babies. She fed Robert until he was 3, weaning him only two weeks before giving birth to Joyce, whom she also breast-fed. Joyce died at 4 months of a 'cold which struck in many red spots all over her body and face'. Alice was still suckling her at this time. Her last child, Christopher, took readily to the breast and 'he thrived very well and grew strong, being a lovely babe'. However, this infant also contracted smallpox, dying at just under 3 weeks of age.[106]

As we have seen, Alice tried to give her younger five children the best possible start in life by breast-feeding them. This was uncommon for women of her social status. However, life in seventeenth-century England was fraught with deadly perils for those at any age. Infants were most at risk. Despite the evils of wet-nursing, only one of the six babies Alice lost died because of it. Disease and the hazards of pregnancy and birth accounted for the other five.

Alice's pregnancies were all uncomfortable, although she always felt healthier when she was carrying boys.[107] She was pleased when she conceived seven weeks after her marriage.

However, she was unwell until the child quickened, had a severe nosebleed when about four months pregnant and developed a 'putrid fever' at nearly eight months after journeying to her mother's house at Hipswell, where she planned to bear the baby. This illness was very dangerous, but her 'old doctor', Mr Mahum, 'could do little towards the cure, because of being with child'. Alice wanted to be let blood, a procedure generally frowned upon for pregnant women. This treatment was finally ordered by another physician, Dr Wittie, after an argument with Mr Mahum. Six days later, Alice's labour began. At this point, she had not felt the baby move for several days. The labour lasted for about twenty-four hours, the infant dying before it could be baptised. Alice suffered from the effects of her illness for a long time after the birth. She had a 'terrible shaking ague' for three months, which gave her two fits a day. Her hair and nails fell out and her teeth grew loose and black. Finally, 'upon great and many means used and all remedies', she recovered.[108]

This was not the only eventful and hazardous pregnancy and birth Alice underwent. As indicated above, she had several falls while pregnant which she feared would cause her to miscarry or would harm the baby. Indeed, concerning the pregnancy with her son Robert, she wrote that she had had 'five great trials and hazards of miscarriage'. The first was an illness she suffered; the second, 'a fright which came on me by surprise of the sight of a penknife which was nigh to have hurt me'. This shock caused the child to be born with 'a mark of a deep bloody colour upon the child's heart'. The third and fourth 'hazards of miscarriage' resulted from business troubles; the fifth was a fall down stairs.[109] Alice's fears reveal how perilous the world seemed to pregnant women in the seventeenth century. The bearing of children was important for both estate and personal reasons to women of her class. Sons were particularly precious. When William died, Alice was terribly grieved, and reported that her husband was sorely 'afflicted for his loss, and being a son he takes it more heavily, because I have not a son to live'.[110] With the threat of miscarriage ever-present, it is no wonder that Alice felt triumphant when she carried a baby full term and produced it alive.

Alice's labours were long and her deliveries difficult. For example, with her fifth child she experienced contractions for three days before 'sharp travail' began on Wednesday, 9 December. Her pains were so strong that the midwife felt she would deliver soon. However, the position of the baby was such that he could not be born. This

> condition continued till Thursday morning between two and three o'clock, at which time I was on the rack in bearing my child with such exquisite torment, as if each limb were divided from other, for the space of two hours; when at length, being speechless and breathless, I was, by the infinite providence of God, in great mercy delivered.

This birth was so traumatic for the baby that he lived only half an hour after it.[111]

Not all of Alice's labours were this difficult. However, they all weakened her terribly; and her troubles were not over once the baby was born. After several of her deliveries Alice lost a great deal of blood. In the first instance Alice was frightened by her daughter Naly's attack of convulsions after she had delivered Elizabeth. She experienced 'so great floods that I was spent, and my breath lost, my strength departed from me, and I could not speak for faintings'.[112] Sometimes in her weakened condition after childbirth, Alice fell prey to only tangentially related ailments. For instance, after the birth of her fifth child, she suffered 'the bleeding of the hemords every day for half a year together', along with lameness in her left knee. At the same time, her physician felt that she was 'deeply gone in a consumption, and if it continued longer I should be barren'.[113] And her three months of illness after the birth of her first child has been described above.

Despite the hazards of childbearing, Alice very much wanted children. As we have seen, she was very happy when she became pregnant shortly after her wedding, worried about miscarriages while she carried her babies, enjoyed feeding them once they were born and watched over them carefully as they grew. However, she was very aware of the dangers of childbirth. This awareness began before she ever had children herself. At the age of 19 Alice was present when her only sister, Catherine Danby, died after giving birth to her sixteenth child. Catherine had suffered more than her share of obstetrical troubles: she had miscarried six babies 'when she was above half gone with them . . . upon frights by fire in her chamber, falls, and such like accidents happening'. She was ill while carrying her last child. This, combined with 'the horrid rudeness of the soldiers and Scots quartered then amongst them', caused her to fall into labour prematurely. The 'child came double into the world, with such extremity that she

[Catherine] was exceedingly tormented with pains, so that she was deprived of . . . sleep for fourteen days . . . neither could she eat'. After one month of fever she died, having disposed of her worldly responsibilities and committed herself to God.[114] For Alice, Catherine's illness and death surely served as a warning of what married life had in store for her.

Alice did not voice her fears about carrying and bearing children until after the birth and survival of her son Robert. About her pregnancy with her eighth child, Joyce, she wrote that

> It pleased God to give me a new hope of comfort of bearing Mr. Thornton another child, although these are accompanied with thorny cares and troubles, and more to me than others.

When her delivery approached, she 'being terrified with my last extremity, could have little hopes to be preserved in this' without the help of God. She prepared for her ordeal by making recommendations for the education of her three living children and disposing of her own estate. Her labour was 'sharp and perilous', and she felt she only narrowly escaped with her life.[115] Thus, when she became pregnant again, she wrote

> and if it had been good in the eyes of my God I should much rather . . . not to have been in this condition. But it is not a Christian's part to choose anything of this nature, but what shall be the will of our heavenly Father, be it never so contrary to our own desires.

She was so tormented by her labour that her daughter Naly, 'with fear and grief for me, fell so sick . . . that she was in much danger of death'.[116]

As indicated in the previous chapter's discussion of Jane Josselin's experience, Alice's fears concerning her deliveries were certainly not unique.[117] Indeed, it would have been surprising if women did not fear something which was likely to bring them close to death. However, the bearing and rearing of children was viewed by both sexes as the divinely appointed duty of women – the only excuse for their creation. Women rarely attained more social importance than when they were giving birth. That God and the world of men approved of their condition was surely some comfort to such women as Jane and Alice.

In addition to the ills surrounding pregnancy and childbirth,

Alice and her relations suffered a multitude of ailments. Her mother had recurring bouts of the stone. Her brother Christopher had fits of the spleen. Her husband became a chronic sufferer from palsy in 1665, three years before his death. Her cousin died of pleurisy.[118]

An important cause of disease, in Alice's experience, was surfeit. As we have seen, she came down with measles after a surfeit upon improperly prepared beef. Her cousin Edmund Norton died after eating melons which were 'too cold for him'. Naly had a choking fit in her sleep after a surfeit upon turbot.[119] The dangers of surfeit reveal the importance of moderate and careful diet for subscribers to the humoral view of illness. Eating too much or the wrong kind of food might cause a serious imbalance in the body's humours.

Another frequent cause of illness was emotional upset. William Thornton developed an ague as a result of 'sadness and discontent' occasioned by the money matters surrounding his marriage. We have seen that Naly became ill with worry when Alice was in labour with her last child. However, Alice herself was the principal sufferer from this kind of disorder. It would not be an exaggeration to say that Alice's usual reaction to the illnesses of her family members was to become ill herself. She had to be sent home from Catherine Danby's death-bed because she had become very weak. Her excessive bleeding after giving birth to her third child resulted from worry about Naly's convulsions. Alice was pregnant and ill with business worries when her daughter Katherine contracted smallpox. She became so distressed about the child's illness and so disturbed by her 'crying night and day, that I was forced to be removed . . . into the scarlet chamber, for want of rest'. Upon receiving the news of her husband's first attack of palsy, she

> was brought into a violent passion of grief and sorrow, with fits
> of sounding [swooning], which I never knew before; and
> prevailed so exceedingly that I immediately went sick to bed,
> being so weak upon that occasion that all gave me for dead, so
> that it was an impossibility to carry me alive to see my dear
> husband.

And when he suffered a later attack, she took to her bed again.[120]

Other sorts of upsets made her ill as well. Her illness on her wedding day may well have been due to her doubts about marrying at all. Business troubles weakened her. And her anger at the slanders directed at her by Mrs Anne Danby caused her to fall 'into a very great and dangerous condition of sickness, weakness of body, and afflicted mind'. Indeed, it is likely that illness was a refuge for Alice, however uncomfortable it made her. In bed, she was cared for and could muster her strength for her return to the cares of the world.[121]

Like Margaret Hoby, Alice Thornton routinely consulted physicians. Most important of these was Dr Wittie or Witty of Hull, who first attended her during her first pregnancy. It is probable that Alice obtained the services of this physician along with her married name, for she recorded that Wittie had treated William Thornton before their wedding. In any case, the physician treated the Thorntons at least until William's death, often travelling long distances to do so. While she was living with her mother at Hipswell, Alice was treated by Mr Matrum or Mahum, who also attended her during the illness surrounding her first delivery. And another physician, Alice's brother-in-law Timothy Portington, treated the Thorntons during the period 1666 to 1669.[122] On a number of occasions these healers consulted together over the condition of their patient, sometimes disagreeing about the proper course of treatment.

From these healers the Thorntons received the conventional therapy of the time. They were purged, vomited and let blood. Like their contemporaries, they sometimes suffered the consequences of 'heroic' physic. Alice's mother-in-law died as the result of taking an antimony vomit which caused 'a flux of blood by siege, as it was supposed to have a vein broken inwardly'. And both Naly and Alice's nephew contracted smallpox after taking physic to prevent the disease.[123]

The relationships between Alice and her relatives and the healers they consulted were generally good. Alice and William deferred to Dr Wittie's judgment and were content with his therapies for many years. However, there is more than a suggestion that they, like their contemporaries, suggested many of the treatments administered to them. As we have seen, when Alice fell ill during her first pregnancy, she felt that only phlebotomy would cure her, despite Mr Mahum's objections. One may even suppose that she called upon the services of Dr Wittie because she assumed he would support her. Clearly the human frailties of physicians were recognised. Alice's mother was annoyed when her husband lay dying because when she 'desired the physicians to give her a true state of his condition, whom she perceived grew weaker . . . , they would not deal truly, nor acknowledge his desperate case'. Both she and the dying man realised the truth of the matter when the physicians prescribed 'pigeons cut' to be 'laid to the soles of the feet' – a measure which Christopher recognised as 'the last remedy'.[124]

Despite their consultation of learned healers, it is clear that the Wandesfords and Thorntons conformed to the contemporary pattern of self- and lay-treatment. After both of the serious injuries Alice had during her childhood, Alice's mother nursed and healed her. Her mother also treated her, her brother John and Frank Kelly when they had smallpox.[125] Alice followed this pattern by treating her own children when they fell ill. Her knowledge of children's disorders and medicines is revealed in her description of baby William's illness. The baby

> began to be very angry and forward; so that I perceived him not to be well, upon which I gave him Gascoyne powder and cordial, lest it should be the red gum in children, usual at that time, to strike it out of his heart at morning after his dressing.[126]

She also rendered first aid to her servants, on one occasion removing a piece of goose pinnion from her maid's throat when it was choking her.[127] However, unlike Margaret Hoby and Jane Josselin, Alice does not appear to have acted as an amateur healer to her friends and neighbours. Her attention was fully absorbed by her own health problems and those of her family.

Alice's approach to illness was quite conventional. Concern about surfeit and cold reveal a basically humoral orientation. Convictions about the mutability of diseases depending upon the circumstances and the blending of emotional and physical disorders are common in the diaries and autobiographies consulted. As far as one can tell, the remedies she and her relatives used were also quite usual. Blood-letting, clysters, vomits, visits to spas and various herbal preparations are mentioned. Only remarkable is her religious orientation to disease and injury.

Scholars such as Alan Macfarlane have analysed the providential views of such Puritan sufferers as Ralph Josselin. The unspoken assumption is that people of other religious persuasions had a different orientation to disaster.[128] However, the royalist and Anglican Alice Thornton, like Ralph Josselin, listed her family's providential escapes from disaster.[129] She clearly felt that God caused and cured illness. Thus, although 'secular' therapies were used, for instance, when her daughter Naly had smallpox, Alice wrote of her recovery,

> But oh that our hearts were enlarged in thankfulness to the great Lord our God for the preservation of this my eldest child, whose special deliverance must not be forgotten, to give glory to the great God of Israel, which had pity upon myself, husband, and three children, by restoring their lives when they were all so nigh many deaths. [130]

Each page of Alice's autobiography reveals her deep religious faith. While she did not, like Margaret Hoby, spend her days in formal spiritual exercise, hearing sermons and talking to religious advisers, she was none the less guided in her behaviour and general attitudes by her religion. This fact, then, raises the issue of how different Puritans were from their High Church contemporaries. [131] Certainly English medical behaviour appears to have been determined more by social and sexual status than by religious conviction, despite the rather distracting example provided by Ralph Josselin.

III CONCLUSION

The title of this chapter, 'The Character of a Good Woman: Women and Illness', is appropriate because all of the women whose writings have been consulted self-consciously aspired to be, and to have the reputation for being, good. Indeed, unlike their male counterparts, female diarists and autobiographers wrote their personal accounts partly in order to demonstrate or protest their goodness. Female virtue was achieved by sound religious convictions and dutiful behaviour. A woman's duty involved both suffering (particularly childbearing) and healing. Her nature and her social utility were combined in the medical arena. So important was her medical role in determining her goodness that it sometimes was mentioned in the catalogue of virtues appearing in epitaphs of the period. Lady Grace Mildmay's monument recalls a

> most devout, unspotedly chaste Maid, Wife, and Widow, compassionate in Heart, and charitably helpful with Physic, Clothes, Nourishment, or Counsel to any in Misery. She was most careful and wise in managing worldly estate so as her life was a blessing to hers and in her death she blessed them, which happened July 27th, 1620. [132]

Thus, chastity, charity (including healing) and good management characterised the ideal seventeenth-century gentle-woman. These attributes certainly belonged to Lady Margaret Hoby and Mrs Alice Thornton. They also described others.

For instance, Lady Anne Halkett wrote her autobiography both to describe the dramatic events of her youth (mainly having to do with the Civil War) and to vindicate her own behaviour.[133] Like Alice Thornton, she was both royalist and highly connected. Hers was a busy life, occupied for many years in flitting between a number of gentry households in England and Scotland. At one point, she became engaged to a married man, and her chief preoccupation for some years was to extricate her good name intact from this predicament. She also was embroiled in several petty household scandals. Throughout these events, she protested her piety and devotion to duty. And, despite her full schedule, she acted as an amateur healer. Along with 'Ar.Ro.', probably a surgeon, she treated at least sixty soldiers injured in the battle of Dunbar. And when staying in Fife, she helped 'the sick and wounded persons [who] came to me'.[134] She attended confinements and treated herself when she became ill.[135]

Even Anne's ailments, like Alice Thornton's, testified to her virtue. On several occasions she took to her bed as a result of emotional upsets associated with her unfortunate engagement. And when she came down with bloody flux in 1653, her illness was the result of toil and want of sleep.[136] By the same token, her escapes from accidental injury were marks of the favour of God.[137]

The experiences of a number of women have been considered in this study. Some, like Jane Josselin and Elizabeth Pepys, are known to us only through the diaries of their husbands. Others, like Lady Anne Clifford and Dorothy Osborne, have left such brief records that their medical experiences can be only hazily conceptualised. Seen as a group, they are a motley crew. They range from gentry to middling status; from Roman Catholic to Puritan religious orientations. They were married and unmarried; childless and the mothers of many. Some were young at the time the records were written; some far older. However, there are many similarities. None of these women suffered from true poverty; some, indeed, were very wealthy. All were literate. All were pious. Many were good business women, deeply involved in the management of and litigation regarding their estates. All were knowledgeable in medical matters, treating themselves and others. And, of course, all were women living in a male-dominated society.

In which respects did the male and female experiences of illness and medicine differ in the period under discussion? With the obvious exception of obstetrical and gynaecological conditions and certain urological problems affecting men, the sexes suffered from the same ailments. Both sexes also engaged in self-treatment and amateur healing.

None the less, the duties of most lay-men took them far from medical spheres. When they offered medical advice, it was because of personal experience or special interest. When they suffered, their disorders came as a result of individual or collective sin, or an imbalance of humours. Neither their ailments nor their healing activities were specifically attributable to their sex.

Women, on the other hand, had a special relationship with illness and healing by virtue of their sex. Their physiology made them particularly vulnerable to disease. Their experience of menstruation, pregnancy, childbirth, breast-feeding and menopause identified, unified and segregated them. Their particular talents for nurturing and healing were seen as inherent in their female nature. Regardless of their social status, their medical advice and services were accepted by men from all social and occupational groups. They were the nurses, pharmacists and 'natural' medical authorities of seventeenth-century England.

9

CONCLUSION:
THE EXPERIENCE OF ILLNESS

Before embarking upon a discussion of the experience of illness, it would be appropriate to say something about that elusive and indefinite state of being – the experience of health. Health is notoriously difficult to define, yet most people have a notion of what it means for them. For instance, Joseph Binns regarded a patient as 'well' when the condition for which he was treating him or her had either totally disappeared or had so stabilised as to cause no inconvenience or handicap.[1]

Seventeenth-century diarists frequently thanked God for their health. Sometimes this gratitude was expressed at regular intervals. Ralph Josselin gave a summary of his family's health every Sunday. Although weeks during which no one had been ill were rare indeed, he always specially remarked them.[2] Samuel Pepys was most likely to comment on his overall physical state on 26 March, when he celebrated his having been successfully cut for the stone. For instance, in 1665 he noted that he was in 'very perfect good health and have long been'.[3]

For both the diarists and the medical practitioners, good health could apparently be defined as the absence of illness. It was something to be maintained by sensible living habits and something to be sought after in times of illness. Humorally speaking, health was balance. Religiously speaking, health was the great gift of God. However one thought of it, health was a rare possession. Too many ailments hovered around for the owner to keep it long.

Thus far, this study has considered the experience of illness largely from the point of view of the individual sufferer. We have been concerned with his or her sensations, fears and medical choices. To some extent, this concentration is fair. Although one can sympathise, or even empathise, with a sufferer's complaints, much of illness is a lonely business. Each person experiences discomfort idiosyncratically. Illness experience, therefore, is determined by individual physiological and psychological factors as much as it is by the surrounding culture which provides the medical options for dealing with it.

However, illness affects many people beside the sufferer. In seventeenth-century England it involved friends, relations, neighbours, servants, masters and healers. Epidemic diseases affected whole communities. This concluding chapter will address itself, then, to the social experience of illness. It will attempt to draw together the miscellany of source material consulted in the preceding chapters in order to widen our viewpoint on seventeenth-century illness.

Illness experience varied depending upon the disorder. Minor ailments, such as colds, were least disruptive to both the sufferer and his or her social circle. However, even colds set the sufferer apart from the surrounding 'healthy' population. The sufferer complained. He or she sometimes went to bed. Occasionally remedies were taken. These were either obtained from apothecaries' shops or prepared within the home. Friends, relatives and servants sympathised and sometimes administered medication. Wives, daughters and maids prepared remedies, soothed rumpled bed-linen, offered fresh nightclothes and were awakened during the night to comfort the sufferer.

Disorders which confined the sufferer to bed for more than a day or two were far more disruptive. Even when the sick person's life was not felt to be in serious danger – in normal childbirth, for instance, or in ordinary ague attacks – the household reorganised itself around the sufferer. Sometimes nurses were hired. As we have seen, the Josselins hired a special nurse to help out during Jane's confinements. Pepys hired a nurse to look after his brother Tom when he was seriously ill.[4] And Pepys's relief that no nurse would have to be engaged to care for his wife during the treatment of her genital fistula has been noted.[5]

Even when nurses were not hired, a great deal of support was demanded from those surrounding the person who had taken up a sick role. It should be emphasised that this role change was often a matter of choice. Then as now, people frequently carried on as usual, despite unpleasant symptoms. Taking to bed was and is the signal for alterations in the behaviour of the sufferer and those around him or her.[6] Thus, the Josselins summoned neighbours in the middle of the night on more than one occasion.[7] Roger Lowe was called upon, both to pray with ailing neighbours and to make their wills.[8]

The Pepyses sometimes slept apart when one or both of them were ill.

Joseph Binns's casebook implies a great deal about the special services demanded of servants and/or housewives during long periods of illness. Fractured legs, for instance, required lengthy bedrest. Patients had to be lifted from their beds – often to pallets on the floor, so that beds could be made. Presumably patients in this condition used bedpans, which had to be carried and emptied. Linen fouled by excrement, sweat, vomit or wound drainage required changing and laundering.

The more serious the disorder, the more extraordinary the demands placed on those surrounding the sufferer. Robert Hooke's servant, Tom Gyles, became ill 9 September 1677, with what was at first diagnosed as the measles. By 11 September he was suffering acutely from smallpox. That day he received two visits from three different medical practitioners. (The surgeon, Mr Gidly, came twice.) He was watched all night. On 12 September Hooke himself visited Mr Gidly at 5 am because Tom was so ill. Gidly sent him to 'old Dr. King', who felt that Tom's illness was mortal. This opinion was confirmed by Dr Mapletoft and Dr Diodati, who met with Hooke at 9 am. Tom died just after noon.[9]

Other masters were likewise concerned with their servants' illnesses. Pepys allowed his 'boy' Will to lie on his own bed when the servant had a severe headache during the 1665 plague.[10] And the Pepyses also contemplated sending a maid-servant, Sarah, to the country for a change of air when Sarah had an attack of ague.[11] The Josselins' concern about their servants' illnesses has been discussed above.

It is tempting to see the above examples of masters caring for servants during times of illnesses as evidence of the patriarchal relationship which was piously advocated by seventeenth-century moralists and which has been referred to nostalgically by those wishing to see in pre-industrial England a golden age.[12] However, such a conclusion would be both romantic and incorrect. A major reason for employers' concern about servants' health was the inconvenience a servant's illness caused within the household.[13] For instance, Pepys wrote in 1660, 'This day or two my maid Jane hath been lame, that we cannot tell what to do for want of her'.[14] Further, as we shall see, if a servant contracted an illness which might endanger the employer's family, that servant was speedily removed from the household in a way an ailing family member would not have been, despite the conventional inclusion of the servants as part of the master's 'family'.

Whether or not a sufferer went to bed, he or she sometimes decided to become a patient, that is to consult a healer. In many cases the healer visited the patient in his or her own home. Sometimes visits were made daily or even more often. Occasionally the healer was able to send a servant or apprentice to do routine dressing changes or administer emergency first aid.[15] But healers frequently travelled long distances at inconvenient times and in bad weather in order to attend patients. Often, more than one healer was involved in caring for a single patient. Indeed, the Barbersurgeons' Company required that patients in danger of death be examined by several surgeons to make certain that the treatment applied was proper and sufficient. Joseph Binns participated in a number of cases where he was invited to consult by the attending physician or surgeon.[16] Such consultations helped to reassure patients and their families that everything possible was being done. They also served as protection for the medical practitioners involved, should the patient fail to improve or die.

In addition, patients sometimes chose to consult several healers, particularly when suffering from an acute or chronic disorder. As we have seen, Hooke consulted four healers when Tom Gyles had smallpox. Ralph Josselin sought help from two physicians and two surgeons regarding his diseased leg during the last ten years of his life.[17] And Pepys consulted both a physician and a surgeon when he feared a recurrence of bladder stones.[18]

Regardless of whether or not a medical practitioner was consulted, family members and friends continued to help, give advice and sometimes even undermine the healer's authority. We have seen that the medical writers were suspicious of the activities of the well-meaning but 'ignorant' women who surrounded their patients.[19] Disagreements between healers and such women sometimes led to the healer being dismissed or leaving the case.[20] Male friends might also challenge a medical practitioner's decisions. Two examples of this sort of interference have already been cited from Pepys's diaries. In one instance, Pepys took a remedy for itching recommended by Sir J. Mennes in preference to any prescribed by a surgeon.[21] And, when his brother Tom was dying, Pepys himself challenged the diagnosis of syphilis made by Tom's physician.

Whether minor or serious, acute or chronic, most disorders entitled the sufferer to visits from friends, relatives and acquaintances. Even when physic-taking confined an individual to his or her chamber, and no illness existed, visitors were welcomed. Modern conventions which protect the privacy of people excreting excrement or giving birth simply did not exist in seventeenth-century England. Apparently no one ever wanted to be left alone. Thus, visiting the sick or confined was a social duty.

Such visits served a number of purposes. As we have seen, both clerical and lay visitors prayed with the sick. Ralph Josselin was summoned in his dual role as vicar and friend to pray with ailing parishioners on a number of occasions. Roger Lowe prayed with fellow-Presbyterians. A good deal of moral support found its way into these visits. The fact that Josselin stayed the night with his friend Mr R. H. during a spiritual crisis surely did R. H. as much good as the prayers they said and the physician Josselin summoned to let R. H.'s blood.[22]

Sometimes practical secular services were performed during visits. Roger Lowe was asked to draw up wills for dying acquaintances on more than one occasion. Any educated person might be asked to write a will. Lowe was a mercer. Perhaps more frequently approached were ministers, physicians and lawyers.[23]

In addition, visitors undertook nursing care and household tasks. Mothers routinely travelled to be with married daughters when the daughters gave birth.[24] They also frequently visited adult children in times of illness. In return, adult children hurried to the bedsides of ailing parents. The Josselin daughters returned to Earls Colne to visit and nurse their parents during serious illnesses.[25] John Evelyn spent nearly four weeks at his mother's death-bed.[26] And he spent the period June to October 1640 travelling between Oxford and his father's house when the elder Evelyn was suffering from the illness which finally killed him.[27] More distant relatives also helped each other. Lady Margaret Hoby offered her help during the confinements of her cousins.[28]

Friends sometimes performed nursing services for one another during illnesses. Jane Josselin applied leeches to Mary Church's leg when Mary, a close friend, was unwell. And Dorothy Osborne attended Lady Diana Rich when Lady Diana was staying with a nearby gentlewoman who was treating her for sore eyes. Dorothy said that she would not leave the area until Lady Diana did.[29]

In addition, as indicated above, it was customary for married women to be present at childbirth. They sometimes helped deliver the babies. More often they provided moral support, took care of the housework and other children, and acted as witnesses of the birth.

Helping out during times of illness was a service people offered their patrons. The best examples of this kind of behaviour come from Samuel Pepys's diary. Not only did Pepys visit Lord Sandwich himself when the great man was ill, but also he supervised the care taken of at least one of the Montague children during medical treatment. In 1660 Lady Jemima Montague was living at the house of Mr Scott, a surgeon, for treatment of 'malformation of the neck'.[30] Pepys and his wife visited her frequently, even consulting with Scott about the collar he wished to fit to the lady's neck to correct her condition.[31]

Visiting persons confined to bed sometimes took on a kind of ritual character. The Pepyses went to several christening parties held in the new mother's bedroom.[32] Even when there was no party, it was certainly traditional to visit a recently delivered woman before her month of lying-in was over.[33]

It was also traditional to visit the dying. Evelyn described the scene in his dying mother's chamber as follows:

> Therefore, summoning all her Children then living . . . she expressed herself in a manner so heavenly, with instructions so pious, and Christian, as made us strangely sensible of the extraordinary loss then imminent; after which, embracing every one of us in particular, she gave to each a Ring with her blessing, and dismissed us. Then taking my Father by the hand, she recommended us to his care . . . and so having importuned him that what he designed to bestow on her Funeral, he would rather dispose among the poor. . . . She laboured to compose herself for the blessed change which she now expected.[34]

And Pepys, who had spent two days at his brother's death-bed, left when he thought he heard the death rattle beginning, because 'I had no mind to see him die'.[35]

Most visits made to sufferers were simply courtesy visits. All of the diarists made this sort of visit. Pepys and Hooke reported the greatest number of sick visits. However, this is not surprising since they lived in London, had large numbers of acquaintances, and depended on the goodwill of others for their social opportunities, promotions and increases in income. None the less, the identity of those they visited makes obvious that personal interest did not consciously affect their visiting habits. For instance, Hooke visited the Bishop of Chester three times in five days, when the bishop was dying of the stone.[36]

He also visited his ex-servant and -mistress, Nell, after she miscarried of a baby girl.[37] By the same token, Pepys made numerous visits to ailing members of Lord Sandwich's family.[38] He also visited Mrs Betty Michell, a poor woman of his acquaintance, after her babies were born.[39]

On only one occasion recorded in a diary were visitors turned away from a sick-room. This was when Samuel and Elizabeth Pepys attempted to visit Samuel's cousin Scott who lay dying after a miscarriage. Samuel wrote, 'My wife could not be admitted to see her, nor anybody'.[40]

Even diseases known to be contagious did not prevent sufferers from receiving visitors. Pepys visited Lady Jemima Montague when it was feared she had smallpox.[41] As it happened, she only had chickenpox. He also visited Sir R. Slingsby, 'our Comptroller, when Slingsby lay ill of the "new disease" – an ague and fever'. Slingsby died the following week.[42]

The above discussion has concentrated upon conventional behaviour and the benefits the sufferer derived from sick-room visits. It should not be forgotten that the visitor also benefited. In an age when illness and death took place at home, suffering cemented relationships between people. Supplying services and comfort to the sufferer allowed visitors to feel that they were helping. Proximity prevented the mystification of illness and death and the alienation of sufferers and the dying which are so apparent today. Visitors, confronted with the truth of their own mortality, were both comforted by the assurance that they also would have social support during their own crises and taught behaviour which they might themselves employ. Pious responses to suffering and the spiritual satisfaction of a 'good' death fulfilled the needs of both sufferers and visitors.

The evidence indicates that seventeenth-century sufferers expected to be visited and seventeenth-century men, women and children expected to visit. However, social responses to diseases varied.[43] There were respectable illnesses, such as gout and ague; frightening, but nearly inevitable diseases, such as smallpox; disreputable diseases, such as syphilis; and terrifying diseases, such as the plague.

Non-infectious chronic disorders, although unpleasant, could bring the sufferer years of sympathy and attention from those surrounding him or her. Pepys visited Lord Brouncker during attacks of gout in the 1660s.[44] Hooke visited him when he suffered from the same disorder in the 1670s.[45]

Infectious diseases, because they were more feared, were

also avoided. Although no coherent 'theory of infection' was articulated in the diaries and autobiographies consulted, people certainly distinguished between infectious and non-infectious ailments, feeling much safer in the presence of the latter. Ralph Josselin, for instance, found comfort, after his daughter Mary's death from worms, in the fact that her 'disease was not infectious'.[46] Infection was believed to pass directly from person to person. It also could lurk in contaminated clothing or bed-linen.[47] John Evelyn was certain he had contracted smallpox by sleeping in a bed previously occupied by a girl whose mother had reported as recently recovered from an ague. Evelyn concluded 'by the smell of franc incense . . . [that] she had been newly recovered of the Small Pox'.[48] Although sufferers from contagious diseases were visited, they were approached with caution.

The response to disfiguring diseases was not always sympathetic. Lady Anne Clifford reported in February 1619,

> My Lady of Suffolk at Northampton House about this time had the smallpox which spoiled that good face of hers, which had brought to others much misery, and to herself greatness which ended with much unhappiness.[49]

And individuals were distressed by even transitory alterations of their own appearances due to minor ailments. When Pepys was troubled with itching and swelling in February 1663, he wrote that he was 'not only sick but ashamed of myself to see myself so changed in my countenance'.[50] And when he developed cold sores in September 1664, he reported 'my mouth very scabby, my cold being going away – so that I was forced to wear a great black patch'.[51]

The shame attached to such temporary problems or even the scarring produced by smallpox was minor. So many people survived smallpox that its effects were almost to be expected and, except in severe cases, unworthy of remark. Patches and make-up disguised pits in the face. Wigs and gloves concealed hair loss and disfigurement of the hands.

The same cannot be said about syphilis. It was indeed the foul disease. Its symptoms, which have been described above, were disgusting to both the sufferer and those caring for him or her.[52] And its foul reputation caused social responses ranging from snide gossip to ostracism. It is no wonder that attempts were made to deny the presence of syphilis in the living and to conceal it as a cause of death.[53] Rather than pity, the stereotyped reaction to the pox was humour.

Indeed, syphilis provided subject matter for a large number of seventeenth-century dramatists. Sufferers were figures of fun. Shadwell's character Crazy was typical of the genre.

Crazy.	Good morrow Mrs. Errant.
Errant.	How does the pain in your head?
Crazy.	Oh I am on the rack: no primitive Christian under Diocletian ever sufferd so much as I do under this rascal: this villain that like a hangman destroys mankind, and has the law for 't. Oh abominable quacks! that devour more than all the diseases would do, were they let alone, which they pretend to cure.
Errant.	Ay, but sir, yours is a French surgeon, and who so fit to cure the French Disease as a French-surgeon?
Crazy.	Yes, as one poison expels another; but if this rogue should cure me, he can cure me of nothing but what he has given me himself; 'twas nothing when I put myself into his hands; he brought it to what it is, and I think I must deal with him as they do that are bitten with a viper, crush the rogue's head and apply it to the part, for if I do not kill him, he'll be the death of me.[54]

Dramatists ridiculed the symptoms of the pox, the practitioners who treated it, the people who suffered from it, the remedies taken for it, and even its name.

Syphilis was no respecter of social class. It tarnished the reputation of Court ladies. Thus a character in a Restoration drama commented:

> Your proud women are a company of proud, vain, fops and jilts, abominably daubed and painted; and I had rather kiss a blackamoor, with a natural complexion, than any such: and, besides, many of them are so unsound, that making love is as dangerous as making war; and the wounds and scars are dishonourable to boot.[55]

And as early as 1619 Beaumont and Fletcher wrote:

Leontius.	Here's one has served now under Captain Cupid, And crack't a pike in' youth: you see what's come on't.
Lieutenant.	No, my disease will never prove so honourable.
Leontius.	Why, sure, thou hast the best pox.
Lieutenant.	If I have 'em, I am sure I got 'em in the best company.[56]

However, the pox afflicted those of lower status as well. Whores were well known to give and receive syphilis when they sold their services.

Regarding syphilis, drama mirrored the attitudes found in general society. Pepys's shock at the news that his brother Tom had the pox has already been described.[57] However, despite his fear of malicious gossip causing shame to his own family, he was more than willing to participate in gossip about other people. For instance, in 1667 he noted that

> Mr.Lowder is come to use the Tubb, that is, to bathe and sweat himself, and that his Lady is come to use the Tubb too; which he [Pepys's informant] takes to be that he hath and hath given the pox.[58]

Later in the year, Mr Lowther was known to have a sore mouth. Still later, Pepys reported that he could no longer look at Lady Lowther with any pleasure because she had developed a sore nose.[59]

John Aubrey, whose appetite for gossip was even larger than that of Pepys, wrote that Eleanor Ratcliffe, Countess of Sussex was

> a great and sad example of the power of lust and slavery to it. She was as great a beauty as any in England and had a good wit. After her lord's death (he was jealous) she sends for —— (formerly) her footman, and makes him groom of the chamber. He had the pox and she knew it; a damnable sot. He was not very handsome but his body of an exquisite shape. . . . His nostrils were stuffed and borne out with corks in which were quills to breathe through. About 1666 this countess died of the pox.[60]

Apparently the shame of syphilis was not sufficient to deter either Mr Lowther or Lady Eleanor Ratcliffe in their pursuit of pleasure. None the less, this shame was very real, motivating numerous attempts to disguise its presence. John Graunt's remarks about the routine concealment of syphilis as a cause of death have been quoted above. And Joseph Binns's syphilis patients who attempted to obtain treatment while remaining unwilling to name their illness have also been referred to.

While syphilis was the only killing disease which was generally ridiculed, it was certainly not the only one people wished to avoid. More fearful than the pox, and never a subject for humour, was the plague. The plague was a disaster set apart from other diseases by both societal and individual reactions to it.

As indicated above, the plague was so dreaded that even people dwelling out of its range, such as Ralph Josselin, lived in fear of it.[61] It was the only illness concerning which embryonic public health legislation was passed. From 1564, plague regulations required that when a person contracted the plague, he or she and all other persons living in the same dwelling (which might house as many as six families in poor neighbourhoods) were ordered to be confined within the building. Houses thus closed were marked with a cross on the door.[62] Needless to say, these regulations were unpopular. In 1603, 'The spread of plague to Westminster discovered a "very unruly" body of citizens "near St. Clements Church and the fields" who had to be forcibly imprisoned in their infected houses'.[63] And early in the 1665 outbreak, Noorthouck reported that

> At the beginning of the disorder there were great knavery and collusion in the reports of deaths, for while it was possible to conceal the infection, they were attributed to fevers of all kinds, which began to swell the bills [of Mortality]; this was done to prevent their houses being shut up, and families shunned by their neighbours.[64]

Thus, not only did plague sufferers have to cope with the discomfort of their symptoms and the fear of death, but also they were faced with the frantic terror of those immured with them. They also had to endure isolation from friends, neighbours and family members. Considering what has been said above about conventions regarding visiting the sick, such isolation must surely have been nearly as painful as the disease itself.

Beginning in the 1590s pest-houses were set up in plague-stricken localities to deal with epidemics. In 1665 there were five pest-houses in London.[65] For the pest-house established for the sixteen parishes outside the walls of the City of London, mortality has been estimated at 98.1 per cent during 1665.[66] Plague sufferers must surely have viewed being sent to a pest-house as a death sentence.

Prevailing theory held that plague was passed directly from person to person. Thus, the Royal College of Physicians approved of the plague legislation, although few of its members stayed around to help deal with the resulting terror and mortality. In their dread of the disease, people became afraid of each other, avoiding one another on the streets and particularly shunning those who had recently come from a plague-stricken area.[67] Masters deserted servants, ministers abandoned congregations, adults were cruel to children, and healers abandoned patients.

Fear of the plague thus caused a breakdown in normal social relations and conventions. It even separated families. When Sir Dudley North and his younger sister Mary contracted the plague as children, they 'were confined to their father's house in London'. Their father moved out 'because of his promiscuous converse'.[68]

According to Pepys, when Mr Wright's serving-maid came down with the plague in early August 1665, Wright put her in an outhouse, presumably to avoid having his house shut up. The maid escaped, so when her master caught her he had her taken to the pest-house. On the way, two young men, presumably in search of flirtation, looked into the coach which was carrying her, 'and there saw somebody look very ill, and in a sick dress and stunk mightily'. One of the young men was nearly frightened to death when he realised the girl had the plague.[69]

Pepys himself had his maid Susan removed from his house in 1666 when he thought she might have the plague. Although he offered to pay the nurse hired to care for her, he was mightily relieved at her departure. However, he was quite pleased to take her back a week later when it was discovered that she merely had ague.[70]

And he told the story, with more distaste than surprise, of a man who in September 1665 had taken

> a child from London from an infected house . . . it was the child of a very able citizen in Gracious Street, a saddler, who had buried all the rest of his children of the plague; and himself and his wife now being shut up, and in despair of escaping, did desire only to save the life of this little child; and so prevailed to have it received stark-naked into the arms of a friend, who brought it (having put it into fresh clothes) to Greenwich.

A complaint was lodged against this Good Samaritan for his pains.[71]

Those who were even suspected of having had contact with a plague sufferer were avoided. Pepys told of Captain Cocke whose man-servant was reputed to have died of the plague.

> By and by Captain Cocke came to the office, and Sir W. Batten and I did send to him that he would either forbear the office or forbear going to his own office. However, meeting with the

Searchers with their rods in their hands coming from his house, I
did overhear them say that the fellow did not die of the plague.[72]

It is no wonder that those who had to stay within reach of the
plague grew reckless. In some cases the sick openly flouted the
plague regulations.

They abused constables who tried to enforce household
segregation and broke out of their houses in Westminster and
Southwark in 1630. One widow got out and marched deliberately
into Westminster Abbey, to the horror of the people there. In
Holborn a watchman went round tearing padlocks off the doors
of infected houses.[73]

Mr Caesar, the lutemaster Pepys hired to teach his boy,
reported that at the height of the 1665 plague in Westminster,

bold people there were to go in sport to one another's burials.
And in spite to well people, would breathe in the faces (out of their
windows) of well people going by.[74]

Such folk had indeed become abandoned – abandoned by God,
by medicine, by their government, by their neighbours. They,
in turn, abandoned courtesy, common sense and, finally,
fear.[75]

The plague was no more typical of seventeenth-century
diseases than a hurricane is of rainstorms. In cases of almost all
other illnesses, medical practitioners were more than eager to
attend patients – provided, of course, that the patients could
afford their services. Even in plague time, when physicians
and many surgeons left London, the city was not totally
deprived of medical care. People dosed themselves with
prophylactics in enormous quantities.[76] In addition, many
apothecaries remained in London, both selling medications
and giving medical advice. The fact that they stayed,
'providing that general medical care which the mass of the
population needed', was not forgotten by the general public.[77]
The apothecaries' star was rising, despite the physicians'
attempt to subordinate them.

The seventeenth-century experience of illness included the
activities of medical practitioners. These practitioners served,
sometimes as learned authorities, sometimes as skilled craftsmen, sometimes as suppliers of necessary commodities,
sometimes as experts in the occult. Despite the physicians'
efforts to ignore the financial relationship existing between

themselves and their patients, all healers sold their services. To a great extent these services were determined and defined by the clients purchasing them. White witches diagnosed witch-craft as the cause of illnesses partly because the patients seeking their help already suspected that they were tormented by witches. Surgeons let blood, made issues and applied blisters on demand. Apothecaries gave medical advice because visitors to their shops requested it. Physicians continued to examine urine long after the Royal College of Physicians denounced the practice as useless, because patients believed in uroscopy. The medical marketplace, then, operated on a supply and demand basis.

At this point in our discussion, it must be reiterated that there was no seventeenth-century medical profession. Although occupational organisations existed and aspired to the kind of control over the provision of medical services their descen-dants would actually attain, in the seventeenth century they supervised the activities of relatively few healers and affected the behaviour of the lay public almost not at all. Even within licensed groups of practitioners, there was little unity. Learned surgeons despised unlearned ones. Fellows of the Royal College of Physicians distrusted licentiates and physicians authorised to practise by universities and bishops. Female midwives were suspicious of man-midwives: man-midwives, in turn, were contemptuous of their female rivals.

Between groups of authorised practitioners there was even greater dissension. Physicians accused surgeons and apothe-caries of usurping their own rights by prescribing internal medicines. Surgeons and apothecaries, in their turn, rejected the subservient roles the physicians recommended for them. Surgeons claimed the right to prescribe internal medication to their patients without first asking the permission of a physician. Apothecaries demanded official recognition of their already habitual practice of giving advice to the clients patronising their shops. And, of course, between licensed healers and unlicensed ones there was only competition and enmity.

The authorities, although basically sympathetic with the aims of those who wished to raise the standards of medical and surgical care, were unreliable supporters. As the 1543 'Quacks' Charter' demonstrates, unlearned and unlicensed practice had its protectors.[78] In addition, seventeenth-century courts and parliaments were fickle, switching support from the physicians to the apothecaries and back again in the controversy over who should be allowed to participate in the practice of general internal medicine.[79] This is not surprising, because courtiers and MPs, like other members of the lay population, reserved the personal right to consult any healer they wished to consult. They patronised medical renegades, such as Simon Forman and Gideon Harvey, along with orthodox physicians and surgeons. Even on them, the medical propaganda promulgated by such writers as the anti-quack authors had a less than successful effect.[80] Thus, although learned and licensed physicians sound very 'modern' in their defence of high standards in medical education and practice, theirs were indeed lonely voices crying in the wilderness. The classical learning they defended was doomed to obsolescence. The privileges they coveted would descend to bastard heirs emerging from surgery and apothecary as well as physic.

All healers claimed expertise in their own areas of practice. However, the question of what constituted such expertise was an open one in seventeenth-century England. Indeed, many lay-people claimed to be expert in the treatment of certain ailments. Sometimes their recipes were even adopted by licensed physicians and surgeons.[81]

Of all licensed healers, the surgeons were best able to sell their services by claiming expertise. Despite the prevalence of self-treatment, rare indeed was the man who would let himself blood, set his own fractured bones, 'cut' himself for the stone or amputate his own limbs. Surgeons routinely performed these and other procedures with success. It is therefore ironic that the diaries and correspondence consulted give so little information about surgery, and so much about internal medicine. With the exception of the Pepyses, the people mentioned in these sources depended mainly on self-treatment and on physicians. Joseph Binns's casebook, therefore, is helpful in giving insight into the career of at least one practising surgeon. Without this insight, this study might have passed over in silence the too-often neglected work of seventeenth-century surgeons. Unlike those of the physicians, the surgeons' services were rarely suspected of being unnecessary. If they were criticised, it was for lack of skill.

Yet even surgery was undertaken by lay-people. The Barbersurgeons' Company of London issued special licences to experts in a number of surgical procedures, regardless of a lack of proper apprenticeship.[82] Lady Margaret Hoby's surgical activities have already been cited, as have those of the two female bone-setters mentioned in Ralph Josselin's diary. Thus, not even surgeons could claim a monopoly over expertise in their area of practice.

In physic and apothecary, of course, such claims were even less secure. Almost everyone diagnosed his or her own ailments. Most people either bought remedies from apothecaries' shops, made their own medicines, or both. Laywomen considered healing a 'natural' duty. Indeed, considering the evidence, one wonders why licensed healers were ever consulted and paid.

The answer lies outside the realm of reason and expertise. At no time are human beings more emotionally vulnerable than during illness. The more acute the symptoms and the longer they last, the more desperate the sufferer and his or her loved ones become to find relief. The promise or hope of a cure supplied by a respectable licensed healer provides at least temporary ease. Perhaps more important, the medical practitioner assumes responsibility for decisions and therapy for a period of time.

Thackeray's explanation, published in 1850, although perhaps more appropriate in the twentieth century, none the less applied in the seventeenth:

> It is not only for the sick man, it is for the sick man's friends that the Doctor comes. His presence is often as good for them as for the patient, and they long for him yet more eagerly. How we have all watched after him! What an emotion the thrill of his carriage-wheels in the street, and at length at the door, has made us feel! How we hang upon his words, and what a comfort we get from a smile or two, if he can vouchsafe that sunshine to lighten our darkness! . . . Over the patient in fever, the wife expectant, the children unconscious, the doctor stands as if he were Fate, the dispenser of life and death.[83]

The doctor is, to a great extent, what patients have made him – not only what his teachers and organisations expected him to be. The Latin phrases, velvet gowns, luxurious coaches and huge fees of the seventeenth-century society physician increased his value in the eyes of prospective patients, even while he was ridiculed for them.

To the aid of both healers and sufferers of the seventeenth century came natural death. This boon to humanity covered a multitude of sins. It excused the healers' failure to cure, while reassuring survivors that they had done everything possible for the deceased. Along with the promise of heavenly health, it comforted the grief-stricken. And if a sufferer, whose survival had been given up by friends and medical practitioners alike, should happen to recover, such an event could be hailed as the providential intervention of a beneficent God.

Natural death came in many guises. It was considered natural for infants and the very old to die of almost any illness. Indeed, these age groups were so at risk that mention of the age group itself was sufficient explanation of the cause of death.[84] It was also natural for people to die of epidemic diseases, childbirth and certain chronic disorders, such as cancer. Even death from minor ailments could be regarded as natural if the symptoms were unusually severe and the sufferer's needs had not been neglected.

Certain deaths were not natural. Murder and suicide were unnatural causes of death. So were deaths caused by witchcraft. However, such calamities were outside the realm of medicine, either in the hands of healers or in the hands of laypeople.

Thus, death was usually not considered to be anyone's fault. Only in rare cases was a healer blamed for causing death. For instance, when the Duke of Gloucester died of smallpox in 1660, Pepys reported that he had perished through 'the great negligence of the Doctors' who 'had forecast recovery and had prescribed nothing'.[85] Of course, healers insulted each other by accusing one another of murder. Sometimes such accusations resulted in trials for malpractice.[86] More often these accusations were merely a part of the general attack made on one sort of healer by another.[87] Although lay-people amused themselves with cynical jokes about the harm the foul-tasting remedies they took might do, they almost never blamed any individual for the death of a loved one. Indeed, approaching death virtually removed the dying person from the realm of medical responsibility.

The process of dying, although often surrounded by healers and medical treatment, was both conventionally and actually a situation where therapeutics gave way to economic, family and spiritual concerns. In his seminal study *The Hour of our Death*, Philippe Aries describes the 'good' death in traditional Europe as one in which the dying person was able to put his or her spiritual and temporal house in order before taking leave of earthly life.[88] Worldly goods were distributed, funerals described and provided for. In addition, the dying sufferer made peace with God and set an example for the living by his or her pious behaviour.

As we have seen, death in seventeenth-century England was often a leisurely affair. Loved ones often spent weeks in or near death-chambers. While the suffering of the dying relative or friend was pitied and occasionally abhorred, time was necessary to produce the desirable end. Sudden death, death alone, death under disreputable circumstances were bad deaths, feared and avoided. Like illness, death was encompassed by general personal and social responsibilities. It was not relegated to professionals.

This book has concentrated, not upon death, but upon illness, an important part of life in any era. It has returned repeatedly to the joint issues of responsibility and power. Sufferers and healers shared the responsibility of dealing with illness, injury, handicap, childbirth and ageing. They also shared the power of decision-making, although ultimately that power rested in the hands of sufferers and their 'friends'.

Neither sufferers nor healers had a great deal of power over illness itself. That power, when it arrived as the gift of medical science and public health initiatives, transformed the relationship between sufferers and healers so dramatically that it is difficult for present-day scholars to avoid seeing in the sufferers and healers of earlier ages their modern counterparts. This book attempts, however imperfectly, to improve the clarity of our vision regarding the medical world of seventeenth-century England. Its exploration is woefully incomplete, but it may perhaps suggest directions for further investigation.

ABBREVIATIONS

Aveling, *English Midwives*: J. H. Aveling, *English Midwives: their History and Prospects*, London (1872).

Barker: British Library Sloane MS 78 or 663.

A Brief Account: *A Brief Account of Mr. Valentine Greatraks*, London (1666 and 1668).

Clark, *Royal College*: G. N. Clark, *A History of the Royal College of Physicians of London*, vols I and II, Oxford (1964).

Clifford, *Diary*: *The Diary of the Lady Anne Clifford with an introductory Note by V. Sackville-West*, London (1923).

Cotta, *A Short Discovery*: J. Cotta, *A Short Discovery of the Unobserved Dangers of Several Sorts of Ignorant and Unconsiderate Practisers of Physic in England*, London (1612).

Evelyn, *Diary*: *The Diary of John Evelyn*, E. S. de Beer, ed., London (1959).

Halkett: *The Autobiography of Anne Lady Halkett*, J. G. Nichols, ed., Camden Society, new series, 13 (1875).

Hoby, *Diary*: *Diary of Lady Margaret Hoby, 1599–1605*, D. M. Meads, ed., London (1930).

Hooke, *Diary*: *The Diary of Robert Hooke, 1672–1680*, H. W. Robinson and W. Adams, eds, London (1968 and 1935).

Josselin, *Diary*: *The Diary of Ralph Josselin, 1616–1683*, A. Macfarlane, ed., Oxford (1976).

Lowe, *Diary*: *Diary of Roger Lowe of Ashton-in-Makerfield, Lancashire, 1663–74*, W. L. Sachse, ed., London (1938).

MacDonald, *Mystical Bedlam*: M. MacDonald, *Mystical Bedlam: Madness, Anxiety and Healing in Seventeenth-Century England*, Cambridge (1981).

Macfarlane, *Family Life*: A. Macfarlane, *The Family Life of Ralph Josselin. A Seventeenth-Century Clergyman: An Essay in Historical Anthropology*, Cambridge (1970).

Macfarlane, *Witchcraft*: A. Macfarlane, *Witchcraft in Tudor and Stuart England: A Regional and Comparative Study*, London (1970).

Osborne, *Letters*: *The Letters of Dorothy Osborne to William Temple*, G. C. Moore Smith, ed., Oxford (1928).

Pelling, 'Appearance and Reality': M. Pelling, 'Appearance and Reality: Barbersurgeons, the Body and Venereal Disease in Early Modern London', in A. L. Beier and R. Finlay, eds, *The Making of the Metropolis: London 1500–1700*, London (1986), pp. 82–112.

Pelling, 'Occupational Diversity': M. Pelling, 'Occupational Diversity: Barbersurgeons and the Trades of Norwich, 1550–1640', *Bulletin of the History of Medicine*, LVI (1982), 484–511.

Pepys, *Diary*: *The Diary of Samuel Pepys*, R. Latham and W. Matthews, eds, vols I–IX, London (1970–82).

Roberts, thesis: R. S. Roberts, 'The London Apothecaries and Medical Practice in Tudor and Stuart England', unpublished London University Ph.D thesis (1964).

Roberts, 'The Personnel and Practice': R. S. Roberts, 'The Personnel and Practice of Medicine in Tudor and Stuart England', *Medical History*, VI (1962), 363–82, and VII (1964), 217–34.

Sl. 1112:: 'The casebook of a provincial physician, 1619–1622', British Library Sloane MS 1112.

Slack, 'Metropolitan Government': P. Slack, 'Metropolitan Government in Crisis: London's Response to Plague, 1563–1665', in A. L. Beier and R. Finlay, eds, *The Making of the Metropolis: London 1500–1700*, London (1986), pp. 60–81.

Stone, *The Family, Sex and Marriage*: L. Stone, *The Family, Sex and Marriage in England, 1500–1800*, London (1977).

Symcotts: *A Seventeenth-Century Doctor and his Patients: John Symcotts, 1592?–1662*, F. N. L. Poynter and W. J. Bishop, eds, Bedfordshire Historical Record Society, vol. 31, Streatley, Beds (1950).

Thomas, *Religion and Magic*: K. Thomas, *Religion and the Decline of Magic*, Harmondsworth (1973).

Thornton: *The Autobiography of Mrs. Alice Thornton of East Newton, Co. York*, C. Jackson, ed., Surtees Society, vol. 62 (1875).

Young, *Barber-Surgeons*: S. Young, ed., *The Annals of the Barber-Surgeons*, London (1890).

NOTES

1. INTRODUCTION

1. C. Singer, *A Short History of Anatomy and Physiology from the Greeks to Harvey*, New York (1957, first published 1925); E. H. Ackerknecht, *A Short History of Medicine*, New York (1955); L. S. King, *The Growth of Medical Thought*, Chicago, Ill. (1963).
2. K. Dewhurst, *Thomas Willis as a Physician*, Los Angeles (1964); G. Keynes, *The Life of William Harvey*, Oxford (1966).
3. E.g. P. Slack, *The Impact of Plague in Tudor and Stuart England*, London (1985); E. Shorter, *A History of Women's Bodies*, Harmondsworth (1984); J. Donnison, *Midwives and Medical Men: A History of Inter-Professional Rivalries and Women's Rights*, London (1977).
4. K. Thomas, *Religion and the Decline of Magic*, Harmondsworth (1973); L. Stone, *The Family, Sex and Marriage in England, 1500–1800*, London (1977).
5. A. Macfarlane, *Witchcraft in Tudor and Stuart England: A Regional and Comparative Study*, London (1970).
6. C. Webster, ed., *Health, Medicine and Mortality in the Sixteenth Century*, Cambridge (1979).
7. M. MacDonald, *Mystical Bedlam: Madness, Anxiety and Healing in Seventeenth-Century England*, Cambridge (1981).
8. P. Slack, op. cit.
9. H. Cook, *The Decline of the Old Medical Regime in Stuart London*, London and Ithaca (1986).
10. See e.g. R. Porter, ed., *Patients and Practitioners: Lay Perceptions of Medicine in Pre-Industrial Society*, Cambridge (1985); M. Pelling, 'Appearance and Reality: Barbersurgeons, the Body and Venereal Disease in Early Modern London', in A. L. Beier and R. Finlay, eds, *The Making of the Metropolis: London 1500–1700*, London (1986).

2. THE MEDICAL MARKETPLACE

1. G. S. Holmes, *Augustan England: Professions, State and Society 1680–1730*, London (1982), p. 3.
2. Ibid., p. 170; J. H. Raach, *A Directory of English Country Physicians, 1603–1643*, London (1962).

3. See Chapter 5.
4. 'Medical Practice in the Early Modern Period. Trade or Profession?', *The Society for the Social History of Medicine Bulletin*, XXXII (1983), 27–8.
5. M. Pelling, 'Occupational Diversity: Barbersurgeons and the Trades of Norwich, 1550–1640', *Bulletin of the History of Medicine*, LVI (1982), 490–1.
6. The best information about the licensing of English physicians, surgeons and midwives is to be found in M. Pelling and C. Webster, 'Medical Practitioners', in C. Webster, ed., *Health, Medicine and Mortality in the Sixteenth Century*, Cambridge (1979), pp. 165–235.
7. See R. S. Roberts, 'The London Apothecaries and Medical Practice in Tudor and Stuart England', unpublished London University Ph.D thesis (1964).
8. J. Oberndoerffer, *The Anatomies of the True Physician and Counterfeit Mountebank . . .* , F. H[erring], trans., London (1602), pp. 29–30.
9. For information on the education of physicians, see P. Allen, 'Medical Education in Seventeenth-Century England', *Journal of the History of Medicine*, I (1946), 115–43; G. N. Clark, *A History of the Royal College of Physicians of London*, vols I and II, Oxford (1965); V. L. Bullough, *The Development of Medicine as a Profession*, Basel and New York (1966); Pelling and Webster, op. cit.; A. H. T. Robb-Smith, 'Cambridge Medicine', in A. G. Debus, ed., *Medicine in Seventeenth-Century England*, Los Angeles (1974), pp. 327–70.
10. Robb-Smith, op. cit., p. 329.
11. 3 Henry VIII *cap.* 11, An Act for the appointing of physicians and surgeons, 1512: *Statutes of the Realm*, London (1810–28, repr. 1963), III, pp. 31 2.
12. Pelling and Webster, op. cit., p 185.
13. *Statutes*, loc. cit.
14. M. MacDonald, *Mystical Bedlam: Madness, Anxiety and Healing in Seventeenth-Century England*, Cambridge (1981). See also *Diary of the Rev. John Ward, A.M., Vicar of Stratford-upon-Avon*, C. Severn, ed., London (1839).
15. Pelling and Webster, op. cit., p. 185.
16. Ibid.
17. G. Keynes, *Dr. Timothy Bright, 1550–1615: A Survey of his Life with a Bibliography of his Writings*, London (1962).
18. R. S. Roberts, 'The Personnel and Practice of Medicine in Tudor and Stuart England', *Medical History*, VI (1962), p. 366.
19. The best description of these efforts is to be found in Roberts, thesis.
20. Clark, *Royal College*, I, pp. 208–10; Pelling and Webster, op. cit., p. 185.
21. M. Pelling, 'Appearance and Reality: Barbersurgeons, the Body and Venereal Disease in Early Modern London', in A. L.

Beier and R. Finlay, eds, *The Making of the Metropolis: London 1500–1700*, London (1986), p. 83.

22. *Statutes of the Realm*, III, p. 31.
23. Pelling, 'Appearance and Reality', p. 83, and Pelling, 'Occupational Diversity', 489.
24. Pelling, 'Appearance and Reality', p. 84.
25. *Certain Works of Chirurgerie*, London (1564), p. 1.
26. E.g. T. Brugis, *Vade Mecum: or, A Companion for a Surgeon*, London (1652); G. Fabrice, *His Experiments in Chyrurgerie*, London (1642); J. Cooke, *Mellificum Chirurgerie. Or the Marrow . . .* , London (1648); J. Woodall, *The Surgeon's Mate . . .* , London (1655, numerous earlier eds, first published 1617).
27. S. Young, ed., *The Annals of the Barber-Surgeons*, London (1890), pp. 77, 119, 182, 316, 336, 341, 342.
28. Ibid., pp. 335–6, 340.
29. See Chapter 3.
30. See Roberts, thesis. See also C. Wall, H. C. Cannon and E. Ashworth Underwood, *A History of the Worshipful Society of Apothecaries of London*, vol. I, 1617–1815, Oxford (1963).
31. See Roberts, thesis; also the small body of polemical literature on the subject, e.g. Dr Cox, *A Discourse Wherein the Interest of the Patient in Reference to Physick and Physicians is Soberly Debated . . .* , London (1699); *An Essay for the Regulation of the Practice of Physick . . .* , London (1673); *A Letter Concerning the Present State of Physick . . .* , London (1665).
32. For an important provincial case of an apothecary winning the right to prescribe, see Roberts, 'The Personnel and Practice', VI (1962), 371–4.
33. See Roberts, thesis.
34. See J. H. Aveling, *English Midwives: their History and Prospects*, London (1872). He indicates that in 1577 baptism by midwives became illegal for Protestants. None the less, baptismal records show that even among Protestants the practice continued for some time. See also W. D., 'Midwives Formerly Baptized Infants', *Gentleman's Magazine*, LV, 2 (1785), 939.
35. J. Hitchcock, 'A Sixteenth-Century Midwife's License', *Bulletin of the History of Medicine*, XLI (1967), 75–6.
36. M. Stocks, in her *A Hundred Years of District Nursing*, London (1960), p. 123, indicates that nurse-midwives of the late nineteenth century sometimes performed like services. Florence Nightingale disapproved of nurses and nurse-midwives doing housework because of her desire to raise the status of nursing.
37. P. Willughby, *Observations in Midwifery*, H. Blenkinsop, ed., Yorkshire (1972).
38. Ibid., p. 305.
39. E.g. E. Roesslin, *The Byrth of Mankynde*, R. Jonas, trans., London (1540); J. Rueff, *The Expert Midwife*, London (1637). For a review of the sixteenth- and seventeenth-century

literature on midwifery, see A. Eccles, *Obstetrics and Gynaecology in Tudor and Stuart England*, London (1982). See also E. Shorter, *A History of Women's Bodies*, Harmondsworth (1984), pp. 35–47.

40. J. H. Aveling, *The Chamberlens and the Midwifery Forceps*, London (1882).
41. Ibid., pp. 20–1.
42. Ibid.
43. Ibid. See also Clark, *Royal College*, I, pp. 253–4.
44. *Harleian Miscellany*, IV, London (1744); J. Donnison, *Midwives and Medical Men: A History of Inter-Professional Rivalries and Women's Rights*, London (1977), p. 19; A. Fraser, *The Weaker Vessel: Woman's Lot in Seventeenth-Century England*, London (1985), pp. 513–22.
45. Aveling, *English Midwives*, p. 2.
46. Quoted in Donnison, op. cit., p. 34, from M. Stephen's *The Domestic Midwife*, London (1795), p. 105.
47. Examples of works attacking man-midwives on moral grounds are J. Blunt, *Man-midwifery Dissected: or the Obstetric Family-Instructor*, London (1793), and [P. Thickness], *Man-Midwifery Analysed: And the Tendency of the Practice Detected and Exposed*, London (1765). Sairey Gamp is a character in Dickens's *Martin Chuzzlewit*, London (1843–4).
48. C. Goodall, *The Royal College of Physicians of London . . .* , London (1684), pp. 1–2.
49. No good general study of unlicensed practitioners exists, although there are some popular works on 'quacks'. R. S. Roberts's thesis contains a discussion of the Royal College of Physicians' attacks on many such healers. Pelling and Webster's article in *Health, Medicine and Mortality* has good information about the activities and numerical strength of unlicensed healers in sixteenth-century England. K. Thomas's *Religion and the Decline of Magic*, Harmondsworth (1973), pp. 209–300, and A. Macfarlane's *Witchcraft in Tudor and Stuart England: A Regional and Comparative Study*, London (1970), pp. 115–34, 178–85, pay particular attention to magical healers. And Pelling's article, 'Appearance and Reality', contains information about seventeenth-century unlicensed healers operating in London and its environs. For a discussion of vagrancy, I depend upon A. L. Beier's *Masterless Men: The Vagrancy Problem in England, 1560–1640*, London (1985).
50. See Chapter 2.
51. Pelling and Webster, op. cit., p. 183.
52. Fioravanti, *A Short Discourse of the Excellent Doctor . . .* , J. Hester, trans., London (1580), The Proheme.
53. Quoted in K. Dewhurst, *Dr. Thomas Sydenham (1642–1689). His Life and Original Writings*, London (1966), p. 124.
54. I have identified at least forty books published in the period 1500–1700 which fall into this category.

55. J. Goeurot, *The Regiment of Life* . . . , T. Phayer, trans., London (1544), Translator's Preface.
56. The large number of do-it-yourself medical handbooks published in the period might, in this context, be considered works by empirical writers.
57. Roberts, thesis, p. 100, and Young, *Barber-Surgeons*, pp. 330 and 340.
58. Ralph Josselin's family employed two local bone-setters. See Chapter 6. The best account of itinerant practitioners is J. Halle's 'An Historical Expostulation . . . ', in Lanfranc of Milan, *A Most Excellent and Learned Work of Chirurgery* . . . , London (1565).
59. Halle, op. cit., no pagination.
60. See Chapter 3.
61. Brain, London (1637), Preface.
62. See Chapter 6.
63. For a discussion of some popular applications of astrology, see B. Capp, *Astrology and the Popular Press: English Almanacs 1500–1800*, London (1979).
64. *The Infallible True and Assured Witch*, 2nd ed., London (1624).
65. See Thomas, *Religion and Magic*; Pelling and Webster, op. cit., p. 183; A. L. Rowse, *Simon Forman: Sex and Society in Shakespeare's Age*, London (1974); 'The Diary of John Dee', J. O. Halliwell, ed., *Camden Society*, XIX (1847).
66. MacDonald, *Mystical Bedlam*; J. Aubrey, *Aubrey's Brief Lives*, O. L. Dick, ed., Harmondsworth (1972), p. 78.
67. J. O. Halliwell, ed., *The Autobiography and Personal Diary of Simon Forman the Celebrated Astronomer from A.D. 1552 to A.D. 1602*, London (for private circulation only) (1849), e.g. pp. 15–19.
68. Clark, *Royal College*, I, p. 259; *A Brief Description of the Notorious Life of J. Lambe*, Amsterdam and London (1628); M. Parker, *The Tragedy of Doctor Lambe*, London (1628).
69. See Thomas, *Religion and Magic*; Macfarlane, *Witchcraft*; also E. Poeton, 'The Winnowing of White Witchcraft', British Library Sloane MS 1954; Cotta, *The Infallible, True and Assured Witch*, London (1624, second edition).
70. Thomas, *Religion and Magic*, pp. 244–5 and 296–8.
71. Ibid., p. 216.
72. Ibid., pp. 217–22.
73. MacDonald, *Mystical Bedlam*, pp. 17–19. See D. P. Walker, *Unclean Spirits: Possession and Exorcism in France and England in the Late Sixteenth and Early Seventeenth Centuries*, London (1981), pp. 57–9, for a case of a cunning-man, hired to heal children thought to be bewitched, who was executed for conjuring.
74. Thomas, *Religion and Magic*, pp. 237 and 240–2.
75. *A Brief Account of Mr. Valentine Greatraks*, London (1666 and

1668) and *The Great Cures and Strange Miracles of Mr. Valentine Gertrux* [sic] (1666). Thomas, *Religion and Magic*, p. 241, lists several other pamphlets which I have not seen.

76. *A Brief Account*, p. 30.
77. In one case he did lance a wen: ibid., p. 65.
78. Ibid., p. 40.
79. Ibid., p. 37.
80. Ibid., p. 1.
81. Thomas, *Religion and Magic*, p. 240.
82. M. Bloch, *The Royal Touch: Sacred Monarchy and Scrofula in England and France*, J. E. Anderson, trans., London (1973), and Thomas, *Religion and Magic*, pp. 192–201.
83. Thomas, *Religion and Magic*, p. 228, based on entries in the King's Register of Healing.
84. Ibid., p. 227.
85. British Library Sloane MS 153, 259/506. (See Notes for Chapter 3 for explanation of case notation.)
86. Thomas, *Religion and Magic*, p. 228.
87. Ibid., pp. 235–6.
88. Ibid., p. 235.
89. 34 and 35 H VIII *cap*. 8, *Statutes of the Realm*, III, p. 906. For information on the use of this act as a defence against prosecution by the RCP, see Roberts, thesis.
90. Macfarlane, *Witchcraft*, p. 120.
91. Pelling and Webster, op. cit., p. 183.
92. J. H. Raach, *A Directory of English Country Physicians, 1603–1643*, London (1962), p. 14.
93. Ibid.
94. Ibid., pp. 13–14.
95. Roberts, 'The Personnel and Practice', VI (1962), 364.
96. Pelling, 'Occupational Diversity', 495.
97. Roberts, 'The Personnel and Practice', VI (1962), 376.
98. Ibid.
99. *Diary of Lady Margaret Hoby, 1599–1605*, D. M. Meads, ed., London (1930), p. 184.
100. See Roberts, thesis, and 'The Personnel and Practice' for information on the blurring of these distinctions. Also see Clark, *Royal College*, I, and Young, *Barber-Surgeons*, for discussions of occupational organisations – particularly the RCP – attempting to enforce monopolies over certain types of practice.
101. See Z. Cope, *The Royal College of Surgeons of England*, London (1959), and C. Wall, *The History of the Surgeon's Company, 1745–1800*, London (1937).
102. Pelling, 'Occupational Diversity', 504–5.
103. Aveling, *English Midwives*, p. 2.
104. Act III, scene 1.
105. *A Most Excellent and Learned Work of Chirurgery*, Epistle.
106. D. Landy, ed., *Culture, Disease and Healing: Studies in Medical*

Anthropology, New York and London (1977), pp. 468–81 and 495–503.

107. F. N. L. Poynter, ed., *Medicine and Culture*, London (1969), p. 2.
108. *Devils, Drugs and Doctors: The Story of the Science of Healing from Medicine Man to Doctor*, London (1929), p. 384.
109. E.g. C. Singer, *From Magic to Science: Essays on the Scientific Twilight*, New York (1958), ch. IV, 'Early English Magic and Medicine'.
110. See U. Maclean, 'Some Aspects of Sickness Behaviour among the Yoruba', in J. B. Loudon, ed., *Social Anthropology and Medicine*, London and New York (1976), pp. 294–5.
111. Thomas, *Religion and Magic*, pp. 223–5.
112. A good example of a compilation of this lore, combined with the basic principles of natural magic, is contained in A. Magnus, *Secrets of the Vertues of Herbes*, London (1549).
113. Robert Hooke, for instance, took chemical remedies and 'Galenicals' in order to purge his system. See Chapter 5.
114. Thomas, *Religion and Magic*, p. 224.
115. Sloane MS 153 op. cit., 105/171, 318/666.
116. Thomas, *Religion and Magic*, p. 225.
117. One edition is Sir Kenelm Digby, *Of the Sympathetic Powder*, London (1669).
118. See P. Slack, 'Mirrors of Health and Treasures of Poor Men: The Uses of the Vernacular Medical Literature of Tudor England', in C. Webster, ed., *Health, Medicine and Mortality in the Sixteenth Century*, Cambridge (1979), pp. 237–73.
119. See Roberts, thesis; Clark, *Royal College*, I. The surgeons' efforts to control surgical practice in London have received less attention than the physicians' activities, but many examples of the Barbersurgeons' Company's efforts in this direction appear in Young, *Barber-Surgeons*.
120. *The Anatomie of the Bodie of Man*, F. J. Furnivall and P. Furnivall, eds, Early English Text Society, extra series, LIII (1888, repr. 1975), p. 6.
121. J. Guillemeau, *Childbirth . . .* , London (1635), Introduction. The eighteenth-century *accoucheur*, William Smellie, called Hippocrates the Father of midwifery: *A Treatise on the Theory and Practice of Midwifery*, 3 vols, London (1779), I, xxx.
122. Cotta, *A Short Discovery of the Unobserved Dangers of Several Sorts of Ignorant and Unconsiderate Practisers of Physic in England*, London (1612), p. 119.
123. Arcaeus, *A Most Excellent and Compendious Method of Curing Wounds in the Head, and in Other Parts of the Body . . .* , J. Read, trans., London (1588).
124. *A Short Discourse of Discovery of Certain Stratagems, Whereby our London Empericks have been Observed Strongly to Oppugne, and oft times to Expugne their Poore Patient's Purses*, London (1602), p. 24.

125. Boorde, *The Breviary of Health*, London (1587), Prologue. This book was published in many editions; I have also seen the 1552 edition.
126. *The Copy of a Letter Written by E. D., Doctor of Physick, to a Gentleman* . . . , London (1606), p. 335.
127. *A Detection and Querimonie of the Daily Enormities and Abuses Committed in Physick* . . . , London (1566), Preface.
128. *A Right Profitable Book of all Diseases, called the Pathway to Health* . . . , London (1632), 'To the Reader'.
129. *The Marrow of Physick* . . . , London (1640), Preface.
130. P. P. Valentinus, *Enchiridion Medicum: Containing an Epitome of the Whole Course of Physic* . . . , London (1608), fo. 3.
131. J. Hart, *KΛINIKH, or the Diet of the Diseased* . . . , London (1633).
132. Boorde, op. cit. (1552), p. 2.
133. W. Folkingham, *Panala Medica* . . . , London (1628), 'To the Reader'.
134. *The Character of a Quack Doctor*, London (1676); Cotta, *A Short Discovery*; Cotta, *Cotta contra Antonium* . . . , Oxford (1625); E. D., *The Copy of a Letter*, op. cit.; P. Forestus, *The Arraignment of Urines* . . . , J. Hart, trans., London (1623); J. Halle, 'An Historicall Expostulation', op. cit.; J. Hart, *The Anatomy of Urines* . . . , London (1624); J. Oberndoerffer, *The Anatomies of the True Physician and Counterfeit Mountebank*, London (1602); E. Poeton, 'Medical Treatises', British Library Sloane MS 1954; J. Securis, *A Detection and Querimonie*, op. cit.; F. Herring, *A Short Discourse of Discovery of Certain Stratagems*, London (1602); [C. Merret], *A Short View of the Frauds* . . . , London (1669).
135. Oberndoerffer, op. cit., Preface.
136. Cotta, *A Short Discovery*, pp. 11, 17.
137. E. D., op. cit., p. 16.
138. Halle, op. cit. [no pagination].
139. Ibid.
140. Cotta, *A Short Discovery*, p. 4.
141. Cotta, *Cotta contra Antonium* . . . , Oxford (1625), Preface.
142. Gale, *Certain Works of Chirurgerie*, London (1564), Preface.
143. Securis, op. cit. [no pagination].
144. Cotta, *A Short Discovery*, p. 42.
145. Hart, op. cit., Preface.
146. E. D., op. cit., p. 17.
147. E.g. *Here Beginneth the Seeing of Urines* . . . , London (1525), 2nd edn, London (1526); *Hereafter Followeth the Judgement of all Urines* . . . , London (? early sixteenth century).
148. Forestus, op. cit., p. 16.
149. See p. 23.
150. Principally Forestus, Hart, Poeton and Cotta, *A Short Discovery*.
151. Forestus, op. cit., pp. 45–6.

152. Cotta was also worried about the problem of itinerants: *A Short Discovery*, pp. 113–14.
153. Halle, op. cit. [no pagination].
154. Cotta, *A Short Discovery*, p. 34.
155. Ibid., p. 112.
156. Ibid., pp. 113–14.
157. Ibid., p. 25.
158. See Young, *Barber-Surgeons*, p. 260.
159. Some general works reflecting seventeenth-century mysogynism are F. Beaumont, *The Woman Hater*, London (1648); W. Blake, *The Trial of the Ladies*, Hyde Park (1656); *A Brief Anatomy of Women: Being An Invective*, London (1653); *A Description of Wanton Women*, [1690?]; *An Invective Against the Pride of Women*, [London (1657)]; [J. Swetnam], *The Arraignment of Lewd, Idle . . . Women*, London (1645).
160. J. Rueff, *The Expert Midwife*, London (1637), Preface.
161. Ibid.
162. Willughby, *Observations in Midwifery*, op. cit., p. 9.
163. Ibid., p. 57.
164. Ibid., p. 135.
165. Smellie, op. cit., Preface.
166. See Donnison, *Midwives and Medical Men*, op. cit., pp. 21–41. For objections to men-midwives, see [Thickness], *Man-Midwifery Analysed*, op. cit.; Blunt, *Man-Midwifery Dissected*, op. cit.; S. Stone, *A Complete Practice of Midwifery*, London (1737); and J. Sharp, *The Midwives Book*, London (1671).
167. Poeton, 'The Winnowing of White Witchcraft', op. cit.
168. Oberndoerffer, op. cit., p. 15.
169. Forestus, op. cit., p. 53.
170. G. Gifford, *A Discourse of the Subtle Practices of Devils by Witches and Sorcerers*, London (1587) [no page numbers]; see also Hart, *The Anatomy of Urines*, op. cit., Conclusion.
171. Cotta, *A Short Discovery*, p. 86. See also Forestus, op. cit., 'To the Reader'.
172. Cotta, *A Short Discovery*, p. 87.
173. Ibid., p. 88.
174. Securis, op. cit. [no pagination].
175. See Oberndoerffer, op. cit., p. 21.
176. N. Culpeper, *A Directory for Midwives*, London (1651), p. 4.
177. Sharp, op. cit., Introduction.
178. P. Barrough, *The Method of Physick . . .* , London (1583), Introduction.
179. E. D., op. cit., p. 17.
180. See E. Freidson, *Profession of Medicine: A Study of the Sociology of Applied Knowledge*, New York (1972); J. L. Berlant, *Profession and Monopoly: A Study of Medicine in the United States and Great Britain*, Los Angeles (1975); N. Parry and J. Parry, *The Rise of the Medical Profession*, London (1976).
181. Freidson, op. cit., pp. 19–20.

3. A LONDON SURGEON'S CAREER: JOSEPH BINNS

★General note: Most of the notes for this chapter refer to a numbering system devised to locate individual cases in a transcription made of Joseph Binns's surgical casebook, British Library Sloane MS 153. The numbers given are double, referring to page numbers of the transcription and individual case numbers.

1. Napier's treatment of patients with emotional disorders has been explored in M. MacDonald's *Mystical Bedlam: Madness, Anxiety and Healing in Seventeenth-Century England*, Cambridge (1981).
2. See e.g. British Library Sloane MS 663, Dr Barker of Shrewsbury's 'Observations on cases in physick, 1595–1605'; British Library Sloane MS 1112, 'The casebook of a provincial physician, 1619–1622'.
3. Sloane MS 153.
4. Mayerne's casebook for the years 1607–51 is housed in the Library of the Royal College of Physicians, MS 444. King's casebook for 1676–96 is British Library Sloane MS 1589.
5. Guildhall Library, MS 5625/1 fo. 89; V. C. Medvei and J. L. Thornton, eds, *The Royal Hospital of St. Bartholomew 1123–1973*, London (1974), p. 388.
6. Public Record Office, PCC 1664, 47, 52.
7. Ibid., PCC 1664, 47. See C. Gittings, *Death, Burial and the Individual in Early Modern England*, London (1984), pp. 117–25, for a discussion of such bequests.
8. 214/429, 311/621, 313/633.
9. PCC 1664, 47.
10. Young, *Barber-Surgeons*, p. 345.
11. 229/450.
12. 39/78.
13. 199/393.
14. 191/372.
15. Young, *Barber-Surgeons*, pp. 77, 119, 182.
16. Pelling, 'Appearance and Reality', pp. 3–4.
17. 185/358.
18. E.g. 168/325, 252/497, 289/561.
19. E.g. 53/86, 100/146, 140/250.
20. E.g. 57/89, 191/372, 259/506, 265/519.
21. 191/372.
22. 12/31.
23. 168/327.
24. 192/379.
25. 217/437–8.
26. 152/288–91.
27. 241/473.
28. 217/437–8.
29. 8/22.
30. 12/31.

31. 6/17, 10/25.
32. 192/379.
33. 123/217, 19/45.
34. 96/142.
35. 24/55.
36. 205/411.
37. 111/190.
38. 123/215.
39. 105/171.
40. 197/388.
41. *The Diary of John Evelyn*, E. S. de Beer, ed., London (1959), p. 264.
42. L. Stone, *The Crisis of the Aristocracy, 1558–1641*, Oxford (1965), pp. 223–4.
43. 213/427.
44. 190/370.
45. E.g. 23/53, 198/391.
46. 176/343, 190/371, 34/67.
47. 125/219.
48. 139/249.
49. 190/371.
50. 213/427.
51. 96/142.
52. 190/370. See also A. L. Beier, *Masterless Men: The Vagrancy Problem in England, 1560–1640*, London (1985).
53. See K. Thomas, *Religion and the Decline of Magic*, Harmondsworth (1973), pp. 628–37; and A. Macfarlane, *Witchcraft in Tudor and Stuart England: A Regional and Comparative Study*, London (1970), pp. 173–6.
54. 191/372.
55. 156/300.
56. 155/297.
57. 155/297.
58. 155/299.
59. 200/394.
60. 12/31.
61. 72/102.
62. 201/396.
63. 86/129.
64. 134/231.
65. 188/365.
66. 163/317.
67. 66/93.
68. 78/115.
69. 140/251.
70. 85/128.
71. 105/171.
72. 29/61.
73. 159/309.

74. 202/402.
75. 67/96.
76. 8/21.
77. 213/425.
78. 141/253.
79. Explanation of this and other medical terms supplied by Dr R. M. McCray, MD.
80. 89/134.
81. 157/301.
82. 100/145.
83. 214/429, 311/621, 313/633.
84. J. Woodall, *The Surgeon's Mate* . . . , London (first published 1617). See also W. J. Bishop, *The Early History of Surgery*, London (1961), pp. 92–3 and 95–6.
85. 96/142, 85/128.
86. 214/429.
87. 207/416.
88. Head wounds are discussed at greater length below.
89. 163/317.
90. 147/269.
91. E.g. 86/129, 147/269.
92. 147/269.
93. 66/93.
94. 239/465.
95. E.g. 116/202.
96. E.g. 72/102, 122/213.
97. 140/251.
98. 8/21, 8/22, 9/24, 167/323.
99. 8/21, 9/24, 167/323.
100. 8/21, 9/24.
101. 198/391.
102. 8/22.
103. 167/323.
104. 32/13.
105. 219/441.
106. E.g. 236/459, 208/417.
107. 200/394.
108. E.g. 29/61, 105/281, 202/401.
109. 202/401.
110. 105/171. The practice of treating certain ailments by touching the hand of a recently hanged criminal is discussed in C. Gittings, *Death, Burial and the Individual in Early Modern England*, London (1984), pp. 67–8.
111. 29/61.
112. This might have been a case where a seriously injured patient was presented to the Court of the Barbersurgeons' Company, and a senior surgeon was called in to consult.
113. 150/281.
114. 112/191.

115. 16/42.
116. 203/404.
117. See Pelling, 'Appearance and Reality', pp. 89–95.
118. 369/526.
119. 169/330.
120. 27/60.
121. For a similar case, see 43/81. In both cases autopsies were performed.
122. 140/250.
123. E.g. 168/325, 229/450, 257/505.
124. 214/429, 294/567.
125. E.g. 25/55, 197/389, 210/421, 278/542, 300/579, 301/583.
126. E.g. 46/83, 81/122, 105/166, 139/248.
127. E.g. 80/121, 82/123, 94/140, 137/244.
128. E.g. 80/121, 89/135.
129. E.g. 81/122, 137/244.
130. 159/310.
131. 95/141.
132. 220/442.
133. E.g. 236/460.
134. E.g. 89/135.
135. 181/352.
136. 46/83.
137. Binns mentioned assistants very infrequently. While it is likely that he trained apprentices, his casebook says so little about them that no comment is possible.
138. 195/386. One cannot help thinking that Binns and his surgical colleagues neglected a golden opportunity for research on the stomach's function similar to that pursued by William Beaumont between 1824 and 1833.
139. 104/164.
140. 271/530.
141. 259/507.
142. 241/471.
143. 311/623.
144. E.g. 227/449, 229/450, 198/390, 199/393.
145. E.g. 71/101, 297/573.
146. 111/190.
147. Pelling, 'Appearance and Reality', p. 83.
148. 197/387. See also 310/618.
149. 265/520.
150. 267/525.
151. 16/42.
152. 288/556.
153. 259/506.
154. 277/541.
155. 43/81, 27/60.
156. 53/85.
157. 307/605. See also 23/52.

158. 212/424.
159. 213/428.
160. E.g. 314/638, 127/223, 241/473, 312/625.
161. The distinction is unclear. See discussion of gonorrhoea as symptom above.
162. E.g. 102/151, 192/377, 191/373, 275/536. See also I. Veith, *Hysteria: The History of a Disease*, Chicago, Ill. (1965).
163. E.g. 41/80, 141/255.
164. T. Sydenham, *Works*, Dr Greenhill, trans., London (1848), vol. II, pp. 35–6.
165. Beaumont and Fletcher, *Knight of the Burning Pestle*, Act III, scene 1, reprinted in *The Dramatic Works in the Beaumont and Fletcher Canon*, F. Bowers, ed., Cambridge (1966), vol. I, p. 57. See also H. Silvette, *The Doctor on Stage: Medicine and Medical Men in Seventeenth-Century England*, Knoxville, Tenn. (1967), pp. 182–234.
166. E.g. 12/30, 20/47, 36/69.
167. E.g. 30/60, 162/316.
168. 129/226.
169. E.g. 65/90.
170. 209/420–2.
171. 209/415–16.
172. 114/200.
173. 54/87.
174. E.g. 18/44, 131/228.
175. 131/228.
176. 97/143.
177. E.g. 274/534, 57/39.
178. 14/36, 33/65–6, 36/69, 158/304, 183/354, 317/657.
179. 56/88.
180. 131/228.
181. 238/464.
182. 92/138.
183. 122/214.
184. 154/295.
185. 165/320.
186. See Chapter 9.
187. 121/210.
188. 102/154–5.
189. 136/242.
190. 192/379 (316/653).
191. E.g. 216/435, 191/373, 275/536.
192. 191/374. For an in-depth discussion of this disorder, see E. Jorden, *A Brief Discourse of a Disease called the Suffocation of the Mother*, London (1603).
193. 292/565.
194. M. MacDonald, *Mystical Bedlam*, p. 20.
195. Ibid., p. 26.

4. THE PHYSICIAN'S TALE

1. Cambridge (1981).
2. Ibid., p. 16.
3. See Chapter 3.
4. Some of his notes for the years 1607–51 are housed in the Library of the Royal College of Physicians, MS 444.
5. F. N. L. Poynter and W. J. Bishop, eds, *A Seventeenth-Century Doctor and his Patients: John Symcotts, 1592?–1662*, Bedfordshire Historical Record Society, vol. 31, Streatley, Beds (1950), hereafter referred to as *Symcotts*.
6. *Symcotts*, p. x.
7. Ibid., pp. xxi–xxiii.
8. Ibid., p. xi.
9. Ibid.
10. Ibid., p. xii.
11. Ibid., pp. 105–8.
12. Ibid., p. xxvi.
13. Ibid., pp. 57, 70, 72, 76, 77, 81, 82.
14. Ibid., pp. 17, 55, 56, 58, 70, 75.
15. Ibid., pp. 75–6.
16. See G. J. Witkowski, *Accoucheurs et Sages-Femmes Célèbres*, Paris (1891), for some diagrams of midwifery instruments used by surgeons.
17. *Symcotts*, p. 81.
18. Ibid., p. 80.
19. Ibid., p. 81.
20. Ibid., p. 62.
21. Ibid., p. 59.
22. Ibid., p. 68.
23. Ibid., p. 76.
24. Ibid., p. 58.
25. Ibid., p. 52.
26. Ibid., p. xxx.
27. Ibid., p. 73.
28. Ibid., pp. 87–8.
29. Ibid., p. 81.
30. Ibid., p. 82.
31. Ibid., pp. 79–80.
32. Ibid., pp. 38, 51.
33. Ibid., p. 77.
34. Ibid., pp. xix-xx.
35. Ibid., pp. 6–7.
36. Ibid., p. 71.
37. Ibid., pp. 71–2.
38. Ibid., pp. 96–7.
39. Ibid., p. 103.
40. Ibid., p. 70.
41. Ibid., pp. 11–12.

42. Ibid., p. 89.
43. Ibid., pp. 87–8.
44. The Royal College of Physicians codified its disapproval of physicians diagnosing from a carried urine sample in 1601. G. N. Clark, *A History of the Royal College of Physicians of London*, p. 178. See Chapter 2.
45. *Symcotts*, p. 25.
46. Ibid., pp. 15, 41.
47. Ibid., p. 39.
48. Ibid., p. 17.
49. Ibid., p. xiii.
50. E.g. ibid., pp. 30, 37, 39.
51. Ibid., pp. 43, 59.
52. Ibid., p. 19.
53. Ibid., p. 43.
54. Ibid., p. 72.
55. Ibid., p. 81.
56. Ibid., p. 7.
57. Ibid., pp. 9–11.
58. Ibid., p. 38.
59. Ibid., p. 28.
60. Ibid., pp. 28–9.
61. See Chapter 2.
62. *Symcotts*, pp. 55–6, 80–1.
63. Ibid., p. 56.
64. See Chapter 3.
65. See Chapter 3.
66. See L. Stone, *The Crisis of the Aristocracy 1558–1641*, Oxford (1965), p. 41, for a brief discussion of the social position of physicians. 'John Ferne thought it not a very honourable profession, and as late as the middle of the seventeenth century a gentleman was refusing the offer of marriage with the daughter of a rich doctor since "the very thought of the Blister-pipes [*recte* clyster pipe] did Nauseate his Stomach"!'
67. See Chapter 6.
68. *Symcotts*, p. 29.
69. K. Thomas quotes Gregory King in calculating that 'in 1688 over half the population were "decreasing the wealth of the kingdom", that is to say earning less than they consumed. There can be no doubt that between a third and a half of the population lived at subsistence level and were chronically under-employed', *Religion and Magic*, p. 3.
70. *Symcotts*, p. 76.
71. Ibid., pp. 12–13.
72. See Chapter 6.
73. *Symcotts*, pp. 11–12.
74. Ibid., pp. 15–17.
75. Ibid., p. 88.
76. Ibid., p. 20.

77. Ibid., p. 23.
78. Ibid.
79. Ibid., p. 33.
80. Ibid., pp. 40–1.
81. Ibid., pp. 25–6.
82. Ibid., p. 45.
83. Ibid., p. 37.
84. Ibid., p. 35. See also p. 47.
85. Ibid., p. 46.
86. Ibid., p. 47.
87. Ibid., p. xxvi.
88. Barker's casebook, hereafter referred to as *Barker*, is the British Library Sloane MS 78 or 663. Another early healer whose work is mentioned above is the magical practitioner Simon Forman. See Chapter 2.
89. *Barker*, 7/4.
90. Ibid., 22/13, 132/78.
91. Ibid., 27/17.
92. Ibid., 56/40.
93. Ibid., 49/34, 124/73.
94. E.g. ibid., 102/66, 105/68, 110/69, 124/73, 137/82.
95. E.g. ibid., 19/11, 24/14, 27/17, 44/28.
96. See Clark, *Royal College*, p. 178.
97. *Barker*, 120–22b/72.
98. Ibid., 112/69.
99. Ibid., 99/65.
100. *Symcotts*, p. 86.
101. *Barker*, 21/13.
102. E.g. ibid., 14/8, 18/9, 23/14, 33/22, 48/34.
103. The *Oxford English Dictionary* states that betony is a 'plant of the Labiate order, having spiked purple flowers and ovate crenate leaves'. It quotes Burton's *Anatomy of Melancholy* to the effect that the Emperor Augustus used this herb to drive out demons.
104. *Barker*, 33/22.
105. Ibid., 61/45.
106. Ibid., 3/2, 4/3, 49/34, 72/49.
107. Ibid., 134/79.
108. Ibid., 90/59.
109. Ibid., 49/34.
110. British Library Sloane MS 1112, hereafter referred to as *Sl. 1112*.
111. *Sl. 1112*, 14/5, 15/5, 21/7, 22/7, 29/7, 48/12, 51/13.
112. Ibid., 1/1, 6/2, 13/5, 23/7, 47/12, 79/16.
113. Ibid., 3/1.
114. Ibid., 8/2.
115. Ibid., 5/15.
116. Ibid., 19/6.
117. Ibid., 5–6.

118. T. R. Forbes, *The Midwife and the Witch*, London (1966), pp. 64–79.
119. *Sl. 1112*, 29/7, 50/12.
120. I. Veith, *Hysteria: The History of a Disease*, Chicago, Ill. (1965).
121. *Sl. 1112*, 78/16.
122. Ibid., 1/1, 2/1, 3/1, 4/1, 33/9, 61/14.
123. *Symcotts.*, pp. 13, 41.
124. *Sl. 1112*, 1/1, 79/16.
125. Although Binns employed a 'man', there was nothing this apprentice or assistant did which Binns did not also do himself.
126. Sloane MS 153, 267/525.
127. *Symcotts*, pp. 13, 41.
128. See Chapter 6.
129. Ibid.
130. Ibid.
131. *Symcotts*, p. 102.
132. Ibid., p. 34.
133. Ibid., pp. 12–13.
134. Ibid., p. 33.

5. SUFFERERS AND PATIENTS: THE DISEASES OF THE PEOPLE

1. *Leviathan*, pt I, ch. 13, London (1973 edn), p. 65.
2. Thomas, *Religion and Magic*, p. 7.
3. Stone, *The Family, Sex and Marriage*, p. 69; and R. Schofield and E. A. Wrigley, 'Infant and Child Mortality in England in the late Tudor and early Stuart Period', in C. Webster, ed., *Health, Medicine and Mortality in the Sixteenth Century*, Cambridge (1979), pp. 61–96.
4 L. Stone, *The Crisis of the Aristocracy, 1558–1641*, Oxford (1965), pp. 223–4.
5. See C. Creighton, *A History of Epidemics in Britain*, Cambridge (1894 and 1965); J. F. D. Shrewsbury, *A History of Bubonic Plague in the British Isles*, Cambridge (1971); H. Zinsser, *Rats, Lice and History*, London (1935 and 1943); *The Plague Reconsidered: A New Look at its Origins and Effects in Sixteenth- and Seventeenth-Century England*, Matlock, Derbyshire (1977).
6. P. Slack, 'The Local Incidence of Epidemic Disease: The Case of Bristol, 1540–1650', in *The Plague Reconsidered*, op. cit., p. 51.
7. Thomas, *Religion and Magic*, p. 3.
8. J. Graunt, *Natural and Political Observations Made Upon the Bills of Mortality*, P. Laslett, ed., *The Earliest Classics*, Gregg International (1973, first edn 1662), p. 70.
9. Interesting commentary on these sources is made in T. R. Forbes's *Chronicle from Aldgate: Life and Death in Shakespeare's London*, London (1971), pp. 25–51.
10. Graunt, 'The Table of Casualties', op. cit., pp. 76–7.

11. Ibid.
12. Ibid.
13. Ibid., p. 32.
14. W. A. Littledale, *The Registers of St. Vedast, Foster Lane,* London: Harleian Society, Vol. XXX (1903), pp. 199–227.
15. Graunt, op. cit., pp. 25–6.
16. Ibid., pp. 26–8.
17. Ibid., p. 29.
18. Ibid., p. 11.
19. Ibid., p. 13.
20. Ibid., p. 14.
21. Ibid., pp. 23–4.
22. Ibid.
23. Ibid., p. 29.
24. *The Diary of Samuel Pepys*, R. Latham and W. Matthews, eds, London (1970–82), e.g. II, p. 17, IV, p. 59, VIII, p. 198, I, p. 283.
25. *The Diary of Ralph Josselin, 1616–1683*, A. Macfarlane, ed., Oxford (1976), e.g. 5/1/51, 16/3/51, 4/2/55, 3/59. See Chapter 6.
26. *The Diary of Robert Hooke, 1672–1680*, H. W. Robinson and W. Adams, eds, London (1968 and 1935).
27. Ibid., 14/2/78.
28. *The Diary of Lady Margaret Hoby, 1599–1605*, D. M. Meads, ed., London (1930), 13/5/1605, p. 220.
29. Pepys, *Diary*, 13/2/61, II, p. 36.
30. Josselin, *Diary*, 26/4/49 and 30/4/49.
31. *The Diary of John Evelyn*, E. S. de Beer, ed., London (1959), p. 240.
32. Pepys, *Diary*, 1/12/68, IX, p. 381.
33. See Chapter 2.
34. Pepys, *Diary*, IX, pp. 564–5.
35. Ibid., p. 248.
36. Ibid., pp. 507, 537.
37. Evelyn, *Diary*, p. 271.
38. E.g. Hooke, *Diary*, 30/1/74, p. 84; Josselin, *Diary*, 15/6/45; *The Letters of Dorothy Osborne to William Temple*, G. C. Moore Smith, ed., Oxford (1928), letter 4, p. 10.
39. See Chapter 6.
40. Osborne, *Letters*, p. 96.
41. Ibid., p. 40.
42. Ibid., p. 41.
43. *The Diary of the Lady Anne Clifford with an Introductory Note by V. Sackville-West*, London (1923), pp. 51–62.
44. Ibid., pp. 51–2.
45. Evelyn, *Diary*, pp. 380–5.
46. Pepys, *Diary*, IV, p. 21.
47. Ibid., p. 28.
48. Ibid., p. 58.

49. Ibid., 11/3/61, II, p. 53.
50. Ibid., 8/5/61, p. 96.
51. Josselin, *Diary*, 17/7/46.
52. Ibid., 28/2/47.
53. Pepys, *Diary*, 19/8/63–11/12/63, IV.
54. Hooke, *Diary*, p. 98; Josselin, *Diary*, p. 149.
55. Lady Anne Clifford believed a nosebleed had ended her daughter's attack of ague in 1617: Clifford, *Diary*, p. 54.
56. Ibid., pp. 108–10. See Chapter 8.
57. See Chapter 7.
58. See Chapter 7.
59. Evelyn, *Diary*, 5/1/64, p. 458.
60. Ibid., pp. 300, 412, 487.
61. Ibid., p. 300.
62. Ibid., p. 412.
63. Ibid., p. 487.
64. D. McLaren, 'Fertility, Infant Mortality and Breast Feeding in the Seventeenth Century', *Medical History*, XXII (1978), 378–96.
65. Evelyn, *Diary*, p. 4.
66. Ibid., p. 459.
67. See Chapter 7.
68. Ibid.
69. Josselin, *Diary*, 31/1/46, p. 54, and 19/7/46, p. 64.
70. Evelyn, *Diary*, p. 7.
71. Pepys, *Diary*, I, p. 1.
72. Ibid., V, p. 277.
73. Ibid., VIII, p., 177, Lady Margaret Hoby, also childless, attended one cousin's confinement in November 1601, and another's in February 1602: Hoby, op. cit., pp. 191–2 and 195.
74. Pepys, *Diary*, IX, p. 102.
75. Notably Stone, *The Family, Sex and Marriage*, p. 552.
76. Pepys, *Diary*, I, p. 213.
77. Ibid., p. 276.
78. Ibid., II, p. 98.
79. Ibid., IV, p. 384.
80. Ibid., p. 386.
81. Ibid., p. 384.
82. Ibid., p. 386.
83. Ibid.
84. Ibid., V, p. 87.
85. Ibid., IX, p. 211.
86. Ibid., p. 265.
87. Josselin, *Diary*, 6–14/2/47, p. 86.
88. Hooke, *Diary*, 14/2/78.
89. Pepys, *Diary*, IV, p. 118.
90. Ibid., I, pp. 283–310.
91. Ibid., VII, p. 36.

92. Evelyn, *Diary*, p. 529.
93. Ibid., p. 537.
94. Ibid., p. 722.
95. Ibid., p. 952.
96. Ibid., p. 1119.
97. Ibid., p. 1123.
98. Hooke, *Diary*, p. 156.
99. Pepys, *Diary*, VIII, p. 218.
100. Ibid., IX, p. 136.
101. Hooke, *Diary*, p. 14.
102. Pepys, *Diary*, IV, p. 59.
103. Evelyn, *Diary*, p. 529.
104. Pepys, *Diary*, VI, p. 51.
105. E.g. ibid., II, 10/10/61, p. 194, 3/12/61, p. 226; III, 1/8/62, p. 152.
106. Ibid., VI, p. 51.
107. Ibid., p. 52.
108. Ibid., V, p. 167.
109. Ibid., p. 194.
110. Ibid., p. 241.
111. Ibid., IV, p. 329.
112. Ibid., p. 328.
113. Ibid., p. 333.
114. Ibid., pp. 38–9.
115. Ibid., VI, p. 4.
116. *Diary of Roger Lowe of Ashton-in-Makerfield, Lancashire, 1663–74*, W. L. Sachse, ed., London (1938).
117. Hooke, *Diary*, xiv.
118. Ibid., xv.
119. Ibid., xxvi.
120. See Chapter 6.
121. Evelyn, *Diary*, p. 334; Hooke, *Diary*, pp. 60, 92.
122. Evelyn, *Diary*, p. 388.
123. Ibid., p. 387.
124. Osborne, *Letters*, pp. 70–1.
125. Clifford, *Diary*, p. 73; Osborne, *Letters*, p. 7.
126. Josselin, *Diary*, 6–27/6/52.
127. Evelyn, *Diary*, p. 264.
128. Ibid.
129. See Chapter 7.
130. Hooke, *Diary*, p. 312.
131. Ibid.
132. Ibid., pp. 418–27.

6. SUFFERERS AND PATIENTS: APPROACHES TO ILLNESS

1. See Chapter 2.
2. M. W. Bullen and A. H. Bullen, eds, Early English Text

Society, extra series, LII (1888 and 1875). Also published in 1564 and 1573.

3. Ibid., p. 119.
4. Ibid., p. 120.
5. R. Burton, *The Anatomy of Melancholy*, F. Dell and P. Jordan-Smith, eds, New York (1948), p. 156.
6. Ibid., p. 384.
7. Ibid., p. 385.
8. Pepys, *Diary*, III, p. 10.
9. A. Anderson, London (1593).
10. Ibid.
11. Pepys, *Diary*, VI, p. 120.
12. Ibid., p. 186.
13. Ibid., p. 201.
14. Ibid., p. 233.
15. Ibid., p. 268.
16. Evelyn, *Diary*, p. 481.
17. Ibid., p. 480.
18. Pepys, *Diary*, VI, pp. 155, 163.
19. Ibid., p. 174.
20. Ibid., VII, p. 35.
21. Ibid., VI, pp. 125, 205.
22. Ibid., VII, p. 21.
23. See Chapter 7.
24. Josselin, *Diary*, pp. 180–1.
25. Ibid., p. 201.
26. Ibid., p. 447.
27. Ibid., p. 430.
28. Ibid., p. 407.
29. Lowe, *Diary*, p. 83.
30. *Diary of the Rev. John Ward, A.M., Vicar of Stratford-upon-Avon*, C. Severn, ed., London (1839).
31. Pepys, *Diary*, VI, p. 67.
32. Ibid., IV, p. 339; IX, p. 32.
33. Hooke, *Diary*, p. 307.
34. Sloane MS 153, 105/171.
35. Pepys, *Diary*, IX, p. 197.
36. P. Willughby, *Observations in Midwifery*, H. Blenkinsop, ed., Yorkshire (1972), p. 205.
37. See Chapter 2.
38. Cotta, *A Short Discovery*, Preface.
39. E. Poeton, 'The Winnowing of White Witchcraft', British Library Sloane MS 1954, Introduction.
40. Burton, *Anatomy of Melancholy*, op. cit., p. 383.
41. Ibid.
42. Ibid.
43. Poeton, op. cit., pp. 5, 7.
44. A publication issued at intervals after 1618 with the endorsement of the Royal College of Physicians. It was

designed to keep physicians and apothecaries up to date concerning approved medicines.

45. Thomas, *Religion and Magic*, p. 226.
46. There exists a large body of work on the intellectual history of medicine. Examples of works which shed light on the diversity of educated medical opinion in seventeenth-century England are T. M. Brown, 'The College of Physicians and the Acceptance of Iatromechanism in England, 1665–1695', *Bulletin of the History of Medicine*, XIIV (1970), 12–30; N. G. Coley, 'Cures without Care: "Chemical Physicians" and Mineral Waters in Seventeenth-Century English Medicine', *Medical History*, XXIII, 2 (1979), 191–214; H. L. Coulter, *Divided Legacy: A History of the Schism in Medical Thought*, Washington (1973–7); W. Pagel, *Paracelsus: An Introduction to Philosophical Medicine in the Era of the Renaissance*, Basel and New York (1958); P. Rattansi, 'The Helmontian–Galenist Controversy in Restoration England', *Ambix*, XII (1964), 1–23; O. Temkin, *Galenism: Rise and Decline of a Medical Philosophy*, Ithaca, NY and London (1973); C. Webster, 'Alchemical and Paracelsian Medicine', in C. Webster, ed., *Health, Medicine and Mortality in the Sixteenth Century*, Cambridge (1979), pp. 301–34; C. Webster, *The Great Instauration: Science, Medicine and Reform, 1626–60*, London (1975).
47. Evelyn, *Diary*, p. 1.
48. Ibid., p. 264.
49. Ibid., p. 1.
50. See B. Capp, *Astrology and the Popular Press, English Almanacs, 1500–1800*, London (1979).
51. The diaries of Hoby, Josselin, Pepys, Evelyn and Hooke all give evidence of this practice.
52. Pepys, *Diary*, III, p. 247.
53. Ibid., VI, p. 244.
54. Ibid., IV, p. 333.
55. Hooke, *Diary*, p. 246.
56. Ibid., p. 16.
57. E.g. S. Bradwell, *Helps for Sudden Accidents Endangering Life. By which those that live far from Physicians or Chirurgeons may happily preserve the life of a poor Friend or Neighbour, till such a Man may be had to perfect the cure*, London (1633); *The Englishman's Doctor. Or the School of Salerne*, London (1607); P. Levins, *A Right Profitable Book of all Diseases, called the Path-way to Health . . .*, London (1632); *The Countryman's Physician . . .*, London (1680).
58. See J. O'Hara-May, *Elizabethan Dyetary of Health*, Lawrence, Kan. (1977), for a list of such publications.
59. Slack, 'Mirrors of Health and Treasures of Poor Men: The Uses of the Vernacular Literature of Tudor England', in C. Webster, ed., *Health, Medicine and Mortality*, op. cit., p. 237.
60. Hooke, *Diary*, pp. 15, 28, 173, 317, 331.

61. Hoby, *Diary*, p. 52.
62. Ibid.
63. Josselin, *Diary*, pp. 154, 181.
64. F. Beaumont and J. Fletcher, *Monsieur Thomas*, Act II, scene 3, *The Works of Francis Beaumont and John Fletcher*, A. R. Waller, ed., vol. IV, pp. 116–17, Cambridge (1906).
65. E.g. Josselin, *Diary*, p. 117; Pepys, *Diary*, V, p. 241; Hooke, *Diary*, p. 65.
66. Osborne, *Letters*, p. 8.
67. Pepys, *Diary*, VII, p. 208.
68. Hooke, *Diary*, p. 7.
69. Ibid., p. 280.
70. Ibid., p. 58.
71. Ibid., p. 203.
72. Ibid., p. 52.
73. Ibid., p. 99.
74. Ibid., p. 28.
75. Ibid., p. 172.
76. Hooke, *Diary*, p. 172.
77. Pepys, *Diary*, III, p. 57.
78. Osborne, *Letters*, p. 23.
79. Josselin, *Diary*, p. 207.
80. Pepys, *Diary*, e.g. IV, p. 246; IX, p. 233.
81. Ibid., IV, p. 246.
82. Evelyn, *Diary*, p. 321; Osborne, *Letters*, p. 7; Josselin, *Diary*, p. 586.
83. Evelyn, *Diary*, pp. 300, 304, 319.
84. Pepys, *Diary*, IX, p. 261.
85. British Library Sloane MS 153, 214/424, 278/542.
86. Ibid., 294/567.
87. Evelyn, *Diary*, p. 333.
88. Pepys, *Diary*, III, p. 77.
89. Evelyn, *Diary*, pp. 355–6.
90. Hoby, *Diary*, p. 102.
91. Clifford, *Diary*, xxiii.
92. E.g. Josselin, *Diary*, pp. 186, 566.
93. Ibid., p. 131.
94. See Chapter 7.
95. Pepys, *Diary*, IV, p. 39.
96. Ibid., p. 329.
97. Osborne, *Letters*, p. 40.
98. Hooke, *Diary*, p. 368.
99. Ibid., p. 67.
100. Ibid., p. 17.
101. Ibid., p. 25.
102. See Chapter 7.
103. Josselin, *Diary*, p. 112.
104. E.g. Evelyn, *Diary*, pp. 241, 264–8, 271, 277–8, 301, 319, 333, 335.

105. Ibid., pp. 31, 163, 241.
106. Ibid., pp. 284–5.
107. Ibid., p. 570.
108. Ibid., p. 387.
109. See e.g. Hooke, *Diary*, pp. 4, 163, 240; Pepys, *Diary*, II, p. 17; V, pp. 1–2; IX, p. 522.
110. Pepys, *Diary*, VI, p. 226.
111. Ibid., V, p. 194.
112. Pepys, *Diary*, V, p. 165.
113. Ibid., V, p. 241.
114. Ibid., p. 86.
115. Ibid., p. 84.
116. E.g. ibid., I, pp. 215, 276.
117. Hooke, *Diary*, p. 105.
118. Ibid., pp. 106 and 115.
119. E.g. Hoby, *Diary*, pp. 114, 120, 123, 146.
120. Lowe, *Diary*.
121. E.g. T. Brown, *Physick Lies a Bleeding or the Apothecary Turned Doctor . . .* , London (1697); G. Harvey, *The Conclave of Physicians, Detecting their Intrigues, Frauds and Plots Against their Patients . . .* , London (1683); P. Mexia, *A Delectable Dialogue wherein is contained a Pleasant Disputation between two Spanish Gentlemen, concerning Physick and Physicians with Sentence of a learned master given upon their argument*, T. N., trans., London (1580); *The Skillful Mountebank . . .* , London (1638).
122. See Chapter 2.
123. An extreme example of this tendency is L. R. C. Agnew's 'Quackery', in A. G. Debus, ed., *Medicine in Seventeenth Century England*, Los Angeles (1974), pp. 313–26.
124. Harvey, op. cit., p. 5.
125. Mexia, op. cit. (no pagination).
126. Mexia, op. cit.
127. Harvey, op. cit., pp. 8–9.
128. *All's Well that Ends Well*, Act I, scene 1.
129. *Volpone*, Act I, scene 4: *Ben Jonson*, C. H. Herford and P. Simpson, eds, Oxford (1937), pp. 35–6.
130. Beaumont and Fletcher, *Thierry and Theodoret*, Act I, scene 5, *The Works*, op. cit., vol. X, p. 64.
131. Lacy, *Dumb Lady*, V, quoted in H. Silvette, *The Doctor on Stage: Medicine and Medical Men in Seventeenth-Century England*, Knoxville, Tenn. (1967), p. 128.
132. Chapman, *All Fooles*, Act III, scene 1: *The Plays of George Chapman*, T. M. Parrott, ed., New York (1961), vol. I, pp. 139–40.
133. See Chapter 2.
134. *Macbeth*, Act IV, scene 1.
135. *The Comedy of Errors*, Act V, scene 1.
136. Mexia, op. cit.

7. IN SICKNESS AND IN HEALTH: THE JOSSELINS' EXPERIENCE

1. *The Diary of Ralph Josselin, 1616–1683*, A. Macfarlane, ed., London (1976), hereafter cited as Josselin, *Diary* with dates (unless cited in text) and page references.
2. A. Macfarlane, *The Family Life of Ralph Josselin. A Seventeenth-Century Clergyman: An Essay in Historical Anthropology*, Cambridge (1970).
3. L. Lessius' *Hygiasticon, or the Right Course of Preserving Life and Health unto Extreme Old Age*, London (1634), and D. Sennertus' *Institutionum Medicinae* (many Latin and English eds). See Josselin, *Diary*, 22/1/49 and 9/10/49, pp. 154, 181.
4. See e.g. Stone, *The Family, Sex and Marriage*, pp. 66–7, and R. Schofield and E. A. Wrigley, 'Infant and Child Mortality in England in the late Tudor and early Stuart Period', in C. Webster, ed., *Health, Medicine and Mortality in the Sixteenth Century*, Cambridge (1979), pp. 61–96.
5. See Chapter 5.
6. Macfarlane, *Family Life*, p. 87.
7. E.g. Josselin, *Diary*, 28/12/44, p. 30; 7/10/44, p. 24; 18/7/50, p. 210.
8. Definite mention is made of Jane feeding her first, second, third and sixth babies. The weaning of all the children is noted. Since Josselin would probably have remarked upon the employment of wet-nurses (which he did not), and since conception of the next child usually followed the weaning of the preceding one by a few months, I think it can safely be assumed that Jane fed all of her children herself.
9. Josselin, *Diary*, 18/6/56, p. 371.
10. E.g. Josselin, *Diary*, 3/4/45, p. 37; 24/11/45, p. 50; 5/9/47, p. 102; 5/12/47, p. 108; 30/10/53, p. 313.
11. Ibid., pp. 313 and 315.
12. Ibid., 23/10/53, p. 313.
13. Ibid., 20/3/47, p. 89.
14. See Chapter 2. I deliberately avoid mentioning the notorious forceps of the Chamberlen family, since very few women had the benefit of this family monopoly, and no other surgeons knew about it. See also A. Fraser, *The Weaker Vessel: Woman's Lot in Seventeenth-Century England*, London (1985), pp. 65–88.
15. E. Jocelin, *The Mother's Legacy to her Unborn Child*, New York and London (1894, repr. of 1632 edn) from 'The Approbation'.
16. Josselin, *Diary*, 23/6/57, pp. 402–3.
17. Ibid., 24/11/45, p. 50. See also 29/3/49, p. 162.
18. Ibid., 5/12/47, p. 108.
19. Ibid., 31/1/46, p. 54, and 19/7/46, p. 64.
20. Ibid., 25/8/61, p. 482.
21. See e.g. J. Hitchcock, 'A Sixteenth-Century Midwife's Licence', *Bulletin of the History of Medicine*, XLI (1967), 75–6. These women witnessed the mother's conversation during

labour and could report on statements made concerning the paternity of the child. They could also protect the mother and the midwife from accusations of infanticide in cases of stillbirth. See A. Wilson, 'Participant or Patient? Seventeenth-Century Childbirth from the Mother's Point of View', pp. 129–44, in R. Porter, ed., *Patients and Practitioners: Lay Perceptions of Medicine in Pre-Industrial Society*, Cambridge (1985), for a discussion of the social ritual surrounding birth.

22. Josselin, *Diary*, p. 50.
23. Ibid., 11/2/48, p. 110.
24. E.g. ibid., 7/9/50, p. 215; 21/10/73, p. 570; 4/11/77, p. 604; 27/10/78, p. 615.
25. Ibid., 7/9/50, p. 215.
26. Ibid., 25/11/45, p. 50; 14/1/58, p. 415; 20/6/60, p. 465; 26/11/63, p. 502.
27. Ibid., 11/2/48, p. 110; 5/5/49, p. 165.
28. Ibid., 14/1/58, p. 415.
29. Ibid., 12/4/42, p. 12.
30. Ibid., 24/2/48, p. 115.
31. E.g. ibid., 27/1/50, p. 189; 17/7/46, p. 64; 9/8/58, p. 429; 30/9/55, p. 354.
32. Ibid., 8/7/56, p. 374; 10/8/56, p. 376.
33. Ibid., 18/6/56, p. 371.
34. Ibid., 27/11/72, p. 566.
35. Ibid., 14/11/80, p. 630.
36. Ibid., 7/11/48, p. 145; 27/12/48, p. 150.
37. See Chapter 5.
38. Ibid., 17/2/48, p. 145; 27/12/48, p. 150.
39. Ibid., 20/2/48, p. 113.
40. Ibid., 17/2/48, p. 112.
41. Ibid., 21/2/48, p. 114.
42. Ibid., 25/11/49, p. 184.
43. Ibid., p. 185.
44. Ibid., p. 186.
45. Ibid., p. 190.
46. Ibid.
47. Ibid., p. 192.
48. Ibid., p. 194.
49. Ibid., p. 197.
50. Ibid., p. 200. See also Chapter 5.
51. Ibid., p. 205.
52. Ibid., p. 198.
53. Ibid., p. 200.
54. Ibid., p. 201.
55. Ibid., p. 202.
56. Ibid.
57. Ibid., p. 203.
58. Ibid., p. 212.
59. Ibid. Similar feelings were expressed by John Evelyn when his

5-year-old son, Richard, died in January 1658. See Evelyn, *Diary*, pp. 385–7.
60. Josselin, *Diary*, p. 203.
61. E.g. ibid., 27/10/44, p. 26; 20/12/46, p. 80; 25/11/49, p. 184; 18/2/52, p. 272.
62. Ibid., 23/10/45, p. 48; 14/1/49, p. 152; 28/3/52, p. 275; 23/5/54, p. 508.
63. Ibid., 1/12/44, p. 29; 23/3/45, p. 37; 21/1/55, p. 338.
64. E.g. ibid., 8/12/44, p. 29; 17/7/47, p. 64; 13/1/50, p. 187; 18/2/50, p. 190.
65. Ibid., 21/12/49, p. 186; 20/6/47, p. 97.
66. Ibid., 8/7/49, p. 172.
67. Ibid., 23/3/56, p. 364.
68. Ibid., p. 428.
69. Ibid., 1/8/52, p. 283.
70. Ibid., 11/6/59, p. 447; 18/4/69, p. 546; 10/11/68, p. 545; 3/11/78, p. 615.
71. E.g. ibid., 24/11/44, p. 28; 14/1/55, p. 337.
72. Ibid., 25–8/5/45, pp. 40–1.
73. Ibid., 13/11/44, p. 27.
74. Ibid., 3/2–14/4/61, pp. 475–8.
75. Ibid., 7–19/2/48, pp. 111–13.
76. Ibid., p. 24.
77. Ibid., pp. 113, 156.
78. Ibid., 9/12/60, p. 473.
79. Ibid., p. 433.
80. Ibid., 13/1/69, p. 545.
81. Ibid., p. 565.
82. Ibid., p. 210.
83. Ibid., p. 314.
84. Ibid., p. 330.
85. Ibid., 22/8/60, p. 468.
86. Ibid., p. 113.
87. Ibid., 1/9/54, p. 330.
88. Ibid., 28/12/44, p. 30.
89. Ibid., 27/1/72, p. 566.
90. Other marginal notes refer to such topics as the weather, Josselin's income, religious events, and so on.
91. E.g. ibid., 16/11/45, p. 49; 12/9/47, p. 103; 7/9/48, p. 134; 9/5/50, p. 200.
92. Ibid., p. 63.
93. Ibid., p. 79.
94. Ibid., 21/10/77, p. 603.
95. He took hyssop syrup made by his wife for a cold: 13/10/50, p. 218.
96. See above, this chapter.
97. Ibid., 5/9/47, p. 102.
98. E.g. ibid., 8/12/44, p. 29; 15/6/45, p. 42; 19/3/46, p. 56; 23/5/47, p. 94.

 99. E.g. ibid., 2–3/12/46, p. 77; 16/10/46, p. 72; 18/9/47, p. 103.
100. Ibid., 4/2/47, p. 86.
101. Ibid., p. 152.
102. E.g. ibid., 23/9/46, p. 70; 24/12/46, p. 81.
103. Ibid., 6/12/52, p. 290.
104. Ibid., 20/4/46, p. 58.
105. Ibid., 17/12/48, p. 149.
106. Ibid., 10/8/59, p. 450.
107. Ibid., pp. 319, 566.
108. Ibid., 21/3–8/5/55, pp. 342–5.
109. Ibid., 10/5/55, pp. 345–6.
110. Ibid., p. 348.
111. E.g. ibid., 10–11/5/50, p. 200.
112. Ibid., p. 64.
113. Ibid., 7–20/2/48, pp. 111–13.
114. Ibid., pp. 544–6.
115. Ibid., 15/10/48, p. 141, to 18/4/52, p. 277.
116. Ibid., p. 159.
117. Ibid., p. 253.
118. Ibid., 27/11/72, p. 566.
119. Ibid., 26/12/72, p. 566.
120. Ibid.
121. Ibid., 18/2/83, p. 642; 25/2/83, p. 642; 17/3/83, p. 642.
122. Ibid., 15/4/83, p. 643.
123. Ibid., p. 644.
124. Macfarlane, *Family Life*, p. 119.
125. Josselin, *Diary*, p. 567.
126. Ibid.
127. Ibid.
128. Ibid., p. 568.
129. By the end of his life he was also employing a man-servant: ibid., 8/8/80, p. 629.
130. Ibid., 28/4/45, p. 39.
131. Ibid., 6/3/48, p. 118.
132. Ibid., 10/3/50, p. 192.
133. Ibid., 23/1/49, p. 154.
134. Ibid., 4/8/58, p. 429.
135. Ibid., 3/9/44, p. 19.
136. Ibid., p. 62.
137. E.g. ibid., 16/4/47, p. 91; 19/8/48, p. 131; 7/9/50, p. 215; 9/5/52, p. 278.
138. Ibid., p. 18.
139. Ibid., p. 68.
140. Ibid., p. 402.
141. Ibid., 17/3/57, p. 394.
142. Ibid., 19/2/60, p. 460.
143. E.g. ibid., 9/5/52, p. 278; 6/6/52, p. 280; 27/6/52, p. 281; 18/7/52, p. 282.
144. Ibid., 25/2/61, p. 476.

145. Ibid., 18/3/75, p. 583.
146. Ibid., 26/2/53, p. 297.
147. Ibid., 4/8/50, p. 212.
148. Ibid., 27/10/49, p. 183.
149. Ibid., 19/5/51, p. 246.
150. Ibid., 9/8/58, p. 429; 27/9/74, p. 579.
151. Ibid., 28/1/45, p. 33.
152. Ibid., 22/5/65, p. 518.
153. Ibid., 4/3/48, p. 117.
154. Ibid., 28/4/45, p. 39.
155. Ibid., 14/2/48, p. 112.
156. Ibid., p. 76.
157. Ibid., 23/5/47, p. 94; 7/5/50, p. 200; 20–7/6/52, p. 281.
158. Ibid., 27/10/50, p. 219.
159. Ibid., 20–1/12/49, p. 186.
160. Ibid., 31/5/46, p. 61, and 13/10/50, p. 218.
161. E.g. ibid., 13/10/50, p. 218; 9/12/57, p. 412; 25/4/75, p. 584; 4/11/77, p. 604; 21/10/73, p. 570.
162. E.g. ibid., 27/1/50, p. 189; 23/5/64, p. 508.
163. Ibid., p. 595.
164. Ibid., p. 91.
165. Ibid., p. 131.
166. Ibid., p. 64.
167. Ibid., 5/9/44, p. 19.
168. Ibid., 17–18/3/45, p. 36; 14/2/48, p. 112; 26/11/48, pp. 147–8.
169. Ibid., 1/3/50, p. 191; 15/6/59, p. 447.
170. Stibium is black antimony, used as an emetic or poison: *Oxford English Dictionary*.
171. Josselin, *Diary*, 18/5/75, p. 584; 16/3/83, p. 642; 4/5/83, p. 643.
172. Ibid., 7/6/75, p. 585.
173. Ibid., 17/5/75, p. 584; 18/6/76, p. 591; 27/6/80, p. 628; 25/7/80, p. 629; 19/9/80, p. 630.
174. Ibid., 13/10/78, p. 615; 14/5/83, p. 644; 20/5/83, p. 644.
175. See Chapter 6.
176. Josselin, *Diary*, 22/5/50, p. 202.
177. Ibid., 23/6/50, p. 207.
178. Ibid., 4/5/83, p. 643.
179. Ibid., 8/5/83, p. 643.
180. Ibid., p. 64.
181. Ibid., 24/12/46, p. 81.
182. Ibid., 28/5/45, p. 41; 21/12/49, p. 186; 27/1/73, p. 566.
183. Ibid., p. 566.
184. Ibid., 22/5/50, p. 212.
185. Ibid., p. 111.
186. Ibid., 4/8/50, p. 212.
187. Ibid., 27–9/11/53, p. 314.
188. Ibid., 22/8/60, p. 460.
189. See above, this chapter.

190. Josselin, *Diary*, 5/5/49, p. 165.
191. Ibid., 21/12/45, p. 51; 28/2/48, p. 116.
192. Ibid., 1/2/58, p. 418.
193. Ibid., 17/2/48, p. 112.
194. Ibid., 2/8/43, p. 14.
195. Ibid., 7/6/75, p. 585; 15/4–4/5/83, p. 643.
196. Ibid., 29/10/76, p. 594; 20/11/76, p. 595; 17/9/78, p. 614.
197. Ibid., 4/5/83, p. 643.
198. Ibid., 1–19/8/64, pp. 510–11.
199. Macfarlane, *Family Life*, pp. 174–6.
200. Josselin, *Diary*, 23/2/48, p. 114.
201. Macfarlane, *Family Life*, pp. 174–6.
202. Josselin, *Diary*, 23/2/48, p. 114.
203. Ibid., p. 121.
204. Ibid., 8/7/56, p. 374.
205. E.g. ibid., 21/11/54, p. 333; 30/9/57, p. 407; 27/3/65, p. 516.
206. Ibid., 15/8/47, p. 101.
207. Ibid., p. 15.
208. Macfarlane, *Family Life*, pp. 28–9.
209. Josselin, *Diary*, 19 and 26/6/59, p. 447.
210. E.g. ibid., 27/5/49, pp. 168–9.
211. Ibid., p. 198.
212. Ibid., p. 71.
213. Ibid., p. 204.
214. E.g. ibid., 5/1/51, p. 230; 16/3/51, p. 238; 4/2/55, p. 339.
215. Ibid., p. 520–1.
216. See K. Dewhurst, *Dr. Thomas Sydenham (1624–1689), His Life and Original Writings*, London (1966), pp. 105–14.
217. Josselin, *Diary*, 15/8/47, p. 101.
218. Ibid., 3/11/67, p. 538.
219. E.g. ibid., 2/9/49, p. 178; 16/3/51, p. 238; 26/6/53, p. 307.
220. Ibid., 4/12/45, p. 51.
221. Ibid., 14/11/51, p. 262.
222. Ibid., 31/7/73, p. 568; 27–8/5/50, pp. 203–4.
223. Stone, *The Family, Sex and Marriage*, p. 70. See L. Pollock, *Forgotten Children*, Cambridge (1983) for further development of this argument.
224. Ibid., pp. 67, 69, 71.

8. THE CHARACTER OF A GOOD WOMAN: WOMEN AND ILLNESS

1. J. Hoch-Smith and A. Spring, 'Introduction' in J. Hoch-Smith and A. Spring, eds, *Women in Ritual and Symbolic Roles*, London (1978), p. 20.
2. Morningside Heights, NY (1943).
3. Ibid., p. 62.

4. K. C. Hurd-Mead, *A History of Women in Medicine*, Haddam, Conn. (1938).
5. A. Clark, *Working Life of Women in the Seventeenth Century*, London (1919), p. 285. For critiques of Clark's seminal theory, see J. Thirsk, 'Foreword', in M. Prior, ed., *Women in English Society 1500–1800*, London (1985), pp. 8–12, and L. Charles, 'Introduction', in L. Charles and L. Duffin, eds, *Women and Work in Pre-Industrial England*, London (1985), pp. 1–23.
6. S. Young, *The Annals of the Barber-Surgeons of London*, London (1890), p. 260.
7. A. Clark, op. cit., p. 260.
8. V. L. Bullough, 'Medieval Medical and Scientific Views of Women', *Viator*, 4, (1973), 499.
9. I. Maclean, *The Renaissance Notion of Woman: A Study in the Fortunes of Scholasticism and Medical Science in European Intellectual Life*, Cambridge (1980), p. 30.
10. P. Crawford, 'Attitudes to Menstruation in Seventeenth-Century England', *Past and Present*, 91 (1981), 59.
11. Ibid., 61.
12. *The Woman's Doctor or an Exact and Distinct Explanation of all such Diseases as are Peculiar to that Sex*, London (1652), p. 4.
13. V. L. Bullough, op. cit., 495.
14. M. Summers, ed., London (1928 and 1971).
15. Ibid., Question VI, 'Contents'.
16. Ibid., Question IX, 'Contents'.
17. B. Ehrenreich and D. English, *Witches, Midwives and Nurses: A History of Women Healers*, Oyster Bay, NY (n.d.).
18. I. Maclean, op. cit., p. 46.
19. *Character of a Good Woman*, London (1697), pp. 42–3. Italics in original.
20. See Chapters 2 and 4.
21. Quoted from R. Thompson, *Women in Stuart England and America*, London (1974), p. 208.
22. Quoted in the *Diary of Lady Margaret Hoby*, D. M. Meads, ed., London (1930), p. 50, hereafter referred to as Hoby, *Diary*.
23. Ibid., p. 53.
24. See Chapter 2.
25. See Chapter 4.
26. A. Clark, op. cit., pp. 243–52.
27. See Chapter 2.
28. See Chapter 7.
29. Hoby, *Diary*, p. 5. See also A. Fraser, *The Weaker Vessel: Woman's Lot in Seventeenth-Century England*, London (1985), pp. 502–3.
30. Hoby, *Diary*, pp. 8–11.
31. Ibid., pp. 12–28.
32. Ibid., p. 29.
33. Ibid., pp. 30–1.

34. Ibid., pp. 39, 43.
35. Ibid., pp. 168, 170, 180.
36. Ibid., p. 100.
37. Ibid., p. 96.
38. Ibid., p. 72.
39. E.g., ibid., pp. 102–5, 108–12.
40. Ibid., p. 193.
41. Ibid., p. 220.
42. E.g. ibid., pp. 167, 169, 189.
43. Ibid., p. 160.
44. Ibid., pp. 67, 106, 146, 161, 171, 174, 186.
45. Ibid., pp. 165, 179.
46. Ibid., pp. 103, 107, 159, 201, 220.
47. Ibid., p. 68.
48. Ibid., pp. 72, 220.
49. Ibid., p. 106.
50. Ibid., pp. 113–15.
51. Ibid., p. 73.
52. Ibid., p. 68.
53. E.g. ibid., pp. 147, 153, 155.
54. Ibid., p. 147.
55. Ibid., p. 157.
56. Ibid., p. 159.
57. Ibid. Mrs Thornborowe was the wife of the Dean of York.
58. Ibid., p. 147.
59. E.g. ibid., pp. 162, 181, 191–2.
60. Ibid., p. 100.
61. Ibid., pp. 101–3.
62. Ibid., pp. 168–70.
63. Ibid., pp. 145, 168.
64. See Chapter 2.
65. Hoby, *Diary*, pp. 131, 134.
66. Ibid., pp. 63, 191–2, 195.
67. *The Autobiography of Mrs. Alice Thornton of East Newton, Co. York*, C. Jackson, ed., Surtees Society, vol. 62 (1875), p. vii, hereafter referred to as *Thornton*. See also A. Fraser, op. cit., pp. 83–4, 86, 88, 108, 143, 150, 154, 169, 504.
68. *Thornton*, p. 43.
69. Ibid., p. viii.
70. Ibid., pp. 78–9.
71. Ibid., p. 75.
72. Ibid., pp. 78–9.
73. Ibid., p. 83.
74. Ibid., pp. xi–xii.
75. It has already served as an important source of information on breast-feeding and child mortality. See D. McLaren, 'Fertility, Infant Mortality and Breast Feeding in the Seventeenth Century', *Medical History*, XXII (1978), 378–96.
76. *Thornton*, p. 3.

77. Ibid., p. 129.
78. Ibid.
79. Ibid., p. 91.
80. Ibid., pp. 139–42.
81. Ibid., pp. 5–6.
82. John Evelyn's physician told him that, had he not been bled in the early stages of smallpox, his disease might have turned to plague or spotted fever.
83. *Thornton*, p. 91.
84. Ibid., pp. 128–9.
85. Ibid., p. 6.
86. Ibid., pp. 33–4.
87. Ibid., pp. 34–5.
88. See P. Aries, *The Hour of our Death*, H. Weaver, trans., London (1981) for lengthy discussion of the good death and changes in conventions over time.
89. *Thornton*, p. 124.
90. Ibid., p. 166.
91. Ibid., pp. 157–9.
92. Ibid., p. 4.
93. Ibid., p. 11.
94. Ibid., p. 133.
95. Ibid., pp. 129–30.
96. See Chapter 6.
97. *Thornton*, p. 164.
98. Ibid., p. 65.
99. Ibid., p. 273.
100. Ibid., p. 95.
101. Ibid., p. 139.
102. Stone, *The Family, Sex and Marriage*, pp. 74–5, 114; D. McLaren, op. cit.
103. *Thornton*, p. 87.
104. Ibid., p. 94.
105. Ibid., pp. 96, 123–4.
106. Ibid., pp. 139–42, 145, 148, 150–1, 166.
107. Ibid., p. 98.
108. Ibid., pp. 84–8.
109. Ibid., p. 140.
110. Ibid., p. 126.
111. Ibid., p. 95.
112. Ibid., pp. 92, 141.
113. Ibid., pp. 96–7.
114. Ibid., pp. 51–3.
115. Ibid., pp. 144–8.
116. Ibid., pp. 164–5.
117. See Chapter 7.
118. *Thornton*, pp. 13, 39–42, 54, 98, 149, 165, 172–5.
119. Ibid., pp. 5–6, 54, 151.
120. Ibid., pp. 81, 52, 157, 149, 173.

121. Ibid., p. 235.
122. Ibid., pp. 39, 81, 87, 157, 172–5, 223.
123. Ibid., pp. 93, 158, 164.
124. Ibid., p. 23.
125. Ibid., pp. 4, 10–11, 33–5.
126. Ibid., pp. 124, 133.
127. Ibid., p. 130.
128. Macfarlane, *Family Life*, pp. 172–7.
129. *Thornton*, pp. 9, 28–32, 48–9, 133, 144, 151, 157.
130. Ibid., p. 159.
131. P. White sees the main difference as being Puritans' 'rigid predestinarian doctrines' – an issue which does not arise in medical matters. See 'The Rise of Arminianism Reconsidered', *Past and Present*, 101 (1983), 34–54. For a discussion of 'Puritan Perceptions of Illness in Seventeenth Century England', see A. Wear, in R. Porter, ed., *Patients and Practitioners: Lay Perceptions of Medicine in Pre-Industrial Society*, Cambridge (1985), pp. 55–100.
132. Hoby, *Diary*, p. 54.
133. *The Autobiography of Anne Lady Halkett*, J. G. Nichols, ed., Camden Society, new series, 13 (1875), hereafter referred to as *Halkett*. See also A. Fraser, op. cit., pp. 68–9, 162–3, 211–13.
134. *Halkett*, pp. 62–3.
135. Ibid., pp. 82, 32–3.
136. Ibid., pp. 32–3, 36, 65, 87.
137. Ibid., pp. 104–5.

9. CONCLUSION: THE EXPERIENCE OF ILLNESS

1. See Chapter 3.
2. See Chapter 7.
3. Pepys, *Diary*, VI, p. 67.
4. Ibid., V, p. 78.
5. See Chapter 5.
6. See D. Mechanic, *Medical Sociology: A Selective View*, London and New York (1968), p. 116.
7. See Chapter 7.
8. Lowe, *Diary*, pp. 19, 100, 109.
9. Hooke, *Diary*, pp. 311–12.
10. Pepys, *Diary*, VI, p. 174.
11. Ibid., III, p. 65.
12. E.g. P. Laslett, *The World We have Lost*, London (1971).
13. See Chapter 7.
14. Pepys, *Diary*, I, p. 187.
15. See e.g. Chapter 3.
16. See Chapter 3.
17. See Chapter 7.
18. See Chapter 6.
19. See Chapter 2.

20. See e.g. Sloane MS 153, 37/76.
21. See Chapter 6.
22. See Chapter 7.
23. See M. Spufford, *Contrasting Communities: English Villages in the Sixteenth and Seventeenth Centuries*, Cambridge (1974 and 1979), p. 322.
24. E.g. Chapter 7; also Evelyn, *Diary*, p. 1023.
25. See Chapter 7.
26. Evelyn, *Diary*, pp. 8–9.
27. Ibid., pp. 14–16.
28. See Chapter 6.
29. Osborne, *Letters*, p. 10.
30. Pepys, *Diary*, I, p. 5.
31. Ibid., p. 36.
32. E.g. ibid., VII, pp. 49, 329–30.
33. Ibid., VI, p. 55; IX, p. 265.
34. Evelyn, *Diary*, p. 8.
35. Pepys, *Diary*, V, pp. 78–86.
36. Hooke, *Diary*, p. 13.
37. Ibid., p. 160.
38. E.g. Pepys, *Diary*, I, p. 5; IV, p. 24; V, p. 136.
39. E.g. ibid., IX, p. 264.
40. Ibid., V, p. 40.
41. Ibid., I, p. 15.
42. Ibid., II, p. 200.
43. See Chapters 5 and 6.
44. Pepys, *Diary*, IX, p. 546.
45. Hooke, *Diary*, p. 44.
46. Josselin, *Diary*, p. 204.
47. See below, this chapter.
48. Evelyn, *Diary*, p. 263.
49. Clifford, *Diary*, p. 87.
50. Pepys, *Diary*, IV, pp. 38–9.
51. Ibid., V, p. 280. See also Pelling, 'Appearance and Reality'.
52. See Chapter 3.
53. See Chapters 3, 5 and 6.
54. T. Shadwell, *The Humorists*, Act I, scene 1, *The Complete Works of Thomas Shadwell*, M. Summers, ed., vol. I, p. 193, London (1968 and 1927).
55. Shadwell, *Bury Fair*, Act III: *The Complete Works*, op. cit., IV, p. 337.
56. F. Beaumont and J. Fletcher, *Humourous Lieutenant*, Act I, scene 1, *The Works of Francis Beaumont and John Fletcher*, A. R. Waller, ed., vol. II, pp. 291–2, Cambridge (1906).
57. See Chapter 6.
58. Pepys, *Diary*, VIII, p. 219.
59. Ibid., VIII, p. 435.
60. *Aubrey's Brief Lives*, O. L. Dick, ed., Harmondsworth (1972), pp. 414–15.

61. See Chapter 7.
62. See P. Slack, 'Metropolitan Government in Crisis: London's Response to Plague, 1563–1665', in A. L. Beier and R. Finlay, eds, *The Making of the Metropolis: London 1500–1700*, London (1986), pp. 65–7.
63. J. F. D. Shrewsbury, *A History of Bubonic Plague in the British Isles*, Cambridge (1971), p. 269.
64. Quoted in ibid., p. 446.
65. Slack, 'Metropolitan Government', p. 67.
66. Shrewsbury, op. cit., p. 476.
67. Ibid., p. 450.
68. Ibid., p. 479.
69. Pepys, *Diary*, VI, p. 181.
70. Ibid., VII, p. 116.
71. Ibid., VI, p. 212.
72. Ibid., p. 283.
73. Slack, 'Metropolitan Government', p. 73.
74. Pepys, *Diary*, VII, p. 41.
75. For a description of social unrest in a plague-stricken Italian village, see C. M. Cipolla, *Faith, Reason and the Plague: A Tuscan Story of the Seventeenth Century*, Brighton (1979).
76. Shrewsbury, op. cit., pp. 464, 480.
77. Roberts, thesis, p. 358.
78. See Chapter 2.
79. See Roberts, thesis.
80. See Chapter 2.
81. See e.g. F. N. L. Poynter and W. J. Bishop, eds, 'A Seventeenth-Century Doctor and his Patients: John Symcotts, 1592?–1662', *Bedfordshire Historical Record Society*, vol. 31, Streatley, Beds (1950), xx–xxi; *Diary of the Rev. John Ward, A.M., Vicar of Stratford-upon-Avon*, C. Severn, ed., London (1839).
82. See Chapter 2.
83. Thackeray, *History of Pendennis*, II, New York (1968), pp. 174–5.
84. See Chapter 5.
85. Pepys, *Diary*, I, p. 244.
86. See Clark, *Royal College*; Young, *Barber-Surgeons*; Roberts, thesis.
87. See Chapter 2.
88. P. Aries, *The Hour of our Death*, H. Weaver, trans., London (1981).

BIBLIOGRAPHY

MANUSCRIPT SOURCES

Barker, Dr, 'Observations on cases in physick, 1595–1605', British Library Sloane MS 78 or 663.

Binns, J., 'Surgical Casebook, 1633–1663', British Library Sloane MS 153.

'The casebook of a provincial physician, 1619–1622', British Library Sloane MS 1112.

Guildhall Library, London, MS 5625/1 fo. 89.

King, Sir Edmund, 'Casebook, 1676–1696', British Library Sloane MS 1589.

Mayerne, Sir Theodore Turquet de, Casebook, Library of the Royal College of Physicians, MS 444.

Poeton, E., 'Medical Treatises', including 'The Winnowing of White Witchcraft', British Library Sloane MS 1954.

Public Record Office, PCC 1664, 47, 52: Joseph Binns's wills.

SIXTEENTH- AND SEVENTEENTH-CENTURY WORKS

Anderson, A., *An Approved Medicine Against the Deserved Plague*, London (1593).

Andrewes, L., *A Sermon of the Pestilence*, London (1636).

Arcaeus, F., *A Most Excellent and Compendious Method of Curing Wounds in the Head, and in Other Parts of the Body . . .* , J. Read, trans., London (1588).

Aubrey's Brief Lives, O. L. Dick, ed., Harmondsworth (1972).

The Autobiography and Personal Diary of Simon Forman the Celebrated Astronomer from A.D. 1552 to A.D. 1602, J. O. Halliwell, ed., London: for private circulation only (1849).

The Autobiography of Anne Lady Halkett, J. G. Nichols, ed., Camden Society, new series, 13 (1875).

The Autobiography of Mrs. Alice Thornton of East Newton, Co. York, C. Jackson, ed., Surtees Society, vol. 62 (1875).

Barrough, P., *The Method of Physick . . .* , London (1583).

Beaumont, F., *The Woman Hater*, London (1648).

Beaumont, F. and J. Fletcher, *Humourous Lieutenant,* in *The Works of*

Francis Beaumont and John Fletcher, A. R. Waller, ed., vol. II, Cambridge (1906).

Beaumont, F. and J. Fletcher, *Monsieur Thomas,* in *The Works of Francis Beaumont and John Fletcher*, A. R. Waller, ed., vol. IV, Cambridge (1906).

Beaumont, F. and J. Fletcher, *Thierry and Theodoret,* in *The Works of Francis Beaumont and J. Fletcher*, A. R. Waller, ed., vol. X, Cambridge (1906).

Beaumont, F. and J. Fletcher, *Knight of the Burning Pestle,* in *The Dramatic Works in the Beaumont and Fletcher Canon*, F. Bowers, ed., vol. I, Cambridge (1966).

Blake, W., *The Trial of the Ladies*, Hyde Park (1656).

Blunt, J., *Man-midwifery Dissected: or the Obstetric Family-Instructor*, London (1793).

Boorde, A., *The Breviary of Health*, London (1587).

Bradwell, S., *Helps for Sudden Accidents Endangering Life . . .* , London (1633).

Brain, T., *The Piss-Prophet, or Certain Piss-Pot Lectures . . .* , London (1637).

A Brief Account of Mr. Valentine Greatraks, London (1666 and 1668).

A Brief Anatomy of Women: Being an Invective, London (1653).

A Brief Description of the Notorious Life of J. Lambe, Amsterdam and London (1628).

Brown, T., *Physick Lies a Bleeding or the Apothecary Turned Doctor . . .* , London (1697).

Brugis, T., *The Marrow of Physick . . .* , London (1640).

Brugis, T., *Vade Mecum: or, a Companion for a Surgeon*, London (1652).

Bullein, W., *A Dialogue against the Fever Pestilence*, M. W. Bullen and A. H. Bullen, eds, Early English Text Society, extra series, LII (1888 and 1975). Also published in 1564 and 1573.

Burton, R., *The Anatomy of Melancholy*, F. Dell and P. Jordan-Smith, eds, New York (1948, first published 1621).

Cellier, E., 'Petition . . .', *Harleian Miscellany*, vol. IV, London (1744).

Chapman, G., *All Fooles,* in *The Plays of George Chapman*, T. M. Parrott, ed., vol. I, New York (1961).

Character of a Good Woman, London (1697).

The Character of a Quack-Doctor, London (1676).

Cooke, J., *Mellificium Chirurgerie. Or the Marrow . . .* , London (1648).

Cotta, J., *Cotta Contra Antonium . . .* , Oxford (1625).

Cotta, J., *The Infallible True and Assured Witch*, 2nd edn, London (1624).

Cotta, J., *A Short Discovery of the Unobserved Dangers of Several Sorts of Ignorant and Unconsiderate Practisers of Physic in England*, London (1612).

The Countryman's Physician . . . , London (1680).

Cox, Dr, *A Discourse Wherein the Interest of the Patient in Reference to*

Physick and Physicians is Soberly Debated . . . , London (1699).

Culpeper, N., *A Directory for Midwives*, London (1651).

D. E., *The Copy of a Letter Written by E. D., Doctor of Physick, to a Gentleman* . . . , London (1606).

A Description of Wanton Women, (1690?).

The Diary of John Dee, J. O. Halliwell, ed., *Camden Society*, XIX (1847).

The Diary of John Evelyn, E. S. de Beer, ed., London (1959).

Diary of Lady Margaret Hoby, 1599–1605, D. M. Meads, ed., London (1930).

The Diary of Ralph Josselin, 1616–1683, A. Macfarlane, ed., Oxford (1976).

The Diary of Robert Hooke, 1672–1680, H. W. Robinson and W. Adams, eds, London (1968 and 1935).

Diary of Roger Lowe of Ashton-in-Makerfield, Lancashire, 1663–74, W. L. Sachse, ed., London (1938).

The Diary of Samuel Pepys, R. Latham and W. Matthews, eds, vols I–IX, London (1970–82).

The Diary of the Lady Anne Clifford with an introductory note by V. Sackville-West, London (1923).

Diary of the Rev. John Ward, A.M., Vicar of Stratford-upon-Avon, C. Severn, ed., London (1839).

Digby, Sir Kenelm, *Of the Sympathetic Powder*, London (1669).

The Englishman's Doctor. Or the School of Salerne, London (1607).

An Essay for the Regulation of the Practice of Physick . . . , London (1673).

Fabrice, G., *His Experiments in Chyrurgerie*, London (1642).

Fioravanti, L., *A Short Discourse of the Excellent Doctor* . . . , J. Hester, trans., London (1580).

Folkingham, W., *Panala Medica* . . . , London (1628).

Forestus, P., *The Arraignment of Urines* . . . , J. Hart, trans., London (1623).

Gale, T., *Certain Works of Chirurgerie*, London (1564).

Gifford, G., *A Discourse of the Subtle Practices of Devils by Witches and Sorcerers*, London (1587).

Goeurot, J., *The Regiment of Life* . . . , T. Phayer, trans., London (1544).

Goodall, C., *The Royal College of Physicians of London* . . . , London (1684).

Graunt, J., *Natural and Political Observations Made Upon the Bills of Mortality*, P. Laslett, ed., *The Earliest Classics*, Gregg International (1973, first edn 1662).

The Great Cures and Strange Miracles of Mr. Valentine Gertrux [sic], n.p. (1666).

Guillemeau, J., *Childbirth* . . . , London (1635).

Halle, J., 'An Historical Expostulation . . .', in Lanfranc of Milan, *A Most Excellent and Learned Work of Chirurgery* . . . , J. Halle, trans., London (1565).

Hart, J., *The Anatomy of Urines* . . . , London (1624).

Hart, J., *KΛINIKH, or the Diet of the Diseased*, London (1633).

Harvey, G., *The Conclave of Physicians, Detecting their Intrigues, Frauds and Plots Against their Patients . . .* , London (1683).

Hereafter Followeth the Judgement of all Urines . . . , London (? early sixteenth century).

Here Beginneth the Seeing of Urines . . . , London (1525 and 1526).

Herring, F., *A Short Discourse of Discovery of Certain Stratagems, Whereby our London Empericks have been Observed Strongly to Oppugne, and oft times to Expugne their Poore Patient's Purses*, London (1602).

Hobbes, T., *Leviathan*, London (1973).

An Invective Against the Pride of Women, [London (1657)].

Joceline, E., *The Mother's Legacy to her Unborn Child*, New York and London (1894, repr. of 1632 edn).

Jonson, B., *Volpone, in Ben Jonson*, C. H. Herford and P. Simpson, eds, Oxford (1937).

Jorden, E., *A Brief Discourse of a Disease called the Suffocation of the Mother*, London (1603).

Lanfranc of Milan, *A Most Excellent and Learned Work of Chirurgerie*, J. Halle, trans., London (1565).

Lessius, L., *Hygiasticon, or the Right Course of Preserving Life and Health unto Extreme Old Age*, London (1634).

A Letter Concerning the Present State of Physick . . . , London (1665).

The Letters of Dorothy Osborne to William Temple, G. C. Moore Smith, ed., Oxford (1928).

Levins, P., *A Right Profitable Book of all Diseases, called the Pathway to Health . . .* , London (1632).

Magnus, A., *Secrets of the Vertues of Herbes*, London (1549).

[Merrett, C.], *A Short View of the Frauds . . .* , London (1669).

Mexia, P., *A Delectable Dialogue . . .* , T. N., trans., London (1580).

Oberndoerffer, J., *The Anatomies of the True Physician and Counterfeit Mountebank . . .* , F. H[erring], trans., London (1602).

Parker, M., *The Tragedy of Doctor Lambe*, London (1628).

Roesslin, E., *The Byrth of Mankynde*, R. Jonas, trans., London (1540).

Rueff, J., *The Expert Midwife*, London (1637).

Securis, J., *A Detection and Querimonie of the Daily Enormities and Abuses Committed in Physick . . .* , London (1566).

Sennertus, D., *Institutionum Medicinae* (many Latin and English editions, mid-seventeenth century).

Shadwell, T., *The Humorists, in The Complete Works of Thomas Shadwell*, M. Summers, ed., vol. I, London (1968 and 1927).

Shadwell, T., *Bury Fair, in The Complete Works of Thomas Shadwell*, M. Summers, ed., vol. IV, London (1968 and 1927).

Shakespeare, W., *The Comedy of Errors* (1592–3).

Shakespeare, W., *All's Well that Ends Well* (1602–3).

Shakespeare, W., *Macbeth* (1605–6).

Sharp, J., *The Midwives Book*, London (1671).

The Skillful Mountebank . . . , London (1638).

[Swetnam, J.], *The Arraignment of Lewd, Idle* . . . *Women*, London (1645).

Sydenham, T., *Works*, vol. II, Dr Greenhill, trans., London (1848).

Valentinus, P. P., *Enchiridion Medicum: Containing an Epitome of the Whole Course of Physic* . . . , London (1608).

Vicary, T., *The Anatomie of the Bodie of Man*, F. J. and P. Furnivall, eds, Early English Text Society, extra series, LIII (1888 and 1975).

Willughby, P., *Observations in Midwifery*, H. Blenkinsop, ed., Yorkshire (1972).

The Woman's Doctor or an Exact and Distinct Explanation of all such Diseases as are Peculiar to that Sex, London (1652).

Woodall, J., *The Surgeon's Mate* . . . , London (1655, numerous earlier edns, first published 1617).

SECONDARY SOURCES

Ackerknecht, E. H., *A Short History of Medicine*, New York (1955).

Agnew, L. R. C., 'Quackery', in A. G. Debus, ed., *Medicine in Seventeenth-Century England*, Los Angeles (1974), pp. 313–26.

Allderidge, P., 'Management and Mismanagement at Bedlam, 1547–1633', in C. Webster, ed., *Health, Medicine and Mortality in the Sixteenth Century*, Cambridge (1979), pp. 141–64.

Allen, P., 'Medical Education in Seventeenth-Century England', *Journal of the History of Medicine*, I (1946), 115–43.

Aries, P., *The Hour of our Death*, H. Weaver, trans., London (1981).

Aveling, J. H., *English Midwives: their History and Prospects*, London (1872).

Aveling, J. H., *The Chamberlens and the Midwifery Forceps*, London (1882).

Beier, A. L., *Masterless Men: The Vagrancy Problem in England, 1560–1640*, London (1985).

Beier, A. L. and R. Finlay, *The Making of the Metropolis: London 1500–1700*, London (1986).

Berlant, J. L., *Profession and Monopoly: A Study of Medicine in the United States and Great Britain*, Los Angeles (1975).

Bishop, W. J., *The Early History of Surgery*, London (1961).

Bloch, M., *The Royal Touch: Sacred Monarchy and Scrofula in England and France*, J. E. Anderson, trans., London (1973).

Boss, J., 'The Medical Philosophy of Francis Bacon (1561–1626)', *Med. Hypotheses*, IV (1978), 208–20.

Brown, T. M., 'The College of Physicians and the Acceptance of Iatromechanism in England, 1665–1695', *Bulletin of the History of Medicine*, XLIV (1970), 12–30.

Bruce-Chwatt, L. J. and J. de Zulueta, *The Rise and Fall of Malaria in Europe: A Historico-Epidemiological Study*, Oxford (1980).

Bullough, V. L., *The Development of Medicine as a Profession*, Basel and New York (1966).

Bullough, V. L., 'Medieval Medical and Scientific Views of Women', *Viator*, 4 (1973).

Capp, B., *Astrology and the Popular Press: English Almanacs, 1500–1800*, London (1979).

Charles, L. and L. Duffin, eds, *Women and Work in Pre-Industrial England*, London (1985).

Cipolla, C. M., *Faith, Reason and the Plague: A Tuscan Story of the Seventeenth Century*, Brighton (1979).

Clark, A., *Working Life of Women in the Seventeenth Century*, London (1919).

Clark, G. N., *A History of the Royal College of Physicians of London*, vols I and II, Oxford (1964).

Coley, N. G., 'Cures without Care: "Chemical Physicians" and Mineral Waters in Seventeenth-Century English Medicine', *Medical History*, XXIII, 2 (1979), 191–214.

Cope, Z., *The Royal College of Surgeons of England*, London (1959).

Copeman, W. S. C., *Doctors and Disease in Tudor England*, London (1960).

Coulter, H. L., *Divided Legacy: A History of the Schism in Medical Thought*, Washington (1973–7).

Crawford, P., 'Attitudes to Menstruation in Seventeenth-Century England', *Past and Present*, 91 (1981).

Creighton, C., *A History of Epidemics in Britain*, Cambridge (1894 and 1965).

D., W., 'Midwives Formerly Baptised Infants', *Gentleman's Magazine*, LV, 2 (1785).

Dainton, C., *The Story of England's Hospitals*, London (1961).

Debus, A. G., *The English Paracelsians*, New York (1966).

Debus, A. G., ed., *Medicine in Seventeenth-Century England*, Los Angeles (1974).

Dewhurst, K., *Thomas Willis as a Physician*, Los Angeles (1964).

Dewhurst, K., *Dr. Thomas Sydenham (1624–1689). His Life and Original Writings*, London (1966).

Dickens, C., *Martin Chuzzlewit*, London (1843–4).

Dingwall, R. and P. Lewis, eds, *The Sociology of the Professions: Lawyers, Doctors and Others*, London and Basingstoke (1983).

Donnison, J., *Midwives and Medical Men: A History of Inter-Professional Rivalries and Women's Rights*, London (1977).

Eccles, A., *Obstetrics and Gynaecology in Tudor and Stuart England*, London (1982).

Ehrenreich, B., and D. English, *Witches, Midwives and Nurses: A History of Women Healers*, Oyster Bay, NY (n.d.).

Forbes, T. R., *The Midwife and the Witch*, London (1966).

Forbes, T. R., *Chronicle from Aldgate: Life and Death in Shakespeare's London*, London (1971).

Fraser, A., *The Weaker Vessel: Woman's Lot in Seventeenth-Century England*, London (1985).

Freidson, E., *Profession of Medicine: A Study of the Sociology of Applied Knowledge*, New York (1972).

Freidson, E., 'The Theory of Professions: State of the Art', in R. Dingwall and P. Lewis, eds, *The Sociology of the Professions: Lawyers, Doctors and Others*, London and Basingstoke (1983), pp. 19–37.

Gittings, C., *Death, Burial and the Individual in Early Modern England*, London (1984).

Guthrie, D., *A History of Medicine*, London (1945 and 1946).

Haggard, H. M., *Devils, Drugs and Doctors: The Story of the Science of Healing from Medicine Man to Doctor*, London (1929).

Harleian Miscellany, IV, London (1744).

Hitchcock, J., 'A Sixteenth-Century Midwife's Licence', *Bulletin of the History of Medicine*, XLI (1967), 75–6.

Hoch-Smith, J., and A. Spring, eds, *Women in Ritual and Symbolic Roles*, London (1978).

Holmes, G., *Augustan England: Professions, State and Society, 1680–1730*, London (1982).

Hughes, M. J., *Women Healers in Medieval Life and Literature*, Morningside Heights, NY (1943).

Hurd-Mead, K. C., *A History of Women in Medicine*, Haddam, Conn. (1938).

Keynes, G., *Dr. Timothy Bright, 1550–1615: A Survey of his Life with a Bibliography of his Writings*, London (1962).

Keynes, G., *The Life of William Harvey*, Oxford (1966).

King, L. S., *The Growth of Medical Thought*, Chicago (1963).

King, L. S., ed., *A History of Medicine: Selected Readings*, Harmondsworth (1971).

Landy, D., ed., *Culture, Disease and Healing: Studies in Medical Anthropology*, New York and London (1977).

Laslett, P., *The World We Have Lost*, London (1971).

Littledale, W. A., ed., *The Registers of St. Vedast, Foster Lane*, London: Harleian Society, vol. XXX (1903).

MacDonald, M., *Mystical Bedlam: Madness, Anxiety and Healing in Seventeenth-Century England*, Cambridge (1981).

Macfarlane, A., *The Family Life of Ralph Josselin. A Seventeenth-Century Clergyman: An Essay in Historical Anthropology*, Cambridge (1970).

Macfarlane, A., *Witchcraft in Tudor and Stuart England: A Regional and Comparative Study*, London (1970).

McLaren, D., 'Fertility, Infant Mortality and Breast Feeding in the Seventeenth Century', *Medical History*, XXII (1978), 378–96.

Maclean, I., *The Renaissance Notion of Woman: A Study in the Fortunes of Scholasticism and Medical Science in European Intellectual Life*, Cambridge (1980).

Maclean, U., 'Some Aspects of Sickness Behaviour among the Yoruba', in J. B. Loudon, ed., *Social Anthropology and Medicine*, London and New York (1976).

Mechanic, D., *Medical Sociology: A Selective View*, London and New York (1968).

Medvei, V. C. and J. L. Thornton, eds, *The Royal Hospital of St.*

Bartholomew 1123–1973, London (1974).
O'Hara-May, J., *Elizabethan Dyetary of Health*, Lawrence, Kan. (1977).
Pagel, W., *Paracelsus: An Introduction to Philosophical Medicine in the Era of the Renaissance*, Basel and New York (1958).
Parry, N. and J. Parry, *The Rise of the Medical Profession*, London (1976).
Pelling, M., 'Occupational Diversity: Barbersurgeons and the Trades of Norwich, 1550–1640', *Bulletin of the History of Medicine*, LVI (1982), 484–511.
Pelling, M., 'Medical Practice in the Early Modern Period. Trade or Profession?', *The Society for the Social History of Medicine Bulletin*, XXXII (1983), 27–8.
Pelling, M., 'Appearance and Reality: Barbersurgeons, the Body and Venereal Disease in Early Modern London', in A. L. Beier and R. Finlay, eds, *The Making of the Metropolis: London 1500–1700*, London (1986).
Pelling, M. and C. Webster, 'Medical Practitioners', in C. Webster, ed., *Health, Medicine and Mortality in the Sixteenth Century*, Cambridge (1979), pp. 165–235.
The Plague Reconsidered: A New Look at its Origins and Effects in Sixteenth- and Seventeenth-Century England, Matlock, Derbyshire (1977).
Pollock, L., *Forgotten Children*, Cambridge (1983).
Porter, R., ed., *Patients and Practitioners: Lay Perceptions of Medicine in Pre-Industrial Society*, Cambridge (1985).
Poynter, F. N. L., ed., *Medicine and Culture*, London (1969).
Poynter, F. N. L., and W. J. Bishop, eds, *A Seventeenth-Century Doctor and his Patients: John Symcotts, 1592?–1662*, Bedfordshire Historical Record Society, vol. 31, Streatley, Beds (1950).
Prior, M., ed., *Women in English Society 1500–1800*, London (1985).
Raach, J. H., *A Directory of English Country Physicians, 1603–1643*, London (1962).
Rattansi, P., 'The Helmontian–Galenist Controversy in Restoration England', *Ambix*, XII (1964), 1–23.
Robb-Smith, A. H. T., 'Cambridge Medicine', in A. G. Debus, ed., *Medicine in Seventeenth-Century England*, Los Angeles (1974), pp. 327–70.
Roberts, R. S., 'The London Apothecaries and Medical Practice in Tudor and Stuart England', unpublished London University Ph.D thesis (1964).
Roberts, R. S., 'The Personnel and Practice of Medicine in Tudor and Stuart England', *Medical History*, VI (1962), 363–82, and VII (1964), 217–34.
Rowse, A. L., *Simon Forman: Sex and Society in Shakespeare's Age*, London (1974).
Schofield, R. and E. A. Wrigley, 'Infant and Child Mortality in England in the late Tudor and early Stuart Period', in C. Webster, ed., *Health, Medicine and Mortality in the Sixteenth Century*, Cambridge (1979), pp. 61–96.

Shorter, E., *A History of Women's Bodies*, Harmondsworth (1984).
Shrewsbury, J. F. D., *A History of Bubonic Plague in the British Isles*, Cambridge (1971).
Silvette, H., *The Doctor on Stage: Medicine and Medical Men in Seventeenth-Century England*, Knoxville, Tenn. (1967).
Sinclair, H. M., 'Oxford Medicine', in A. G. Debus, ed., *Medicine in Seventeenth-Century England*, Los Angeles (1974), pp. 371–92.
Singer, C., *A Short History of Anatomy and Physiology from the Greeks to Harvey*, New York (1957, first published 1925).
Singer, C., *From Magic to Science: Essays on the Scientific Twilight*, New York (1958).
Singer, C., and E. Ashworth Underwood, *A Short History of Medicine*, Oxford (1962).
Slack, P., 'The Local Incidence of Epidemic Disease: The Case of Bristol, 1540–1650', in *The Plague Reconsidered: A New Look at its Origins and Effects in Sixteenth- and Seventeenth-Century England*, Matlock, Derbyshire (1977), pp. 49–62.
Slack, P., 'Mirrors of Health and Treasures of Poor Men: The Uses of the Vernacular Medical Literature of Tudor England', in C. Webster, ed., *Health, Medicine and Mortality in the Sixteenth Century*, Cambridge (1979), pp. 237–73.
Slack, P., *The Impact of Plague in Tudor and Stuart England*, London (1985).
Slack, P., 'Metropolitan Government in Crisis: London's Response to Plague, 1563–1665', in A. L. Beier and R. Finlay, eds, *The Making of the Metropolis: London 1500–1700*, London (1986), pp. 60–81.
Smellie, W., *A Treatise on the Theory and Practice of Midwifery*, 3 vols, London (1779).
Spufford, M., *Contrasting Communities: English Villages in the Sixteenth and Seventeenth Centuries*, Cambridge (1974 and 1979).
Statutes of the Realm, London (1810–1828; repr. 1963).
Stephen, M., *The Domestic Midwife*, London (1795).
Stocks, M., *A Hundred Years of District Nursing*, London (1960).
Stone, L., *The Crisis of the Aristocracy, 1558–1641*, Oxford (1965).
Stone, L., *The Family, Sex and Marriage in England, 1500–1800*, London (1977).
Stone, S., *A Complete Practice of Midwifery*, London (1737).
Summers, M., ed., *Malleus Maleficarum*, London (1928 and 1971).
Temkin, O., *Galenism: Rise and Decline of a Medical Philosophy*, Ithaca, NY and London (1973).
Thackeray, W. M., *History of Pendennis*, New York (1968).
[Thickness, P.], *Man-Midwifery Analysed: And the Tendency of the Practice Detected and Exposed*, London (1765).
Thomas, K., *Religion and the Decline of Magic*, Harmondsworth (1973).
Thompson, R., *Women in Stuart England and America*, London (1974).
Veith, I., *Hysteria: The History of a Disease*, Chicago, Ill. (1965).
Walker, D. P., *Unclean Spirits: Possession and Exorcism in France and*

England in the Late Sixteenth and Early Seventeenth Centuries, London (1981).

Wall, C., *The History of the Surgeon's Company, 1745–1800*, London (1937).

Wall, C., H. C. Cannon and E. Ashworth Underwood, *A History of the Worshipful Society of Apothecaries of London*, vol. I, 1617–1815, Oxford (1963).

Webster, C., 'Alchemical and Paracelsian Medicine', in C. Webster, ed., *Health, Medicine and Mortality in the Sixteenth Century*, Cambridge (1979), pp. 301–34.

Webster, C., *The Great Instauration: Science, Medicine and Reform, 1626–60*, London (1975).

White, P., 'The Rise of Arminianism Reconsidered', *Past and Present*, 101 (1983), pp. 34–54.

Wilson, A., 'Participant or Patient? Seventeenth-Century Childbirth from the Mother's Point of View', in R. Porter, ed., *Patients and Practitioners: Lay Perceptions of Medicine in Pre-Industrial Society*, Cambridge (1985), pp. 129–44.

Witkowski, G. J., *Accoucheurs et Sages-Femmes Célèbres*, Paris (1891).

Young, S., ed., *The Annals of the Barber-Surgeons*, London (1890).

Zinsser, H., *Rats, Lice and History*, London (1935 and 1943).

GLOSSARY

ague: an intermittent fever, sometimes identified with malaria. The form of an ague is determined by the interval between fits. A quotidian ague is characterised by daily fits, a tertian ague by fits every second day, and a quartan ague by fits every third day.

apostem: a matter-filled swelling.

clyster or **glister:** an enema.

cachexia: a depraved condition of the body characterised by pervasive malnutrition.

cupping: letting blood by means of suction.

dropsy: a condition characterised by the accumulation of fluid in one or more parts of the body.

fistula: a hollowness, usually long and narrow, which will not heal.

issue: an artificially produced ulcer which is not allowed to heal.

ligature: a thread of silk, flax wire, or other material, used by surgeons to tie arteries or other parts of the body.

livergrown: a condition, primarily affecting children, which involved having an enlarged liver.

pannado: bread boiled to a pulp and flavoured with sugar, nutmeg, etc.

phlebotomy: therapeutic bleeding.

pleagett: a bandage or dressing.

posset: hot milk which has been curdled by means of wine.

rheum: mucous discharge, common in colds.

rotula: patella or knee-cap.

scarification: letting blood by means of shallow cuts.

scrofula or King's Evil: swellings, sometimes ulcerated, on the neck and other parts of the body.

squinsey or quinsy: a severe sore throat.

suffocation of the Mother: fits caused by a wandering womb.

tent: a roll of dressing used to keep an orifice open.

trepan or trephine: instruments used to open the skull.

INDEX